The Spartan Army

MACEDONIA

CHALKIDIKE

Amphipolis

Olynthos

Mt.Olympos

Tempe

Mt.Ossa

THESSALY

MAGNESIA

EPIRUS

SKIATHOS

Pharsalos •

ARKANANIA

Lamia

Artemision

SKYROS

Thermopylai

LOKRIS

EUBOEA

AITOLIA

Orchomenos

r.Kephisos

Amphissa

Chaironeia

Chalkis

Delphi

Koroneia

Kopais

Tanagra

Delion

Eretria

ITHAKA

Thespiai

Thebes

Dekeleia

KEPHALLENIA

GULF OF CORINTH

Leuktra

Plataea

ACHAEA

Aigosthena

Pellene •

Megara

Athens

Sikyon •

SALAMIS

ELIS

Phleious

Corinth

ZAKYNTHOS

Olympia

Orchomenos

Mycenae

AIGINA

Heraia

Epidauros

ANDROS

Mantineia

Argos

KEOS

Lepreon

Hysiai

Nauplion

• Phigalia

Tegea

Trozen

Megalopolis

r.Eurotas

Hermione

Ithome

Karyai

MESSENIA

Sparta

Sellasia

Prasiai

Pylos

Geronthrai

Methone

Amyklai

Asine

Cytheion

MELOS

c.Malea

KYTHERA

The Spartan Army

J. F. Lazenby

Pen & Sword
MILITARY

First published in Great Britain in 1985 by
Aris & Phillips Ltd

Reprinted in this format in 2012 by
Pen & Sword Military
an imprint of
Pen & Sword Books Ltd
47 Church Street
Barnsley
South Yorkshire
S70 2AS

ISBN 978–1–84884–533–6

A CIP catalogue record for this book is available from the British Library.

Typeset in 11pt Ehrhardt by
Mac Style, Beverley, E. Yorkshire

Printed and bound by CPI Group (UK) Ltd, Croydon, CR0 4YY

Pen & Sword Books Ltd incorporates the Imprints of Pen & Sword Aviation, Pen & Sword Family History, Pen & Sword Maritime, Pen & Sword Military, Pen & Sword Discovery, Wharncliffe Local History, Wharncliffe True Crime, Wharncliffe Transport, Pen & Sword Select, Pen & Sword Military Classics, Leo Cooper, The Praetorian Press, Remember When, Seaforth Publishing and Frontline Publishing.

For a complete list of Pen & Sword titles please contact
PEN & SWORD BOOKS LIMITED
47 Church Street, Barnsley, South Yorkshire, S70 2AS, England
E-mail: enquiries@pen-and-sword.co.uk
Website: www.pen-and-sword.co.uk

Contents

Preface xx
Sources, Select Bibliography and Abbreviations xxiv

Part I: Preparation 1

Chapter 1:   The Age of Xenophon 3

Chapter 2:   The Fifth Century 51

Chapter 3:   Origins 82

Part II: Battle 103

Chapter 4:   Thermopylai 105

Chapter 5:   Plataea 120

Chapter 6:   Sphakteria 140

Chapter 7:   Mantineia 151

Chapter 8:   The Nemea, Koroneia and Lechaion 161

Chapter 9:   Leuktra 176

Part III: Epilogue 189

Chapter 10: After Leuktra 191

Notes 205
Glossary of Greek Terms 228
Index 230

To my friend and colleague of many years
Dick Hope Simpson
with whom, while ostensibly looking for Mycenaean sites,
I contrived to visit most of the battlefields of Greece.

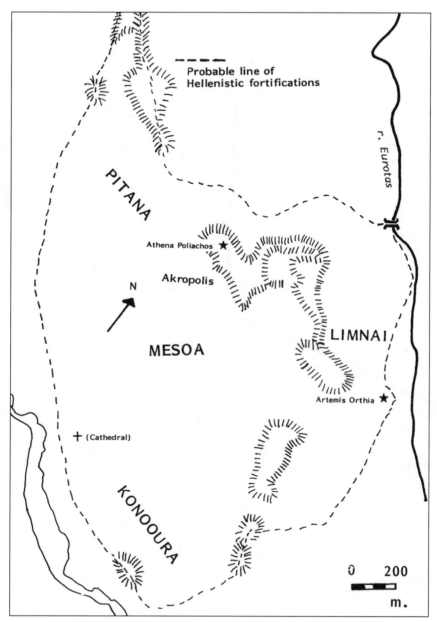

Map 1. Ancient Sparta.

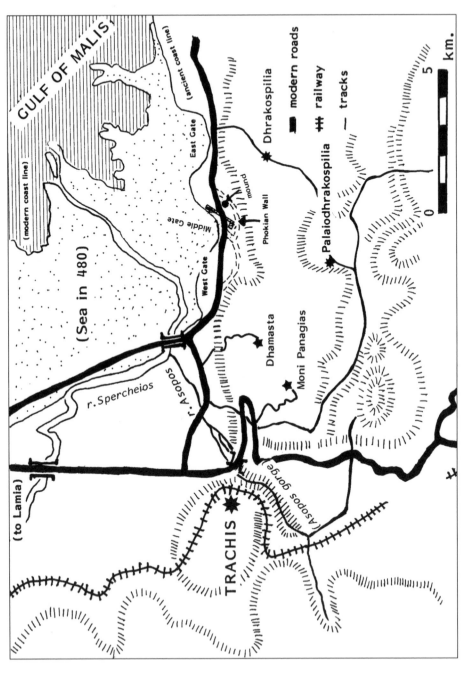

Map 2. Thermopylai.

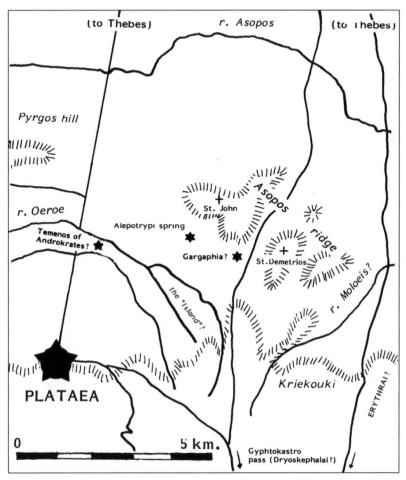

Map 3. Plataea.

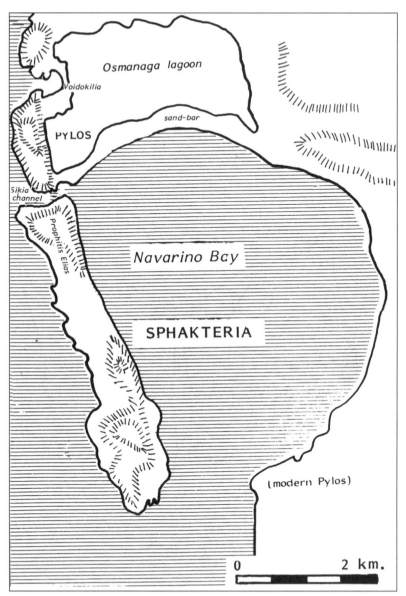

Map 4. Sphakteria.

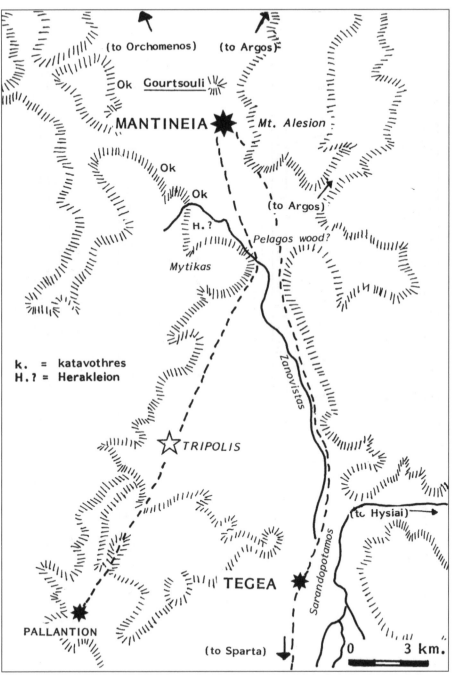

Map 5. Mantineia.

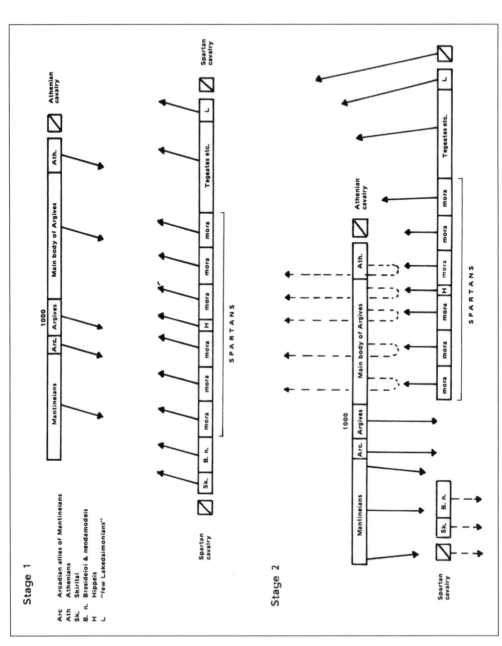

Map 6. Battle of Mantineia (stages 1 & 2).

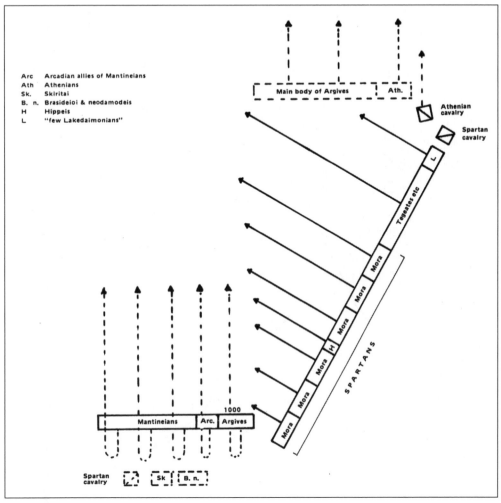

Map 7. Battle of Mantineia (stage 3).

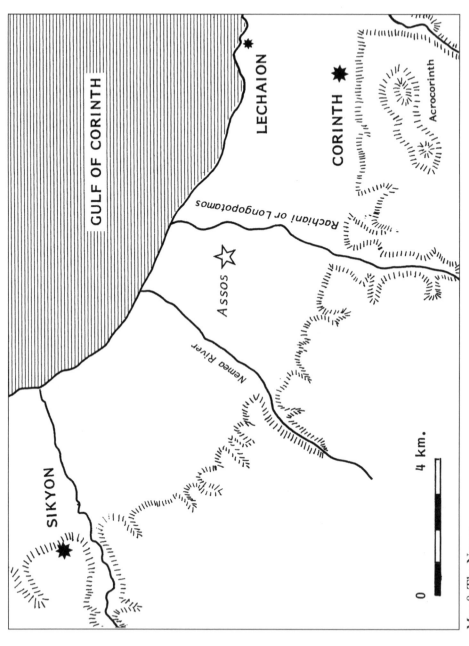

Map 8. The Nemea.

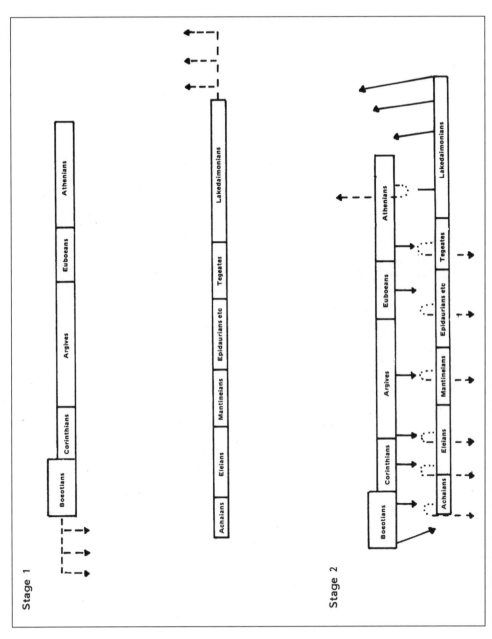

Map 9. The Battle of the Nemea (stages 1 & 2)

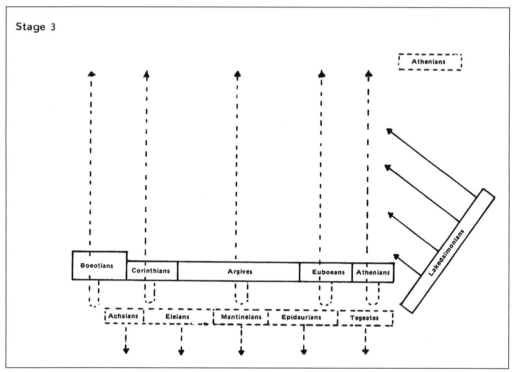

Map 10. The Battle of the Nemea (stage 3).

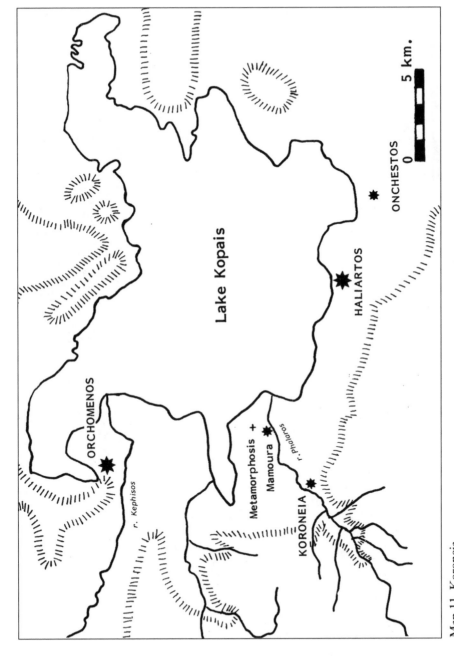

Map 11. Koroneia.

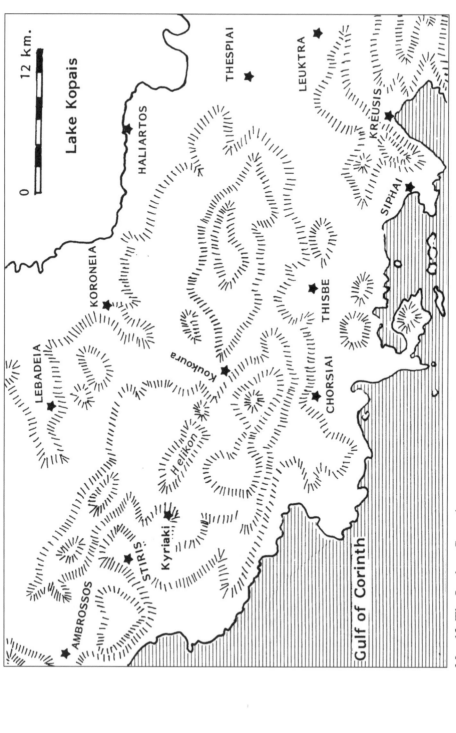

Map 12. The Leuktra Campaign.

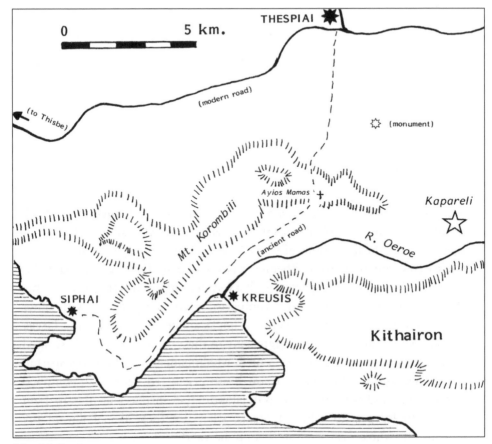

Map 13. Leuktra.

Preface

This book is about the Spartan army: it is not, except incidentally, a book about Sparta, nor a book about Greek warfare, nor yet a military history of Sparta itself. The limitations of scope I have set myself may sometimes seem too narrow, but they are deliberate: more could undoubtedly be said, for example, about how the Spartan military system fitted into the Spartan way of life as a whole, and further comparisons could be drawn with other armies, but there are already plenty of books about Sparta and about Greek warfare, which discuss the Spartan army in these wider contexts. It seemed to me that there was a place for a book which concentrated on the Spartan army itself, and tried to sort out how it was organized, recruited, equipped and trained, and what made it so outstanding an instrument of war. I am content to leave it to others to make what use they like of any of my conclusions which may seem to them to be valid.

It is an old joke among ancient historians that everyone, at one time or another, wants to write a book on Sparta, and it is easy to see why this is so. Although the peculiarities of the Spartan way of life have been exaggerated, both in ancient and modern times, and it is in particular a mistake to project these peculiarities too far back in time, taken as a whole, Sparta remains unique, if only as a totalitarian state which lasted, if not for 'a thousand years', at least for a good few centuries. The study of Sparta is also a marvellous arena for both the beginner and the professional, since there is so tantalisingly little evidence that anyone can think they have a brilliant new solution to some old problem – how many of us, I wonder, have not thought up a new and completely satisfactory version of the *rhetra?* But the truth of the matter is, of course, that the more one studies Sparta, the more questions remain unanswered and perhaps unanswerable. The problem, indeed, about writing any book on Sparta is that one is bound, sooner or later, to slip into a morass of controversy in which one finds oneself disagreeing with someone about almost everything. Plutarch's remark, at the beginning of his life of Lykourgos, that 'in general it is possible to say nothing that is undisputed,' can easily be applied to Sparta as a whole.

One result is that the stream of books and articles about Sparta is seemingly endless, and I am very conscious that I have not read everything that I might have done, on my subject – I am not sure that it would be possible in an average lifetime. I think I have read most of the ancient literary sources, and that I have at least a reasonable knowledge of the other ancient evidence, and it is, after all, on this that all conclusions should be based. It seems to me more worthwhile to set out the conclusions to which one has come on the basis of the ancient evidence, than to argue against all other possible interpretations, and I have tried to avoid what might be categorized as the 'coconut-shy' school of history, whereby one tries to knock down the hypotheses of others, one by one, often leaving the field strewn with hypotheses and not a conclusion in sight. Three of my general conclusions, in particular, I think are new, and if valid, have some importance – that the Spartan army was twice as large in Xenophon's and Thucydides' time as most people think, and still composed exclusively of Spartans, though no longer only of Spartiates, and that its basic organization into *morai* and *lochoi* goes back to the eighth century.

The modern works I have used extensively are listed in the bibliography, and the others are referred to in the notes. Probably the most stimulating to appear in recent years has been Paul Cartledge's *Sparta and Lakonia,* and if I may sometimes appear to have singled it out for criticism, I hope it will be apparent that this is rather the measure of the extent to which it has set me thinking. Of the others, George Huxley's *Early Sparta* remains a marvellous quarry for evidence and erudite information of all kinds, and I still think that everyone should start by reading George Forrest's *A History of Sparta 950–192 BC.* But perhaps the best general introduction is now J.T. Hooker's *The Ancient Spartans.*

I hope that this book will be as intelligible to the layman as some of these, and equally that specialists will find something in it to interest them, and will not be irritated by passages of explanation where to them no explanation is necessary, and by the translation of Greek words and phrases. Non-specialists may feel that some of the discussion of detail might have been left out altogether, or at least relegated to footnotes or appendices, but I find it intensely irritating constantly to have to refer to other parts of a book, and yet I feel that anyone who seriously wants to know about the past, deserves to have the evidence and the problems presented to them, so that to some extent they can make up their own minds. There are too many 'popular' books about the Greeks and Romans which are written as though there were no doubts about the facts and the ancient world were as well known as the modern.

It will also be apparent that I do not entirely share the evident distaste for the Spartans felt by many modern scholars. I am quite sure that I would not have liked to have been a Spartan, even if I had been a full-blown Spartiate, and I can sympathize with Spartan boys, having myself endured an *agoge*-like regime for two years at the Lawrence Memorial Royal Military School at Lovedale in the Nilgiri Hills of southern India. But I feel that criticism can go too far. I doubt whether, for example, the majority of helots normally led worse lives than the majority of slaves elsewhere in the Greek world, and although the Spartans could be brutal and cruel, so could other Greeks – the Spartans were not guilty of worse crimes against others than the Athenians at Skione or on Melos, or against their own citizens than the Corcyreans or Corinthians, Thebans or Argives. I am not convinced that the Spartans were wholly to blame for the outbreak of the Peloponnesian War, and when all is said and done, they rejected the clamours of their allies for the destruction of Athens – one wonders how the Athenians might have behaved, if they had won, and they might even have learned a lesson from that archetypical Spartan, Lysander, who told the harmost Kallibios that he did not know how to rule free men. Of course, by comparison with the Athenians in particular, the Spartans do appear intellectually and artistically barren in the classical period, but one must ask oneself how far it was the Athenians, and not the Spartans, who were the exceptions, and I am not sure that the Spartans were really as philistine as they are sometimes made out to be – it is significant, for example, how many of them were evidently skilful diplomats. To some extent I suspect that they deliberately played up to the image the rest of the world had of them, while being secretly amused at it – this may be what Aristophanes meant when he described them as 'διειρωνόξενοι' in the *Peace* ('fond of poking fun at strangers'), and is not this the point of the famous story of the barbarian king who, on finding the Spartan black broth not to his taste, was blandly informed that he had first to bathe in the Eurotas to appreciate it?

Another hazard that a book on the Spartan army faces is that many people find the whole subject of war distasteful. I can only say that I am not a bloodthirsty militarist, and that any admiration I may appear to show for the

Spartan army should not be construed as admiration for war in general or for the particular uses to which the Spartan army was put – though I think one can at least admire courage, even in a bad cause, and not all the causes for which the Spartans fought were bad. But, in any case, if one is interested in Greek history, it is important to understand the principal instrument which made Sparta one of the dominant powers in Greece for so long – to study Sparta without studying her army would be an absurdity, and one cannot understand what made her army what it was without studying the details of the fights in which it took part. I should, perhaps, add that I have never taken part in, or even seen, any kind of battle, other than on film, and to that extent cannot begin to understand what it is like. On the other hand, I doubt whether anyone alive today really knows what it is like to take part in a hand-to-hand conflict involving thousands of men, and the ancient evidence is such that we frequently do not even know precisely what happened, let alone the feelings of those who participated.

My thanks are as usual due to my colleagues in the Department of Classics at Newcastle upon Tyne, who have patiently endured my latest craze, and helped me with their expert knowledge in their several fields. Brian Shefton, in particular, helped me with some of the illustrations, Jerry Paterson read the original typescript and discussed many points, and Tony Spawforth also read the typescript and patiently allowed me to pick his brains, particularly on later Spartan history. I was lucky enough to have George Forrest as my tutor at Oxford, and he it was who first introduced me to the fun of studying early Spartan history; since 1957 I have also enjoyed the friendship of another eminent Spartan scholar in George Huxley, and more recently I have had the opportunity to discuss some ideas with John Davies – to all of these my thanks. My thanks also to my wife, who drew the maps and helped prepare the index, and to my children, who once again kept out of the study with as much patience as anyone could reasonably expect. Finally, my thanks to my publishers, Adrian and Lucinda Phillips and their staff, who have produced the book with their usual courteous friendliness and efficiency.

J.F. Lazenby
Newcastle upon Tyne
May, 1984

Sources, Select Bibliography and Abbreviations

1. Sources

The following is – I hope – a complete list of the ancient sources I have used, with a word of explanation about each for the benefit of readers to whom some of the names may not be familiar. Many are now available in translation in the Penguin Classics series, and, if not, nearly all appear in the Loeb Classical Library series, published by William Heinemann of London, and the Harvard University Press, Cambridge, Massachusetts.

Aelian (Claudius Aelianus):	3rd century AD writer of – among other things – a 'Ποικίλη ἱστορία' ('Miscellaneous History'), usually known as 'Varia Historia' (VH).
Alkman:	Spartan poet of the seventh century of whose works only fragments survive.
Appian:	2nd century AD Greek historian of Rome.
Aristophanes:	Athenian comic playwright (c. 444–c. 380).
Aristotle:	Greek philosopher and scientist (384–322).
Arrian:	Roman general of Greek origin, who wrote an account of Alexander (*Anabasis*), and a book on tactics (*Tactica*); he lived from c. 90 to c. 165 AD.
Athenaios:	3rd century AD grammarian, author of '*Deipnosophistai*' ('Philosophers at Dinner'), a collection of anecdotes and quotations from earlier authors, many of whose works are now lost.
Asklepiodotos:	1st century writer on tactics.
Cassius Dio:	Roman senator and historian from Bithynia (155–c. 235 AD).
Cornelius Nepos:	Roman biographer, contemporary and friend of Cicero.
Curtius (Q. Curtius Rufus):	Roman historian of unknown date, but probably 1st century AD.

Demosthenes:	Athenian orator and statesman (c. 385–322).
Diodoros (Diodorus Siculus):	Sicilian historian, contemporary of Caesar and Augustus.
Diogenes Laertius:	2nd century AD biographer of philosophers.
Ephoros:	4th century Greek historian, whose work, now lost, was used extensively by later writers (e.g. Diodoros).
Frontinus (Sextus Iulius Frontinus):	Roman general of the 1st century AD who wrote a book on strategems.
Harpokration:	Alexandrian grammarian of uncertain date, but probably of the 1st or 2nd century AD.
Hellanikos:	5th century Greek historian whose work has perished.
Herodian:	Greek historian of the Roman empire, 2nd to 3rd century AD.
Herodotos:	Greek historian (c. 484–c. 428).
Hesychios:	4th century AD Alexandrian grammarian.
Homer:	Greek epic poet, probably of the eighth century.
Isokrates:	Athenian orator (436–338).
Justin:	Roman historian, probably of the 4th or 5th century AD.
Kallisthenes:	a relation and pupil of Aristotle, who accompanied Alexander until executed by him, and wrote an account of his campaigns; he also wrote a history of Greece, but none of his work survives.
Ktesias:	5th-4th century Greek historian who wrote a history of Persia, now lost.
Livy (Titus Livius):	Roman historian (probably 64 BC–12 AD).
Lycurgus:	Athenian orator (c. 396–323).
Lysias:	Athenian orator (458–378).
Pausanias:	Greek traveller of the 2nd century AD, who wrote a guidebook to Greece.
Philochoros:	Athenian historian, whose work is now lost (c. 320–c. 260).
Photius:	9th century AD Byzantine bishop and scholar.
Phylarchos:	Greek historian of the 3rd century whose work only survives in fragments.
Pindar:	Boeotian poet (c. 522–c. 442).
Plato:	Athenian philosopher (428–347).
Plutarch:	Greek biographer and essayist, who, apart from the well-known lives, wrote a large number of miscellaneous essays, usually referred to collectively as '*Moralia*' ('Moral Writings').

Polyainos:	Greek rhetorician of the 2nd century AD, who wrote a book on strategems.
Polybios:	Greek historian (c. 200–c. 118).
Sosylos:	Spartan historian who accompanied Hannibal to Italy, but whose work has now perished.
Stobaeus:	(?) 6th century AD scholar who collected extensive excerpts of earlier writers for his son.
Strabo:	Greek geographer (c. 54 BC–AD 24).
Thucydides:	Athenian historian (c. 470–c. 400).
Tyrtaios:	Spartan poet of the 7th century.
Xenophon:	Athenian soldier and writer, whose work included an account of his own experiences as a mercenary (*Anabasis*), a fictitious account of the education of Cyrus, founder of the Persian empire (*Cyropaedia*), a life of King Agesilaos of Sparta, and the *Hellenika* (=XH), a history of Greece from 410 to 362. A treatise on the *Constitution of the Lakedaimonians* (=LP) is also attributed to him.

2. Select Bibliography and Abbreviations

This is not intended to be a complete list of all the modern works I have used – for those see the notes – and in particular omits articles. I list books which readers may find useful for various aspects of Sparta and Greek military history.

Adcock = F.E. Adcock, *The Greek and Macedonian Art of War* (Berkeley & Los Angeles, 1957).

AJA = The American Journal of Archaeology

Anderson = J.K. Anderson, *Military Theory and Practice in the Age of Xenophon* (Berkeley & Los Angeles, 1970).

Andrewes, A., *The Greek Tyrants* (London, 1956).

BCH = Bulletin de Correspondance Hellénique

BSA = The Annual of the British School at Athens

Buckler, J., *The Theban Hegemony 371–362 BC* (Cambridge, Mass., & London, 1980).

Burn = A.R. Burn, *Persia and the Greeks* (London, 1962).

CAH = The Cambridge Ancient History (first edition).

Cartledge = Paul Cartledge, *Sparta and Lakonia* (London, 1979).

Cawkwell, G.L., *Philip of Macedon* (London, 1978).

Chrimes, K.M.T., *The Respublica Lacedaimoniorum ascribed to Xenophon* (Manchester, 1948).

Chrimes = K.M.T. Chrimes, *Ancient Sparta* (Manchester, 1949).

Coldstream, J.N., *Geometric Greece* (London, 1977).

Connolly, Peter, *Greece and Rome at War* (London, 1981).

CQ = *The Classical Quarterly*

Delbrück, H., *History of the Art of War* (trans. Renfroe, Westport, Connecticut & London, 1975).

Desborough, V.R.d'A., *The Last Mycenaeans and their Successors* (Oxford, 1964).

Desborough, V.R.d'A., *The Greek Dark Ages* (London, 1972).

FHG = F. Jacoby, *Die Fragmente der griechische Historiker*

Fitzhardinge, L.F., *The Spartans* (London, 1980).

Forrest = W.G. Forrest, *A History of Sparta 950–192 BC* (London, 1968).

GHI = M.N. Tod, *Greek Historical Inscriptions*

Gomme, A.W., & others, *A Historical Commentary on Thucydides,* vols, i–v (Oxford, 1945–81).

GRBS = *Greek, Roman and Byzantine Studies*

Green = Peter Green, *The Year of Salamis* (London, 1970).

Greenhalgh, P.A.L., *Early Greek Warfare* (Cambridge, 1973).

Grundy, G.B., *The Great Persian War and its Preliminaries* (London, 1901).

Hamilton, Charles D., *Sparta's Bitter Victories* (Ithaca & London, 1979).

HCT = *A Historical Commentary on Thucydides* (see above, under Gomme).

Hignett = C. Hignett, *Xerxes' Invasion of Greece* (Oxford, 1963).

Hooker = J.T. Hooker, *The Ancient Spartans* (London, 1980).

How and Wells = W.W. How & J. Wells, *A Commentary on Herodotos* (Oxford, 1912).

Huxley = G.L. Huxley, *Early Sparta* (London 1962).

IC = *Inscriptiones Graecae*

Jeffery, L.H., *Archaic Greece. The City States c. 700–500 BC* (London, 1976).

JHS = *The Journal of Hellenic Studies.*

Jones = A.H.M. Jones, *Sparta* (Oxford, 1968).

Kagan, D., *The Archidamian War* (Ithaca & London, 1974).

Kagan, D., *The Peace of Nicias and the Sicilian Expedition* (Ithaca & London, 1981).

Keegan, John, *The Face of Battle* (London, 1978).

Michell = H. Michell, *Sparta* (Cambridge, 1964).

Oliva = P. Oliva, *Sparta and her Social Problems* (Amsterdam & Prague, 1971).

PCPhS = *Proceedings of the Cambridge Philological Society.*

Pritchett, W.K., *Studies in Ancient Greek Topography I* (Berkeley & Los Angeles, 1965).

Pritchett, W.K., *Studies in Ancient Greek Topography II* (Berkeley & Los Angeles, 1969).

Pritchett, W.K., *Studies in Ancient Greek Topography III* (Berkeley & Los Angeles, 1980)

Pritchett, W.K., *The Greek State at War I* (Berkeley & Los Angeles, 1971).

Pritchett, W.K., *The Greek State at War II* (Berkeley & Los Angeles, 1974).

RE = Pauly-Wissowa's *Real-Encyclopädie der classischen Altertumswissenschaft*

Ste. Croix = G.E.M. de Sainte Croix, *The Origins of the Peloponnesian War* (London, 1972).

Snodgrass = A.M. Snodgrass, *Arms and Armour of the Greeks* (London, 1967).

Snodgrass, A.M., *Early Greek Armour and Weapons* (Edinburgh, 1964).

Snodgrass, A.M., *The Dark Age of Greece* (Edinburgh, 1971).

Sylloge = *Sylloge Inscriptionum Graecarum*

Toynbee = A.J. Toynbee, *Some Problems of Greek History* (Oxford, 1969).

Vernant, J.-P. (ed.), *Problèmes de la Guerre en Grèce Ancienne* (Paris, 1968).

Wade-Gery, H.T., *Essays in Greek History* (Oxford, 1958).

Walbank, F.W., *A Historical Commentary on Polybius I* (Oxford, 1957).

Wilson, J.B., *Pylos 425 BC* (Warminster, 1979).

τύχῃ μέν, ὡς ἐδόκουν, κακιζόμενοι
Vνώμῃ δὲ οἱ αὐτοί ἔτι ὄντες

'They might seem to have been worsted by Fortune,
but in spirit they were still the same'
Thucydides 5.75.3

Part I

Preparation

Chapter 1

The Age of Xenophon

When the Theban general, Epameinondas, went marching down the valley of the Eurotas at the end of 370, it had been nearly six hundred years, as Plutarch says (*Agesilaos* 31.2)[1], since the beautiful land of 'hollow Lakedaimon' had seen an invader, and even then it was to be nearly another century and a half before Sparta itself was occupied by foreign troops. Nor had the Spartans merely successfully defended their own homeland, in splendid isolation, during all this long time: ever since about the middle of the sixth century their *polis* had been recognized as one of the greatest powers in the Greek world (cf. Herodotos 1.56.1–2), and for a generation, since the end of the Peloponnesian War, it had been the dominant power. Yet there had probably never been more than eight or nine thousand full Spartan citizens of military age.[2]

Other Greeks had little doubt why this was so: apart from praising the excellence and stability of Sparta's institutions in general (cf., e.g., Thucydides 1.18.1), it was, above all, to the superiority of her army to which they bore witness. Herodotos' account of the 'three hundred' at Thermopylai, for example, though there may be much in it of the stuff of legend, surely reflects something of the awe in which Spartan soldiers were held (cf. 7.208.3 and 218.2), and later writers again and again say that their enemies either feared to face them in battle, or gave way at the first onset.[3] An incident recorded by Xenophon (XH 4.4.10) is especially revealing: a Spartan cavalry officer, seeing some hoplites from Sparta's ally, Sikyon, reeling back before an Argive attack, dismounted his men, tied their horses to trees, and, taking the shields from the Sikyonians, boldly advanced against the enemy, while the Argives, seeing the *sigmas* on the advancing shields, 'feared nothing from them as though they were Sikyonians.' The implication is clear: the Argives would have felt very differently had the shields borne the dreaded *lambdas*.[4] If this is how most of Sparta's foes felt, it is perhaps not so surprising that her army does not appear to have suffered any significant defeat in pitched battle between the disastrous fight against the Tegeates early in the sixth century (Herodotos 1.66), and Leuktra in 371.

It is clear, too, that the Greeks were aware of the main reason for the superiority of Spartan soldiers – what Thucydides calls, in one passage (4.33.2), their 'practised skill' or 'experience' (ἐμπειρία). Elsewhere (2.39.1) Thucydides has Perikles sneer at their 'laborious training' (ἐπίπονος ἄσκησις), while Herodotos describes them as 'past masters' (ἐξεπιστάμενοι: 7.211.3), and the Persians, by contrast, as 'lacking in professional skill' (ἀνεπιστήμονες: 9.63.2). Aristotle, perhaps, puts his finger on the point when he says (*Politics* 1338b27ff.) that it was not so much the methods the Spartans used to train their young men which made them superior, as the fact that they trained them at all, and that this was also true of the adults is the point of the story told by Plutarch in his life of Agesilaos (26.4–4), and repeated by Polyainos (2.17). On one occasion, having received complaints from Sparta's allies about the comparative fewness of the troops she had fielded, Agesilaos ordered the whole army to sit down, and then first the potters, then the smiths, then the carpenters and builders, and so on, to stand up, until almost all the allied soldiers were on their feet, but still not a single Spartan. The point, of course, was that the contingents of the allies were composed of essentially part-time soldiers, the Spartan of full-time professionals – Spartan soldiers knew no other trade.[5] Well might Antisthenes the philosopher say of the Thebans after Leuktra that they were 'no different from little boys strutting about because they had thrashed their tutor' (Plutarch *Lykourgos* 30.6).

It was not, however, so much the skill-at-arms of the individual Spartan that was important, as his training as part of a unit, for hoplite fighting left little scope for the display of individual skills (see pp. 35–6, 45–6). Thus one of the speakers in Plato's dialogue *Laches* makes the point (182a–d) that skill-at-arms was only really important when one side or the other had given way and the combatants were in pursuit or in flight: what mattered before this happened was clearly the ability of the individual soldiers to fight together as one man, and in this Spartan soldiers were unsurpassed: as Herodotos has the exiled Spartan king, Demaratos, tell Xerxes (7.104.4), Spartans fighting as individuals were 'no worse' than other men, but fighting together were the best of all men. Thus, at Thermopylai, only troops trained to move as one and instantaneously obey words of command could have carried out the series of feigned retreats Herodotos describes (7.211.3), and at Plataea, he implies (9.63.2), the lack of expertise and skill shown by the Persians lay precisely in their inability to combine together. At Mantineia, in 418, King Agis' last-minute attempt to adjust his line, although it nearly led to disaster (Thucydides 5.71.2–3), shows his supreme confidence in the ability of his men to carry out such manoeuvres, and both in this battle, and at the Nemea in 394, Spartan commanders were evidently able to keep their men in check and wheel them to the left to roll up the enemy line, whereas their opponents were allowed to pursue too far. At Koroneia, also in 394, and in Arcadia in 370, Agesilaos was able to carry out – in the very face of the enemy – the kind of manoeuvres we associate with the ceremony of 'Trooping the Colour'.

All this too must have had a profound effect on the morale of Spartan soldiers, producing in them what has been well-described[6] as 'a cool steadiness born of ingrained, rigorous discipline that shuts the mind to fear.' This is the point of the well-known stories Herodotos tells of Spartan behaviour at Thermopylai, for example – of how they calmly went on with their exercises and with combing their hair, when the Persian scout rode up to view the position (7.208.3), or of how Dienekes welcomed the news that there were so many Persian archers that their arrows would hide the sun (7.226). On Sphakteria, in 425, though surprised by the Athenian attack before dawn, the Spartans at first advanced confidently against the Athenian hoplites, though they must have seen that they were outnumbered two to one, and Thucydides' description of their advance at Mantineia conveys a vivid impression of professionals who knew just what they were doing – the Spartans, he says (5.69.2), needed no encouragement from their commanders, but instead encouraged themselves with martial songs, 'knowing that long-continued practice in action is a more effective safeguard than any hurried verbal exhortation however well-delivered.' Similarly, in Xenophon's time, we find Spartan soldiers holding the enemy in contempt – for example before their disastrous fight with Iphikrates' peltasts near Lechaion (cf. XH 4.5.12) – or so eager to fight that their officers had difficulty in restraining them, as before the so-called 'Tearless Battle' in 368 (XH 7.1.31).

Yet for all this, we know very little about the organization, training and equipment of the Spartan army, partly, perhaps, due to the secretiveness to which Thucydides bears witness in the fifth century (2.39.1, 5.68.2), but mainly to the lack of attention paid to military details by most ancient writers. What little good evidence there is comes mostly from the late fifth and early fourth centuries, when we have Thucydides' remarks about the composition of a Spartan force trapped on the island of Sphakteria in 425 (4.8.9 and 38.5), and his detailed description of the Spartan army at the battle of Mantineia in 418 (5.68.3), and, above all, the writings of Xenophon, who, though born an Athenian, was a soldier himself, and spent much of his life in Spartan territory, and fought alongside Spartans both in Asia Minor and in Greece.

It seems best, then, to begin at the end, as it were, and to look first at what Xenophon has to say,[7] then to look at Thucydides and Herodotos, and finally to look at the beginnings of Spartan military history. This *hysteron-proteron* approach produces its own problems – for example, it is not really possible to treat the accounts of Xenophon and Thucydides completely in isolation, and the first chapter will be much longer than the rest – but it would be difficult to say anything very much about the early Spartan army without constantly referring forwards to its later history, and it will be one of the main conclusions of this book that we can trace the organization known to Xenophon at least back into the early fifth century, and, perhaps, in its essentials, even to the eighth.

If, then, we begin with what Xenophon says in his history of Greece (*Hellenika*), we find that from at least 403 (2.4.31) to the time of Leuktra (6.4.17), the regular infantry of the Spartan army was divided into units called '*morai*' (μόραι), apparently six in number (cf. 6.1.11 and 4.17), and each commanded by an officer called a 'polemarch' (πολέμαρχος: cf. 4.4.7, 5.4.46, etc). In addition, there were subordinate officers called '*pentekosteres*' or '*pentekonteres*' (3.5.22, 4.5.7; *Anabasis* 3.4.21), implying the units called '*pentekostyes*', which, although not mentioned in the *Hellenika*, are mentioned in the *Anabasis* (3.4.22), though there the reference is, of course, not to the Spartan army. The smallest unit seems to have been called an '*enomotia*' (ἐνωμοτία: XH 6.4.12), implying the officer called '*enomotarches*' or '*enomotarchos*' (ἐνωμοτάρχης, ἐνωμοτάρχος), again referred to in the *Anabasis* (3.4.21, 4.3.26), but not in the *Hellenika*. As for numbers, there appear to have been not more than thirty-six men in each *enomotia* at Leuktra, when seven-eighths of the army had been called up (cf. XH 6.4.12 and 17), and there are said to have been about 600 hoplites in the *mora* which met with disaster near Lechaion in 390 (XH 4.5.12).

This is about all the information we can glean about the organization of the regular army from the first six books of the *Hellenika*, but three passages in the last book (7.1.30, 4.20 and 5.10) refer to units called '*lochoi*' (λόχοι), and the last two of these passages imply that there were in all twelve such units in the army, whereas *morai* are never referred to in the seventh book. Nevertheless, it is simplest to assume that this is due to mere coincidence, and that there were both *morai* and *lochoi* in the Spartan army in Xenophon's time, each *mora* being divided into two *lochoi,* and this is partially confirmed by the references to polemarchs in the seventh book of the *Hellenika* (1.17 and 25), by the statement in the treatise on *The Constitution of the Lakedaimonians,* attributed to Xenophon, that there were officers in the *morai* called '*lochagoi*' (i.e., 'commanders of *lochoi*': *LP* 11.4, cf. 13.4), and by references elsewhere in Xenophon to *lochoi* and *lochagoi* in forces which were either clearly modelled on the Spartan army or were commanded by Spartan officers, though not consisting of regular Spartan troops. Thus he refers to *lochoi, pentekostyes* and *enomotiai* in the special unit formed by his fellow-mercenaries after Kounaxa (*Anabasis* 3.4.21–2, cf. 4.3.26), and to *lochagoi* in both Derkylidas' and Agesilaos' armies in Asia Minor (XH 3.1.28, 3.2.16, 4.1.26), and in Mnasippos' force on Kerkyra (6.2.18).

The most cogent evidence against the view that the *morai* were subdivided into *lochoi,* as well as into *pentekostyes* and *enomotiai,* is that Xenophon twice refers to the summoning of polemarchs and *pentekosteres* to a conference (XH 3.5.22, 4.5.7), but does not mention *lochagoi,* who would presumably have outranked *pentekosteres,* and elsewhere (*Hellenika* 4.3.15, *Agesilaos* 2.6) refers to half a *mora* and to a *mora* and a half, where he might have been expected to refer to *lochoi.*[8] However, for what it is worth, *lochagoi* are said to have attended sacrifices with polemarchs and *pentekosteres,* in the *Constitution* (*LP* 13.4), and if Xenophon's failure to mention them at the conferences is not just another coincidence – there are, after all, only two such passages – it is just possible that they were deliberately left with their units in case of a surprise attack – there is, perhaps, a pattern to be discerned in the attendance of polemarchs and *pentekosteres,* but the absence of *lochagoi* and *enomotarchai.* As for the argument that Xenophon would not have referred to half a *mora* or to a *mora* and a half if he had been able instead to refer to a number of *lochoi,* it must be borne in mind that half a *mora* was not necessarily the same thing as one or more *lochoi,* since such a force could have been made up of *enomotiai* drawn from more than one of a *mora*'s component *lochoi.* In any case, what is the alternative to believing that the *morai* were subdivided into *lochoi* before 368, when *lochoi* are first mentioned? It has been suggested, for example, that *morai* were abandoned in favour of *lochoi* after Leuktra,[9] but there is no compelling reason why this should have been so, and the casual way in which Xenophon first refers to

lochoi (XH 7.1.30) belies the notion that he was suddenly talking about a new
kind of unit.

But if there were *lochoi* in the Spartan army between 403 and 368, as there
almost certainly were, how many of them were there in each *mora*? As was
suggested above, the simplest hypothesis is that the two references in the
Hellenika (7.4.20 and 5.10) to 'the twelve *lochoi*' mean that there were two
lochoi in each of the six *morai*, and this is probably right: as we shall see
(below, p. 57), there is some reason to believe not only that there were *lochoi*
in the Spartan army during the Peloponnesian War, but that there were
already twelve of them at least by 425, if not by 480, and, indeed, as far back
as we can trace (see pp. 70, 90). The treatise on the *Constitution*, however,
appears to say that each *mora* contained four *lochagoi*, and this clearly implies
that there were four *lochoi*, for although it has been suggested that two of the
lochagoi might have been attached to the polemarch as staff-officers,[10] this is
very forced. Alternatively, it has been suggested that there may have been
four *lochoi* in each *mora* before Leuktra, but that after that disaster the
number was halved,[11] but this would either mean our having to abandon the
plausible hypothesis that there were already twelve *lochoi* at the time of the
Pylos campaign, or our having to suppose that the number was subsequently
doubled sometime before the date reflected by the *Constitution*, and then
halved again after Leuktra. There is also the point that if what the
Constitution says is to be accepted, we would have to accept that at one time
there were only two *pentekostyes* in each *lochos*, since the *Constitution* also
says that there were eight *pentekosteres* in each *mora*. But in Thucydides'
description of the army at Mantineia, there are four *pentekostyes* in each
lochos (5.68.3), and although we shall see reason to believe that he may have
been mistaken about the number of *lochoi* which took part in the battle, there
is no reason to doubt that he was right about their internal structure. Thus
we would have to posit yet another change in the organization of the army
between Mantineia and the date reflected by the *Constitution*, and all this is,
surely, to place far too much weight on a single passage, and on a series of
numbers at that, when numbers are notoriously susceptible to corruption in
ancient texts – in this case, for example, a copyist may easily have read 'δύο'
(two) as 'δ″' (four).[12] It is more sensible to take the view that the reference in
the *Constitution* to four *lochagoi* in each *mora* is either a simple mistake by its
author, or is due to an error in the copying of our manuscripts.

If, then, there were two *lochoi* in each *mora*, we can at least accept the
statement in the *Constitution* that each *mora* contained eight *pentekosteres*

(*LP* 11.4), implying eight *pentekostyes*, for this is not contradicted by anything said in the *Hellenika*, and is supported by what Thucydides says about the internal composition of the *lochoi* at Mantineia. Moreover, since this would mean that there were forty-eight *pentekostyes* in the army as a whole, the term '*pentekostys*' itself could be explained: the word could mean either a 'fifty' or a 'fiftieth', and although the former might seem the more obvious, there is, in fact, no evidence that there ever was a unit of fifty men in the Spartan army – at Mantineia, for example, each *pentekostys* is implied to have contained about 128 men (Thucydides 5.68.3) – and although a *pentekostys* may not, strictly speaking, have been a 'fiftieth' of the army, it would surely have seemed absurdly cumbersome to refer to such units and their commanders as '*tessarakostogdyes*' and '*tessarakostogderes*'![13]

But the most important question of numbers is the number of *enomotiai* in each *mora*, for one of the few relatively certain things about the Spartan army at this period is that each *enomotia* had a total strength of 40 men (see p. 16 below), and if we knew how many *enomotiai* there were in a *mora*, it would be a simple matter not only to calculate how many men there were in a *mora*, but how many men there were in the army as a whole. Unfortunately, Xenophon never even hints how many *enomotiai* there were in a *mora*, in the *Hellenika*, but the *Constitution* says that each *mora* had sixteen *enomotarchoi* (*LP* 11.4), implying sixteen *enomotiai*, and this agrees well enough with what Xenophon says about the strength of the *enomotiai* at Leuktra (6.4.12, cf. 17), and of the *mora* which got into difficulties near Lechaion (4.5.12). At Leuktra each *enomotia* is said to have been drawn up in three files of not more than twelve men, and since later it is said that only thirty-five of the forty age-classes had been called up, this probably means that in fact the *enomotiai* at Leuktra each contained thirty-five men, their full strength being forty men. Thus, if there were sixteen *enomotiai* to the *mora*, each *mora* at Leuktra would have contained 560 men, and the full strength of a *mora* would have been 640 men: the Lechaion *mora* is said to have had about 600 men.

Plausible as this view is, however, and widely as it is held, there is one serious, if not fatal, objection to it: it requires us to accept that the total strength of Sparta's regular army, at the height of her imperial power, was only 3840 men (6 × 640), excluding cavalry and other infantry such as the *Hippeis*, *Skiritai* and *neodamodeis*. But it is barely credible that at a time when Argos, for example, could allegedly field 7,000 hoplites for a campaign not fought in her territory, and even Euboea 3,000 (XH 4.2.17), Sparta could hardly have fielded 4,000, even if all six *morai* were present, as well as the *Hippeis*. It is true that there is very little good evidence for the size and composition of Spartan armies at this period, and what little there is is difficult to interpret because of the equivocal use of the term 'Lakedaimonians' (see p. 19 below). But Xenophon says that there were 13,500 hoplites on the Spartan side at the Nemea – in fact there were probably more (see p. 163 below) – including 6,000 Lakedaimonians (XH 4.2.16), and since there were probably five *morai* present (see p. 163 below), if we allow only 560 men to each *mora*, this would mean a total of only 2,800 Spartan hoplites, or 3,100, if we add three hundred *Hippeis*. Similarly, if Diodoros is right to say that when Agesilaos invaded Boeotia in 377, he had an army of 18,000 men, it is difficult to believe that he was also right in saying that of these only 2,500 were Spartan hoplites (five *morai* of 500 men each: 15.32.1). Again, there is good reason to believe that there were 7,000 hoplites on the Boeotian side at Leuktra, of whom 4,000 were Thebans (see p. 179 below), and Plutarch's figure of 10,000 for the Spartan side (*Pelopidas* 20.1) is plausible – Frontinus (*Strategemata* 4.2.6) gives them 24,000 foot alone and Polyainos (2.3.8 & 12) 40,000 men! – but can we really believe that there were only 2,540 Spartan hoplites there (four *morai* of 560 men each and 300 *Hippeis*)? Apart, however, from any particular difficulties which may arise from the figures given by the sources for individual campaigns, it is too much of a strain on one's credulity to have to believe that the state which from time to time was the arbiter of Greek affairs from Byzantion to the Peloponnese could ultimately only rely upon an army of just over 4,000 hoplites.[14]

In Thucydides' description of the Spartan army at Mantineia, however, there are not two *enomotiai* in each *pentekostys*, as implied by the *Constitution*, but four (5.68.3), and if this was the case in the army of Xenophon's time, each *mora* would have had not sixteen *enomotiai*, but thirty-two, assuming that there were eight *pentekostyes* in each *mora*. This, in turn, means that the full strength of a *mora* would have been 1,280 men (32×40), instead of 640 (16×40), and the whole number of the Spartan regular infantry, excluding the *Hippeis*, would have been 7,680 men ($6 \times 1,280$). Thus, at the Nemea, if five of the *morai* were present and thirty-five age-classes had been called up, as later for Leuktra, the Spartan hoplites would have numbered 5,600 men ($5 \times 32 \times 35$), which is near enough Xenophon's figure for the 'Lakedaimonians' (XH 4.2.16) – the correspondence would be even closer if we should add the 300 *Hippeis* and at Leuktra, similarly, where there were four *morai* (cf. 6.4.17), each would have numbered 1,120 men (32 × 35), giving a total of 4,780 Spartans, including the *Hippeis* (4 × 1,120 + 300), which fits Plutarch's total of 10,000 infantry for the Spartan side far better than 2,540 (4 × 560 + 300).

There are, at first sight, two main objections to believing that there were thirty-two *enomotiai* in each *mora*: firstly, the statement in the *Constitution* that each *mora* had sixteen *enomotarchoi*, and, secondly, the fact that all the figures given by ancient sources for the strength of a *mora* are less than 1,280. However, we have already seen reason to doubt the *Constitution* when it apparently says that each *mora* had four *lochagoi*, and we should, perhaps, not pay too much attention to what it says about the number of *enomotarchoi* – its author may have confused the number of *enomotarchoi* in a *mora* with the number in a *lochos*[15] – and it is arguable that Thucydides' evidence about the number of *enomotiai* in a *pentekostys*, and thus in a *lochos*, should carry more weight, even though for him the *lochos* was apparently the largest unit (see below, p. 51ff.).

More serious is the second objection – that the figures in ancient sources for the size of *morai* are all less than 1,280 – but even this is not as serious as it may seem: there are, in fact, very few references to the size of *morai* in ancient sources, and of these, only one need be taken seriously in this context – Xenophon's statement (XH 4.5.12) that the *mora* caught by Iphikrates' peltasts near Lechaion in 390 contained about 600 hoplites. Apart from this, we have only Diodoros' assertion (15.2.1) that the *morai* in Agesilaos' army in Boeotia in 377 each contained 500 men, Plutarch's report, in his life of Pelopidas (17.2), that Ephoros said that there were 500 men in a *mora*, Kallisthenes 700, and 'certain others, of whom one was Polybios' 900, and the entries in Photios (s.v. μόρα) that each *mora* contained either 1,000 or 500 men. Of these, we need not pay too much attention to the statements of Kallisthenes, Polybios and the 'certain others', and of Photios, since we have no means of knowing whether they refer to *morai* in general or to particular *morai* on particular occasions, nor what period they are talking about, though it is worth noting that both Kallisthenes and Polybios wrote after Leuktra and yet apparently both mentioned *morai*. Diodoros' figure is presumably derived from Ephoros, but is also very dubious: it occurs in a passage in which it is stated that the *Skiritai* were stationed near the king and were largely responsible for many a Spartan victory, both of which are almost certainly wrong (see below) – they look like general conclusions wrongly drawn from a particular exploit of the *Skiritai* in 377, described by Xenophon (XH 5.4.52–3), possibly confusing them with the *Hippeis* – and, as was argued above, a total of 2,500 for the Spartans in Agesilaos' army hardly fits the figure of 18,000 men given by Diodoros for the whole army. Photios' figure of 1,000, of course, would be very nearly right, particularly for the campaign-strength of a *mora*, when 35 age-classes were called up, if there were 32 *enomotiai* in a *mora* ($32 \times 35 = 1,120$).

This leaves Xenophon's *mora* at Lechaion, and it is straight away arguable that we should place no more reliance upon a single statement about a particular *mora* for the size of *morai* in general than upon some of the figures for Caesar's legions, for example, for the size of legions. In the case of this particular *mora*, indeed, there is reason to believe that it was under strength: in the first place, all the men from Amyklai in it had presumably been given furlough to go home for the festival of the Hyakinthia, like their fellow-Amyklaians in the rest of the army (XH 4.5.11–12), and, in the second place, detachments from the *mora* may have been stationed in the forts at Sidous and Krommyon, captured in 392, in Epieikeia, fortified at the same time (XH 4.4.13), and in Oinoe, captured by Agesilaos just before the disaster (XH 4.5.5). We also have no means of knowing how many age-classes had been called upon on this occasion: if it was thirty-five, as for the Leuktra campaign, then the full strength of the *mora* would have been 1,120 men, if there were thirty-two *enomotiai* in a *mora*, and thus, when it made its fatal march back towards Lechaion, it would have been at only just over half strength, if Xenophon's figure of 'about 600' is correct; but if only twenty-five age-classes had been called up on this occasion, for example, the *mora* would originally only have mustered 800 men and the absence of about 200 would be easily explained.

On the other hand, if a *mora* really only contained sixteen *enomotiai*, it would only have had a full strength of 640 men, even when all forty age-classes were called upon, and it would be very difficult to understand how this particular *mora* came to be so nearly at full strength on this occasion: it must have been very rare for all forty age-classes to be called up – the last five were only called up after Leuktra, for example (XH 6.4.17) – and we know that the Amyklaians were absent on this occasion. It is easier to understand how this *mora* may have become seriously depleted than how it came to have only about forty men short of its full complement, and thus Xenophon's figure for the size of this particular *mora*, far from supporting the view that there were only sixteen *enomotiai* in a *mora*, in fact turns out to suggest that there were more.

In view of the lack of evidence, and the conflicting nature of the evidence we have, it is obviously not possible to be certain about even the basic organization of the Spartan army in Xenophon's time. But the most likely view to be right seems to be that at least from the end of the Peloponnesian War to the 360's, the regular infantry were divided into six *morai* commanded by polemarchs, and subdivided into two *lochoi*, eight *pentekostyes* and thirty-two *enomotiai*, commanded respectively by *lochagoi*, *pentekosteres* and *enomotarchai*. It is fairly certain that each *enomotia* at full strength contained 40 men, and this would mean that a full-strength *pentekostys* consisted of 160 men, a *lochos* of 640 men, and a *mora* of 1,280 men.

There were, in addition, probably three other units or types of unit in the regular army at the same period – the *Skiritai*, the *Hippeis* and the cavalry. From time to time forces of *neodamodeis* also appear, but they do not seem to have formed part of the regular establishment. The *Skiritai* are mentioned in connection with only two episodes in the *Hellenika*, and Diodoros surely exaggerates when he declares (15.32.1) that the *lochos* of *Skiritai* 'creates many an important turn of the scale in battle and is mostly responsible for victory.' The origin and meaning of the name is obscure, but probably derives from the district of Skiritis mentioned by Xenophon (XH 6.5.24–5, 7.4.21):[16] presumably the people who inhabited it were *perioikoi*, but the unit obviously had a different status from that of normal perioecic contingents. At Mantineia, in 418, for example, they fought in the battle-line (Thucydides 5.67.1), when, if we are to believe Thucydides at least, no other perioecic contingents were present, and they are singled out for special mention in Xenophon's description of the army Agesipolis took to Olynthos in 383, when other *perioikoi* are mentioned (XH 5.2.24). There is nothing in either of these references to them to suggest that they were anything else than hoplites, but there are some hints that they may have had a skirmishing role: in 377, for example, during Agesilaos' second campaign in Boeotia, they boldly followed the Thebans up the hill to the very walls of Thebes (XH 5.4.52–3), and according to the *Constitution* (*LP* 12.3 and 13.6), they were used as pickets, outside the lines, at night, and as advanced guards on the march.

The *Hippeis* are mentioned even more rarely in the *Hellenika* – indeed, there is possibly only one reference to them (6.4.14), and that depends upon an emendation (see below). However, the reference to the '*hippagretai*' in the account of Kinadon's conspiracy (3.3.9) is some confirmation that the *Hippeis* still existed, for the word seems to mean something like 'choosers of the *Hippeis*' – the *Constitution* says they were the officers responsible for recruiting the corps (4.3) – and it is possible that some of the references to '*hippeis*' which are usually interpreted to mean 'horsemen' (i.e. cavalry), in fact refer to the *Hippeis*. When Agesilaos, for example, after crossing the frontier and marching to Tegea in 387, is said to have sent 'some of the *hippeis*' (τῶν μὲν ἱππέων: XH 5.1.33) in various directions to hurry up the *perioikoi*, although the meaning could be 'some of the cavalry' since speed was obviously important, it is possible that members of the corps of *Hippeis* are meant, since the cavalry ranked low in the Spartan military hierarchy (see p. 16 below), and such a task really required men of some authority.

According to the *Constitution* (loc.cit), the three hundred *Hippeis* were chosen by the *hippagretai*, who were appointed by the ephors from 'the men in their prime' (ἐκ τῶν ἀκμαζόντων), and since the context is concerned with the methods used by Lykourgos to instil a spirit of rivalry into the young men (cf. τοὺζ ἡβῶνταζ: *LP* 4.2), it seems clear that the author thought all the *Hippeis* were young men. In some sense they also probably still constituted a 'Royal Guard' who fought around the king in battle, as they had done at Mantineia (cf. Thucydides 5.72.4), for in Xenophon's account of Leuktra, although the manuscripts would have it that 'the horses' (οἱ ἵπποι: 6.4.14) fell back before the Theban attack on the right wing, this makes no sense and the obvious emendation is 'the *Hippeis*' (οἱ ἵππεῖς) – nor could this mean 'the cavalry' in this particular passage, for they are already said to have been routed (XH 6.4.13).

It is not certain, however, whether the *Hippeis* formed a separate unit, or were incorporated into one of the *morai*,[17] and in particular whether they are to be identified with the '*agema*' referred to in two passages of the *Constitution* (ἄνημα: *LP* 11.9 and 13.6), which have to do with the positioning of the commander of the army in certain circumstances. In the first passage, which explains how the commander – here called the *hegemon* (ὁ ἡνεμών) – can be transferred from the left to the right wing, if need be, the phrase used is 'having wheeled the *agema* to the flank, they countermarch the phalanx'; in the second, the author is explaining what happens when the army is on the march and 'they think there will be a battle': 'taking the *agema* of the first *mora*,' he says, 'the king, having wheeled to the right, leads on until he is between two *morai* and two polemarchs.' What is meant by these manoeuvres will be discussed below (see p. 35, 39), but is the *agema*, and in particular the *agema* of the first *mora*, to be regarded as a special unit, and, if so, is it the *Hippeis*, or does it simply mean the unit which happens to be leading on each occasion? Certainty is not possible, but although the term *agema* came to be used of various *corps d'elite* in the

Macedonian and Hellenistic armies, the original meaning of the term is, just, 'leading unit', and this is probably the meaning in the *Constitution*: it would then correspond with the term '*to hegoumenon*' used by Xenophon in a passage in the *Hellenika* (XH 4.2.19). In any case, it is very unlikely that the *agema* is to be identified with the *Hippeis,* for in that case one of the *morai* would have had a different structure from the other five, since the number 300 is not a multiple of 40 and was not therefore divisible into normal *enomotiai,* and the *Hippeis* were all probably young men, as we have seen, whereas normal *enomotiai* seem to have contained representatives of all the age-classes (see p. 16 below). Nor will it do to suppose that the *Hippeis* formed a special corps for purely ceremonial purposes, but were incorporated into regular units for practical purposes, for in that case there would have been no point in Xenophon's saying that the *Hippeis* fell back before the Theban onslaught at Leuktra: if that is what Xenophon wrote (XH 6.4.14), he clearly meant that a particular group of men fell back. Finally, Xenophon's use of the term 'δορυφόροι' (*doryphoroi,* i.e. 'spear-bearers': XH 4.5.8) of the actual bodyguard of Agesilaos on another occasion, does not preclude the *Hippeis* from forming the king's guard in battle, as the Leuktra passage certainly implies, and as is also implied by the heavy losses among the Spartiates at that battle (see p. 187) – there is a difference between the king's bodyguard and the Guard. In any case, Agesilaos' 'spear-bearers' could conceivably have been a unit of the *Hippeis,* since the latter were certainly armed with spears.

Despite their title, the *Hippeis* in the sense of the Guard had nothing to do with *hippeis* in the sense of cavalry, as indeed the account of Leuktra in the *Hellenika* indicates, for the Spartan cavalry is said to have already been routed before the Theban infantry attack developed and the *Hippeis* fell back before it (XH 6.4.13). The *Hippeis* in the sense of the Guard almost certainly fought on foot in Xenophon's time as they had done in Thucydides' (cf. Thucydides 5.72.4 and Strabo 10.4.18), and it is indeed doubtful that the *Hippeis* had ever fought as true cavalry.[18] Xenophon, who wrote treatises on commanding cavalry and on horsemanship, had precious little use for Spartan cavalry: at Leuktra, he says (XH 6.4.10–11), it was at its worst, since the richest Spartans reared the horses, but the troopers only appeared when war was declared, and then they were amongst the least strong, physically, and the least ambitious (cf. also, XH 4.5.16). It has been suggested that this means that the troopers were not full Spartan citizens,[19] but on at least one other occasion Spartan cavalrymen are said to have included Spartiates (cf. XH 5.4.39), though these may, of course, have been officers. The cavalry was apparently organized in units called *morai*, like the infantry, six in number and each under the command of a *hipparmostes* (ἱππαρμοστής: cf. XH 4.5.12), but it is not known how many troopers there were in a cavalry *mora*: at the Nemea, in 394, there were 600 Lakedaimonian cavalry (XH 4.2.16), which might imply five *morai* of 120 troopers each, since there were probably five infantry *morai* present (see p. 163), but it is not absolutely certain that all the 600 were Spartans.

The call up of the Spartan army, or at least of the infantry, seems to have been organized in a simple but effective way: for the Leuktra campaign, for example, Xenophon tells us (XH 6.4.17), the age-classes 'up to those thirty-five years from manhood' (μέχρι τῶν πέντε καὶ τριάκοντα ἀφ᾽ ἥβης) were originally called up, and after the battle men 'up to those forty years from manhood' (μέχρι τῶν τεττταράκοντα ἀφ᾽ ἥβης) Such a system enabled the Spartan government to put into the field, quickly and easily, a force of any size it wished (cf. *LP* 11.2). Liability for military service apparently extended up to 'those forty years from manhood', for King Agesilaos once asked to be excused on the ground that he was 'beyond forty years from manhood' (ὑπὲρ τετταράκοντα ἀφ᾽ ἥβης: XH 5.4.13), and this probably meant from a man's twenty-first to his sixtieth year, inclusive. After this he was at least not liable for service outside Spartan territory, as Agesilaos implied. Probably also each *enomotia* was made up of representatives from all forty age-classes, or, perhaps, more strictly, each of the eight groups of five year classes was represented by five men in each *enomotia*, thus producing a full strength of forty men for each *enomotia*.[20] The Spartan government would, of course, have known how many *enomotiai* there were in each *mora*, even if we do not, and so, if it wanted an army of 4,480 men, for example, it would have known that four *morai*, with thirty-five age-classes represented, were required, assuming that there were thirty-two *enomotiai* in a *mora*.

It seems, further, that not only were the *enomotiai* formed on the basis of age-classes, but that they were also deployed for battle on a similar basis, with the younger men stationed in the front ranks. This emerges from several incidents in which 'those ten years from manhood' or 'fifteen years from manhood' (τὰ δέκα/δεκάπεντε ἀφ᾽ ἥβης) were ordered to charge out from the phalanx (cf. XH 2.4.32, 4.5.14 & 16, 4.6.10, 5.4.10). This would clearly have been more easily achieved if the younger men were in the front ranks: in a full-strength *enomotia*, for example, ranged in five files, eight deep, orders to 'those ten years from manhood' could have referred to the front two ranks, orders to 'those fifteen years from manhood' to the front three. If all forty age-classes had not been called up, as they probably very rarely were for active service, or if the *enomotiai* were deployed in greater depth, these simple arrangements would no longer have worked, but modification would have been easy: at Leuktra, for example, where the *enomotiai* were in three files, with an average depth of twelve men (XH 6.4.12), orders to 'those ten years from manhood' could have been interpreted to mean the front three ranks, and so on.

There is, however, one problem here: according to the *Constitution* (*LP* 11.5), the 'front rank men' (οἱ πρωτοστάται) were all, in some sense, 'leaders' (ἄρχοντες), and it is doubtful whether the Spartans, of all people, would have made the youngest men in the files their commanders. If the author of the *Constitution* is right here – and certainly the file-leaders would have been of considerable importance in some of the manoeuvres the *enomotiai* were expected to perform – it is possible that the front rank men were older, and that only the other ranks were made up according to age-classes, so that if orders were given to 'those ten years from manhood', for example, the front rank men stood firm and only a certain number of ranks behind them complied. An alternative possibility is that the front rank men were 'leaders' only in the literal sense that they led the files, not that they were some kind of officers.

It has been suggested[21] that the *enomotiai* were composed of a certain number of the messes – variously called '*syssitia*', '*phiditia*', '*andreia*' or '*syskenia*' (cf. Aristotle *Politics* 1271a27, 1272a2; *LP* 5.2, etc.) – to which all adult male Spartans of full citizen status had to belong (cf. Aristotle *Politics* 1271a26ff.), and there is something to be said for this view: the *syssitia* clearly had strong military overtones (cf., e.g., Herodotos 1.65.5; Plutarch *Lykourgos* 12.3; Polyainos 2.3.11), and mobilization would have been all the easier, and *esprit de corps* all the stronger, if members of the same *enomotia* were accustomed to eat together, and the younger, at least, to sleep together (cf. Plutarch *Lykourgos* 15.3–4). Unfortunately, we do not know how many men there were in each *syssition*, in Xenophon's day. The only evidence is in Plutarch, but he was writing over four centuries later, when Sparta was a very different place, and we thus have no means of knowing whether what he says is true, or, if true, of what period it was true. In one passage (*Lykourgos* 12.2), he says that there were about fifteen men in each *syssition*, but in another (*Agis* 8.1–2) he says that when King Agis IV attempted to revive Spartan institutions in the third century, he created *syssitia* of 200 and 400 members. In theory the two sets of figures could be reconciled, since it is possible that when the number of full Spartan citizens declined (see below), the number of men in each *syssition* was reduced. However, on the face of it, it seems more likely that the traditional number of men in each *syssition* would have been maintained, and the number of *syssitia* reduced, if only because the smaller number seems right for such a gathering.[22] But whatever the size of the *syssitia* in Xenophon's time, it is very improbable that they continued to form the basis for the *enomotiai*, even if they had ever done so, for by then there were far too few Spartans of full citizen status to form more than two or three *enomotiai* in each *mora*, and it is more likely that they were distributed fairly evenly throughout the *morai*, with a marked concentration of the younger ones in the *Hippeis*. It is suggestive that in 390 there appears to have been Amyklaians in all the *morai* (cf. XH 4.5.11), and that men in other *morai* are said to have had sons, fathers and brothers amongst those killed in the *mora* so roughly handled by Iphikrates' peltasts (XH 4.5.10).

In Xenophon's time there were certainly no longer enough Spartans of full citizen-status to form six *morai*, whether these had a total strength of 640 or 1,280 men, for even if the former was true, the four *morai* at Leuktra, for example, would have contained 2,240 men, since only thirty-five age-classes had been called up, and yet Xenophon explicitly says (XH 6.4.15) that only 700 '*Spartiatai*' took part, and of these 300 were almost certainly brigaded separately in the *Hippeis*. Who, then, were the other men who formed these *morai*?

The problem is bedevilled from the start by the equivocal use in even contemporary sources of the terms 'Lakedaimonians' (Λακεδαιμόνιοι) and 'Spartans' (Σπαρτιᾶται): a passage in Xenophon (XH 5.1.11), for example, relates the death of eight 'Spartans' on Aigina in 388, but a few sentences later (5.1.12) the same men are called 'Lakedaimonians'. We can probably, indeed, only say with any confidence that whereas all 'Spartans' were 'Lakedaimonians' and hence the Spartan state was, officially, 'the Lakedaimonians' and Spartan soldiers bore a *lambda*, not a *sigma*, on their shields (cf. XH 4.4.10), not all 'Lakedaimonians' were 'Spartans', for the 'Lakedaimonians' certainly included the semi-independent communities of *perioikoi*. It is also clear that within the Spartan community, as distinct from those of the *perioikoi*, there were 'Spartans' who were so in the fullest sense, and others who were not. One of the latter groups is easy to distinguish, the '*neodamodeis*' (literally 'new citizens'), who make their first appearance in the 420s (Thucydides 5.34.1), and seem to have been ex-helots, freed for military service.[23] But the *neodamodeis* always seem to have served in separate contingents, often in distant campaigns, and there can surely be no question of their serving in the *morai*.

At the other end of the scale, many of the officers, special commissioners and so on, referred to by name by Xenophon, are explicitly described as 'Spartans' (Σπαρτιᾶται), and there can be little doubt that they were 'Spartans' in the fullest sense. But apart from these individuals, the only men explicitly described as 'Spartans' by Xenophon, are the king, ephors, *gerontes* and about forty others counted in the *agora* by the man who informed against Kinadon in 397 (XH 3.3.5), the various groups of thirty sent to advise Agesilaos in Asia and Agesipolis at Olynthos (XH 3.4.2, 8, 20; 4.1.5, 23; 5.3.8), and two smaller groups – the eighteen killed with the polemarch, Gylis, in Lokris in 394 (XH 4.3.23), and the eight killed on Aigina in 388, who are later called 'Lakedaimonians' (XH 5.1.11–12). By far the largest number of 'Spartans', as opposed to 'Lakedaimonians', ever mentioned by Xenophon, are the seven hundred who fought at Leuktra (XH 6.4.15), and thereafter the only ones he mentions are the 'very few' who defended Sparta in 370 and 362 (XH 6.5.28 and 7.5.10), and those captured at Kromnos in 365 (XH 7.4.27). In these cases, except perhaps those of the men killed in Lokris and on Aigina, we can be reasonably sure that we are dealing with full citizens, since either their importance or their fewness is emphasised, and we can probably accept that the word '*Spartiatai*' could be used, in a technical sense, to mean such citizens: in this book the Anglicized form 'Spartiate(s)' is used to mean Spartans in this sense.

It is, then, certain that there were not enough Spartiates even to man the four *morai* which fought at Leuktra, whether they contained 2,240 or 4,480 men, and we are left with the problem of who the other men in these *morai* were. One view that has gained widespread acceptance is that they were *perioikoi*,[24] but there are serious objections to it. In the first place, none of the passages which have been cited to show that *perioikoi* did serve in the same units as Spartiates, proves any such thing. It is, for example, surely going too far to argue that when Isokrates, of all people, remarks in the *Panathenaikos* (180) that '(the Spartans) station the *perioikoi* individually alongside themselves, and station some in the front rank' (κατ ἄνδρα συμπαρατάττεσθαι σφίσιν αὐτοῖς, ἐνίους δὲ καὶ τῆς πρώτης τάττειν), he reveals a knowledge of the composition of Spartan military units: all he is saying is that 'man for man' the *perioikoi* are made to share the same dangers as Spartans, sometimes to take a disproportionate share, without having any of the privileges – he goes on to say that they were often sent on particularly hard, dangerous or lengthy expeditions.

Better evidence is the inscription from Geronthrai (*IC* V i 1124), recording the death 'in war at Mantineia' of one Eualkes, which by its letter-forms should refer to the first battle of Mantineia in 418, rather than the second in 362.[25] The natural assumption, since the inscription comes from perioecic Geronthrai, is that Eualkes was a *perioikos,* and since Thucydides does not mention *perioikoi* as serving in separate contingents at the battle, it is arguable that Eualkes must have served in one of the Spartan units – indeed, it has been argued,[26] that Eualkes is commemorated 'exactly as if he had been a Spartiate.' However, it is difficult to see how else he might have been commemorated – would not the *perioikoi* have tended to 'ape' the Spartiates? – and, of course, he may have been a Spartiate, whose estates, for example, lay near Geronthrai. On the other hand, if he was a *perioikos,* it is possible to account for his presence at Mantineia without having to suppose that he was serving in one of the Spartan units: Thucydides may have omitted to mention the perioecic contingents (though it will be argued below – p. 42ff. – that this is not the case), or Eualkes may have been a 'volunteer' like the *perioikoi* who accompanied King Agesipolis to Olynthos (XH 5.3.9), in which case he may have died fighting near King Agis himself, for the *Constitution* says (13.7) that any 'volunteers' who joined the Spartans, formed part of the king's staff. In any case, one inscription recording a possible *perioikos,* who may have been a member of a Spartan unit in 418, can hardly be regarded as proof that by then Spartan military units did contain *perioikoi.*

More serious, perhaps, are a number of passages in which Xenophon appears to include *perioikoi* in expressions like 'the citizens' (οἱ πολῖται) or 'the citizen army' (τὸ πολιτικὸν στράτευμα), with which we may compare the expression 'the citizen *morai*' (τῶν πολιτικῶν μορῶν) in the *Constitution* (*LP* 11.4, cf. XH 7.1.28).[27] The most telling of these passages is one in which Archidamos is said to march out 'with the citizens' (μετὰ τῶν πολιτῶν) to take Kromnos, and to leave there 'three of the twelve *lochoi*' (τῶν δώδεκα λόχων τρεῖς: XH 7.4.20), for later prisoners from this force are said to have included *perioikoi* (7.4.27). But Xenophon can hardly have consciously included *perioikoi* among what he calls 'the citizens', since he would have been well aware that *perioikoi* were not citizens of Sparta, and it is much more likely that he simply omitted to mention that Archidamos' army included *perioikoi* until he had cause to mention them. The same is probably true of his failure to mention *perioikoi* in his account of the end of Agesilaos' campaigns in Boeotia in 378 and 377, where he uses the formulaic expression 'he dismissed the allies and led the citizen army (τὸ πολιτικὸν στράτευμα) back home' (XH 5.4.41 & 55), for at least one *perioikos* is said to have been killed in 378 (XH 5.4.39). But it should not be assumed that Spartan armies always included *perioikoi* even when they are not specifically mentioned by the sources, for there may have been reasons, unknown to us, why *perioikoi* served in some campaigns and not in others. It is, for example, suggestive that until Agesilaos' campaign against the Arcadians in 370, *perioikoi* do not seem to have been specifically said by either Xenophon or Thucydides to have served against a Peloponnesian enemy: they seem always to have served outside the Peloponnese, or, in the case of the Pylos campaign in 425, against an enemy from outside the Peloponnese,[28] and it is perhaps significant that at the end of his account of the campaign against the Arcadians in 370, Xenophon varies his usual formula and specifically mentions the *perioikoi* (XH 6.5.21). Thus, when he uses the expression 'the citizen army' at the end of his accounts of the campaigns of 391 against Argos (XH 4.4.19) and of 379 against Phleious (XH 5.3.25), he may mean, precisely, the Spartan army.

There are, in any case, a considerable number of passages in which Xenophon refers to *perioikoi* in such a way as strongly to suggest that they were still providing separate contingents,[29] and this would be very odd if a large part of their manpower had now been absorbed into the Spartan army itself (cf. XH 3.3.6, 5.7; 5.1.33, 2.24, 3.9, 4.39; 6.5.21 & 32; 7.2.2, 4.27). Some of these passages make it particularly difficult to believe that *perioikoi* now served in Spartan units: Agesipolis' army at Olynthos, for example, which apparently did not contain any regular Spartan units, unless one counts the *Skiritai* (cf. XH 5.2.24), is said to have contained 'many gentlemen-volunteers of the *perioikoi*' (πολοὶ ... τῶν περιοίκων ἐθελονταὶ καλοὶ κἀγαθοί: XH 5.3.9), and these were, surely, just the sort of men who would have been drafted into the Spartan army, if any were, and one can hardly believe that they were allowed to leave their units to serve as 'volunteers' on so distant a campaign. Several times, too, after the Spartan army had mobilized and had even advanced beyond the frontier, it had to wait for contingents of the *perioikoi*: in 395, for example, King Pausanias is said to have waited at Tegea for 'the soldiers of the perioecic states' (XH 3.5.7), and, similarly, eight years later, Agesilaos crossed the frontier to Tegea and then 'sent out some of the *Hippeis* (see p. 13 above) in various directions to hurry up the *perioikoi*' (XH 5.1.33). In both these passages the natural interpretation is that the Spartan units were complete and that the *perioikoi* formed quite separate units: if there had been *perioikoi* serving in the same units as Spartans, we would have to suppose either that these units had crossed the frontier incomplete, or that the *perioikoi* in them had already joined up, before the rest, and both explanations seem very forced.

A second objection to the hypothesis that *perioikoi* served in the same units as Spartiates is that one of the strengths of the Spartan army clearly lay in the professional training of its soldiers, both as individuals and as members of units, training which began, in the case of Spartiates at least, at the age of seven, and which kept boys and men of the same age together in age-classes which ultimately formed the basis for mobilization. But even if the *perioikoi* had the same basic social structure as the Spartiates – which is not impossible – it is very unlikely that some of them can have been semi-permanently away from home, training day-in and day-out with their Spartiate counterparts. Yet to intermingle highly-trained Spartiates with less well-trained *perioikoi*, unaccustomed to the kind of tactical unit-drill which probably formed part of the daily lives of Spartiate hoplites, would surely have nullified the whole point of the Spartan military system. Xenophon's description of the end of the 370 campaign certainly suggests that the *perioikoi* were not permanently barracked at Sparta, for he says (XH 6.5.21) that Agesilaos 'released the Spartiates to their homes and sent the *perioikoi* off to their own cities.'

But if the extra men the Spartans used to make up the numbers required for their regular army were not *neodamodeis* or *perioikoi*, who were they? The answer must be, surely, that they were 'Spartans' in the sense that they were born of Spartan parents and were not helots; *neodamodeis* or *perioikoi*, but that they were not *Spartiates*, in the technical sense – they were not '*homoioi*' ('equals' or 'peers'), as the full-citizens of Sparta were called (cf. XH 3.3.5) – either because they were too poor to contribute their dues to the *syssitia* (cf. Aristotle *Politics* 1271a26ff.), or because they were debarred from full rights for some other reason (cf., e.g., Thucydides 5.34.2). Xenophon once uses the term '*hypomeiones*' (ὑπομείονες, i.e. 'inferiors') of some kind of second-class members of the Spartan community distinct from *neodamodeis*, *perioikoi* and helots (XH 3.3.6), and this was probably the technical term for Spartans who were not classed as 'peers', though since the word is never used elsewhere of Spartans – it is once used by Cassius Dio (38.35) to mean 'inferior officers' in the army – its precise significance must remain uncertain.

Despite the rareness of an ⬛⬛⬛ ce to them in the sources, the passage from the *Politics* cited above (⬛⬛⬛) proves that there were such Spartans, and there is no particular reason to believe that they were few in number – on the contrary, as the number of Spartiates declined, so presumably the number of 'inferiors' rose, as is indeed implied by Aristotle in a previous passage (*Politics* 1270b1–6). It is true that the same author in a famous sentence in this part of the *Politics* (1270a33–34) ascribes the eclipse of Sparta to 'ὀλιγανθρωπία' (fewness of men), but it is clear from the whole context that he is thinking of the decline in the number of *Spartiates*, not a decline in the whole population of Sparta, and despite natural disasters like the famous earthquake in the 460s, continuous wars, infanticide, primitive methods of contraception, and intermarriage within a relatively small group of families, it would be difficult to account for an absolute decline in the total population.[30] The only good evidence for it in Xenophon is, perhaps, his references to the 'ἐρημία' (desertion) of Spartan territory in 370 (cf. XH 6.5.23 & 25), but he is there purporting to give the arguments of those who were seeking to persuade the Thebans to invade Lakedaimon, and he is also surely thinking of the catastrophic losses the Spartiates again had suffered at Leuktra, where well over half – 400 out of 700 (XH 6.4.15) – of those who were present, had perished, representing about forty per cent of the total number.[31]

It is, of course, true that the implication of some of the things that are said about the necessity for Spartiates to go through the *agoge* ('training') and to belong to a *syssition* is that those who were unable to do so were debarred from the army. But the *agoge*, though it would have had the effect of toughening and disciplining those who had to go through it, was as much a part of the social and religious life of the Spartiates as it was of their real military training, and we have already seen, too, that the *syssitia*, for all their military overtones, were probably not part of the military organization. In any case, there is no question of the *perioikoi* participating in the *agoge* or belonging to the *syssitia*, and some at least of the *hypomeiones* will have passed through the *agoge* and only later have been debarred from the *syssitia*. The *hypomeiones* were, presumably, permanently domiciled in Spartan territory, and would have been available for military training to an extent that the *perioikoi* probably were not: it would have been absurd for the Spartiates to ignore this potential source of first-class recruits in favour of *perioikoi*, and it is incredible that in emergencies they can actually have recruited helots, as they did increasingly from 424 onwards, in one way or another (cf. Thucydides 4.80.5, and, e.g., XH 6.5.29), unless they were already making full use of Spartans who were admittedly 'inferiors', but Spartans none the less. Obviously using such men would have meant abandoning some of the old ideals of an army of 'peers' (see p. 95ff. below), but this may have seemed far less deplorable than admitting to their cherished regiments men who were not even Spartans by birth.

It is, indeed, possible that the sources sometimes use the term '*Spartiatai*' in the sense of Spartans who were not Spartiates, but at the same time were certainly not *neodamodeis* or helots, let alone *perioikoi,* and one may well wonder how else a Greek could describe non–Spartiate Spartans, since the term '*Lakedaimonioi*' clearly could include *perioikoi.* Thus it seems possible that not all the eighteen '*Spartiatai*' killed with the polemarch, Gylis, in Lokris in 394 (XH 4.3.23), for example, were really Spartiates, and the same may be true of the eight '*Spartiatai*' killed with Gorgopas in Aigina in 388 (XH 5.1.11: see above). It would be characteristic of the Spartans if while sticking rigidly to the rules as far as the full rights of citizens were concerned, they should have sought to blur the distinction between Spartiates and other Spartans in other respects, just as they sought to blur the distinction between Spartans and *perioikoi* by calling them all '*Lakedaimonioi*'. On the other hand, when Xenophon, in his account of the losses at Leuktra (XH 6.4.15), says that 'of the Lakedaimonians as a whole' (συμπάντων Λακεδαιμονίων) nearly 1,000 died, whereas 'of the Spartiates themselves' (αὐτῶν Σπαρτιατῶν) about 400 were killed, although he may include *perioikoi* among the former, it is possibly more likely that he was trying to distinguish other Spartans from Spartiates.

A careful reading of the passage in which Xenophon mentions *hypomeiones,* moreover, leads one to believe that they did serve alongside Spartiates in the army. The passage occurs in his account of the conspiracy of Kinadon, in the first year of Agesilaos' reign (398): he says that an informer told the ephors that Kinadon had declared that the leaders of the conspiracy were in the plot with all the rest – helots, *neodamodeis, hypomeiones* and *perioikoi* – 'for whenever there was talk among these of Spartiates, not one of them could conceal that he would not gladly eat them even raw' (XH 3.3.6). But then he goes on to say that when the informer was asked where Kinadon proposed to get weapons, he replied that Kinadon had said that 'those of us who serve with them (οἱ μὲν δήπου συντεταγμένοι)[32] have weapons of our own', while the rest could get them from the iron – store. Now Kinadon was no disgruntled Spartiate, for Xenophon specifically says that he was not one of the *homoioi* (XH 3.3.5), and he was probably an 'inferior' – in response to a question from the ephors as to the purpose of his plot, he is said to have replied, that he wished 'to be less than no one in Lakedaimon' (μηδενός ἥττων εἶναι ἐν Λακεδαίμονι: XH 3.3.11) – yet not only did he apparently serve alongside Spartiates in the army, but he had evidently been employed by the ephors on missions of some responsibility (cf. XH 3.3.9). Here, surely, was just the kind of man – 'of youthful physique and stout of heart' (XH 3.3.5) – that the Spartiates would have wanted in their army, provided that it was understood that they were not to share their political or social privileges.

It might be argued that to arm and train *hypomeiones* would have been dangerous, and would have had a bad effect on the morale of the army, but it is questionable whether it was any more dangerous or bad for morale than to arm and train *perioikoi*, and, indeed, helots, and there is a question of psychology here: all *hypomeiones*, however badly off and however much they may have resented their 'inferiority', would at least have realized that they were better off than helots, and if they did have a chance of serving in the army, they would then probably have regarded themselves as better off than those who were not so lucky and felt that loyal service might well secure the patronage of a Spartiate for their sons (see below). Morale in the army might have been enhanced by the rivalry of Spartiates and non-Spartiates, the one striving to show that they were still the best, the others that they were just as good. Nor need the political and social privileges of the Spartiates have seemed so overwhelmingly attractive, since probably few even of the Spartiates really had much political influence, and when all is said and done, who would want to participate in some of the more brutal aspects of the *agoge* in return for the dubious honour of eating black bread and gruel in a *syssition*?

In any case, one should not imagine that overnight thousands of disgruntled *hypomeiones* suddenly found themselves with arms in their hands and a thorough military training. The process would have been very gradual: at first only a few *hypomeiones* would have been recruited into the *morai*, and they would probably have regarded themselves as specially privileged, and would have looked down on those they had left behind rather than up to those who were still above them, and this feeling may still have persisted even when the majority of Spartan soldiers were in fact *hypomeiones*. Except when a man like Kinadon came along, with a special 'chip on his shoulder', there may have been little resentment among the *hypomeiones*, or fellow-feeling for the less privileged among themselves or for *perioikoi* or helots, and even Kinadon's conspiracy seems to have collapsed without any serious trouble for the authorities. Of course the conspiracy is revealing of the problems which beset Sparta at the time, but it is the only recorded instance in classical times of opposition to the established order from within the Spartan community, as opposed to opposition from helots or *perioikoi* (though cf. n.41 below). If Sparta really did contain the seething mass of malcontents that Kinadon implied in his conversation with the informer, over a considerable period of time, it is difficult to see why the thousand or so Spartiates who remained, were not swept away. But if beyond the privileged class of the Spartiates, there was a series of ever-widening circles of the less and less privileged, the secret of the survival of the Spartiates might be explained. The Roman system of alliances shows, on a larger scale, the advantages of so grading the under-privileged that an 'us and them' attitude does not arise, and to an 'inferior' in the army, one who was not might seem just as much one of 'them' as a Spartiate.

There may also have been a certain amount of movement between the classes of Spartiates and inferiors: it is obvious that some Spartiates were degraded, but it is also possible that some 'inferiors' were up graded. This may be the explanation, for example, of the mysterious '*mothakes*' or '*mothones*' (μόθακες, μόθωνες).[33] They are often thought to have been the sons of helot mothers by Spartiate fathers, but this view seems to be based mainly on the statement of Hesychios (s.v.) that they were 'slave boys' (δοῦλοι παῖδες), and on the assumption that they are to be equated with the '*nothoi*' mentioned in a passage in Xenophon (XH 5.3.9). Other evidence, however, suggests that some at least may have been of quite different origin: Phylarchos, for example, apparently said that they were 'free, though not Lakedaimonians' (ἐλεύθεροι μέν, οὐ μὴν Λακεδαιμόνιοι: ap. Athenaios 6.271e-f), where one suspects that he should have said 'free, though not Spartiates,' and if he was right that Lysander was a *mothax*, it hardly seems possible that his mother was a helot – Plutarch (*Lysander* 2.1) claims that he was a Heraklid – and the same is true of Gylippos and Kallikratidas, who are also said to have been *mothakes*, though not on such good authority (Aelian *VH* 12.43). If we can believe Plutarch, however, Lysander's family was very poor, and since Gylippos' father, Kleandridas, was exiled in 445 (Plutarch *Perikles* 22, *Nikias* 28), it is a fair guess that his property was confiscated, leaving Gylippos without the wherewithal to fulfil his obligations as a Spartiate. In other words, both Lysander and Gylippos were probably *hypomeiones,* and yet belonged to distinguished families, and this provides a clue as to why they were lucky enough to be 'adopted' as *mothakes* by Spartiates and put through the *agoge* with their sons, for this is how Phylarchos explains what *mothakes* were. Presumably most or all *mothakes* became Spartiates, and if it is true that Lysander, Gylippos and Kallikratidas were all *mothakes*, it is clear that such men could attain high rank, although it is, perhaps, significant that Gylippos became famous as a result of being sent to Sicily, where he never commanded regular Spartan troops, and that both Kallikratidas and Lysander were navarchs, though Lysander, of course, commanded on land after the Peloponnesian War. This suggests that the highest ranks in the army may have been closed to such men, at least until they had 'won their spurs' in another capacity – one wonders whether a *mothax* ever became polemarch, for example.

Command at the highest level, at least on land, was normally held by one or other of the two kings, or, if they were unavailable for some reason, by a close relative. Thus, of the six battles that we shall be considering, excluding Sphakteria and the fight near Lechaion, in four (Thermopylai, Mantineia, Koroneia and Leuktra) a king was in the field, while at Plataea the command was held by the regent Pausanias, cousin and guardian of Leonidas, young son, Pleistarchos (Herodotos 9.10.1–2), since the other king, Leotychidas, was commanding the fleet, and at the Nemea the Spartan side was led by Aristodemos, guardian of the young king, Agesipolis, since Agesilaos was then away in Asia (XH 4.2.9). Command at sea, on the other hand, was rarely exercised by a member of one of the royal houses – the only exceptions seem to be Leotychidas in 479 and Pausanias in 478, when their fleets included ships from allies outside the Peloponnesian League, and Agesilaos' brother, Teleutias, in the 390s (XH 4.4.19, 8.11, etc.), where the explanation may be either Agesilaos' own influence, or the exceptional ability of Teleutias himself.

Supreme command at sea was normally held by navarchs (ναύαρχοι),[34] who seem to have been appointed strictly for a year, and apparently, technically, could not be reappointed – this led to Lysander's supersession by Kallikratidas in 406, for example (XH 1.6.1, cf. 2.1.7). The admirals were supported by a vice-admiral called *'epistoleus'* (ἐπιστολεύς, i.e. 'secretary'), who seems to have enjoyed something of an independent existence, as is suggested by the use of the office to give Lysander effective command of the fleet again in 405, by appointing him *epistoleus* to the navarch, Arakos (XH 2.1.7). As we have seen, it is possible that at least two *mothakes*, Kallikratidas and Lysander, held the office of navarch, and this suggests the post may have been open to merit, to some extent. This is supported by what Xenophon says about the appointment of Peisander to command the fleet in 394: he says (XH 3.4.29) that Agesilaos, who was married to Peisander's sister, appointed him 'although he was rather inexperienced in making the necessary dispositions,' and although Xenophon may have been thinking of his failure at Knidos, where he was killed (XH 4.3.10–12), he implies that normally a navarch might be expected to know something of his duties. At least once, too, we know of an *epistoleus* who went on to become navarch (Pollis: cf. XH 4.8.11 and 5.4.61), and Thucydides records (8.22.1) one case of a *perioikos* commanding at sea, though he was not a navarch. On the other hand, Pharax, navarch in 397 (XH 3.2.12–14), if he was the same man as the Theban *proxenos* ('consul') at Sparta (XH 4.5.6), and the ambassador to Athens in 370 (XH 6.5.33), looks as though he belonged to the aristocracy, and he may have been related to Styphon, son of Pharax, who surrendered the Spartan force on Sphakteria (Thucydides 4.38.1: see below).

Some of the harmosts ('fixers')[35] appointed with increasing frequency in the last years of the Peloponnesian War and after it, particularly to take charge of 'allied' cities, may have been of comparatively humble origin, if we are to believe the Theban ambassador reported by Xenophon (XH 3.5.12) to have declared that even helots were made harmosts – perhaps they were *mothakes* – and Xenophon also twice describes harmosts as 'Lakonians' (XH 1.1.32 and 2.2.2), which might suggest that they were *perioikoi*. But other harmosts were probably of aristocratic origin: Labotas, harmost of Herakleia, for example, bore a royal name (XH 1.2.18), and although this probably does not prove anything, and Herakleia was in any case a Spartan colony (cf. Thucydides 3.92), Klearchos, a notorious harmost of Byzantium (XH 1.1.35, 1.3.15–9), was apparently the son of the Ramphias sent to Athens as ambassador in 432 and later a commander in Chalkidike (Thucydides 1.139.3 & 5.12–4), and Sphodrias, who was left as harmost of Thespiai by Kleombrotos in 379, and who later led the ill-fated raid on the Peiraeus (XH 5.4.15 & 20), is said to have been close to the king's 'friends' – they are described (XH 5.4.25) as Sphodrias' '*hetairoi*', a term used for the 'companions' of an aristocrat – and he was subsequently begged off by Agesilaos' son, Archidamos, who was in love with his own son, Kleonymos (XH 5.4.25ff.). It seems likely, then, that although in the special circumstances created by Sparta's final victory over Athens in 404, some surprising choices were made to take charge of the growing number of places which now came under Sparta's control, perhaps particularly under the influence of the *mothax* Lysander, these were still the exceptions rather than the rule.

On land, and nearer home, we would expect most high-ranking Spartan officers to have been of aristocratic origin, and some of what we are told about them seems to confirm this. Brasidas, for example, was apparently ephor in 431/0 (XH 2.3.10), and was presumably elected to this office just after his first recorded command in Messenia (Thucydides 2.25.2) – he was probably the son of the Tellis who is named as one of the signatories of the Peace of Nikias and of the subsequent treaty with Athens (Thucydides 5.19.2 & 24.1), and was evidently of some importance. Similarly, Alkamenes, one of the commanders of a force of *neodamodeis* sent to Euboea by King Agis in 413 (Thucydides 8.5.1), may have been the son of the famous ephor of 432/1, Sthenelaidas, and himself bore a royal name. But of the six polemarchs named by Xenophon, including the enigmatic Geranor (see n. 7 on p. 226 below), we know nothing but their names, though Plutarch says (*Pelopidas* 17.3) one of the polemarchs killed at Tegyra was called Theopompos, which may suggest that he was of high birth. We do not even know the names of any of the other 'tent companions' (οἱ περὶ δαμοσία – XH 4.5.8, 6.4.14; οἱ ἀπὸ δαμοσίας – XH 4.7.4; οἱ περὶ τὴν δαμοσίαν – LP 13.7), who formed the king's staff on campaign: according to the *Constitution* (*LP* 13.1 & 7), they included the polemarchs, three *homoioi*, seers, surgeons, pipe-players and any 'volunteers' accompanying the army. We would expect at least the polemarchs and the three *homoioi* to be aristocrats, and one passage in Xenophon possibly indicates this: he names one of two Spartiates killed fighting 'in front of' Archidamos near Kromnos, as Chilon (XH 7.4.23), and although he does not say so, it is possible that Chilon was one of the prince's 'tent companions.' If so, it is possibly significant that the man in question, who was married to the prince's sister, bore the same name as the great sixth century ephor, and thus possibly belonged to a family which had probably twice given brides to Spartan kings in the sixth and fifth centuries (cf. Herodotos 5.41.3 and 6.65.2).

If we cannot be sure of the origins and backgrounds of most of the highest – ranking Spartan officers, it is still less possible to know much about other officers: not a single *lochagos*, *pentekoster* or enomotarch is ever named by either Thucydides or Xenophon, and although Herodotos' Amompharetos may have been a *lochagos*, there are difficulties about his position (see below p. 61ff.): if he was a *lochagos*, it may be significant that he bore the same name as one of the five arbitrators who allegedly awarded the island of Salamis to

Athens early in the sixth century (Plutarch *Solon* 10.4), and may thus have been of ancient lineage. The same may be true of the three officers named by Thucydides as in turn commanding the Spartan force trapped by the Athenians on Sphakteria in 425, which, since it originally numbered only 420 men, should not have rated a very high-ranking commander: if it really did consist of twelve *enomotiai* (see p. 57 below), it was the equivalent of three *pentekostyes*, so perhaps its three commanders were merely *pentekosteres*. Yet the first – Epitadas, son of Molobros (Thucydides 4.8.9) – may have been related to the mysterious ephor, Epitadeus (Plutarch *Agis* 5.3),[36] the name of the second – Hippagretas – was the title of the commanders of the elite *Hippeis*, and the father of the third – Styphon, son of Pharax (Thucydides 4.38) – may have been one of King Agis' 'advisers' at Mantineia, though what our source – Diodoros (12.79.6) – says about him is probably not true (see below, p. 159–60); the navarch, Pharax, may have been a descendant. Thucydides says in general of the Spartiates captured on Sphakteria that they were 'leading citizens' (πρῶτοι: 5.15.1), and apparently that they were related to members of the government, though the passage is unfortunately corrupt;[37] later (5.34.2) he remarks that in 421 some of these men were holding office, and that although they were then temporarily deprived of their rights, these were later restored. It would be interesting to know whether he was here primarily talking about Styphon, Hippagretas and the *enomotarchoi*. Brasidas, too, first turns up in Thucydides (2.25.2) in command of a 'garrison' (φρουρά) in Messenia, and if his whole command consisted of the 100 hoplites with whom he was instrumental in saving Methone, he may have been a *pentekoster* at the time, though the 100 may, of course, not have been Spartan regulars. Brasidas' career, however, exemplifies the difficulties in deciding whether Spartan officers were appointed on merit or because of their social standing: he was obviously a very talented officer, and his successive appointments, culminating in his command in Chalkidike, may have been due to his ability – but one wonders whether he would not have risen to high command in any case, if he did belong to the aristocracy.

On the other hand, if there really were 128 *enomotiai* at Leuktra (4 *morai* each containing 32), and if 300 of the 700 Spartiates who were there were brigaded separately in the *Hippeis*, there would only have been three or four Spartiates, on average, in each of the *enomotiai*, and since some of these would have been young men, it seems likely that some of the enomotarchs, at least, were not even Spartiates. Thucydides, too, remarks (5.66.4) that 'almost all the army of the Lakedaimonians, except for a small part, consists of officers commanding other officers (ἄρχοντες ἀρχόντων), and the responsibility for the execution of orders is the concern of many men,' and although he was, no doubt, primarily remarking on the fact that the Spartan army had such a comprehensive command-structure (cf. 5.66.2–3), what he says suggests that most Spartiates at least might expect to exercise command, if only at a junior level, at some point in their military careers. In this sense the otherwise misleading translation of 'Spartiatai' by 'the Spartan officer class' in the Penguin Classics *Thucydides*, may have some point.

It is, however, not at all clear how Spartan officers were appointed. Navarchs, and possibly even *epistoleis*, may have been elected, as is suggested by their annual tenure of command (cf. also Aristotle *Politics* 1271a40), and the same may have been true of polemarchs, who seem at least to have been to some extent outside the king's authority: it was not apparently King Agis, for example, who dismissed Hipponoïdas and Aristokles after their insubordination at Mantineia (cf. Thucydides 5.72.1), and if Amompharetos was really a polemarch (see below p. 67), this might explain Pausanias' inability simply to replace him with a more compliant officer. Plutarch, too, says (*Lykourgos* 12.3) that when King Agis, on return from campaign on one occasion, wished to dine at home with his wife, and sent for his rations from the mess, the polemarchs refused to send them, and subsequently actually fined him for omitting one of the customary sacrifices. It is not clear who appointed the 'tent companions', but the 'advisers' (ξυμβούλοι; Thucydides 5.63.4) appointed to accompany King Agis on campaign, after his abortive expedition against Argos in mid-summer 418, were clearly not chosen by himself, and it may be significant that he is said only to have consulted one 'of the men in office accompanying him on campaign' (τῶν ἐν τέλει ξυστρατευομένων: Thucydides 5.60.1), when he concluded the truce with Argos, suggesting that he did not see eye-to-eye with his staff. The various groups of thirty Spartiates sent to advize Agesilaos in Asia (XH 3.4.2, 8, 20; 4.1.5) and Agesipolis at Olynthos (XH 5.3.8) were also clearly not chosen by the kings.

But the sources are equivocal about how commanders in general were appointed: Xenophon, for example, says or implies that some were appointed by 'the Lakedaimonians' (e.g. 3.1.4, 4.8.21, 5.2.24) which might suggest some kind of vote in the Spartan assembly, unless he is just using a loose expression – as we might say 'appointed by Sparta'. Elsewhere he implies that the ephors at least had a hand in such appointments: Anaxibios, for example, is said to have secured his appointment as harmost of Abydos through having the ephors as friends (XH 4.8.32), and when Eudamidas was appointed to take command of the original Olynthos expedition, he is said to have asked the ephors to allow his brother, Phoibidas, to collect the rest of his troops (XH 5.2.24) – these passages may, of course, mean no more than that the ephors were influential in such appointments, as in so much else. Other appointments, again, are implied to have been made by a king, navarch or other commander-in-chief, on the spot (cf. XH 2.2.2, 3.2.29, 3.4.6 & 20, 4.2.5, 5.1.5 & 6, 5.4.15). The pattern in Thucydides is very similar, except that there does not appear to be any specific reference to ephors' taking a hand, and most appointments are implied to be by 'the Lakedaimonians' (cf. 1.95.6, 2.85.1, 3.16.3 & 100.2, 5.56.1, 6.93.2, 7.19.3, 8.6.5, 28.15 & 39.1, 8.107.2) – even King Agis is said to have sent to Lakedaimon for officers to command in Euboea (8.5.1). The only exceptions are one or two appointments by navarchs on the spot (cf., e.g., 8.23.4 & 61.4), and some by Brasidas (4.123.4 & 132.3), all of which are presumably to be explained by the difficulties involved in securing an appointment from Sparta. There is, indeed, no real discrepancy with Xenophon, for most of the latter's references to apparent appointments by commanders-in-chief are probably mostly to be explained by their distance from Sparta, if not by their own forceful personalities – they mostly concern Lysander, Agesilaos and Antalkidas.

Since we know so little about most Spartan officers and the way they were appointed, it is impossible to be certain whether they were appointed on merit or because of the circumstances of their birth: one can only guess that it was mainly the latter, but that some of them owed their rise to talent. But even if most of them owed their positions primarily to their social standing, this would not necessarily have seriously diminished the efficiency of the army, in normal circumstances, or have been resented by the men they led, whether they were Spartiates or *hypomeiones*. The experience of more modern armies[38] suggests that the aristocratic code of honour would have kept the officers steady in the field, and that their steadiness would have been respected and followed by their men. Certainly the number of Spartan officers killed in action suggests that they – perhaps literally – led from the front. By Xenophon's day, too, there were so few Spartiates left that they must all have known each other, to a large extent, and by comparison with *hypomeiones*, have all regarded themselves as 'aristocrats' in a sense: there is some evidence to suggest a certain free-and-easy attitude to officers, judging from the objections voiced against Agis' tactics on the day before Mantineia (Thucydides 5.65.2), and to those of the 'first polemarch' at the Nemea (XH 4.2.22). Some *hypomeiones*, like Kinadon, may have resented their 'inferiority', if they felt they were passed over for promotion, but the case of Kinadon himself suggests that even some of them could find themselves holding positions of responsibility.

Despite the impression made on Thucydides by the command-system in the Spartan army, we should not suppose that any of the officers were 'professionals' in the sense that they had had a formal training in their duties: there is no evidence for a 'staff college' or for courses for N.C.O.s and junior officers, and one must assume that they simply learned the rudiments of their duties by service in the ranks, and then by experience. The Spartan army, thus, probably depended for its efficiency to a far less extent than the Roman, for example, or the German, on a hard core of expert leaders at the level of their smallest units, unless the enomotarchs were such men. But although nowadays we may think that this would seriously diminish an army's efficiency, we must remember that other Greek armies were even less 'professional' – it was only after Leuktra, Xenophon implies (XH 6.5.23) that the Thebans, for example, seriously began to train. Spartan soldiers would have expected their officers to be able to organize the few relatively simple manoeuvres required in a hoplite battle, but would probably not have expected much more, and such manoeuvres were probably practised endlessly in peace-time.

Above all, we should not imagine that Spartan generals, whether kings or others, were ever given any formal training in tactics or strategy: obviously they could have studied the lessons of the past, and could in many cases have learned something from their fathers or other relatives who had commanded in battle – Agesilaos, for example, might have learned something from his elder brother Agis, if only what *not* to try to do in battle. But the kings certainly did not owe their positions in the army to any ability they might have shown, but to their birth, and the same was probably normally true of other commanders-in-chief, though some of them, of course, either through innate intelligence or through experience, proved to be competent commanders. On the other hand. Spartan soldiers probably did not expect much more of their generals than that they did not make complete fools of themselves, and the presence on the battlefield of the king himself probably itself had a marked effect on morale,[39] and no doubt something of that 'divinity (which) doth hedge a king' also reflected on commanders such as

Pausanias or Aristodemos. Plutarch (*Lykourgos* 22.4) tells the story of the Spartan wrestler at Olympia who was offered large sums to 'throw' a fight, and who, when he had refused and won, was asked what advantage he had gained: 'I shall be stationed in front of the king when I fight the enemy,' he replied – and Xenophon mentions the Olympic victor, Lakrates, who was killed outside the Peiraeus in 403, no doubt fighting in front of King Pausanias (XH 2.4.33). Sphodrias' son, Kleonymos, too, died at Leuktra defending his king, and both there and at Thermopylai the fall of the king was the signal for an even more ferocious display of valour on the part of the Spartans (cf. XH 6.4.13 and Herodotos 7.225.1) – at Mantineia Thucydides says (5.72.4) that it was especially where 'King Agis was and about him the three hundred called the *Hippeis*' that the enemy gave way.

Even though their officers had probably had little or no tactical or strategic training, all Spartiates at least, with the exception of the heirs to the thrones (cf. Plutarch *Agesilaos* 1.2–3), had to pass through the *agoge*, a training system for boys, allegedly from the age of seven, which probably had its origins in ancient religious initiation-rites connected particularly with the worship of Artemis Orthia, but which also must have had the effect of instilling the military virtues of discipline, toughness, self-reliance and courage.[40] How far other Spartans called up for military service participated is problematical – presumably those born *hypomeiones* did not, unless they were lucky enough to be 'adopted' as *mothakes*, for these are said (Phylarchos ap. Athenaios 6.271e-f) to have shared 'all the education' (τῆς παιδείας πάσης) of their patrons' sons. Perhaps even more important than the actual ritualistic training of the *agoge* was the code of honour with which Spartiates at least must have been imbued from their earliest days, a code which made them as boys accept pain and hardship without flinching (cf., e.g., *LP* 2.2–11, 3.1–4.6; Plutarch *Lykourgos* 16–18), and as men prefer death to dishonour (cf., e.g., *LP* 9.1–2), so much so that – according to Xenophon (XH 4.5.10, 6.4.16) – after defeats like those near Lechaion and at Leuktra, it was the relatives of the fallen who went about with cheerful faces, while those whose kin had survived were filled with gloom. There were penalties for cowardice (cf., e.g., *LP* 9.3–6, and Plutarch *Agesilaos* 30.2–4), but more potent, one feels, was the whole atmosphere in which the Spartans lived their lives, and here the women played an important role: the most famous example is the injunction of the Spartan mother to her son to come back with his shield or on it (cf., e.g., Plutarch *Moralia* 241f16), but Plutarch's essay on '*The Sayings of Spartan Women*' is filled with such aphorisms. Nor is there any reason to believe that the attitude of Spartan soldiers changed as more and more of them came to be *hypomeiones*, for they would surely have tended to be imbued with much the same kind of attitude: there is no evidence that Sparta's defeats were due to any lowering of morale.[41]

But although their training as boys, and the attitudes with which they were imbued, were no doubt of immense value in turning out good soldiers, battles are not really won 'on the playing fields of Eton',[42] and the real military training of Spartan men probably began when they were enrolled in one of the *enomotiai* at the age of twenty. It was then that they must have learned to march in step to the sound of the pipe (cf. Thucydides 5.70), and the necessary arms-drill – for bringing the spear down from the upright or slope position, for example, in readiness for the underarm or overarm thrust (cf., e.g., Xenophon *Anabasis* 1.2.17 and 6.5.25–7), and for handling the heavy shield (cf., e.g., Diodoros 15.32–3).[43] In Plato's dialogue *Laches*, Laches himself says that those who professed to teach arms-drill (ὁπλομαχία: 181e-183d, cf. *Laws* 813e, 833e), steered clear of Sparta, and although his argument is that such instruction was useless, we should clearly not imagine that it was not taught at Sparta.

But Nikias in the same dialogue may well reflect reality in saying that arms-drill was not of great importance until one side or the other gave way, and it was probably their training in tactical manoeuvres which really gave Spartan soldiers the edge on the battlefield. The manoeuvres in question were mainly for deploying from column into line-of-battle to meet attacks from various directions, with forming line to different depths, counter-marching to reverse front or flanks, inclining or extending a wing to take the enemy in flank, and, probably, for forming in open or close order. The principle upon which all these manoeuvres seem to have depended, except for counter-marching to the flank (see below), was to regard the file and not the rank as the basic unit (cf. *LP* 11.5) – thus, basically, the men in the rear ranks of each file had simply to follow the file-leader and do whatever he did.

It is not always easy to see how some of the manoeuvres on actual campaign, described in the *Hellenika*, were performed – we can only guess, for example, how the Spartans managed to get themselves onto the left flank of the opposing army at the Nemea, and so bring about a classic case of 'rolling up the line'. All Xenophon says (XH 4.2.19) is that they 'led to the right' (ἦγον ... ἐπὶ τὰ δεξιά), and this could mean either that they literally all turned to the right into column and marched to the right until they overlapped the enemy line, or that they simply inclined to their right as they advanced.[44] Again, at Koroneia, a little later in the same year, when Agesilaos learned that the Thebans had broken through the contingent from Orchomenos on his left and got among the baggage-train in his rear, he is said to have 'countermarched the phalanx and led it against them' (ἐξελίξας τὴν φάλαγγα ἦγεν ἐπ'αὐτούς: XH 4.3.18),[45] but one is left to assume that this was done in the manner mentioned in the *Constitution* (*LP* 11.8), and distinguished by later tactical writers as the 'Lakonian' countermarch as opposed to the 'Macedonian' or 'Cretan': in the Lakonian version each file about-turned and while the original rear-man stood fast, the file-leader led the rest of the file to take up position in front of the rear-man, thus giving the impression of moving towards the enemy, whereas in the other version, the file-leader about-turned and stood fast, and his file then took up position behind him. In either case, the result would be that the commander of the phalanx would now be on the left of the line, instead of in his normal place on the right, but as the author of the *Constitution* explains (*LP* 11.9), this could be an advantage, for if the enemy attempted to outflank in the usual way, by extending his right, then the commander would be on the spot to counter this threat. On the other hand, if it seemed desirable to have the commander in his normal place on the right, then the whole phalanx could be counter-marched *by ranks,* to the right, though one doubts whether this was ever carried out in practice in the face of the enemy.[46]

At Koroneia, too, it is alleged by later writers (Frontinus, *Strategemata* 2.6.6; Polyainos 2.1.19) that Agesilaos opened ranks to let the Thebans through, in the final stage of the battle, and although Xenophon's account (XH 4.3.19) rather suggests that the Thebans forced their way through, there probably was a Spartan drill for forming into close or open order, as there was for the Greek mercenaries at Kounaxa (Xenophon *Anabasis* 1.8.20 & 10.7), and later for the Macedonian phalanx (cf. Asklepiodotos 4.1.4 & 12.8.9). In battle a hoplite held his shield in such a way that it roughly covered the left half of his trunk, and relied upon the man to his right to protect the right half of his body (cf. Thucydides 5.71.1): this presupposes a relatively close order, with the shields forming a continuous line, if not overlapping, but the counter-march described above required a more open order, and so too did ordering those 'ten (or fifteen) years from manhood' to charge out from the phalanx, if these younger men did not literally form the front ranks (see above, p. 16).

The only other manoeuvre described in the *Hellenika* is the *anastrophe* (ἀναστροφή, literally 'wheeling back'), used for increasing the depth of a phalanx in the face of the enemy. It involved units on the left or right wing about-turning and marching to the rear, then wheeling to come up behind the new wing. On the first occasion Xenophon describes (XH 6.2.21), the right wing of a Spartan force, ranged eight deep, was considered too weak to withstand an attack, but the men were charged as they began the movement to the rear and did not complete the wheel. It may be of some significance that this force did not include regular Spartan troops, for on the second occasion, when regular troops were certainly involved, the manoeuvre was a complete success (XH 6.5.18). This time Agesilaos was caught in a valley near Mantineia, and threatened with an attack on his rear, if he retreated, by enemy forces gathering on the hills to the rear of his line of retreat. Realizing this, he himself, with the right wing – which would have formed the van had he retreated in the normal way – stood fast and faced the enemy, ordering those on his left, which would have constituted the rear, to 'wheel back to the spear-side (i.e. right) and march towards him behind the phalanx' (ἀναστοέψαντας τοὺς ἀπ᾿ οὐρᾶς εἰς δόρυ ὄπισθεν τῆς φάλαγγος ἡγεῖσθαι πρὸς αὐτόν), i.e., presumably, to about-turn and march to the rear, then left-turn into column and march behind the right wing, this being termed 'wheeling back to the right' because the new position was behind and to the right of the old. In this way, the king both extricated his phalanx from the narrow confines of the valley and made it steadily deeper, as Xenophon says (οὕτως ἅμα ἔκ τε τοῦ στενοῦ ἐξῆνε καὶ ἰσχυροτέραν ἀεί τὴν φάλαννα ἐποιεῖτο). Then, when the phalanx had doubled in depth, he moved it out into the plain 'with the hoplites in this formation' (οὕτως ἔχοντι τῷ ὁπλιτικῷ: XH 6.5.19), i.e., one assumes, with his men just about-turning and marching to the rear so that if they were attacked, they could simply about-turn again to face the enemy, and thus be in their correct positions. Finally, when the plain was reached, the king 'extended his army back to a depth of eight or ten shields' (ἐξέτεινε πάλιν ἐπ᾿ ἐννέα ἢ δέκα τὸ στράτευμα ἀσπίδων XH ibid.), presumably by reversing the process by which he had doubled his depth in the first place.

Xenophon's description of this episode, which he may have witnessed, conveys a vivid impression of the parade-ground efficiency of the Spartan army, but it must be remembered that as artificial as it may all sound nowadays, these manoeuvres were not then just for ceremonial purposes, as the episode shows: on the battlefield, this ability to manoeuvre gave Spartan soldiers a distinct advantage, as the Nemea and Koroneia demonstrated, though it almost led to disaster at the first battle of Mantineia in 418, and was possibly partly responsible for the disaster at Leuktra forty-seven years later.

The *Constitution of the Lakedaimonians* (*LP* 11.8ff., 13.6) describes a number of other manoeuvres mainly for deploying from column-of-march into line-of-battle when the enemy appeared in front or on one or other flank.[47] In a possibly slightly corrupt passage (11.4), the *Constitution* apparently first talks about deploying the *enomotiai* in single file, or in three or six, though one wonders if they ever were really drawn up in single file: at Leuktra they were in three (XH 6.4.14).[48] The *Constitution* then goes on to make the point that Spartan drill was not complicated, apparently because it depended upon the principle of each file following its leader (there is again a possibly corrupt passage at 11.5), though orders for deploying the phalanx at a greater or lesser depth were given by the *enomotarchoi*: the author claims that none of this was difficult to learn, but stresses that it was not easy, except for troops trained under 'the laws of Lykourgos', to fight equally well with anyone who happened to be alongside, if they were thrown into confusion (11.7). The Spartans were also able to carry out, with complete ease, manoeuvres which seemed difficult to 'drill-instructors' (ὁπλομάχοι). Thus, when they marched in column, *enomotia* followed *enomotia*, but if an enemy phalanx appeared in front, the command was given to each enomotarch to deploy into line to the left until the phalanx was formed. If the enemy then appeared in the rear, each file countermarched, and if it was then felt desirable to have the commander on the right as usual, the whole phalanx countermarched by ranks (11.8–9 – see above, p. 35). If, on the other hand, an enemy appeared on the right when they were marching in column, they did no more than wheel each *lochos* to the right to front the enemy 'like a trireme bow on,' so that the rear *lochos* formed the right of the line. Here it is possible that the author was thinking of a threat to the column from light troops, for he seems to imply that the *lochoi* would not deploy into line, but would advance on the enemy in column, and this was a formation sometimes used by hoplites against light troops (cf. Xenophon *Anabasis* 4.8.9–13; 4.2.12, 3.17; 5.4.22).[49] Alternatively he may mean that each individual *lochos* was wheeled through 180 degrees, so that the men at its head became its right, as was normal, though this still meant that the rear *lochos* was on the right of the line, instead of on the left, as would have been the case with the deployment to the left to meet a threat from the front. This interpretation is possibly borne out by the next section in the *Constitution* which seems to imply that if a threat materialized from the left of the column, a different manoeuvre was used, though there is unfortunately some doubt about the text. The point is that in this case a simple left-turn of each individual man would do, since the head of the column would now form the right of the phalanx, whereas a simple right-turn of each individual man would not do, if the column was threatened from the right.

An even more puzzling passage later in the *Constitution* (13.6) appears to describe what the king did if a battle was expected when he was leading the army in column: apparently only the *Skiritai* and mounted scouts went ahead of him, but 'if ever they think there will be a battle, taking the *agema* of the first *mora*, the king wheels to the right and leads on until he is between two *morai* and two polemarchs.' This has been interpreted to mean that the king and the first *mora* wheeled to the right until they were facing back the way they had come, and then marched back until they reached the head of the second *mora*, whereupon they about-turned and the march continued with the king and what had been the head of the *mora* now at its rear.[50] But to describe the king's position as a result of the manoeuvre as 'between two *morai* and two polemarchs,' would then be a little odd, even if it was literally true that he was now positioned between the first and second *morai*, and in any case the Spartans would probably not have wanted to reverse the head and rear of a *mora* like this, even on the march, since if it then had to deploy into line-of-battle, what should have been its left would become its right, if it deployed to the left in the usual way (cf. *LP* 11.8). A more natural way to take the passage might be that the king wheeled the first *mora* to the right and led it back the way it had come until it reached the *rear* of the second *mora*, whereupon it wheeled back into the column behind the second *mora*, while the third presumably halted to let it in, thus achieving the desired position 'between two *morai* and two polemarchs' (i.e. the second and third *morai* and their polemarchs). This would have meant that the order of the *morai* in the line-of-battle would not have been the same as in the line-of-march, but at least each *mora* when deployed for battle would have had its head on its right and its rear on its left. Presumably the king and the men with him wheeled to the right, in the first place, rather than to the left, so as to leave room for the rest of the column to deploy to the left, if necessity arose, and an added advantage, on the second interpretation, would have been that the king and his men would have been protected by their own shields on one side, and by the rest of the marching column on the other, as they marched past the second *mora*. An advantage of the whole manoeuvre, whichever of the interpretations is accepted, would have been that if the column did subsequently have to deploy into line-of-battle, the king would then have been between two *morai*, and not in an exposed position on the extreme right of the line.[51]

The equipment used by Spartan infantry soldiers certainly included shield, spear and sword (see plate 1). The shield was apparently the standard hoplite one, usually called '*aspis*', but one of the terms for which – '*hoplon*' – had almost certainly originally given the hoplite his name (cf. Diodoros 15.44.3). Usually a little over eighty centimetres in diameter, slightly convex, but with a flat, offset rim, the shield was made of wood with a bronze rim and a thin bronze facing, which was kept polished (cf. *LP* 11.3). It was carried by inserting the left arm up to the elbow through a bronze arm-band placed centrally (πόρπαξ) and gripping a hand-grip inside the rim (ἀντιλαβή), apparently made of cord (see plate 2).[52] Spartan shields in Xenophon's time probably bore the letter *lambda* (Λ) as a blazon (cf. XH 4.4.10), but earlier, perhaps, had borne individual blazons – Plutarch tells the story of a Spartan who had a life-sized fly as a blazon on his shield, and when taunted that he only wanted to escape notice, replied that on the contrary he got so close to his enemies that his emblem was seen at its true size (*Moralia* 234C–D.41). Shields of high-ranking officers, at least, were apparently often carried by servants (ὑπασπισταί: cf. XH 4.5.14 & 8.9), when not in use, and there is reason to believe that every Spartan hoplite was accompanied on campaign by such a batman, usually a helot (cf. Herodotos 7.229.1 and Thucydides 4.8.9). The *hypaspistai* also seem to have acted as stretcher-bearers, for example carrying the dead and wounded out of the battle near Lechaion (XH 4.5.14).

If the helot-batmen were armed at all, as they probably were, they do not seem to have been particularly effective: one might, for example, have expected them to be useful as skirmishers against light troops, as on Sphakteria and near Lechaion, but they play no part in the accounts of Thucydides and Xenophon, though some were allegedly killed at Plataea (Herodotos 9.85.2): the *Constitution* (*LP* 12.4) says 'the slaves' (τοὺς δούλους, i.e., presumably, the helots) were kept away from the arms, at least in camp. When standing 'at ease' hoplites would often have rested their shields on the ground, leaning against their knees (cf. Xenophon *Anabasis* 1.5.13 and Diodoros 15.32.5): to have to stand guard carrying one's shield was a form of punishment (XH 3.1.9). Spartan spears were apparently of normal pattern, varying from two to two-and-a-half metres in length, with an iron head and butt, but their swords were said to be shorter and straighter than those of other Greeks (cf. Plutarch *Moralia* 191e & 216c, *Lykourgos* 19.2).

It is not certain how much protective clothing Spartan soldiers wore in Xenophon's time. It has been argued that they wore nothing but their crimson tunic and a conical felt or leather cap,[53] but there is evidence which points the other way: for example, the Spartan army retreating from Boeotia in the winter of 379/8, by the difficult route from Kreusis to Aigosthena, is said (XH 5.4.18) to have found it impossible to negotiate a particularly precipitous descent 'with their arms' (σὺν τοῖς ὅπλοις), and many of the men are said to have left their shields (τὰς ἀσπίοας) at the top, weighted down with stones, returning to retrieve them next day. Here, although the shields are of course included in the 'arms' mentioned first, the natural implication is that they were not all the arms the Spartans had, nor that the men just went on with their spears and swords. It is not a convincing argument that Xenophon says (*Agesilaos* 2.7) that Agesilaos made his army look like 'one mass of bronze and crimson' (ἄπαντα μὲν χαλκόν, ἄπαντα δὲ φοινικᾶ), for even if corslets were worn over the tunics, their sleeves and kilts would still have been visible, and Xenophon may also have been thinking here of the famous Spartan military cloak (see plate 3).[54] The matter would be put beyond all doubt if we could believe some of the details of what Plutarch says, for he not only describes Agesilaos as wounded 'through his armour' (διὰ τῶν ὅπλων) at Koroneia (*Agesilaos* 18.3), but later tells the splendid story of Isidas, son of Phoibidas, who, having played a heroic part in the defence of Sparta in 362 'bare of protective equipment and clothes' (γυμνὸς δὲ καὶ ὅπλων τῶν σκεπόντων καὶ ἱματίων), was promptly rewarded for his valour, and then fined by the ephors for fighting 'without equipment' (χωρὶς ὅπλων: 24.7). By this date, if they did continue to wear protective clothing, the Spartans, like other Greeks, would have discarded the earlier solid bronze front and back plates, and would have adopted instead the lighter and more flexible corslet made of quilted linen or leather.[55]

All in all, the idea that Spartan hoplites of the fourth century did not wear corslets is not very convincing, though the evidence that they wore a conical hat of felt or leather, instead of a metal helmet, is more cogent,[56] and it is possible that the Spartans had started to experiment with more lightly equipped hoplites in response to the difficulties traditional hoplites could experience against more lightly equipped skirmishers. However, it is more likely that they tried to counter the threat partly by employing light-armed skirmishers of their own, and partly by developing the tactic of ordering the younger men in the front ranks to charge out from the phalanx and drive the enemy away (see p. 49 below). It must be borne in mind, moreover, that hoplites differed from these lighter troops not just in being more heavily equipped or in using the thrusting-spear rather than missile weapons: hoplites would have been trained to fight as parts of a unit – this certainly must have been true of Spartan hoplites – whereas the lighter troops fought in a looser order and to a large extent as individuals. Moreover, so long as the traditional hoplite shield was retained, it was bound to have an effect on tactics, since it naturally only protected a man's left side and he had to rely on his neighbour on the right to protect his right.

From things that Xenophon says in the *Hellenika* and from some of the details in the *Constitution*, it is possible to catch a glimpse of the daily lives of Spartan soldiers on campaign. According to the *Constitution* (12.1ff.), their camps were circular, rather than square, except where they had a hill, a wall or a river in their rear. At night it was the duty of the *Skiritai*, helped by foreign troops if any were present, to keep watch; by day, sentries faced inwards to watch the stacks of arms, apparently to prevent the 'slaves' (see above) from getting at them, while cavalry watched for the enemy. But despite these precautions, it appears that even the Spartans could be caught unawares: in Arcadia in 370, for example, the early arrival 'with the day' of some troops from Orchomenos and Phleious, who turned out to be friendly in the end, evidently remained undetected until they were quite close, since the Spartans are said to have had to run to their places in the line, and Agesilaos, who was engaged in the morning sacrifice, had to retire precipitately back to camp (XH 6.5.17). In the following year, Epameinondas surprised a force of Spartan troops guarding Oneion, near Corinth, by attacking 'when the night-watches were ending' (XH 7.1.16). These incidents came towards the end of Sparta's hey-day as a military power, but there is no real reason to believe that the discipline or efficiency of the army was declining: the incident involving Agesilaos' army in Arcadia was followed immediately by his masterly use of the *anastrophe* to extricate his army from a defile.

The baggage of the army seems to have been carried by pack-animals (cf. XH 5.4.17), though Thucydides mentions waggons in the fifth century (5.72.3), but it is not clear what kind of baggage there would have been: we do not know, for example, whether all Spartan soldiers slept in tents or under any other kind of covering, while on campaign, but presumably at least the high-ranking officers did; the men surprised by Epameinondas at Oneion were sleeping on straw or rush mattresses (στιβάδες: XH 7.1.16). If it was cold, or the weather was unpleasant, fires would be lit and extra clothing worn. This appears from an incident in 390 when Agesilaos, advancing towards the Perachora peninsula, sent one *mora* up onto what was evidently the ridge above the modern health-resort of Loutraki (cf. τὰ θερμά in XH 4.5.3), and the Spartan soldiers found themselves bivouacking high on the ridge on a cold, wet night – it even hailed during the evening – without fires because none of those carrying food to them (presumably helots) had brought any, and wearing light clothes (σπειρία) suitable for summer. Agesilaos partially solved the problem by sending ten men up to them carrying fire in pots, whereupon the soldiers rubbed themselves down with oil and began the supper they had previously been reluctant to touch (XH 4.5.4).

Nothing seems to be known about the normal rations of Spartan soldiers on campaign, though the sources do tell us a little about the food eaten in the messes (cf. Plutarch *Lykourgos* 12.2–3; Athenaios 4.141c, etc.) back home: it evidently included barley-bread, wine, cheese, figs, fish and game. But Spartan food was notoriously supposed to be austere: their black broth (μέλας ζωμός) was particularly famous – Plutarch tells the story of the king of Pontos who actually bought a Lakonian cook to prepare him some, and when he had tasted it and found it foul, the cook told him that it was necessary to bathe in the Eurotas before eating it (*Lykourgos* 12.7). Similarly, Athenaios says that once a Sybarite after dining in a Spartan mess was constrained to remark that it was reasonable for the Spartans to be the bravest of all men, since any sensible man would choose to die ten thousand deaths rather than have to put up with their wretched diet (4.138d). Thucydides, in his account of the Pylos operations, says that during the truce the Spartan hoplites on Sphakteria were to be allowed just under two kilograms of ready-kneaded barley meal, just over half a litre of wine, and some meat, per man, presumably each day (4.16.1), and later, when some of them were trapped on the island, the provisions smuggled in to them included flour, cheese, wine and 'other food' (4.26.5), while swimmers brought skins containing poppy-seed mixed with honey and pounded linseed (4.26.8).

Sanitary arrangements, as one might have expected, seem to have been non-existent – sentries who wanted to relieve themselves, for example, were only supposed to go far enough away to avoid annoying their comrades (*LP* 12.4) – but there is some evidence for a kind of medical service, at least for the kings and their immediate entourage: Agesilaos was operated on by a Syracusan doctor on returning from Boeotia in 377 (XH 5.4.58), but the

Constitution says that the king's 'tent companions' included doctors (*LP* 13.7). As we have seen, the *hypaspistai* sometimes acted as stretcher-bearers on the field of battle, and the two men suffering from ophthalmia at Thermopylai, were apparently tended by their helot-batmen behind the lines (Herodotos 7.229.1) (see plate 4). But basically, one assumes, ordinary soldiers would have had to patch up wounds for themselves, as best they could.

Unless there was to be a battle, the morning of a normal day seems to have been spent in gymnastics (*LP* 12.5), and although the author of the *Constitution* merely says this gave the Spartans more pride in themselves, and made them appear more free-spirited than other men – an interesting remark in view of the common opinion that Spartans were ground down by iron discipline – it was probably also this attention to physical fitness which enabled at least the younger soldiers to co-operate with cavalry and catch peltasts, if need be. Spartan soldiers were, clearly, very tough, and often surprised the enemy by their speed of march (cf., e.g., XH 4.6.6), or by taking a route which was considered impossible, as during Kleombrotos' retreat from Boeotia in 379/8 (XH 5.4.16–7), and both before and after Leuktra (XH 6.4.3 & 26). After the exercises, the 'first polemarch' – this seems to have been the commander of the so-called 'first *mora*' (cf. *LP* 13.6 and XH 4.2.22) – gave orders to sit and an inspection took place, followed by the morning meal (*LP* 12.6), apparently taken about midday (cf. XH 6.4.8); after this, the men seem to have been free to amuse themselves and to rest until the evening exercises: to this day many Greeks have hardly any breakfast, but eat a fairly substantial lunch and then take a *siesta* until four or five o'clock. Finally came the evening meal, followed by a sacrifice and a hymn to the gods, and then bed (*LP* 12.6–7).

The Spartans were a religious people, and it may at first sight seem surprising to modern readers how large a part religion played in their military life.[57] Sometimes religious taboos inhibited action altogether, for example at the time of Marathon (Herodotos 6.106.3), or at various times during the Peloponnesian War (cf., e.g., Thucydides 3.89.1, 5.54.2). At other times, unfavourable omens could allegedly deter Spartan generals even in fhe face of the enemy, as they are supposed to have done Pausanias when his men were suffering from the enemy archery on the final day at Plataea (Herodotos 9.61.3). It has sometimes been suggested (see p. 71, 136–7) that in circumstances like these religion was being manipulated to suit military or political purposes, but although Herodotos may not have been cynical enough to see this, Thucydides surely was, and yet he, too, thought that even when others manipulated religion, as the Argives did in 419 (5.54.3), the Spartans declined to do so. Xenophon reports an occasion when King Agesipolis actually consulted Olympia and Delphi as to the propriety of ignoring false claims of a 'holy truce' by the enemy (XH 4.7.2), and there is some possibility that the composition of the Spartan force at Thermopylai was deliberately contrived to get round a taboo at the time (see pp. 71–2).

The demands of religion were constantly observed on campaign: before setting out the king sacrificed to Zeus *Agetor* (the Leader), and, possibly, his sons, Castor and Pollux (*LP* 13.2 – the text is uncertain). Then, if this sacrifice proved favourable, a priest called the 'fire-bearer' took fire from the altar and led the way to the frontier where the king again sacrificed, this time to Zeus and Athene (*LP* ibid, cf. Thucydides 5.54.2, XH 4.7.2): the fire used in the sacrifices then accompanied the army, as well as further sacrificial animals. Each day, while it was still dark, the king also sacrificed – thus it was before dawn, on the final day at Thermopylai, that the seer, Megistias, was able to foretell the coming doom of Leonidas and his men (Herodotos 7.219.1). According to the *Constitution* (*LP* 13.4), polemarchs, *lochagoi*, *pentekosteres*, commanders of mercenary contingents, commandants of the baggage-train, and any general from an allied state who wished, all attended the sacrifice. Before battle sacrifice was also offered (cf. Herodotos 9.61.2) – Plutarch (*Lykourgos* 21.4) says to the Muses, but Athenaios (13.561e) to Eros, 'since safety lies in the love of those ranged alongside each other' – and even when the advance had begun, if we are to believe Xenophon (XH 4.2.20), and the armies were less than two hundred metres apart, the Spartans still found time for a final sacrifice to Artemis the Huntress (*Agrotera*).

A famous passage in Thucydides (5.70) reminds us that the Spartans marched to battle to the sound of the pipe, and music was important to them, especially for its martial qualities (cf. Plutarch *Lykourgos* 21, Athenaios 14.630f, etc.). The poems of Tyrtaios were naturally particularly popular as songs (Athenaios 14.630f), and perhaps some of them provided the texts for the martial songs with which the Spartans are said to have encouraged each other as they marched to battle at Mantineia (Thucydides 5.69.2). According to Plutarch (*Lykourgos* 22.2–3), before the final advance into battle began, the king ordered the pipers to pipe the song of Castor, and he himself led the marching-song – we can well believe Plutarch when he says that it was 'a sight at once awesome and terrifying as they marched in step to the pipe, leaving no gap in their line of battle and with no confusion in their hearts, but calmly and cheerfully advancing into danger.'

In the ultimate resort, organization and equipment, diet and training, were all put to the supreme test in battle, and it is almost impossible nowadays for anyone even to begin to imagine what it was like to take part in a fight between hoplites.[58] Missiles – arrows, sling-shots and javelins – clearly played little part in the set-piece engagements, and even cavalry was unimportant: fighting was predominantly hand to-hand between hoplites using their long, thrusting spears, and if these were broken or discarded, their swords – even the Spartan tactic of ordering the young men out to attack was apparently only used to drive off skirmishers. We must imagine, then, the opposing phalanxes – eight, twelve or more deep, as the case might be – closing to within a few feet, but then what happened? Presumably the men in the front ranks thrust at their opponents with their spears, aiming overarm for the throat and upper part of the body, or underarm for thighs or belly; presumably, too, if a man fell, the man behind him stepped over his body as well as he could and took his place. Sometimes, it appears, one side or the other gave way almost immediately, hardly waiting for the enemy to come 'within spear-thrust' (εἰς δόρυ: XH 7.1.31), as happened in the 'Tearless Battle'. But if both sides stood to fight it out, did the phalanxes behave like a kind of armoured rugger – scrum, pushing and shoving until one or the other gave way, or, as has recently been suggested,[59] was there a stage of relatively fluid combat before the 'shoving' started?

It is possible that the analogy of the rugger-scrum has been overdone, but the passages cited to show that hoplite battles were far more fluid until the decisive 'shove' (ὠθισμός) took place (Herodotos 9.62.2 and Thucydides 6.70.1-2), really do not prove any such thing. It is true that they suggest that there was fierce fighting before the 'shove', but it is much more likely that the 'shove' marks the point at which the Spartans in the one case, and the Athenians and Argives in the other, 'with a final heave' as it were, bore their opponents back, than that the combatants had been engaged in anything like individual duels before this moment. The passage from Plato's *Laches* already cited (above pp. 4 & 34–5) suggests that skill-at-arms was only really useful to the hoplite when the ranks were broken, as one side or the other gave way, not that it would also be required in a preliminary stage, before the shoving started.

Xenophon is, unfortunately, vague on the details of actual fighting, but although he says nothing about it in his accounts of the Nemea and of the second battle at Mantineia, in his account of the second stage at Koroneia, when the Thebans had broken through Agesilaos' left wing and the king had counter-marched his phalanx to face them, he does say (4.3.19) that 'they crashed their shields together and shoved' (συμβαλόντες τὰς ἀσπίδας ἐωθοῦντο), before he adds 'they fought, they slew, they died' (ἐμάκοντο, ἀπέκτεινον, ἀπέθνηοκον – a description he repeats in the *Agesilaos* 2.12), and, similarly, in his description of Leuktra, he describes the Spartans on the right falling back 'shoved by the mass' (ὑπὸ τοῦ ὄχλου ὠθουμένοι), and those on the left also giving way 'when they saw the right shoved back' (ὡς ἑώρων τὸ δὲ δεξιον ὠθουμένον: XH 6.4.14). Of course, none of these passages need necessarily mean that actual 'shoving' took place – we still use words like 'push' even in these days of tanks and missiles – but they presumably indicate at least that something like 'shoving' had once taken place, and the description of the Spartans and Thebans 'crashing their shields together' at Koroneia sounds terribly like the crashing together of the front rows in a set scrum. Similarly, the words Epameinondas is supposed to have used at the crisis of Leuktra (Polyainos 2.3.2) 'grant me one pace, and we will have victory' – are just the kind of thing the leader of a scrum might shout to his fellow-forwards, and Thucydides' description of the Thebans at Delion 'shoving little by little at first' (ὠσάμενοι κατὰ βραχὺ τὸ πρῶτον: 4.96.4) reminds one of the relentless pressure of a scrum – at Delion, too, there had apparently been shoving elsewhere in the battle, from the beginning (Thucydides 4.96.2). After all, the whole point of hoplite tactics was that a phalanx of heavily-armed men, fighting as a unit, replaced the individual prowess of 'heroic' warfare, and one would expect cohesion and weight to play a major part in hoplite battles: why else was the depth of the phalanx of such importance from Marathon to Leuktra?

Warfare in Xenophon's time, however, no longer only consisted of the simple clash of hoplite armies, though these did, of course, occur, and one of them at least – Leuktra – has a good claim to being that elusive event, a 'decisive' battle. It might be thought that the Spartans would have become increasingly out of touch when there were fewer of the great set piece engagements for which their training was primarily intended to fit them, and war began more and more to consist of skirmishes and ambushes, assaults on walls and fortresses, the seizing of strategic passes, and even occasionally, as in Boeotia in 378 and 377, what almost amounted to a kind of trench-warfare (cf. XH 5.4.38–41, 47–55). Thus it was an era in which the Greeks began to make greater use of the light–infantry *tirailleurs* they called 'peltasts' after the small shield (πέλτη) they carried, and in which cavalry at last began to come into its own. But the Spartans were not called 'artists in warfare' (τεχνῖται τῶν πολεμικῶν: *LP* 13.5) for nothing, and it is surprising, in fact, how well they coped with the changes.

They began to use peltasts almost as soon as they appeared on the scene: they met them for the first time on Sphakteria (cf. Thucydides 4.28.4, 32.2), and although they were probably not able to hire them until they came into contact with the original sources of supply, in Thrace (cf. Thucydides 4.28.4), Brasidas, inevitably, was already using them soon after his march to Chalkidike, by the winter of 424/3 (Thucydides 4.111.1, cf. 123.4). In the battle outside Amphipolis, in which both he and Kleon lost their lives, the peltasts in the Spartan army routed the right wing of the Athenians, killing Kleon in the process, after the Athenian hoplites had twice or three times held off the hoplites under Brasidas' lieutenant, Klearidas (Thucydides 5.10.9–10). During the rest of the Peloponnesian War we hear no more of peltasts in Spartan service, but when Sparta became involved again in Asia Minor, after the end of the war, we hear of increasing numbers of peltasts being used by Spartan commanders like Derkylidas and Agesilaos (cf. XH 3.2.2 & 16, 3.4.16 & 23, 4.1.3 & 21), and Agesilaos brought a large force of them back with him from Asia Minor (XH 4.2.5): at Koroneia they are said to have been more numerous than those of the enemy (4.3.16).

Thereafter, they again disappear for a time from Xenophon's account of the activities of the Spartan army, and it may be that with Persia now an enemy and increasingly funding Sparta's other enemies in Greece, the Spartans could no longer afford to hire peltasts – it is perhaps significant that their next appearance is in Teleutias' army at Olynthos (XH 5.3.3ff.), after the Peace of Antalkidas had once more patched up relations with Persia. Thereafter we hear of them fairly frequently in the fighting in Boeotia in 378–6: Kleombrotos, for example, used peltasts to seize the pass leading to Plataea, after learning that the usual pass *via* Eleutherai was guarded by Athenian peltasts under Chabrias (XH 5.4.14), and the mercenaries Agesilaos used to seize the pass over Kithairon, in 378 (XH 5.4.36–7), may also have been peltasts – he certainly had peltasts later in Boeotia (cf. XH 5.4.39), and left some of them behind at Thespiai, with Phoibidas (XH 5.4.42–3); Kleombrotos again tried to use peltasts to seize the pass leading into Boeotia, in 376, but they were surprised and beaten off by the enemy (XH 5.4.59). Later, there were some Phokian peltasts on the left wing of Kleombrotos' army at Leuktra (XH 6.4.9). Agesilaos was joined by some from Orchomenos during his campaign in Arcadia in 370

(XH 6.5.17), and they appear for the last time in Xenophon's pages, on the Spartan side, acting as the advanced guard of Archidamos' army as it approached Kromnos in 365 (XH 7.4.22).

It was, then, during the confused and complicated warfare of the period from 394 to 386 that the Spartans perhaps most missed peltasts, possibly because of financial difficulties: we do not even know what became of Agesilaos' numerous peltasts, brought back from Asia Minor, after Koroneia, but they were apparently not present when the polemarch, Gylis, was discomfited by Lokrian missile-troops immediately after the battle (XH 4.3.22–3): perhaps they had accompanied the king on to Megara, and thereafter they may have been disbanded. Thus, at just the time when the war ceased to be an affair of the set-piece battle between citizen armies (cf. XH 4.4.14), Sparta herself still had to depend on her own regulars. This, of course, led to the disastrous occasion when a *mora* was caught in the open near Lechaion by peltasts under one of the experts in the new warfare, the Athenian Iphikrates, backed up by Athenian hoplites, and lost some 250 men killed out of about 600 (XH 4.5.11–17 – see below, p. 173ff.). Xenophon specifically says (XH 4.5.12) that the Spartans were aware that there were many peltasts and hoplites present in Corinth, but that they 'contemptuously assumed that no one would attack them because of their previous successes,' referring particularly to an earlier occasion when the younger men in a Spartan force had even managed to catch peltasts who were no nearer than a javelin's throw (XH 4.4.16).

Contemporaries clearly took the disaster seriously (cf. XH 4.5.7 & 10), and Agesilaos, who had been campaigning on the Perachora peninsula at the time, evidently sought to minimise its effects both on the morale of his own men and on the attitude of Sparta's allies, by avoiding contact with them, as much as possible, on his way home (XH 4.5.18). But Xenophon emphasises that the blow was felt all the more keenly because it was so unusual (XH 4.5.10), and it does not appear that the Spartans were habitually baffled by the new style of warfare during these years. We have already seen that Spartan hoplites, no doubt using the tactic of ordering those 'ten or fifteen years from manhood' to charge at the double, were even able to catch and kill peltasts, in the open (XH 4.4.16), and a couple of years before, they had successfully been able to exploit the treachery that presented them with the walls linking Corinth to Lechaion, in just the kind of operation in which peltasts are supposed to have excelled, using ordinary hoplites, despite the presence of Iphikrates' peltasts at the time (cf. XH 4.4.7–13). Later, too during Agesilaos' campaign in Akarnania, in 389, although the king was initially discomfited by the Akarnanian peltasts (XH 4.6.7–9), in exactly the same way that the Athenian Demosthenes had been in Aetolia in 426 – (cf. Thucydides 3.97–98), the Spartan king managed to extricate his army with more success than Demosthenes, attacking uphill with 'those fifteen years from manhood' and his cavalry, supported by his whole hoplite force (XH 4.6.9–11).

The Spartan army thus did cope with the changing conditions of warfare, in the early fourth century, and although its hoplites could be beaten, particularly if caught in the open by a combination of hoplites and skirmishers armed with missile-weapons, as on Sphakteria and at Lechaion, such troops had to be very skilfully handled, as some of Sparta's enemies learned to their cost, and the fact remains that the Spartan army remained supreme in the set-piece battle, down to Leuktra, and then were beaten by hoplites, led by a general of genius – and some luck – and not by peltasts. Nor despite the changed nature of its composition, and its few defeats, is there really any reason to believe that the morale of the Spartan army was beginning to crack in Xenophon's time: if there were many *hypomeiones* like Kinadon, who resented their 'inferiority', we hear nothing of them, and the army remained steady, even in the depths of adversity. The disaster to the *mora* and the defeat at Leuktra were, after all, nineteen years apart, with only, perhaps, the shadowy defeat at Tegyra in 375 (Plutarch *Pelopidas* 16–17; Diodoros 15.81.2) coming in between. Even after Leuktra, the Spartan army was still formidable, judging from Epameinondas' reluctance to press home his attacks on the still unwalled city in 370 and 362 (cf. XH 6.5.27–31, 7.5.11–14), and from the attitude of the Arcadians at the 'Tearless Battle' in 368 (XH 7.1.31).

The truth of the matter is not that Sparta's army at last failed her, but that after her defeat of Athens in 404, she overstretched herself, and so called upon her army to perform too many tasks for which it was not well fitted, against increasingly bold and enterprising enemies. What is notable is not that in the end Sparta was defeated, but that this took so long to happen.

Chapter 2

The Fifth Century

At first sight, there appears to be one crucial difference between the Spartan army of Xenophon's time and the one known to Herodotos and Thucydides: neither of the latter ever mentions *morai*, and the largest unit they seem to have heard of was the *lochos*. But for this, the natural assumption would be that certainly the army Thucydides knew, and probably even the one known to Herodotos, was similar in all significant respects to the one with which Xenophon appears to have been familiar. Thus Thucydides mentions polemarchs, *lochagoi*, *pentekonteres* and *enomotarchoi* (5.67.3), *lochoi*, *pentekostyes* and *enomotiai* (5.68.3), *Hippeis* (5.72.4) and *Skiritai* (5.67.1, etc.), and a system of call-up by age-classes which produced *enomotiai* of c.32 men at Mantineia (5.68.3), when one sixth of the fighting men, consisting of 'the older and the younger' (5.64.3), and an unspecified number of the remaining 'older' (5.72.3), were absent from the line-of-battle. Herodotos gives far fewer details, but he, too, knew of *enomotiai* (1.65.5) and *lochoi* (9.53.2, 57.1–2), of polemarchs (7.173.2), and of *Hippeis* (1.67.5, 8.124.3).

If there was a change, moreover, between 418, when Thucydides seems to have thought that the largest units in the army at Mantineia were *lochoi* of c.512 each,[1] and 403, when *morai* first make their appearance in the surviving sources (XH 2.4.31), it is difficult to see what the reason for it can have been: Sparta suffered no defeat on land during these years, and although Mantineia had itself not been an unqualified success, it had not apparently revealed any deficiencies in the army's organization, for which Thucydides has nothing but praise. The suggestion that the *mora* was introduced when the army was 'reorganized on a peace footing'[2] seems particularly unfortunate: when was the Spartan army ever put on a 'peace footing'?

If it was just a question of Herodotos' and Thucydides' failure to mention *morai*, one would not be too concerned, since it is not usually the style of either of them to go into such details, and one could suppose either that they themselves were vague about them, or that they deliberately avoided using Spartan military terms in order to avoid confusing their non-Spartan audiences. But the case is different with Thucydides' account of King Agis' army at Mantineia: he obviously took some trouble to find out the details, and to be as precise as possible, and when he bandies about terms like *pentekonteres* and *enomotarchoi*, *pentekostyes* and *enomotiai*, it may be thought that it is asking too much to expect one to believe that he somehow omitted the technical term for the largest units in the army, if such units then existed.

Nevertheless, there does appear to be something wrong with Thucydides' account of the Spartan army at Mantineia, and there are some indications that he somehow contrived to underestimate its size by confusing *lochoi* with larger units.[3] Basically the problem is that although he estimates the total number of Spartan as opposed to allied troops at about 4184 men – apart from the 'few Lakedaimonians' on the extreme right (5.67.1), and, possibly, the *Hippeis* (5.72.4 – see below) – made up of seven *lochoi* of c.512 men each and 600 *Skiritai* (5.68.3), he nevertheless says (5.68.1) that the Spartan army appeared larger than that of the enemy, and later (5.71.2) that the Spartans had the greater army. Now, although there are many variables on either side, it does not seem likely that Sparta's allies on this occasion – Heraia, Mainalia and Tegea – can have furnished more than about 2,500 hoplites at most, and this would mean that the whole Spartan army, allies included, would have been less than 7,000 strong at most. Their opponents, however, can hardly have been less numerous than that: the Mantineians, in whose territory the battle was fought, should have been there in full force, and there is some reason to believe that they could field at least 3,000 hoplites at this date (cf. Diodoros 12.78.4); the main body of the Argive contingent, apart from the picked hoplites whose number Thucydides says was 1,000 (5.67.2), presumably numbered more than 1,000, and may well have been more numerous than the Mantineans; their allies from Kleonai and Orneai should have numbered a hundred or two; and finally there were probably 1,000 Athenian hoplites (cf. 5.61.1). In short, it is hardly possible to believe that the army that faced the Spartans was less than about 7,500 strong, and it could have been nearer 10,000.

One way out of the difficulty would be to suppose that Thucydides has omitted the *perioikoi*, who might have been presumed to have been there in some force,[4] but, as was argued above (pp. 20–1), we have no reason to assume that *perioikoi* always formed part of Spartan armies, even when they are not specifically mentioned by the sources, and it is possible that they were not used against Peloponnesian enemies at this time. In the case of the Mantineia campaign, indeed, as earlier in that of the invasion of the Argolid, Thucydides twice uses the phrase '(the Lakedaimonians) themselves and the helots in full force' (5.57.1, 5.64.2), of the Spartan forces, as if to exclude the *perioikoi*. Of course, the inscription (*IG* V i 1124) recording the death of Eualkes 'in war at Mantineia' may be evidence that one *perioikos* at least was present (see above, p. 20), but Eualkes may have been a 'gentleman – volunteer' like those at Olynthos (cf. XH 5.3.9), as we have seen.

In any case, some of the things Thucydides says point to a different solution. Firstly, it is usually thought that his seven *lochoi* included one consisting of the *Brasideioi* and *neodamodeis* (cf. 5.67.1), and of these Brasidas' soldiers had originally numbered 700 (cf. 4.80.5), and the *neodamodeis* possibly 1,000 (cf. 5.34.1 & 49.1): although some allowance must be made for losses among the former, and some of the latter may have been left to garrison Lepreon, it hardly seems likely that those at Mantineia together only numbered about 512 men. Secondly, it is odd that although Thucydides mentions polemarchs between the king and the *lochagoi* in his description of the Spartan chain-of-command (5.67.3), there was nothing for polemarchs to command if the *lochoi* were really the largest units in the army, since they were presumably commanded by the *lochagoi*. If, on the other hand, the polemarchs commanded the *lochoi* – as may seem to be implied by what is said about Hipponoïdas and Aristokles (5.71.3 – see below) – what did the *lochagoi* command?

A possible solution is, then, that Thucydides somehow confused *morai* and *lochoi*, and that what he should have said was that the main body of the Spartan army, *Brasideioi, neodamodeis* and *Skiritai* apart, consisted of six *morai*, each commanded by a polemarch, and composed of *two* of his *lochoi* commanded by *lochagoi*. If this is so, there were about 6,144 Spartan troops in the main body (6 × 1,024), and not just about 3,072 (6 × 512), and with another unit of 1,024 *Brasideioi* and *neodamodeis*, 600 *Skiritai*, possibly 300 *Hippeis*, and 'a few Lakedaimonians' on the right wing, the Spartan troops alone would have numbered over 8,000 men, easily enough, with their allies, to account for their army's appearing the larger, as Thucydides says it did. The confusion may have arisen because the unit composed of the *Brasideioi* and *neodamodeis*, although the same size as a *mora*, was not called one: if it was called a *lochos*, like the *Skiritai*, Thucydides, knowing that the Spartan army on this occasion consisted of seven main units of equal size, may have mistakenly called them all *lochoi*, when he should have said six *morai* and a *lochos*, and then, when he came to describe their detailed internal organization, forgot that a *lochos* in the Spartan technical sense was only half the size – possibly the fact that the unit of *Skiritai* was only 600 strong, helped the confusion.[5]

A hint that there was some such confusion is contained in the passage (5.71.3) in which Thucydides describes how Agis ordered the polemarchs, Hipponoïdas and Aristokles, to take two *lochoi* from the right and plug the gap on the left caused by the shift to their left of the *Brasideioi*, *neodamodeis* and *Skiritai*. Here it must be presumed that Thucydides ignores the Arcadians and the 'few Lakedaimonians' on the extreme right, and means thai the two *lochoi* were to be drawn from the right of his six *lochoi* of Spartan troops.[6] But it does not seem possible that even Agis can seriously have thought of moving a *third* of his Spartan troops from right to left in the face of the enemy: such a manoeuvre would have left a yawning gap between the Spartans' new right – their unshielded side – and their Arcadian allies, and would completely have nullified any advantage they might gain from overlapping the enemy's left flank. But if here Thucydides correctly uses the term *lochos* to mean half a *mora*, and there were really six *morai* in the Spartan line, Agis was only contemplating the transfer of one sixth of his Spartan troops from right to left, and the two *lochoi* might not even have been contiguous to each other: the manoeuvre would still have left a gap corresponding to a front of 128 men, but at least then there could have been two gaps, each corresponding only to a front of sixty-four men, and this would have been considerably less dangerous. This may be why Thucydides uses the odd phrase 'having two *lochoi*' (δυὸ λόχους ... ἔχουσι) of Hipponoïdas and Aristokles: the two *lochoi* they were to take did not constitute their whole commands, but were, perhaps, the *lochoi* on the right of their respective *morai*, where one might expect the *polemarchs* themselves to have been stationed: possibly the king specifically wanted them to take charge of so dangerous, but – in his eyes – so important a manoeuvre, leaving the remaining two *lochoi* of their commands to continue advancing under their *lochagoi*.

If all this is right, the Spartan army at the time of Mantineia was organized in exactly the same way as – we have argued – it was in Xenophon's time, even to including a special unit of *Skiritai* (Thucydides 5.67.1), and a corps of 300 *Hippeis* who fought 'about the king' (Thucydides 5.72.4).[7] This is, however, only what we should expect, for the Spartans were a conservative people, and it is more likely that they would have clung to the various elements of something as central to their lives as their army, than that they would constantly have been indulging in radical military reorganizations as some modern scholars have thought.[8] Of course, the most obvious objection is that Thucydides does not mention *morai*, but, as has been pointed out,[9] the author of the *Constitution of the Lakedaimonians* does ascribe the creation of the *morai* to Lykourgos (11.4), and although this cannot be taken seriously as evidence for the date of their creation, it does not seem possible to believe that either Xenophon or a contemporary could have said such a thing if the *morai* had in fact come into being in their lifetime, and the further back one puts their creation, the easier it is to understand how it could be ascribed to Lykourgos.

At first sight, too, Thucydides' statement (5.64.3) that a sixth of the Spartan army, consisting of the older and the younger men, was sent home from Orestheion, may seem difficult to reconcile with the view that there were forty age-classes in groups of five, but the difficulty is removed if we take 'the younger' (τὸ νεώτερον) here to mean those in their nineteenth and twentieth years, who did not form part of the adult establishment, but could, no doubt, be used for home-defence, and 'the older' (τὸ πρεσβύτερον) to mean, as one would expect, the five oldest age-classes, consisting of men in their fifty-sixth to sixtieth years. This would mean that when the army marched to Orestheion there were actually forty-two age–classes present, but that after the sixth had been sent home, the army which eventually fought at Mantineia consisted of what Xenophon would have called 'the thirty-five from manhood,' as at Leuktra (cf. XH 6.4.17). This may also be thought to conflict with Thucydides' statement (5.68.3) that the average strength of each *enomotia* in the battle-line was thirty-two, but he himself subsequently says (5.72.3) that some of the 'older men' (πρεσβύτεροι) were guarding the wagons – these could easily have been men in their fifty-third to fifty-fifth years – and that there were also 'a few Lakedaimonians' (Λακεδαιμονίων ὀλίγοι) on the extreme right (5.67.1). Thucydides' remarks about the age-structure of the army at the time of Mantineia can thus be made exactly to fit what Xenophon says about it later, and however speculative these conjectures may appear to be, they are more plausible than the view that Thucydides' army, which clearly resembles Xenophon's in so many respects, was in this respect quite different.

Despite the difficulties we have been considering, Thucydides' account of Mantineia is one of the best descriptions of a hoplite battle that has come down to us, and apart from the precious details, tells us a great deal about the Spartan army. The refusal of Hipponoïdas and Aristokles to obey the king's order, for example, shows that Spartan officers were not necessarily accustomed to blind, automatic obedience, and interesting, too, is the incident Thucydides describes which took place before the final battle, when Agis led his army to 'within stone and javelin throw' of the enemy position on the slopes of a hill, and one of the older Spartans called out to him that he 'had it in mind to cure wrong with wrong' (5.65.2: i.e. 'two blacks don't make a white'), meaning that he appeared to be trying to demonstrate on this occasion how bold he was, in order to wipe out the stigma of his previous failure to fight the Argives. This is reminiscent of Xenophon's account of the Nemea, when a Spartan is said to have called out to his polemarch to 'let the front ranks go by' (XH 4.2.22), before he charged the exposed flank of the enemy: it is clear that Spartan discipline did not prevent their soldiers from expressing their views.

Thucydides was, nevertheless, evidently impressed by the disciplined speed with which the Spartans deployed, despite their initially having been taken by surprise (5.66.2), by their slow and measured advance, in step to the sound of their many pipers, which contrasted with that of the enemy 'full of sound and fury' (5.70), and by their fighting qualities, even when outmanoeuvred (5.72.2). On the latter point, it is worth emphasizing again that few if any other Greek armies could even have contemplated the kind of manoeuvre Agis attempted, though in this case it nearly led to disaster. It is also worth noting that many of the contingents on the left of the enemy line broke and fled at the first onset (5.72.4), and that Agis was able to keep his men from pressing too vigorous a pursuit and so getting out of hand, and to wheel them to the left to support his own hard-pressed left wing – again something few other Greek soldiers would have been able to accomplish in the heat of battle, though the Athenians and Plataeans, miraculously, accomplished it at Marathon (cf. Herodotos 6.113.2). Thucydides, indeed, notes (5.73.4) that it was not Spartan practice to pursue a beaten enemy for any distance or length of time, and one suspects that this was precisely because troops who did so could so easily find themselves in difficulties.

But perhaps the most interesting thing that Thucydides says in his account of the battle is that the right wings of armies tended to drift to the right until they overlapped those opposite them, owing to the individual fear of each man about his shieldless side and consequent desire to stand as close as possible to the man on his right (5.71.1). Thucydides implies that this was a tendency over which generals and officers, even in the Spartan army, had little or no control, and in this instance it led to Agis' near-disastrous idea of trying to switch two *lochoi* from his right to his left. But it is possible that as a result of this battle, the Spartans came to appreciate the possibilities opened up by this tendency, and deliberately set out to exploit them: at the Nemea they 'led to the right' as we have seen (above, p. 35; below, p. 165ff.), and the outflanking of the enemy line which resulted, followed by rolling up his line from left to right, looks deliberate.

The other passage in Thucydides which is particularly interesting for the study of the Spartan army in his day is his account of the Pylos campaign in 425 (4.8ff.). Here we certainly meet *lochoi* again (4.8.9), and when it is said (ibid.) that the relays of men sent across to Sphakteria, were chosen by lot 'from all the *lochoi*' (ἀπὸ πάντων τῶν λόχων), since it seems unlikely that lots can literally have been drawn among thousands of individual soldiers, a plausible suggestion is that each *lochos* was called upon to provide one *enomotia*, drawn by lot, and that the number of men in the final group – 420 – was made up of twelve *enomotiai*, each of thirty-five men.[10] If this is right, it would mean that there were already twelve *lochoi* in the Spartan army at the time, and this would support the view taken above about the Spartan army at Mantineia. However, it is, of course, theoretically equally possible that each of six *lochoi* was called upon to provide two *enomotiai* of thirty-five men, and no doubt other mathematical permutations are possible – that the forces sent to Sphakteria were made up of units of about this size is suggested by Thucydides' statement that the first guard-post overwhelmed by the Athenians, contained about thirty hoplites (4.31.2).

Thucydides' account of the Pylos campaign also again raises the question of the personnel of Spartan units, for he implies (4.8.9) that the various groups of men sent across to Sphakteria were random samples of the army as a whole, since they were 'chosen by lot from all the *lochoi*', and he says (4.38.5) that of the 292 who eventually surrendered, only 'about 120' were Spartiates: who, then, were the remainder? It is usually assumed that they were *perioikoi*, in accordance with the view already discussed (above, p. 18ff.) that as the number of Spartiates declined, *perioikoi* were increasingly drafted in to make up the numbers required.'[11] However, there is no more reason to believe that this was the case in Thucydides' day than in Xenophon's, and it is more likely that these men were Spartans who, for one reason or another, were not Spartiates – this might indeed explain why Thucydides could only say that 'about 120' of the prisoners were Spartiates, for one might have expected him to have been able to find out exactly how many Spartiates there had been, if the rest had been merely *perioikoi*. His account of the mustering of the army at Pylos (4.8.1) also suggests that Spartiates and *perioikoi* did not serve in the same units at the time, for he there distinguishes '*Spartiatai*' from *perioikoi*. Of course, this would mean that – strictly speaking – we would have to suppose that here Thucydides includes non-Spartiate Spartans in the term '*Spartiatai*', whereas elsewhere (e.g. 2.66.2, 3.100.2, and, above all, 4.38.5) he clearly uses it to mean Spartiates in the strict sense. But, as has already been pointed out, it is not easy to see how a Greek could have referred to non-Spartiate Spartans, as opposed to *perioikoi*, except as '*Spartiatai*', since the term '*Lakedaimonioi*' would not do. Whoever the non-Spartiate prisoners may have been, however, if we can assume that the proportion of Spartiates was roughly the same in the army as a whole (excluding the *Hippeis*),[12] it is interesting that roughly forty-one per cent of it was still Spartiate at this time, compared with possibly less than nine per cent at the time of Leuktra.

Thucydides' account of the Pylos operations also raises questions about the equipment of Spartan hoplites in 425. In the first place, their helmets are called '*piloi*' (πῖλοι), and this should mean, strictly, that they were made of felt, and that they were not made of metal is suggested by the statement (4.34.3) that they were not capable of protecting their wearers against arrows, though the thin bronze of the average Greek metal helmet would probably not have withstood a direct hit at close range. But it is not easy to determine whether Spartan hoplites still wore some kind of protective clothing. It is quite clear that the reason why they found it so difficult to come to grips with their opponents in the fight on the island (cf. 4.33.2, 34.1, etc.) was that they had 'hopla' (ὅπλα ἔχοντες), whereas their opponents were 'lightly equipped' (κούφως ἐσκευασμένοι), but this might mean no more than that the Spartans were impeded by their shields. However, in the one passage in which their shields are unequivocally mentioned (4.38.1), they are called 'aspides', as is Brasidas' shield in an earlier passage (4.12.1), and the natural interpretation is that the 'hopla' of the Spartans included more than shields – nor can it refer to their offensive weapons, since their opponents would have had these too. Similarly, when earlier the Lakedaimonians are said to rush into the sea 'with their *hopla*' (ξῦν τοῖς ὅπλοις: 4.12.2), in an endeavour to recover their ships from the Athenians, we are surely to think that this means more than just 'with their shields and spears.' In this connection, too, it should be noted that after his victory at Olpai in 426, Demosthenes dedicated 300 '*panopliai*' (Thucydides 3.114.1), and although no Spartan regular units had fought at Olpai, some of the panoplies at least must have come from Peloponnesians.

Elsewhere, Thucydides does not give any details of the organization or equipment of the Spartan army – what he says about rations has already been discussed (above, p. 43) – and it is usually difficult to determine how many regular Spartan troops there were in Spartan armies. When, for example, the 'Lakedaimonians' went to the aid of Doris, early in the 450s, with 1,500 hoplites 'of themselves' (ἑαυτῶν: 1.107.2) and 10,000 of their allies, it is perhaps natural to suppose that the 1,500 included Spartans and *perioikoi*[13] and that the 10,000 consisted of Arcadians, Corinthians, Sikyonians, and so on. On the other hand, it seems unlikely that the force which later faced and beat an Athenian army of 14,000 hoplites at Tanagra, can have contained fewer than 1,500 Spartan troops, and the qualification that the 1,500 were 'of themselves' rather suggests that they were all Spartans, and that if any *perioikoi* were present, they were either omitted by Thucydides, or included in the 10,000. 1,500 Spartan hoplites could mean two *morai* consisting of twenty-five age-classes – which would actually have come to 1,600 – for there is some reason to think that only twenty–five age-classes were called up earlier, during the Persian Wars (see p. 68ff.).

Conversely, when 1,000 hoplites 'of the Lakedaimonians' are said to have attacked Zakynthos in the autumn of 430 (Thucydides 2.66.2), the fact that the navarch, Knemos, is specifically said to be a Spartiate suggests that none of the rest were – this was obviously a relatively minor campaign, quite unlike the one that culminated at Tanagra, and perhaps thought quite suitable for *perioikoi*.

During the course of the Peloponnesian War, Sparta also began to use helots as soldiers. The first occasion was in 424 when 700 accompanied Brasidas to Chalkidike (Thucydides 4.80.5), and subsequently helot soldiers were also sent to Sicily in 413 (cf. 7.19.3 & 58.3). In view of the shortage of Spartiates implied by what Thucydides says about the prisoners taken on Sphakteria, it would be natural to assume that this was the main reason for using helots, but Thucydides actually says (4.80.2) that the motive was fear of helot unrest, and he goes on to recount the appalling episode of the massacre of 2,000 helots after they had been invited to select those who claimed to have done the best service in the war (4.80.3–4). The helot soldiers who went with Brasidas may have been organized in something like the same way as Spartan regular soldiers, for Thucydides says (4.125.3) that on his retreat from Lynkos in 423, Brasidas gave orders to 'the youngest' (νεωτάτοι) of his men to sally from the column if it was attacked, and this is reminiscent of the orders given for similar action to 'those ten or fifteen years from manhood' in the 4th century. As we have seen, the unit formed by Brasidas' veterans and the *neodamodeis*, at Mantineia, seems to have been organized in exactly the same way as the Spartan units, since Thucydides probably included it for the purposes of his calculations (cf. 5.68.3).

The *neodamodeis* were obviously something like Brasidas' helot soldiers, but distinct from them. They are first mentioned in connection with the return of Brasidas' soldiers from Thrace in 421, when Thucydides says that these latter were voted their freedom and shortly afterwards settled with the *neodamodeis* at Lepreon, on the borders between Spartan territory and that of Elis (5.34.1). Since Thucydides subsequently says (5.49.1) that Elis fined Sparta for sending troops to Lepreon during the time of the Olympic truce, and yet the *neodamodeis* were apparently already at Lepreon in the summer of 421 (5.34.1), it is possible that the *neodamodeis* had been raised and sent to Lepreon during the *previous* Olympic truce, i.e. in 424. The fine imposed on Sparta was 2,000 *minai*, and since Thucydides says that the rule was two *minai* per hoplite, we can conclude that the Spartans had sent 1,000 hoplites to Lepreon: probably all these were *neodamodeis*, the survivors from Brasidas' helot force being in addition. Men from the two groups formed one of the main Spartan units at Mantineia, as we have seen, and subsequently *neodamodeis* are said to have been sent to Sicily and Euboea, both in 413 (Thucydides 7.19.3 & 8.5.1): presumably these were raised in addition to the garrison of Lepreon. By 399, 1,000 *neodamodeis* could be sent to Asia with Thibron (XH 3.1.4), and later 2,000 more with Lysander (XH 3.4.2). *Neodamodeis* are probably to be distinguished from helot-soldiers in being helots freed before service in the army,[14] whereas Brasidas' helots, at least, were freed after returning from Thrace (Thucydides 5.34.1).

The year 424 also saw the raising of a cavalry force for the first time, to counter the threat of Athenian hit-and-run raids, increased by the establishment of their bases at Pylos, on Kythera and elsewhere (Thucydides 4.55.2). Thucydides gives no details, but since only the rich possessed horses, either the force was raised from the Spartan aristocracy, or, more likely, they provided the horses and the troopers were drawn from elsewhere, as in Xenophon's day (cf. 6.4.11), possibly from *hypomeiones*.

This is about all the detailed information on the Spartan army that can be gleaned from Thucydides, and it is a great pity, in particular, that we do not know more about Tanagra, fought at around 457. Thucydides (1.108.1) gives no details except that the Athenians and their allies had 14,000 hoplites, and that the Spartans and their allies won, after a hard fight, with heavy losses on both sides. The Peloponnesian contingents are previously said to have numbered 11,500 men (1.107.2), including, perhaps, two Spartan *morai* of 800 men each (see above, p. 58), but presumably these were joined by considerable numbers of Boeotians before the battle: there are no details of the Spartan army in any of the secondary sources (e.g. Diodoros 11.79.4ff.; Plutarch *Kimon* 17.3ff.). One would also like to know more about the mysterious battles at Tegea, Dipaia and the 'Isthmos' (Ithome?), won by the Spartans, according to Herodotos (9.35.2), between Plataea in 479 and Tanagra, the first against the Tegeates and Argives, the second against 'all the Arcadians except the Mantineians' and the third against the Messenians. They all probably belong to the period of unrest in the Peloponnese culminating in the great Messenian revolt of the 460s, but that is all we know, although Isokrates reports a tradition (*Archidamos* 6.99) that the Spartans fought only one rank deep at Dipaia – a 'thin red line' indeed, if it is true!

About a decade before the battle of Tegea, perhaps, the Spartans and *perioikoi* formed the core of the greatest hoplite army of all, at the battle of Plataea in 479. Herodotos repeatedly refers to the 5,000 Spartan hoplites – as opposed to those of the *perioikoi* – as '*Spartiatai*' (9.10.1, 19.1, 26.7, 28.2 & 3, 29.1), and if he uses the term with strict accuracy, this is by far the largest number of Spartiates ever expressly described as such. However, Herodotos is here trying to distinguish the Spartan contingent from that of the other Lakedaimonians (i.e. the *perioikoi*: cf., e.g., 9.28.2 and 29.1–2), and as has been repeatedly argued, it is difficult to see what other term he could use but '*Spartiatai*'. In other words, we should not just assume that all the 5,000 *Spartiatai* at Plataea were Spartiates – some may already have been non-Spartiate Spartans – and thus we cannot use this figure, without hesitation, to show how the numbers of Spartiates declined.

Unfortunately, the only detail about the organization of the Spartan army provided by Herodotos is the description of Amompharetos as '*lochagos* of the Pitanate *lochos*' (λοχηγέων τοῦ Πιτανήτεω: 9.53.2, cf. 57,1), and although this statement has often been used as one of the lynch-pins of a widely-accepted hypothesis about the organization of the Spartan army at this time, Amompharetos and his unit in fact create more problems than they solve. If one had nothing to go on but the first passage in which he is mentioned (9.53.2ff.), where his behaviour in refusing to obey Pausanias' order to retreat is contrasted with that of the other '*taxiarchoi*', we would naturally assume that he was a senior officer, comparable with an Athenian *taxiarchos*, for example, who commanded the hoplites from one of the ten *phylai* into which adult males were divided, and this is what the hypothesis mentioned above would have us believe – that Amompharetos commanded one of the five *lochoi* into which the Spartan army was allegedly divided at this time. But this can hardly have been the case if he was the same Amompharetos said later (9.85.1) to have been buried among the '(*e*)*irenes*', for this was the term used of young Spartans, probably between twenty and twenty-one or twenty-two, who had just 'graduated' into the army (cf. Plutarch *Lykourgos* 17.2; *LP* 2.11),[15] and if there is one thing that is certain about the Spartan army it is that no twenty year-old or twenty-one year-old ever commanded a fifth of it.

The easiest way out of the problem, of course, would be to assume that Herodotos is talking about two different men of the same name, but that would surely be too much of a coincidence. If, then, he was talking about the same man, either Amompharetos was not an (*e*)*iren,* or the *lochos* he commanded was such that an (*e*)*iren* could conceivably have commanded it, or Herodotos was wrong about his being the commander of a *lochos.* In favour of the first alternative is the manuscript reading in the passage of Herodotos in question (9.85.1–2), which is actually 'ἱρεάς/ἱρεές' (i.e. 'priests') – 'ἱρένας/ἱρένες' is an emendation which requires the further assumption that this is the Ionic form of 'εἱρένας/εἱρένες'. However, it is clear that the ancient commentators on Herodotos read words meaning '*eirenes*' in their texts, and the reading 'priests' does not make much sense, unless we are to suppose that the four men so described held some kind of hereditary priesthoods in addition to any military function they may have had, and that their quasi-sacred position marked them out for separate burial.[16] But even if Herodotos did describe the four men as *eirenes*, it is possible that he was mistaken: it seems odd that the Spartans should have buried *eirenes* in a separate grave, with the other Spartiates in a second and the helots in a third – what about the *perioikoi?* – and Pausanias, if he is referring to the same three graves, says that two of them were those of the Lakedaimonians and Athenians, and the third that of the other Greeks (9.2.5). Furthermore, it seems even more peculiar that four of the five Spartans singled out for special mention by Herodotos – the fifth was Arimnestos, who killed Mardonios (9.64.2) – should all have been *eirenes*, unless the fact that they were all killed is significant, indicating that they had fought in the front rank, as *eirenes* may indeed have done: one of the four –

Kallikrates – was shot in the side while 'sitting in his rank' before the fight began (Herodotos 9.72.1), which might indicate that he at least was in the front rank, and the fact that Herodotos also says that he was the handsomest of all the Greeks there might also suggest that he was a young man. However, one suspects that Herodotos either got the names from some monument, or, more likely, was misled by an informant: he actually says (9.72.2) that Kallikrates told a Plataean called Arimnestos that he was not so much concerned that he was dying for Greece as that he had not lifted a hand or done anything worthy of himself, though he was eager to do so, and one suspects that Arimnestos may have been Herodotos' source for the whole story. Did Arimnestos tell him that Kallikrates was an *eiren* – and perhaps go on to claim that the Spartan who killed Mardonios bore the same name as himself? and what was a Plataean doing near the Spartans at the time of the final fight in any case?

If, on the other hand, Amompharetos was an *eiren*, it has been suggested that the *lochos* he commanded may have been a special force exclusively composed of *eirenes*.[17] This is possible, but most unlikely: there is no good evidence that there ever was such a unit in the Spartan army, and if *eirenes* were really men in their twenty-first and twenty-second years, it is much more likely that they were incorporated into the ordinary units, indeed that they formed the front ranks of the *enomotiai*. In any case, even if there were units exclusively composed of *eirenes*, it remains very doubtful whether they would have been commanded by *eirenes* – one would have expected their commanders to have been older men, just as the *eirenes* themselves were apparently put in charge of younger boys (cf. *LP* 2.11).

However, it is just possible that when Amompharetos was left behind on the morning of the final battle of Plataea, probably to act as a rearguard (see below, p. 133), he was put in command of a force of younger men, many of whom were in fact *eirenes* – that he was given command of what Xenophon would have called 'those five years from manhood' (τὰ πέντε ἀφ' ἥβης), for example, for although such improvised forces were later used primarily in an offensive role, the fitness and speed which qualified them for that would also have qualified them to act as a rearguard. If Amompharetos and his men were really left behind to act as a rearguard, they might have been expected to have had to beat off attacks by Persian cavalry and skirmishers – Herodotos' says that they and the Persian cavalry reached Pausanias' new position simultaneously (9.57.3) – and this would have been a rather similar situation to the one faced by the *mora* near Lechaion, even though that was advancing, not retreating (cf. XH 4.5.14–17). This would not meet the objection that even if he commanded 'those five years from manhood', Amompharetos himself is unlikely to have been a young man, but perhaps he was buried with the young men he had led, and this gave rise to the mistaken belief that he himself was an *eiren*.

The final possibility is that Amompharetos really was an *eiren*, and that Herodotos made a mistake in thinking that he commanded the 'Pitanate *lochos*', whatever that may have been. In favour of this is Thucydides' statement, plainly designed to correct Herodotos, that there never was a 'Pitanate *lochos*' in the Spartan army (1.20.3), and it may well be that Herodotos simply misunderstood a Spartan informant. It so happens that he tells us (3.55) that one of his informants – indeed, one of only three that he expressly names – came from Pitana (which Herodotos calls a 'deme' of Sparta – see below), and it is possible, for example, that Archias told him that the *eiren* Amompharetos of Pitana was killed 'in the front rank' (ἄρχων: cf. *LP* 11.5) of his *lochos* at Plataea, after protesting against running away from 'the strangers', and that Herodotos assumed not only that there was a *lochos* from Pitana, but that Amompharetos commanded it. It is even worth noting that the word '*lochos*' could later mean 'file' as in Arrian's treatise on tactics (4.5ff.), though the usual word for a file in Herodotos' time was probably '*stichos*' (cf. *LP* 11.5 & 8).

On balance, however, it seems more likely that Herodotos was mistaken about Amompharetos' being an *eiren* than about his being an officer, since one would have thought the latter more likely to be remembered than the former. But was he a *lochagos*, as Herodotos implies he was, and, if so, what was the nature of the *lochos* he commanded? The generally accepted view[18] is that, at this date, the Spartan army was divided into five *lochoi*, recruited from five *phylai* ('tribes'), based on the four *obai* ('villages' or 'wards') into which Sparta itself was probably divided – Pitana, Mesoa, Limnai and Konooura – with Amyklai constituting a fifth, and that Amompharetos commanded the *lochos* recruited from the *phyle* of Pitana, even if it was not strictly speaking called the *lochos* of Pitana.

Ingenious as this theory is, however, it is based on the flimsiest of evidence, most of it late. Thus one ancient commentator on a line in Aristophanes' *Lysistrata* (453), in which the Spartan women are said to be divided into four *lochoi*, pedantically remarks that 'the poet seems to have studied Lakonian matters rather carelessly, for there are not four *lochoi* in Lakedaimon, but five – Edolos, Sinis, Arimas, Ploas, and Messoages – but

Thucydides says seven, apart from the *Skiritai.*' Another commentator on the passage in Thucydides (4.8.9) in which he talks about *lochoi* at the time of the Pylos campaign, says that 'there are five *lochoi* of Lakedaimonians - Aidolios, Sinis, Sarinas, Ploas, and Mesoates.' Finally, among ancient lexicographers, Hesychios (s.v. *Edolos*) says that there was a *lochos* of Lakedaimonians so called, and under '*lochoi*' remarks, 'Aristophanes says there are four among the Lakedaimonians, but there are five, as Aristotle says,' while Photios (s.v. *lochoi*) says there were four according to Aristophanes, five according to Thucydides, and seven according to Aristotle, where he has almost certainly got Thucydides and Aristotle the wrong way round.[19]

In all this it should be noted, firstly, that another commentator on the *Lysistrata* says that Aristophanes said that there were four *lochoi* of women 'because there are also four *lochoi* among the Lakedaimonians with which the king has been furnished', which looks as though he may have been talking about *lochoi* among the *Hippeis* (see p. 211 n.28), and not in the ordinary army at all. Secondly, although the first commentator on Aristophanes and the one on Thucydides have obviously somehow got hold of the same list of five names, only one – Mesoates – corresponds with the name of an *oba* – even here there is the variant 'Messoages' – and, as we have seen, Thucydides expressly denied that there was a *lochos* of Pitana, though it is possible that he was just quarrelling with the name, and that one of the commentators' five names was that of the *lochos* of Pitana. But, in any case, the evidence of commentators and lexicographers is not very reliable, since we really do not know where they got their information from or what they were talking about – the only worthwhile source for the five *lochoi* they mention is Aristotle, who may have said something about them in the lost *Constitution of the Lakedaimonians*, though exactly what must remain unclear.

The evidence that Spartans were at some time divided into *phylai* possibly connected with the ancient *obai* is more solid, but probably irrelevant: it is all of comparatively late date – inscriptions of Hellenistic and Roman times – and although three of the four *phylai* commonly mentioned are called *Limnaeis*, *Konooureis* and *Pitanatai*, the fourth is usually called *Neopolitai*. There is one reference to a phyle of *Mesoatai*, for which *Neopolitai* may be the common name, but there is no apparent reference to a *phyle* corresponding to Amyklai. In any case, the *phylai* in question seem to have consisted exclusively of the young Spartans called '*sphaireis*' ('ballplayers'), who engaged in what sounds like the Spartan equivalent of the Eton wall-game.[20] There is no evidence that adult Spartans ever belonged to such *phylai*, and no evidence that any Spartans belonged to them in Herodotos' time. The only *phylai* known to have existed in early Sparta are the three Dorian *phylai* of *Hylleis*, *Dymanes* and *Pamphyloi* (cf. Tyrtaios, fr.19.8 West), and there is some reason to believe that they still existed in Sparta in Herodotos' time: he himself mentions the Sikyonian equivalents in his account of the tyrant Kleisthenes (5.68.2), and Pindar implies that they still existed in Sparta early in the fifth century in his account of the founding of Etna by Hiero of Syracuse (*Pythian* 1.120ff.).

It is probably true that Sparta was, in early times, composed of four villages or wards called '*obai*': Herodotos, as we have seen, says that his informant, Archias, came from what he calls the 'deme' (δῆμος) of Pitana, probably thinking of the demes of Attica, and Thucydides says that Sparta was a 'settlement in villages (κατὰ κώμας) after the ancient fashion of Greece' (1.10.2) – that the 'demes' or '*komai*' of Sparta were called '*obai*' is suggested by Hesychios' glosses on the cognate words '*oai*' and '*oge*' (ὤαι/ὠνή), both of which he explains as '*komai/kome*'; the earliest extant use of the actual word '*oba*' – unless we count the enigmatic phrase '*obas obaxanta*' in the *rhetra* (see below, pp. 93–4) – appears to be its occurrence in an inscription which is no earlier than the second century (*IG* V i 26.11). The names of the original *obai* were probably Pitana, Mesoa, Limnai and Konooura,[21] but the only evidence that Amyklai was also an *oba* occurs in the inscription referred to above, and it seems to be an *oba* of a different kind.[22] Men from Amyklai certainly served in the Spartan army in the fourth century (XH 4.5.11–12), but we do not know what their constitutional position was even then, still less what it was earlier: they still seem to have retained a somewhat separate identity, for example in the worship of Hyakinthos, and do not appear to have been admitted to the ceremonies connected with Artemis Orthia which formed a central part in the rituals associated with the youth of the *obai* of Sparta (cf. Pausanias 3.16.9). There is, then, no good evidence that there were more than four *obai* in Herodotos' time,[23] and the existence of various groups of five officials, for example, the five ephors,[24] no more proves a five-fold division of Sparta, than the nine archons or the *Eleven* prove a nine-fold or eleven-fold division for Athens.

There is, thus, little reason to believe that in 479 the Spartans were divided into five *phylai* based on five *obai*, and even less reason to suppose that their army was then divided into five *lochoi*. It would be very remarkable if a tradition of such a division somehow managed to survive through the period when the army was divided into six *morai* and twelve *lochoi*, to be incorporated into remarks by commentators and lexicographers hundreds of years later, and the only worthwhile evidence would be Aristotle's, if we could be sure that Hesychios quoted him correctly. Even if Aristotle did say somewhere in a lost work that there were five *lochoi*, we have no means of telling whether he was referring to the whole army or to only part of it. One ingenious suggestion is that the commentators and lexicographers somehow got hold of and misunderstood a source which actually meant that each *enomotia*, when at full strength, contained five '*lochoi*' in the sense of files, the name '*Messoages*' being the correct one and referring to the middle file, the other four being mnemonics.[25] Another possibility is that the five *lochoi* had something to do with one or other of the rituals connected with the youth of Sparta – the odd and generally meaningless names are reminiscent of some of the terms applied to the various age-groups.[26]

If these arguments are accepted, there remains nothing in what Herodotos says about the Spartan army which precludes the possibility that it was already organized in *morai, lochoi, pentekostyes* and *enomotiai* in the early fifth century, or even before that. It is true that he does not mention *morai* or *pentekostyes*, but there are only two passages in which he gives any details – the Amompharetos episode (9.53.2, 57.1) and the passage about Lykourgos (1.65.5) – and the one does in fact mention a *lochos* as we have seen, and the other mentions *enomotiai*. The nature of the *lochos* of Pitana must remain problematical, of course, in view of Thucydides' denial that such a thing existed – though even Thucydides could have been wrong – but even if there was no Pitanate *lochos* at this date,[27] this would not necessarily mean that Amompharetos did not command a unit called a *lochos*. On the other hand, it is possible that he was even more senior, for, as we have seen, his behaviour is contrasted with that of the 'other *taxiarchoi*' (Herodotos 9.53.2), and the Spartan rank corresponding most closely to that of an Athenian taxiarch in the fourth century – so far as we know no Spartan officer was actually called a taxiarch – was that of polemarch. The Amompharetos story would make more sense if he was really one of six polemarchs present at the battle. But even if Amompharetos was not a polemarch, Herodotos' description of Euainetos, the Spartan commander at Tempe in 480, as 'chosen from the polemarchs' (7.173.2), is evidence that there were such officers, in the plural, at the time. As was said above, Herodotos ascribes the creation of the *enomotiai* to Lykourgos (1.65.5), and even if this is virtually meaningless as evidence for the date of their creation, it at least shows that *enomotiai*, too, existed in Herodotos' time, and presumably that they were already of some antiquity.

Herodotos also clearly knew of a *corps d'élite* of 300 *Hippeis* (1.67.5, 8.124.3), and although elsewhere (6.56) he speaks of 'a hundred picked men' who guarded the king on campaign, this need not necessarily be a contradiction, since even if the *Hippeis* fought 'about the king' in battle (cf. Thucydides 5.72.4), and so in a sense constituted a 'Royal Guard', that is not necessarily the same thing as the royal bodyguard (see above p. 14-15). Alternatively, 100 of the *Hippeis* may have taken it in turn to guard the king 'on campaign', whereas the whole corps naturally did this duty in actual battle – the treatise on the *Constitution of the Lakedaimonians* attributed to Xenophon actually does suggest that the *Hippeis* were grouped in hundreds (cf. *LP* 4.3). However, the number of soldiers who fought with Leonidas at Thermopylai should not be used as evidence for the number of the *Hippeis*, for these men were almost certainly not the *Hippeis* (see below p. 70). Herodotos also says (1.67.5) that the five 'oldest' men who left the *Hippeis* each year, were known as '*agathoergoi*' ('good-workers'), and this suggests that the corps was recruited year by year on some kind of age-class basis, though it is not possible to be certain how this was done.[28]

In the same passage in which he mentions *enomotiai* (1.65.5), Herodotos also mentions '*triekades*' and '*syssitia*' (τριηκάδες, συσσίτια), all three having something to do with war (cf. '... ἐς πόλεμον ἔχοντα'). Of the three terms, '*triekades*' (the Ionic form of the more usual '*triakades*') is the most obscure: it can mean 'thirties' (as in Aeschylus' *Persai* 339) or 'thirtieths' – its commonest meaning is the thirtieth day of the month – and if it meant the latter, it could be another word for *enomotiai*, there being thirty-two of these to the *mora*, on the analogy of *pentekostyes* (see pp. 8–9); alternatively, if the meaning is 'thirties', it could still be another word for *enomotiai*, on the assumption that there were, at some time, thirty men in each *enomotia*, not forty, or because the usual campaign-strength of an *enomotia* was about thirty men. However, there is some reason to believe that Spartans were already liable for military service for forty years, in the early fifth century, and so that there were already forty age-classes and forty men in a full-strength *enomotia*. In any case, the *triakades* may, of course, have had nothing to do with *enomotiai*. It is of some interest, however, that they imply some kind of triple division in the army, and not a quintuple one.[29]

On *syssitia* we are on firmer ground in that at least we know that they were the 'messes' to which all Spartiates had to belong (see above, p. 17), but what connection, precisely, they had with war, as Herodotos says they did, is uncertain. It is possible that the *enomotiai* were based upon them in the early fifth century, when there may have been enough Spartiates still to fill all the ranks of the army (see below), but if there were already forty men in each *enomotia*, a pair of fifteen – strong *syssitia* (cf. Plutarch *Lykourgos* 12.2) would not have been enough for each *enomotia*, and even if the *enomotiai* were only thirty strong, presumably men of sixty and above continued to belong to *syssitia*, and the younger members would have been competing for places in the *Hippeis*. In any case, it is not certain that there were only fifteen men in each *syssition*, in the light of Plutarch's remarks about the reforms of Agis IV (*Agis* 8.1–2),[30] and it may be that Herodotos' implication that *syssitia*, like *enomotiai* and *triakades*, had something to do with war, means no more than that they had military overtones, as did almost everything in Sparta, not that they literally had something to do with the organization of the army.

None of the figures Herodotos gives for various Spartan forces precludes an organization into *morai* at this date, provided that we can assume that the multiples of 1,000 he gives are round numbers. Thus the 5,000 *Spartiatai* at Plataea could have been six *morai* with twenty-five age-classes called up, *plus* three hundred *Hippeis* ($6 \times 32 \times 25 + 300 = 5,100$), the 2,000 Lakedaimonians who marched to Marathon (Herodotos 6.120) two and a half *morai* with twenty-five age-classes called up ($2\frac{1}{2} \times 32 \times 25 = 2,000$), and so on. Nor is this mere arbitrary guesswork, for a comparison of the implication of Demaratos' statement that there were 8,000 men in Sparta (Herodotos 7.234.2), with the 5,000 *Spartiatai* at Plataea, suggests that five-eighths were called up for that campaign, i.e. twenty-five age-classes out of forty. Even more interesting are the three references in Herodotos to forces of three hundred men (at the Battle of the Champions – 1.82.3, at Thermopylai – 7.202 & 205.2, and in Stenyklaros during the Messenian revolt – 9.64.2), for the first two may give a clue to how and why such a force came into being: if there is any truth in the story of the Battle of the Champions, the Spartans would clearly have needed some mechanism for choosing their champions, assuming that all Spartans would automatically have volunteered for such a task, and a very simple method would have been to choose by lot one *enomotia* 'from all the *lochoi*' as was done for the Sphakteria garrison in 425 (Thucydides 4.8.9): one *enomotia* of twenty-five men from each of twelve *lochoi*, of course, would have produced a force of 300 men.

Leonidas' force is often said to have been the *Hippeis*,[31] but this was almost certainly not the case, for the *Hippeis* were probably all young men and chosen by the *Hippagretai* (see pp. 13–14), whereas Leonidas' men were allegedly chosen by himself and all already had sons (Herodotos 7.205.2). Nevertheless, Herodotos does say of these three hundred that they were 'appointed' or 'assigned' (καθεστεῶτας), and this suggests that Leonidas did not have complete control over whom he took. Again the simplest method of choosing such a force would have been to choose one *enomotia* of twenty-five men from each of the twelve *lochoi*, and this may be all that was done before Thermopylai, for the tradition that all the three hundred already had sons smacks of the legend that Leonidas knew he was going to his death (cf. Herodotos 7.220.2–4). On the other hand, since the alleged reason why Sparta could not send her full forces was that the *Karneia* were being celebrated (Herodotos 7.206.1), it is possible that religion lay not only behind the method used for selecting the force, but also its composition. If the Spartans believed that they were forbidden to fight during the *Karneia*, and yet were convinced of the necessity of sending at least a token force, they may have thought that by drawing lots to determine who was to be sent, they were, as it were, putting the responsibility on the gods. The taboo against fighting during the *Karneia*, moreover, is likely to have applied particularly to the young warriors, and it is possible that this is what really lay behind the tradition that Leonidas only took those who already had sons: Spartan males probably did marry young, and some of them no doubt had sons, but there is some reason to believe that there were ancient taboos against this – Plutarch, for example, says that the young bridegrooms were supposed to visit their brides by stealth, returning to sleep among the other young men (*Lykourgos* 15.3–5). It is possible, then, that young Spartans were, in a sense, not supposed to be married until they were thirty,[32] and thus the *Karneia* taboo on fighting may have particularly applied to the age-groups from twenty to twenty-nine. We then only have to assume that the last five age-groups were not called up for Thermopylai, as was usual, and the composition of Leonidas' three hundred is explained: it consisted of one *enomotia* composed of men of the age-groups from thirty to fifty-four inclusive, drawn by lot from each of twelve *lochoi*. Leonidas himself may have been exempt from the taboo, finally, not so much because he was older than thirty, as because he was altogether beyond military age, having passed his sixtieth birthday:[33] one might have expected any taboos against engaging in fighting to have applied particularly to the king – it is fairly obvious that the oracle foretelling either the destruction of Sparta or the death of one of her kings (Herodotos 7.220.4) was later put about to explain away Leonidas' death – and to send a king who could be regarded as in some sense 'dead' already, might have seemed a way of placating the possible wrath of the gods, for the other king, Leotychidas, was probably a younger man.

We have no means of knowing what considerations governed the composition of Arimnestos' force of three hundred with whom he was destroyed in Stenyklaros, probably during the great Messenian revolt in the 460s (Herodotos 9.64.2), but if he, too, was on some difficult or dangerous mission, his force might also have consisted of twelve *enomotiai* of twenty-five men chosen from the twelve *lochoi*. Thus not only do bodies of three hundred men fit very easily into an army-organization into six *morai* and twelve *lochoi*, but the supposition that this is how the army was organized helps to explain how the three hundred came to be chosen on at least two of the three occasions in question. There is, moreover, one final point and that is that the theoretical total strength of the Spartan army, if it consisted already at this date of six *morai* of 1,280 men each, was 7,680, and this total, especially if we add to it the 300 *Hippeis*, comes very close to the 8,000 men Demaratos declared Sparta had at the time of Xerxes' invasion (Herodotos 7.234.2). Indeed, if we can at all trust the tradition of the Battle of the Champions, and if they were really chosen in the manner suggested, then the organization into six *morai* and twelve *lochoi*, composed ultimately of *enomotiai* recruited on an age-class basis and consisting of forty men at full strength, can be traced back at least to the middle of the sixth century.

Before leaving Herodotos, it is worth considering what else he has to tell us about the Spartan army, in his account of the final fight at Plataea, he emphasizes the value of Greek protective armour (9.62.3, 63.2) – he must mean more than that they just had stouter shields – and the lack of skill displayed by the Persians in this kind of fighting, in comparison with their opponents – where it is clear that he is thinking particularly of the Spartans (cf. the last words of 9.62.3: 'they fell upon the Spartiates and were destroyed.'). He implies, in particular, that the Persians fought as individuals or in small groups, whereas the Greeks fought in a body. Plato, in the *Laches* (191c), has Socrates declare that the Spartans, faced with the wicker shield-wall planted by the Persians (cf. Herodotos 9.61.3 & 62.2), adopted the tactics of feigning flight, only to turn upon the enemy when pursued. Herodotos says nothing of this in his account of Plataea, but does say that the Spartans used these tactics at Thermopylai (7.211.3), where again he emphasizes Spartan skill, and Persian lack of it: if what he says about the tactics is true – and there is no reason to doubt it – it says much for the disciplined expertise of Spartan hoplites, since the manoeuvre required exceptional control if it was not to develop into real flight. Discipline, too, of a different kind, is exemplified by the measured retreat of Amompharetos and his men, though isolated from the main force (9.57.1), and the stolid way in which the Spartan hoplites later endured the galling fire of the Persian archers, apparently sitting in their ranks (cf. 9.72.1). According to Herodotos, Pausanias was waiting for favourable omens, which may well be true in view of the Spartans' scrupulous attention to the demands of their religious beliefs, though he may also have been waiting for what he judged to be the right moment to order the advance. In any case, it is significant that it was the Tegeates who broke first (Herodotos 9.62.1).

The story of Thermopylai is, of course, the *locus classicus* for the discipline of Spartan soldiers, and the complete indifference with which they went about their daily chores even when they must have begun to realize the sheer magnitude of the task that confronted them (Herodotos 7.208.3). The retort of Dienekes to the native of Trachis who told him that when the Persian archers loosed their bows, they blotted out the sun with the number of their arrows – that this was good news because it meant that the battle would be in the shade and not in sunlight (Herodotos 7.226) – illustrates the slightly cynical sense of humour which was characteristic of this strange and – to many – rather unlovable people, as was Leonidas' injunction to his men to have a good lunch because they would be dining in Hades (Diodoros 11.9.4; Plutarch, *Moralia* 225d). The stories of Aristodemos and Pantites, on the other hand (*Herodotos* 7.229–232), illustrate the grimmer side of the Spartan character: both were said to be survivors of the three hundred, Aristodemos having been sent back to Alpenoi suffering from ophthalmia, Pantites because he had been sent on a mission to Thessaly. The latter hanged himself on his return (7.232), even though he could hardly have been blamed for his survival, but Aristodemos, who was perhaps the more blameworthy in that his fellow-sufferer, Eurytos, ordered his helot batman to lead him back to the fight and died in the thick of it, survived to fight another day at Plataea and to perish there, after feats of valour which made him the bravest man on the field, in Herodotos' opinion (cf. 9.71.2). But it is interesting to note that Herodotos says the Spartans declared a man called Poseidonios braver than Aristodemos, partly because he did not want to die, whereas Aristodemos did, but partly because the latter did his deeds 'raging and *leaving the line*' (λυσσῶντά τε καὶ ἐκλείποντα τὴν τάξιν: 9.71.3): in other words, Aristodemos went so far as to forget the supreme duty of the hoplite – not to leave the line and so risk exposing his neighbours, particularly the man on his left. The story also illustrates that it was normal for each Spartan soldier to be accompanied by a helot batman (cf. Herodotos 7.229.1). But perhaps the most interesting detail is the nickname applied to Aristodemos: he was called 'the trembler', Herodotos says (ὁ τρέσας: 7.231), and cowards were apparently still so-called in the time of Agesilaos (cf. Plutarch *Agesilaos* 30.2–4), though then, it appears, they were normally debarred from military service, whereas Aristodemos apparently was not. Again the story illustrates how little changed over the years in Sparta.

Herodotos' story of the Marathon campaign, even though in the end the Spartans arrived too late, tells us something at least about their marching qualities, if it is true that they marched from Sparta to Athens – a distance of about 130 miles – in three days (Herodotos 6.120), and, incidentally, gives the lie to those who believe that the Spartans really did not want to help the Athenians: to march so far and so fast and to arrive just too late would argue too nice a sense of timing even on the part of the Spartan military machine. The Sepeia campaign, finally, gives us a glimpse of the kind of reputation the Spartans were already beginning to enjoy, if it is true that the Argives sought to avoid surprise by conforming to all the orders given to the Spartans (Herodotos 6.77.3ff.). Unfortunately, Herodotos does not say how many men took part, but the 1,000 men Kleomenes took with him to the Argive Heraion (Herodotos 6.81), assuming that they were all Spartans, might have been a single *mora* made up of twenty-five age-classes, together with the *Hippeis* ($32 \times 25 + 300 = 1,100$), and it is notable that helots were also present on this campaign (Herodotos 6.80.1, 6.81). Kleomenes' strategy of perhaps feinting an invasion across the Erasinos, and then making his real attack by sea at Nauplion (Herodotos 6.76), was possibly a product of this king's eccentric genius rather than the strategic skill of Spartan commanders in general, but if it is true that 6,000 Argives perished in the battle and in the massacre that followed (Herodotos 7.148.2), this was one of the most decisive victories ever won by a hoplite army, and it was due to Kleomenes' ruse of ordering his men to attack when the herald next gave the signal for lunch (Herodotos 6.78.1). Anchimolios' abortive invasion of Attica, on the other hand, possibly in 511 (Herodotos 5.63), though it again illustrates the Spartan ability to make use of sea-power at this time, is also an early example of the vulnerability of Spartan hoplites to cavalry, in certain circumstances –

in this case, the cavalry of Hippias' Thessalian allies, for whom the plain near Phaleron had been specially cleared of trees. Unfortunately, Herodotos does not say how many men Anchimolios led, and merely describes him as 'a man of repute among the citizens' (τῶν ἀστῶν ἄνδρα δόκιμον: 5.63.2), but he may have been a polemarch.[34] Subsequently, when Kleomenes invaded Attica by land, the Thessalian cavalry presented no problem (Herodotos 5.64.2).

It is possible that by this time the number of Spartiates was already on the decline, and that the Spartans were already having to take steps to persuade Spartiates to marry and to have sons.[35] However, some at least of the evidence can be interpreted in different ways: the steps taken to ensure that King Anaxandridas had a son, for example (Herodotos 5.39–41), may indicate no more than anxiety lest one of the royal lines die out, and the choice of men who already had sons to serve with Leonidas (Herodotos 7.205.2), if it is not just part of the legend that Leonidas and his men knew that they were doomed, may in reality mean merely that they were all in the age-classes from thirty upwards (see pp. 70–1). The measures taken to persuade Spartiates to have sons, similarly, are usually attributed to Lykourgos (cf. Plutarch *Lykourgos* 15.1–3; *LP* 9.5; Aristotle *Politics* 1270b1ff), and we have no means of knowing when they were really passed – the only concrete evidence is an inscription of c.500 (*IG* V i 713), which records the death of a woman in childbirth, suggesting that by then such a woman was exempt from the rule – again attributed to Lykourgos (Plutarch *Lykourgos* 27.2) – prohibiting the inscribing of names on tombstones except in the cases of men killed in battle or women who held priestly offices.

We do not know, of course, how many Spartiates there may once have been: Aristotle reports a tradition that there had once been 10,000 (*Politics* 1270a37), and there was also a tradition that 9,000 *klaroi* were distributed either by Lykourgos or by him and King Polydoros (Plutarch *Lykourgos* 8.3), but the former looks like a guess, and the latter may be no more than a product of third century propaganda.[36] However, if these figures are anything like the truth – and it is hard to believe that there were ever more than 10,000 Spartiates at most – there had possibly not been much of a decline in their number by 480, for Herodotos believed that Sparta was then 'a *polis* of about 8,000 men' (7.234.2), and implies that he was thinking of men of military age – in other words, if he was right, there would in fact have been more than 8,000 Spartiates, including minors and men beyond their sixtieth birthdays. Certainly, if Herodotos was right, an army of six *morai* of

1,280 men each, plus 300 *Hippeis*, could still all have been found from the Spartiates, and this is borne out by his repeated assertions (cf. 9.10.1, 28.2, etc.) that 5,000 Spartiates fought at Plataea, for this figure could well represent six *morai* of 800 men each (i.e. with twenty-five of the forty age-classes called up), together with 300 *Hippeis* (see pp. 68–9).

However, whether or not there had been a decline in the number of Spartiates before 480, there certainly was a considerable one after that date, for by 425 only about forty-one per cent of the prisoners captured on Sphakteria were Spartiates (120 out of 292: Thucydides 4.38.5), though the implication of the statement (Thucydides 4.8.9) that the relays of hoplites were drawn by lot 'from all the *lochoi*,' is that they all came from the regular Spartan army - the extreme anxiety of the Spartans to recover the prisoners (cf. Thucydides 4.14.2, 4.15; 5.15.1) is also suggestive. By the time of Leuktra the situation seems to have been still worse, for, assuming that the four *morai* which fought there (cf. XH 6.4.17) contained in all 4,480 men, and that 300 of the 700 Spartiates (cf. XH 6.4.15) were brigaded separately in the *Hippeis*, the proportion of Spartiates in the actual *morai* will have been less than nine-per cent.

If, then, there was no appreciable decline in the number of Spartiates before the Persian Wars, but a steep decline after them, factors which should have been relatively constant, like the possible effects of sexual practices or the division of estates between several sons and daughters – thus reducing them to a size too small to provide the dues required for membership of a *syssition* (cf. Aristotle *Politics* 1270b4–6) – cannot be the explanation. We can also, probably, discount actual losses sustained by the Spartiates, for example in the earthquake of c.465 (cf. Thucydides 1.101.2–3; Diodoros 11.63.5ff.; Plutarch *Kimon* 16.6f.), or the constant warfare from the 460s onwards – such losses should have been replaced fairly rapidly. The notorious '*rhetra* of Epitadeus', allowing the disposal of hitherto inalienable property by gift or bequest (Plutarch *Agis* 5.3), is also hardly an explanation, even if it is historical:[37] it is probably true that many Spartiates lost their land for one reason or another, but the reason can hardly be that they willingly gave it up, knowing that the consequence would be that they would be unable to hand over the dues in kind required for membership of their *syssitia*, and thus would cease to be Spartiates.

The ancient sources associate Sparta's downfall with greed for material possessions, particularly after the victory over Athens in the Peloponnesian War (cf. *LP* 14.3; Plutarch *Lykourgos*, 30.1, *Agis* 5.1; Polybios 6.49.10), and it has been suggested that the ultimate cause of the decline in the number of Spartiates was the greed of Sparta's wealthier landowners for ever more land[38]. We have Aristotle's word for it (*Politics* 1270a18, 1307a36) that land in Lakonia did come to be concentrated in the hands of a few rich Spartans – almost two-fifths of it in the hands of women (*Politics* 1270a23–4). But although the rich could, no doubt, have done something about the situation, as Agis IV and Kleomenes III tried to do in the third century, and in that sense their greed was responsible for prolonging and accentuating the problem, presumably they could not have forced even the humblest Spartiate from his land against his will, and it does not appear that someone who failed to pay his mess-bill was thereby deprived of his land, even though he ceased to be a Spartiate (cf. Aristotle *Politics* 1270a16–18, 1270b5–6). In the end, presumably, those who got into difficulties were forced to resort to what was regarded as the disgraceful practice of *selling* their land to the rich (cf. *Politics* 1270a 19–20), and what we need to know is what brought them to this extreme.

A possible explanation is that the constant warfare from the 460s onwards, and particularly from 431, so disrupted the normal way of life on the *klaroi* that the produce needed for the *syssitia* could no longer be grown in sufficient quantities, in many cases. There was, firstly, a certain amount of actual fighting and devastation in both Lakonia and Messenia, for example during the helot revolt in the 460s and as a result of Athenian raids in the 450s (cf., e.g., Thucydides 1.108.5) and in 431 (Thucydides 2.25.1–2) – from 425 to 422, and again from 418 to 409, the existence of permanent Athenian bases on or near the coasts must have had a particularly damaging effect (cf. Thucydides 4.41.2, 55–56.1, 80.1; 5.56.1–3; 6.105.2, 7.18.3). Presumably this did not so much affect inland areas, such as the upper Eurotas valley where the Spartan aristocracy probably had their estates,[39] but it may seriously have affected some of the areas where *klaroi* had been distributed to humbler Spartans in the eighth and seventh centuries – the helot revolt, after all, centred on Mt Ithome below which lay the' 'rich fields' for which the Spartans had striven for nineteen long years in the eighth century (Tyrtaios fr. 5 West). Devastation apart, however, there must have been a constant draining away of the helots who actually worked the land, due either to rebellion and desertion, or to the requirements of military service, whether as soldier-servants or later as hoplites. Thus there would have been a considerable loss of helots when the rebels who had held out on Mt Ithome were allowed to go free (Thucydides 1.103.1), and presumably helots served in the Tanagra campaign (Thucydides 1.107.2–108.2), the so-called 'holy war' (Thucydides 1.112.2), and in the invasion of Attica in 446 (Thucydides 1.114.2), the latter, in particular, probably involving a full levy. It may be that in the crisis of the helot revolt, some Spartans whose *klaroi* were in rebel hands, or whose helots had deserted, were nevertheless retained in the army, even though they were technically *hypomeiones*, and some may never have been able to regain their Spartiate status.

After 446 there followed some fourteen years of peace during which the wounds inflicted on Spartan agriculture should have begun to heal, but then, in 431, the great Peloponnesian War broke out. Helots must have been immediately involved, in considerable numbers, in the annual invasions of Attica in that year, in 430, 428, 427 and 425, and in the siege of Plataea from 429 to 427: even in 426, though the Spartans turned back at the Isthmus because of earthquakes (Thucydides 3.89.1), helots had presumably already been called away from the fields to serve their Spartan masters on campaign. From 425 the situation would have grown far worse, for although the invasions of Attica ceased, Spartan troops were on constant alert in Messenia and Lakonia, and were presumably accompanied by helots, and now the latter had a real opportunity to desert to the Athenian base at Pylos (cf. Thucydides 4.41.2–3, 80; 5.14.3). There was also a massacre of helots in 424 – 2,000 of them are alleged to have disappeared (Thucydides 4.80.3–4) – and in addition they began to be used as hoplites, beginning with the 700 who went with Brasidas to Thrace (Thucydides 4.80.5), and the first 1000 *neodamodeis*, who may have been created this year (cf. Thucydides 5.34.1 & 49.1).

The Peace of Nikias cannot have brought much relief, for although Athenian raids stopped for a few years, and the removal of the Messenians from Pylos suggests that the desertion of helots ceased, helots must have been heavily involved in the campaign in Parrhasia in 421, since the Spartans were in full force (Thucydides 5.33.1), and again in the two abortive mobilizations of 419 (Thucydides 5.54.1–2, 55.3). During the winter of 419/8 the Athenians were persuaded to send the Messenians back to Pylos to recommence raiding (Thucydides 5.56.1–3, cf. 6.105.2 & 7.18.3), and presumably the helots were again encouraged to desert. In his accounts of the two full mobilizations of the Spartan army in 418, Thucydides singles out the helots for mention (5.57.1 & 64.2), and there were further mobilizations at the end of that year and in each of the following four years (Thucydides 5.76.1, 82.3, 83.1, 116.1; 6.7.1, 95.1, 105.1). In 413 the

Spartans invaded Attica in full force again and this time established a permanent base at Dekeleia (Thucydides 7.19.1), operations which must have involved helots in considerable numbers, and some helots were also sent to Sicily as hoplites, alongside *neodamodeis* (Thucydides 7.19.3, cf. 58.3). The Athenians responded by raiding southern Lakonia and establishing a permanent base there, specifically to provide a place of refuge for helots (Thucydides 7.26.2).

From 413 onwards there were presumably many helots permanently stationed at Dekeleia with the Spartan garrison (cf. Thucydides 7.27.4), and although after the defeat of the Sicilian expedition the tide finally began to turn in Sparta's favour, this did not mean that the disruption of Spartan agriculture ceased. It was not until 409, for example, that Pylos was finally evacuated, and even this meant a permanent loss to Sparta of the helots who had taken refuge there – Xenophon says that they came from as far away as Malea (XH 1.2.18). Helots were also still used as hoplites (cf., e.g., Thucydides 8.5.1), and presumably as rowers, at least for the ships Sparta herself manned. There were never very many of these – the largest number mentioned are the thirty Alkibiades heard were being commissioned at Gytheion in 407 (XH 1.4.11), and the largest number at sea appear to have been the ten which fought at Arginusae and of which nine were lost (XH 1.6.34) – but even ten triremes would have required nearly 2,000 rowers.

The twenty-seven years of the Peloponnesian War would thus have seen a serious disruption of the normal way of life on many a *klaros*, and presumably it would have been the smaller estates, with the fewest numbers of helots, which were the hardest hit – the richer landowners would, as usual, have been cushioned against the worst effects of both Athenian raiding and the desertion or call-up of helots. Nor did the victory over Athens bring immediate relief, for there must have been hundreds if not thousands of helots scattered about the Aegean with Spartan garrisons – some even became harmosts according to a passage in Xenophon (XH 3.5.12 – see p. 28 above) – and the Spartan army was almost immediately mobilized again to deal with the situation in Athens in 403 (XH 2.4.29ff.); helots were also elevated to the status of *neodamodeis* in ever increasing numbers – 1,000 were sent to Asia Minor with Thibron, for example (XH 3.1.4), and 2,000 with Agesilaos (XH 3.4.2).

It was, thus, probably from the 460s onwards, and particularly from 431, that the number of Spartiates began to seriously decline. Poorer Spartiates may have seen their farms wrecked and their helots deserting or being called up, and may thus have found it impossible to pay their dues to their *syssitia*.

Many probably found it impossible to recover, and much of their land may thus have eventually passed, in one way or another, into the hands of the rich – the influx of wealth into Sparta after the victory over Athens would have tended to widen the gulf between rich and poor, and it is obviously against this background that we must set the conspiracy of Kinadon (XH 3.3.4–11), early in the fourth century.

But what effect would all this have had upon the Spartan army? Clearly it would have become less homogeneous as it ceased to be an army of 'peers' and more and more *hypomeiones* were admitted to its ranks, and there may have been a certain amount of ill-feeling between the Spartiates and non-Spartiates, exemplified by Kinadon's attitude. But it would be easy to exaggerate the effects: Kinadon and his associates, assuming that he was a *hypomeion*, are the only *hypomeiones* known to have actually plotted to do something about the situation,[40] and his conspiracy collapsed without a fight, suggesting that the number of men in the army who actively supported him, was very small. As was suggested above (pp. 25–6), the process by which *hypomeiones* came to be admitted into the army, would have been gradual, and many of the non-Spartiates in its ranks may well have felt themselves to be the next best thing to Spartiates. Nor is there really any evidence that the dilution of the Spartiate-nature of the army by the admission of non-Spartiates had any appreciable effect on either its morale or its efficiency. The surrender on Sphakteria, for example, may have astonished the Greeks, as Thucydides says (4.40.1), because they believed that 'Spartans would not surrender their arms through hunger or any other form of compulsion,' but this was partly, at least, the product of the Thermopylai-myth, and there is no hint in Thucydides' narrative that the surrender was due to the presence among the survivors of more non-Spartiates than Spartiates – that the enemy missiles had *not* picked out the 'best men' is the point of the story Thucydides tells about the response made by one of the survivors to the taunt flung at the prisoners (4.40.2). As to the efficiency of the Spartan hoplites, they were heavily outnumbered – probably by over twenty-five to one – and, as Thucydides says (4.34.2), 'unaccustomed to this kind of fighting' – he implies (4.33) that if they had been able to come to grips with the Athenian hoplites, the story might have been very different.

It is true that there are some signs of cracks in the army's morale after the Sphakteria episode. Thucydides says (4.55.2) that in the following year, after the Athenian seizure of Kythera, 'they became, if ever, most irresolute in their conduct of the war' (ἔς τε τὰ πολεμικα, εἴπερ ποτέ, μάλιστα δὴ ὀκνηρότεροι ἐνενοντο), and even (4.55.4) that they were 'less bold in battle' (ἀτολμότεροι ... ἐς τὰς μάχας). Garrisons in southern Lakonia remained on the defensive, thinking that they were outnumbered – something which had not disturbed Spartans before – and when one ventured to confront Athenian raiders, it retreated as soon as it came into contact with Athenian hoplites (4.56.1). In the Thyrea, soon afterwards, a Spartan garrison again took up a defensive position, when the Athenians attacked, and made no move, 'since they did not consider themselves a match for the enemy in battle' (ὡς οὐκ ἐνόμιζον ἀξιόμαχοι εἶναι: 4.57.2).

However, it is not certain that all the forces concerned were drawn from the regular Spartan army, and there is no evidence, if they were, that their lack of spirit was due to the presence of *hypomeiones* among them, unless one regards the fact that Tantalos, son of Patrokles, the 'Lakedaimonian' commander, was wounded and captured in the Thyrea (Thucydides 5.57.3), as proof that Spartiates were more resolute than other Spartan troops. Thucydides does, it is true, say that at about this time the Spartans feared 'some kind of revolution in the established state of affairs' (νεώτερον τι ... τῶν περὶ τὴν κατάστασιν: 4.55.1), but what he says later (cf. 4.80.2 & 5.14.3) shows that he was thinking primarily of the helots, not *hypomeiones*, and when elsewhere (5.34.2) he talks of the possibility of revolution from within the Spartan community, involving those who had surrendered on Sphakteria, it is clear that he is talking of Spartiates of the highest rank, who feared that their influence had been irretrievably damaged.

An interesting side-light on the growing 'professionalism' of the Spartan army in these years, which might have had something to do with its ceasing to be exclusively an army of 'peers', is thrown by Thucydides' remarks about the agreement concluded with Argos in 420. This included, at the insistence of the Argives, a clause that it should be open to either party to challenge the other to settle the issue of the Kynourian land by battle, 'as once before, when both claimed to have won' (5.41.2), and Thucydides says (5.41.3) that this seemed 'silly' (μωρία) to the Spartans, which might imply that they no longer took war in quite the same spirit as they had done at the time of the 'Battle of the Champions' in the middle of the sixth century (cf. Herodotos 1.82). But by the time of Mantineia, in 418, the Spartans seem to have completely recovered their morale, judging from Thucydides' description of their advance to battle (5.69.2), and the victory also restored the reputation of Spartan soldiers among the Greeks (5.75.3).

There clearly were changes in the composition of the Spartan army in the fifth century, from the apparently all–Spartiate army of 479 to the army of Spartiates and non-Spartiates of 425. But is very difficult to see any indication that the changes had any deleterious effect: Spartan soldiers seem to have been just as tough, disciplined, efficient and brave at the end of the century as they had been at its beginning, judging from what Xenophon says about them. Xenophon was a biased witness in some ways, but he was a soldier, and he had no qualms about criticizing the performance of Spartan cavalry, for example (cf. XH 4.5.16 and 6.4.10–11), or individual Spartan commanders (cf., e.g., XH 6.5.26 or 7.1.17). But even the disaster which befell the *mora* on the road to Lechaion, he believed (cf. XH 6.5.12), was due to an excess of confidence, rather than the reverse, and elsewhere he has nothing but praise for the conduct of Spartan soldiers (cf., e.g., XH 5.2.7). It may be the case that the admission of *hypomeiones* to the army's ranks had weakened its cohesion and morale, but there is no evidence that it was this that caused its defeats, when they occurred. If the Spartan army began to degenerate after the Persian Wars, it took a long time for its degeneration to become apparent, and it does not look as though its opponents from Sphakteria to the 'Tearless Battle' really believed that they were faced by an army in decline.

Chapter 3

Origins

The origins of the Spartan military system are, in a sense, coeval with the origins of Sparta itself, and it may be thought that there is little point in pursuing the study back to a period where evidence is so slight and controversy so fierce. Nevertheless, an attempt will be made, partly because some features of the later system look so obviously primitive, and partly because it was so bound up with the very nature of the Spartan state that any light thrown on military institutions may help to illuminate other dark corners in early Spartan history. The lack of evidence means that many of the hypotheses advanced in this chapter are bound to be very speculative, but the extreme scepticism advocated by some modern scholars[1] does not seem necessary, and at least for the seventh century we can derive some information from the surviving fragments of the poetry of the contemporary Spartan poet, Tyrtaios.

Judging from what little archaeological evidence there is, it would appear that the ancestors of the historical Spartans, whatever their ultimate origin,[2] were living in Lakonia by at latest about the middle of the tenth century,[3] and this evidence may thus be said to 'confirm' the ancient traditions about the origins of historical Sparta, up to a point. By the fifth century tradition had projected back the 'Dorian invasion', which reputedly brought the historical Spartans to Sparta, some seven centuries,[4] but in fact, if one takes the genealogies of the Spartan kings and allows three generations to the century, as Herodotos did (cf. 2.142.2), the reputed twin ancestors of the two royal houses will have been on the throne towards the beginning of the tenth century, at a date not very far removed from the one archaeology suggests.[5]

The Spartans will have had some kind of an army from the beginning, and it is possible that some elements of their later way of life, like the *agoge,* the age-classes, the *syssitia,* and even, possibly, the basically triple organization of the army, go back to the very earliest times. This is suggested by the fact that some of their institutions were similar to those of the Dorian Cretans,[6] for although this was sometimes explained – e.g. by Herodotos (1.65.4) and Aristotle (*Politics* 1271b24ff.) – as due to Spartan borrowing from Crete, a more plausible explanation might be that the common features derived from the common ancestors of both the Cretans and the Spartans, for both spoke the Doric dialect of Greek. The triple organization, similarly – 300 *Hippeis*, *triakades*, possibly the six *morai* (see below, pp. 88–9) – may have derived from the three *phylai* of *Hylleis*, *Dymanes* and *Pamphyloi*, to one or other of which all Spartans belonged (cf. Tyrtaios frag. 19 West, line 8), and these *phylai* also existed in other Dorian states of the Peloponnese (e.g. Argos – *IG* IV 598, Epidauros – *IC* IV² 1.71.19, and Sikyon – Herodotos 5.68.2). The Karneian month, too, in which took place the great festival of the Spartan year, with considerable military overtones (cf. Demetrios of Skepsis ap. Athenaios 4.141e-f), was sacred to other Dorian communities (cf., e.g., Thucydides 5.54.2–4).

Almost nothing is known, however, about Spartan military activities before, perhaps, the eighth century, for we can hardly believe the stories about fighting in Kynouria and against Argos during the reigns of the early kings Echestratos and his son, Labotas, grandson and great-grandson, respectively, of the eldest twin (Pausanias 3.2.2–3). The first authentic event in Spartan military history may be the conquest of the district known as Aigys, at the northwestern end of Taygetos, south of the modern village of Leondari,[7] in the reign of Archelaos, seventh king of the Agiad line (Pausanias 3.2.5), and if even this seems improbably far-ranging for the early eighth century – Aigys was some thirty kilometres from Sparta – we can surely believe in the defeat of Amyklai, Pharis and Geronthrai in the reign of Archelaos' son, Teleklos (Pausanias 3.2.6), for Amyklai lay only some seven or eight kilometres south of Sparta itself, and even Geronthrai (now Geraki) was less than thirty kilometres to the southeast.

According to tradition, then, Spartan expansion really began in the eighth century, possibly no earlier than its second quarter, and this tradition is again broadly confirmed by archaeology.[8] Yet, by the end of the century, Sparta appears to have conquered not only the whole of Lakonia, but at least the eastern part of Messenia, and is even said to have invaded the Argolid (Pausanias 3.7.4). Teleklos himself is supposed to have been killed by Messenians at the temple of Artemis at the Limnai, which is probably to be located at Volimnos, on the ancient border between Lakonia and Messenia[9] (Pausanias 3.2.6, 4.1.1–3), and his son, Alkamenes, was credited with the conquest of Helos, probably including the whole of the coastal plain bordering the Gulf of Lakonia (Pausanias 3.2.7) – that Sparta at least had access to the sea by the end of the century is indicated by the foundation of Taras (Taranto), traditionally in 706. At the same time,[10] the king of the other line, Theopompos, was completing the conquest of the lower part of the valley of the Pamisos in Messenia, the part dominated by Mt Ithome (cf. Tyrtaios fr. 5 West). Here, then, is one clear sign of a growth in Spartan militarism.

It may also be of some significance for the history of the Spartan army that the double monarchy possibly came into existence at the beginning of this period of expansion. The Spartans themselves affected to believe that it derived from the twin sons of the hero Aristodemos, under whom they claimed – agreeing with no poet, as Herodotos says (6.52.1) – their ancestors had come to Sparta. But, inherent probability apart, there are a number of things wrong with the story of the twins: in the first place it is odd that the two royal houses were not called after the supposed twins themselves, Eurysthenes and Prokles, but after the supposed sons of the twins, Agis and Euryphon – hence, Agi(a)dai and Eurypontidai. Secondly, the Spartans themselves evidently believed that it had been possible to tell which of the twins was the elder (cf. Herodotos 6.52.3ff), and in that case one would have expected there to have been only one royal house, descended from the elder twin, though one might, perhaps, save the credit of the story by supposing that superstition enjoined that both twins should rule. More significant is the evidence that the tombs of the two royal families were in different places (cf. Pausanias 3.12.8 & 14.2), which strongly suggests that they were not originally related to each other, but were descended from the chieftains of different communities.

There are also some very suspicious names amongst the early kings of the junior house, the Eurypontidai, and it looks as though at some point extra names were invented to bring their genealogy into line with that of the Agiadai. Thus, in Herodotos' list of the ancestors of King Leotychidas II (8.131.2), it is difficult to believe in King 'Prytanis' (i.e. 'President') and – in Sparta of all places, where '*eunomia*' ('constitutional well-being') was almost the supreme ideal (Tyrtaios wrote a poem with that title) – in a King 'Eunomos'. There was also an alternative version of the Eurypontid genealogy, used by Plutarch (*Lykourgos* 1.4) and Pausanias (3.7.1ff.), which contained a probably spurious king called 'Soös' ('Saviour'), unknown to Herodotos. It is significant, too, that even less was known about these early

The Royal Houses of Sparta

Although the genealogy of the Agiadai seems to have been fixed (cf. Herodotos 7.204 and Pausanias 3.2.1–6.9), there were different versions of the Eurypontidai, down to Agesikles (cf. Herodotos 8.131, Plutarch *Lykourgos* 1.4, Pausanias 3.7.1–7). I reproduce here the version of Herodotos, which is partially confirmed by the references to an older Leotychidas in *Pap. Ox.*2390, Plutarch *Lykourgos* 13.5 and *Moralia* 224c-d. It goes without saying that the early kings, their relationship and their dates, must be treated with caution.

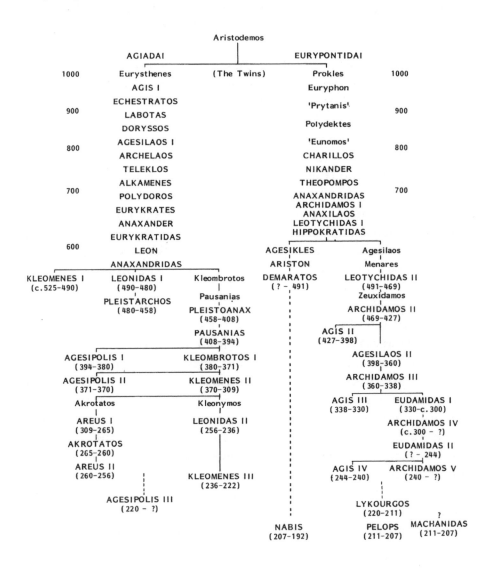

Eurypontid kings than about their Agiad counterparts: King 'Soös' was credited with the subjugation of the helots and with wide conquests in Arcadia (Plutarch *Lykourgos* 2.1), and the hatred between the Spartans and the Argives is said to have begun in the reign of King 'Prytanis' (Pausanias 3.7.2), but that is all. The first Eurypontid king to be associated with an Agiad in tradition is Charillos or Charilaos (Aristotle *Politics* 1271b25; Pausanias 3.2.5), who is said to have helped the Agiad king Archelaos in the conquest of Aigys. This suggests that he may have been the first genuine king of the Eurypontid line,[11] and since his grandson, Theopompos, was credited with at least the final victory in the First Messenian War c. 715 (Tyrtaios frag. 5 West), Charillos was presumably on the throne early in the eighth century.

If the double monarchy really did only come into existence early in the eighth century, this might well have some bearing on the beginnings of Spartan expansion. There was evidently a tradition that there had originally been hostility between the *obai* of historical Sparta, Pitana and Mesoa pairing off against Limnai and Konooura (Pausanias 3.16.9, cf. Polyainos 1.10 and Herodotus 6.52.8). We know, too, that the royal tombs of the Agiadai were in Pitana (Pausanias 3.14.2), and it is a plausible guess that the tombs of the Eurypontidai – 'at the end of Aphetais ('Going-away') street and very close to the walls' (Pausanias 3.12.8) – were in Limnai.[12] It seems possible, then, that the Agiadai were descended from the original chieftains of Pitana-Mesoa, and that they were the original 'kings' of Sparta in the sense that the acropolis lay in their territory, with its sanctuary of Athene Poliachos ('Protectress of the City'), and that, perhaps, their *obai* had been the more powerful from the first, whereas the Eurypontidai represented the original chieftains of Limnai-Konooura. It goes without saying that if these originally hostile *obai* finally patched up their differences in the early eighth century, this would, literally, have doubled 'Sparta's' strength, and would go a long way towards explaining why the expansion of Sparta's power seems to begin at about the same time.

It may also have been then that the *agoge* became so essential in the lives of the young Spartans. According to Pausanias (3.16.9–10), the fights between the rival gangs of Pitana-Mesoa and Konooura-Limnai were ritualized into the notorious 'whipping ordeal' which later formed the most famous feature of the rites associated with the shrine of Artemis Orthia, and the shrine lay in Limnai: this suggests that the *agoge* itself may originally have been particularly associated with the people of Limnai. Possibly the hostility between the warring *obai* came to a head in the claims of the men of Pitana and Mesoa to participate in the rites of Artemis Orthia, and the peace between the *obai* was appropriately symbolized by admitting the Pitanates and Mesoates to the ritual, but retaining the force once used to keep them from the altar in a new, symbolical form.[13] At the same time, the ritual training of the boys may have been reorganized to take in the boys from Pitana and Mesoa, and thus the *agoge* may have been reborn and taken on a fresh meaning.

There is, thus, a cluster of evidence to suggest that something very important was going on in Sparta during the first two or three decades of the eighth century, and here, surely, is the place for the law-giver Lykourgos, if he is a historical figure[14] – not so early that we could not hope to know anything about him, but not so late that it would be surprising that we did not know more. Despite the testimony of Herodotos (1.65.4), which made him the uncle and guardian of King Labotas, third king of the Agiadai, there was a strong tradition which made him uncle and guardian of Charillos, possibly the first real king of the Eurypontidai (cf., e.g., Aristotle *Politics* 1271b25; Plutarch *Lykourgos* 3.1–4), and even Herodotos' elder contemporary, the poet Simonides, at least made him a Eurypontid (cf. Plutarch *Lykourgos* 1.4). He may thus have played a part in establishing the double monarchy, if Charillos really was the first king of the Eurypontidai, and in reconciling the warring *obai* and ritualizing their quarrels into some of the rites associated with the worship of Artemis Orthia and the *agoge*. In this sense, Herodotos would not, after all, have been far wrong in crediting him with establishing some of Sparta's basic military institutions (1.65.5). Later on he would naturally have been credited with many other things – for example the *rhetra* and the ephorate – which in fact only appeared long after his time. It is possible that he only finally began to play the star role in early Spartan history as the influence of the kings began to decline, in the sixth century, for Tyrtaios clearly never mentioned him – if he had, the reference was bound to have been quoted. One suspects that the great ephor, Chilon, who 'first yoked the ephors beside the kings' (Diogenes Laertius 1.68), may have played a part in the creation of the Lykourgos legend.[15]

In any case, whether Lykourgos had anything to do with it or not, it is probable that some of the basic elements in the military way of life of the Spartans had come into being by the time of the era of expansion in the eighth century, though unfortunately we know nothing about the Spartan army before the time of Tyrtaios, probably about the middle of the seventh century. Pausanias may conceivably preserve one authentic detail of the First Messenian War, fought in the time of Tyrtaios' grandfather (cf. fr.5 West), when he says that in one battle the Spartans were marshalled in three divisions (4.7.8). One thinks immediately of the three *phylai* of *Hylleis*, *Dymanes* and *Pamphyloi*, for Tyrtaios appears to say that the Spartans fought in these divisions in his time (cf. fr.19.8 West). But Pausanias actually says that on the occasion in question the right was commanded by King Theopompos of the Eurypontidai, their left by the Agiad, Polydoros, and the centre by Euryleon, a descendant of the hero Aigeus. The tradition is probably spurious, but the Aigeidai (i.e. descendants of Aigeus) were evidently an important clan in Sparta, in historical times (cf. Herodotos 4.149.1), and they may have been associated with Amyklai in particular,[16] so it is just possible that Pausanias here preserves a lingering echo of the division in Sparta between the two pairs of *obai,* and that the men of Amyklai still fought in a separate contingent at this date. But Pausanias can hardly be right in contrasting the hoplite-like tactics of the Spartans with those of the Messenians (4.8.2ff.), for the first Messenian War was probably fought roughly from 735 to 715, and this was before the beginning of hoplite warfare.[17]

It is, however, conceivable that the *morai* already existed in an embryonic form, at this date, for an obvious explanation of their number and their name is that there were originally two *morai* to each of the three *phylai*, each being a 'part' of the fighting men of the *phyle,* as the name itself implies, and this in turn suggests that the division of the army into *morai* goes back to the original division of Sparta into two pairs of *obai*. It is almost certain that the three *phylai* were common to all Spartans, irrespective of the *oba* to which they belonged – in other words that there were *Hylleis, Dymanes* and *Pamphyloi* in all four *obai* – for the same three *phylai* existed in other Dorian communities, as we have seen (above, p. 82), and the two kings of Sparta presumably both belonged to the *Hylleis* since both royal families claimed descent from Herakles, father of Hyllos, eponym of the *phyle* (cf. Herodotos 7.204 & 8.131.2).[18] Thus, when the reconciliation between the men of Pitana and Mesoa, on the one hand, and the men of Limnai and Konooura, on the other, took place, there would have been two groups of *Hylleis,* two of *Dymanes* and two of *Pamphyloi,* and this may have been the origin of the *morai,* each being regarded as 'part' of a now united *phyle.* Perhaps, too, the *syssitia* also originated, or were reorganized, as part of the reconciliation, for in Xenophon's time both kings evidently belonged to the same *syssition* (cf.

XH 5.3.20, Plutarch *Agesilaos* 20.5).

The *lochoi*, too, may have originated here, each being originally formed by the men of each *phyle* in each of the four *obai* – thus, for example, the two *morai* of *Hylleis* would each have comprised two *lochoi*, consisting of the *Hylleis* of Pitana and Mesoa, on the one hand, and those of Limnai and Konooura, on the other. This is, of course, pure speculation, but the later organization of the Spartan army was certainly based on a combination of multiples of two, three and four (six *morai*, twelve *lochoi*, forty-eight *pentekostyes*, probably 192 *enomotiai*), and it is at least plausible that this had something to do with the three *phylai* and the two pairs of *obai*. If this is right, too, Herodotos may not, after all, have been completely wrong to describe Amompharetos as *lochagos* of the *lochos* of Pitana, for there will once, at least, have been three *lochoi* of Pitana, composed of the *Hylleis*, *Dymanes* and *Pamphyloi* of that *oba*, though it is probable that by the fifth century the *lochoi* were no longer recruited in this way (see below).

This is not to say that after the reconciliation of the warring *obai*, the Spartan army was already organized in exactly the same way as it was in Xenophon's day: for one thing, presumably, the original *morai* and *lochoi* contained fewer men, and for another, if the original army was based on locality, one suspects that the smallest units may have been some kind of kinship groups like *phratriai*.[19] But as soon as men who were not originally from the four *obai* of Sparta were admitted into the army, an organization based on kinship-groups would have had to be abandoned, since such groups were notoriously reluctant to admit outsiders, and this is, perhaps, when the *enomotiai* made their appearance, for the term – meaning something like 'sworn-bands' – suggests that their members were not originally bound together by ties of kin. One may guess that when the people of Amyklai finally became 'Spartans', their men were distributed among the *morai*, for they were certainly found in them all later (cf. XH 4.5.11) – indeed, if the Amyklaians were themselves 'Dorians', as has recently been argued,[20] and if they, like the Spartans, were divided into *Hylleis*, *Dymanes* and *Pamphyloi*, it would have been natural for them to join the appropriate *mora*. But the Amyklaians certainly did not belong to one or other of the four *obai* of Sparta,[21] and it is not even by any means certain that Amyklai ever formed an *oba* in this sense (see above pp. 65–6) : thus there could be no question of its men joining an appropriate *lochos*. Perhaps, then, the members of the smallest units, which now came to include Amyklaians, 'swore' to fight loyally together, and so the *enomotiai* came into existence.

The *pentekostyes*, one presumes, came into existence later, when the number of men in the Spartan army reached something like its later strength: it is the only term for a unit, apart from the enigmatic *triakades*, which has a numerical connotation, and this itself suggests that it was the last term to come into use.

We can possibly even date the change over from an army based on kinship – groups to one based on *enomotiai*, for if there is any truth in the tradition that the Aigeid, Euryleon, commanded a third of the Spartan army during the First Messenian War (Pausanias 4.7.8), it suggests that the men of Amyklai were still brigaded separately from the Spartans at this date, and there is some reason to believe that there was still what one might describe as a 'nationalist' feeling in Amyklai at the end of the war: part of the traditions connected with the foundation of Taras associates the problems, which Taras was meant to solve, particularly with Amyklai – Antiochos of Syracuse, for example, is quoted by Strabo (6.3.2) as having said that the conspiracy which led to the foundation of the colony was to have been hatched at the festival of Hyakinthos at Amyklai. The root cause of the problem seems to have been the right of various groups to a share in the conquered land in Messenia, and perhaps in southern Lakonia as well (cf. Aristotle *Politics* 1306b27ff.; Ephoros ap. Strabo 6.3.3), and it is possible that the men of Amyklai felt that they were being denied their rightful share – possibly the Aigeidai, for example, demanded *temene* like those possessed by the kings of Sparta in perioecic territory (cf. *LP* 15.3). If the men of Amyklai were really disaffected at the end of the war, it may well be that the Spartans solved the problem partly by sending disaffected elements to southern Italy, partly by breaking up the Amyklaian division in the army and absorbing its men into their own *morai*.[22]

For the equipment of the primitive Spartan army the one that conquered Lakonia and won the First Messenian War – we have to rely entirely upon archaeological evidence, unless we can accept that the corslet of Timomachos, displayed at the festival of Hyakinthos at Amyklai, was an authentic relic of Sparta's war against that place.[23] This apart, we can probably assume that there would have been little if any metallic armour – the famous Late Geometric armour from Argos is the earliest post-Mycenaean evidence for armour made of bronze. But jerkins of leather or other perishable material may well have been worn, and probably a helmet of leather or felt, with a crest, leaving most of the face exposed. The shield would probably have been round, or, possibly, shaped like an hour-glass (the so-called 'Dipylon' shield), supported by a leather strap across the shoulder, and held by a single, central hand-grip. Offensive weapons were probably predominantly throwing-spears and swords, and battle-tactics would have been rudimentary, allowing for the display of individual prowess in something like the Homeric manner. Except for any advantages they might have enjoyed as a result of their youthful training, it is unlikely that Spartan warriors at this date would have been very different from those of other Greek states.

The next crucial stage in the development of the Spartan army, as was the case with the armies of other Greek states, presumably came with the adoption of hoplite equipment and tactics. Here, too, the evidence is largely archaeological, and controversy about the date – for Greece as a whole - fierce.[24] The really important stage, however, was not so much the coming into use of the individual items of hoplite equipment, even of the hoplite shield with its characteristic double grip – what really mattered was the combining of relatively large numbers of men equipped in this way into a phalanx, and a good case can be made for believing that this had happened by c.675 in some parts of Greece, on the basis of vase paintings of what look like hoplites ranged in such a way[25] (see plate 5). For our purposes the main question is when the Spartans adopted these tactics, and unfortunately archaeological evidence in the shape of figure-decoration on Lakonian vases, is lacking for the crucial period. It will be argued below that surviving fragments of Tyrtaios' poetry provide a *terminus ante quem,* since there should not be much doubt that Tyrtaios was addressing hoplites, but apart from this we have to fall back on argument from inference. There is some reason to believe that the *phalanx* may have made its first appearance in Argos, and indeed that it was the embryonic hoplites of Argos who brought the 'tyrant' Pheidon to power,[26] and in that case it is possible that the reason for Sparta's defeat by the Argives at Hysiai in 669 (Pausanias 2.24.7),[27] was that the Argives were already using the new tactics, whereas the Spartans were not. However, this is obviously not the only possible explanation for Sparta's defeat, and it seems probable, on other grounds, that Sparta had already adopted the new tactics before the battle.

Pheidon's possible connections with hoplites, however, and the repercussions elsewhere in Greece which seem to be connected with the emergence of hoplite armies – e.g. at Corinth and Sikyon[28] – suggest that this may also be the explanation of the *stasis* in Sparta, noted by Herodotos (1.65.2) and Thucydides (1.18.1), which was brought to an end by the establishment of *eunomia*. Tradition, of course, held that it was Lykourgos who was responsible for Sparta's *eunomia*, long before the emergence of hoplites, but we have seen reason to believe (above, pp. 86–7) that if Lykourgos ever existed, he was really connected with the establishment of a unified Spartan state early in the eighth century, and there are hints that the tradition about Lykourgos became confused with a much later period of *stasis* which began with the troubles connected with the foundation of Taras, and ended with a settlement achieved by the kings Theopompos and Polydoros.[29] In particular, the demands of Sparta's hoplites for political recognition may well lie behind the archaic document quoted by Plutarch (*Lykourgos* 6.1), and known as the '*rhetra*'. Plutarch, presumably following the lost Aristotelian '*Constitution of the Lakedaimonians*', believed that Lykourgos was responsible for the *rhetra*, but he goes on to quote some lines of Tyrtaios (fr. 4 West) to show that Theopompos and Polydoros were responsible for an addition (*Lykourgos* 6.4–5), and these lines seem in fact to paraphrase the *rhetra* itself. No certainty is possible, but it is at least fairly certain that Tyrtaios did not ascribe the *rhetra* to Lykourgos, and if Plutarch and, one supposes, Aristotle, quoted his poem to prove something about the two kings, there was presumably something in the rest of it to show that it was about them – perhaps, indeed, that they were the subject of the verb (ἔνεικαν: 'they brought') in the first line quoted by Plutarch. But if Tyrtaios did ascribe the *rhetra* to Theopompos and Polydoros, this is very good evidence that it should be dated to the first half of the seventh century, for these two kings belonged to different generations and are unlikely to have overlapped at any other time. A more precise date may be given by the tradition that the Karneian festival was founded in the twenty-sixth Olympiad (676–3: Sosibios ap. Athenaios 14.635e-f), for this, the most important festival of the Spartan year, may well have been founded to commemorate the ending of the *stasis* and the establishment of *eunomia*.[30] In this case, we can presumably date the emergence of a hoplite army at Sparta some time before the twenty-sixth Olympiad.

It has even been suggested[31] that the *rhetra* itself, with its talk of 'dividing into *phylai* and *obai*' (ιφυλὰς φυλάξαντα καὶ ὠβὰς ὠβάξαντα), embodies a reform in the Spartan army, namely its reorganization into five *lochoi*, drawn from five *phylai* based on five *obai* (Pitana, Mesoa, Limnai, Konooura and Amyklai). However, we have seen reason to doubt that the Spartan army was ever organized in this way (above pp. 64–6), and there is no good reason to believe that the *phylai* and *obai* mentioned in the *rhetra* were anything other than the three *phylai* of *Hylleis*, *Dymanes* and *Pamphyloi* and the four *obai* of Pitana, Mesoa, Limnai and Konooura, for there is no evidence that there were any other *phylai* and *obai* in Sparta before the Hellenistic period.

Connected with the *stasis* which eventually led to the settlement summarized in the *rhetra*, however, was probably the problem of land, and the solution the Spartans eventually adopted – the distribution of land in *klaroi* (land-lots) – was important in the development of the army in two ways: it made it much easier for Spartan soldiers to spend their lives in the full-time practice of their profession, since they had helots to work their *klaroi* for them (cf. Plutarch *Lykourgos* 24.3), and it possibly determined the number of troops the regular army was henceforth to contain. Unfortunately, however, it is not possible to be certain when or how or why the klaros-system came into being. According to Ephoros (ap. Strabo 8.5.4), it was the first king Agis himself who enslaved the helots, and although it is difficult to take such a tradition seriously, it is possible that there were helots and some kind of *klaroi* in Spartan territory from the very earliest times.[32] Again, if we can trust the tradition of the conquest of Aigys in the reigns of Archelaos and Charillos (Pausanias 3.2.5), its inhabitants were enslaved, which may imply the division of their land into *klaroi*, and although the tradition that it was Lykourgos who made the original division (Plutarch *Lykourgos* 8) probably means nothing, if Lykourgos was Charillos' uncle and active at the time, he may have had something to do with it. But the subjugation of Amyklai, Pharis and Geronthrai in the reign of Archelaos' son, Teleklos (Pausanias 3.2.6), would not seem to have led to any further significant distribution of *klaroi*, for the people of Amyklai, at any rate, were later Spartans in some sense, and the inhabitants of Pharis and Geronthrai were later *perioikoi*.

Whatever the truth may be about earlier manifestations of the klaros-system, however, it seems probable that it was first used extensively after the conquest of southern Lakonia and eastern Messenia in the late eighth century. This is suggested by the tradition which connected the origin of the helots with the subjugation of Helos in southern Lakonia (cf. Hellanikos *FGH* 4F188; Theopompos *FGH* 11F13; Pausanias 3.20.6; etc.), even though the tradition is almost certainly false – the word probably just means 'captives' – and by the legend that the Spartan colony at Taras in southern Italy was founded – traditionally in 706 – by colonists disgruntled at not receiving their fair share of the conquered land (cf. Aristotle *Politics* 1306b27ff.; Strabo 6.3.2–3). In the case of Messenia, we also have the

Tyrtaios fragments (5 & 6 West) which stress the fruitfulness of Messenia and the burdens of tribute in kind laid upon the wretched Messenians – the first fragment certainly refers to the first Messenian war – and the traditions which connected King Polydoros with the distribution of *klaroi* in Messenia (Plutarch Lykourgos 8.3 and *Moralia* 231e). Unfortunately, however, what is potentially the best evidence turns out to be equivocal on examination: Aristotle (*Politics* 1306b36ff.) cites Tyrtaios' lost poem on *Eunomia* as evidence that 'at the time of the Messenian War' (ὑπὸ τὸν Μεσσηνιακὸν πόλεμον), certain Spartans demanded that they 'redistribute the land' (ἀνάδαστον ποιεῖν τὴν χώραν), but it is not certain which Messenian War Tyrtaios had in mind – the one in his own day or the one fought in his grandfather's time – nor whether this was the first demand for the distribution of land, or a demand for a re-distribution, as the Greek rather implies (cf. ἀνάδαστον), perhaps because the rebellion in Tyrtaios' time had robbed the original recipients of their land.[33]

A difficulty in all this lies in determining the precise causal relationship between the appearance of hoplites, the distribution of *klaroi,* and the unrest which presumably led to the distribution of *klaroi* and the concessions made to the *damos* in the *rhetra,* for those who had little or no land in the first place would presumably not have been able to equip themselves as hoplites,[34] and if they were not hoplites, would not have had the political 'clout' necessary either to wring land out of the aristocracy or the concessions embodied in the *rhetra.* A possible solution, however, is that those in power at the time, however reluctant they may have been to see land going to a wider group, when faced with the problem of what to do with the newly-conquered land and its inhabitants, and, perhaps, with the pressure of overpopulation which led to colonization elsewhere in Greece, hit upon the klaros-system as a means of both controlling the subjugated territory and its inhabitants, and of satisfying the land-hungry, without envisaging that the new landowners, now able to take their place in the hoplite-phalanx, might no longer be content to leave the running of the state to the old 'establishment'. In much the same way, one suspects, the aristocracies of places like Argos, Corinth and Sikyon were – to an extent – happy to see the increasing numbers of men able and willing to share the burdens of 'military service', without appreciating the danger they constituted to aristocratic privilege.[35] In Argos, perhaps, the storm broke because a king seized upon the newly-emerging 'hoplite-class' as a means of redressing the decline in the monarch's powers in the face of the aristocracy; in Sparta, perhaps, the problem arose at about the same time because the conquest of southern Lakonia and Messenia produced an immediate problem – the land was there and something had to be done about it – whereas in Corinth and Sikyon, for example, it took time before the prosperity arising from trade and colonization percolated down to a wider class and so roused resentment against their aristocracies. In these latter places, the result was the violent overthrow of the aristocracy by a tyrant: in Sparta, the aristocracy, perhaps under the influence of the 'liberal' Polydoros (cf. Pausanias 3.2.2–3), and with the acquiescence at least of the revered Theopompos,[36] woke up in time, and made the *damos* the concessions embodied in the *rhetra* – thus, as Thucydides says (1.18.1), Sparta was 'always without a tyrant.' The *rhetra*, surely, does essentially embody a compromise: it concedes ultimate sovereignty to the *damos*, and provides for the machinery to enable the *damos* to express its wishes, but even if the so-called 'rider' did not in fact give the kings and *gerontes* the power of veto, the privileges of the kings and the class from which the *gerontes* were drawn were still enshrined in the *rhetra*.[37]

The idea of compromise was also, perhaps, expressed by the Spartans themselves in the notion that all Spartiates were 'equals' or 'peers' (ὅμοιοι), for they must have known, at least as well as Aristotle (cf. *Politics* 1270a15ff.), that there were marked inequalities amongst them in reality. Presumably, then, their 'equality' lay in the fact that they all at least owned a *klaros* sufficient to provide them with the dues in kind required for membership of a *syssition* and so for citizenship (cf. Aristotle *Politics* 1271a32–7), that they all had to go through the *agoge* (cf. *Politics* 1294b19ff.), and that they all had an equal vote in the *ekklesia*, whether on questions of policy or in elections (cf. *Politics* 1294b29–31). Possibly, too, as far as the army was concerned, 'equality' lay in uniformity of equipment, training and place in the basic units out of which the phalanx now came to be constituted.[38]

How many *homoioi* were there when the final distribution of *klaroi* had been made? Plutarch, in a well-known passage (*Lykourgos* 8.3), implies that in the end there were nine thousand, though there were evidently variant traditions about how there came to be that number, some saying that it was due to Lykourgos, some that King Polydoros added either 3,000 or 4,500 *klaroi* to those originally distributed by the lawgiver. It has been argued that the figure of 9,000 is simply a projection back from the proposal of King Agis IV, in the third century, to create 4,500 *klaroi*, after the loss of Messenia,[39] but Herodotos reports the ex-king Demaratos as telling Xerxes that Sparta was a *polis* of 'about eight thousand men' (7.234.2), the context implying that men of military age were primarily meant, and Aristotle (*Politics* 1270a36–37) reports a tradition that there were once 10,000 Spartiates, so, even if the figure of 9,000 for the number of *klaroi* rests on no good ancient tradition, it is likely to have been roughly right.

The number of *klaroi* eventually assigned would obviously have determined how large the army was to be, for it was clearly originally intended that the army should consist exclusively of *homoioi*. Some of the *klaroi*, however, were presumably originally assigned to men too old to serve in the army any longer, and some provision may also have been made for minors, at least in the future.[40] Thus the envisaged total for the army may have been more like the 8,000 of Demaratos' reported remarks to Xerxes, and this is very near the total of 7,980 infantry suggested for the army of Xenophon's time (six *morai* of 1,280 men each, + 300 *Hippeis*). By Xenophon's time, of course, the army no longer consisted exclusively of *homoioi*, but the way in which the Spartiates seem to have been scattered about in the various units suggests that some older organization was being rigidly adhered to even though the personnel had changed: we have already seen that the organization into six *morai* and twelve *lochoi* may go back to the establishment of the unified Spartan state in the early eighth century, and it is possible that their size was now finally fixed by the number of *klaroi*. In this case, the army which fought at Hysiai in 669 may have been organized, in all essentials, in exactly the same way as the one which fought at Leuktra almost three hundred years later.

The battle of Hysiai probably formed part of the war against Argos over the Thyreatis, fought when King Theopompos was an old man (Pausanias 3.7.5),[41] and it has often been suggested that it was this defeat which sparked off the second Messenian war.[42] Pausanias actually dates the latter war 685 to 668 (4.15.1,23.4), but he later says (4.27.9) that when the Messenians were freed by Epameinondas (i.e. early in 369), it was two hundred and eighty-seven years since the fall of Eira, the event which marked the end of the struggle with the Spartans (cf. Pausanias 4.23.4), and the tradition that Phigalia was captured by the Spartans in 659 (Pausanias 8.39.3) also suggests that fighting was still going on in Messenia in the 650s, since although Phigalia was in Arcadia, the Arcadians were allegedly allies of the Messenians (cf. Strabo 8.4.10, Pausanias 4.15.7–8). Thus he may have dated the beginning of the war too early. It is even possible that Messenia continued to be the main preoccupation of the Spartans right down to the end of the seventh century, for Epameinondas again is alleged to have declared, according to another tradition (Plutarch *Moralia* 194b), that he re-established Messene after two hundred and thirty years.

It was to inspire the Spartans in this second great struggle against the Messenians that Tyrtaios composed his battle-poetry, and some of the things he says confirm that the Spartans already thought of themselves as *homoioi*. It is true that in one passage (frag. 10 West, lines 9–12) he exhorts his hearers not to shame their *genos* ('clan'), and in another (frag. 12 West, line 24) to bring honour to their fathers, which is typical of aristocratic ideals (cf. the Leipsydrion drinking-song in the Aristotelian *Constitution of the Athenians*, 19.3), but there is also the suggestion that a brave man can, in effect, create a noble *genos* (frag. 12 West, lines 29–30), and the injunction to be brave in order to save or to bring honour to the *laos* ('people': cf. frag. 11 West, line 13, and frag. 12, line 24), is foreign to the aristocratic ideal.[43] Elsewhere, too, Tyrtaios refers to a man acting nobly 'for the state and all the people' (πολήῖ τε παντί τε δήμωι), and, of course, in the well-known fragment (frag. 4 West) in which he appears to paraphrase the *rhetra*, gives the 'men of the people' (δημότες ἄνδρες: line 5) their proper place, and even declares that 'victory and sovereignty are to go with the mass of the people' (δήμου τε πλήθει νίκην καί κάρτος ἕπεσθαι: line 9). Such remarks really make no sense except in the context of a Sparta in which all Spartiates are now at least officially held to be equal, and all virtues to be for the common good. Tyrtaios' warriors, too, are all anonymous – the only beings named in his surviving fragments are gods, heroes and kings – and his appeal is to the solid, dependable, useful virtues of the patriotic hoplite, not the brilliant but egocentric qualities of the aristocratic hero.

It is also, surely, certain – though even this has been doubted[44] – that Tyrtaios is addressing hoplites, in the sense of heavily-armed foot-soldiers accustomed to fight shoulder-to-shoulder in a phalanx. Thus, although much of his language is Homeric, his attitude to warfare is quite different from Homer's: Homer's heroes, with the possible exception of Hektor (cf. *Iliad* 12.243, etc.), fight for themselves and their own glory, and one suspects that this had long been the attitude of Sparta's aristocrats, but Tyrtaios seeks to inspire his hearers to stand together and fight for their country (cf. frag. 10 West, lines 2 & 13; frag. 12, lines 24 & 34); in Homer it is perfectly proper for a hero to leap out from the battle-line and challenge an opposing hero to a duel (cf. *Iliad* 3.19–20, 5.627ff., 6.119ff., 13.445ff., 13.809), and it is an oddity when Nestor exhorts his charioteers to stick together (*Iliad* 4.303–5), but Tyrtaios bids his hearers fight 'standing by each other' (παρ' ἀλλήλοισι μένοντες: frag. 10 West, line 15; frag. 11, line 11), and to remain patiently, even if in the front line, encouraging those standing alongside them (cf. frag. 12 West, lines 15–20): one can imagine what Achilles' reaction would have been had he heard it said that 'this is what makes a good man in war' (οὗτος ἀνὴρ ἀγαθὸς γίνεται ἐν πολέμωι: Tyrtaios frag. 12 West, line 20).

If the fragments are taken as a whole, it is clear, too, that the heavily-armed soldiers, standing in close-packed ranks (cf. frag. 11 West, lines 11–14), are all-important, and that any skirmishers that there are have an essentially subordinate role, just as was the case in hoplite battles: '*gymnetes*' are only mentioned in one passage (frag. 11 West, lines 35–8),[45] and there the implication is that there are not many of them, and that they are not to pursue an independent role – they are to fling their stones and throw their javelins 'crouching beneath the shield, one here, one there … standing near the fully-armed' (ὑπ' ἀσπίδος ἄλλοθεν ἄλλος πτώσσοντες … τοῖσι πανόπλοισιν πλησίον ἱστάμενοι). Obviously this conjures up something rather different from our normal picture of a hoplite battle, but light-armed skirmishers did later participate in hoplite battles,[46] and this is, in any case, an isolated reference in Tyrtaios, though elsewhere (frag. 11 West, line 28, and frag. 19, lines 2 & 19) he mentions the missiles characteristic of skirmishers.

Even less convincing as an argument against the view that Tyrtaios' warriors are hoplites is the alleged implication in two passages (frag. 11 West, lines 30 & 34) that the sword was as alternative weapon to the spear. Hoplites certainly later carried swords for use when their spears were broken (cf., e.g., Herodotos 7.225.3), and there is no compelling reason to read any more than this into Tyrtaios' lines. It is quite clear that for him as for classical hoplites, the spear was the weapon *par excellence*: it gave rise to one of his terms for 'warriors' (αἰχμηταί: frag. 5 West, line 6, and frag. 19, line 13), it was the disgrace of a spear-wound in the back that was to be avoided (frag. 11 West, line 20), spear-wounds in the front that were an honour (frag. 12 West, lines 25–6), and victory could be described as winning 'the glorious boast of the spear' (αἰχμῆς ἀγλαὸν εὖχος: frag. 12 West, line 36). Even the constant exhortation to his hearers to be 'among the front-fighters' (πρόμαχοι: cf. frag. 10 West, lines 1, 21 & 30; frag. 11, lines 4 & 12; frag. 12, lines 16 & 23), which might be thought to fit better a more fluid kind of fighting, would in fact have been perfectly intelligible to hoplites, since it was presumably always the duty of the men in the rear ranks to take the places of those in the front ranks who had fallen, and a shirker was one who hesitated

Scene on an Attic red figure cup, signed by Douris (c. 500–460 BC), now in the Kunsthistorisches Museum in Vienna (No. 3964), showing hoplites arming. Note the complex corslets and the convex shields with their sharply offset rims. (After Furtwängler–Reichhold, pl.53, photograph by the Audio–Visual Centre of the University of Newcastle upon Tyne).

Scene on an Attic red figure calyx crater by the Tyszkiewicz Painter (first quarter of the fifth century), now in the Boston Museum of Fine Arts (No. 97.368), depicting the fight between Diomedes and Aineias. Note the interior arrangements of the shields and the complex corslets. (Photograph courtesy the Museum of Fine Arts, Boston. Perkins Collection)

Archaic bronze statuette of a presumably Spartan warrior, now in the Wadsworth Atheneum, Hartford, Connecticut. Note the long hair and the cloak – the unusual transverse crest may denote an officer. (Photograph courtesy of the Wadsworth Atheneum. Gift of J.P. Morgan).

Scene on an Attic red figure cup by the Sosias Painter (c.500 BC), now in the Staatliche Museen Berlin (No. 2278), showing Achilles bandaging Patroklos. Note the flap of Patroklos' corslet above his left shoulder, loosened for comfort (cf. Pls 1 & 2), and the cap of felt or hide which he appears to be wearing: hoplites may have worn such a cap under their helmets to prevent chafing. Although the scene is heroic, this kind of thing must have been seen after many a real battle. (Photograph courtesy of the Antikenmuseum Staatliche Museen Preussischer Kulturbesitz Berlin).

One of the earliest depictions of hoplites in battle – c.650 BC or a little later – from a Protocorinthian *olpe* (the 'Chigi Vase'), now in the Villa Giulia, Rome (No. 22679). Note the bell–corslets and the individualized blazons, but note also the piper, a feature of Spartan armies down to at least as late as the fourth century. (Drawing by the Author)

Scene on a Lakonian cup by the Hunt painter (c. 550 BC), now in the Staatliche Museen, West Berlin (No. 3404). Roughly contemporary with the 'Battle of the Champions', it presumably depicts young Spartan warriors carrying older, bearded comrades from the field – note the long hair. (Photograph courtesy of the Antikenmusem Staatliche Museen Preussischer Kulturbesitz Berlin).

The modern monument at Thermopylai. It goes without saying that Spartan soldiers did not fight in the nude! Note the inscription 'ΜΟΛΩΝ ΛΑΒΕ' i.e. 'Come and get them!'

Bronze facing of a Spartan shield captured by the Athenians at Pylos, now in the Agora Museum, Athens – the so-called 'Shield of Brasidas'. (Photograph courtesy of the American School of Classical Studies at Athens: Agora Excavations)

Drawing of the above showing the inscription 'ΑΘΗΝΑΙΟΙ ΑΠΟΛΑΚΕΔΑΙΜΟΝΙΩΝ ΕΚ ΠΥΛΟ', i.e. 'The Athenians (dedicated this, taken) from the Lakedaimonians from Pylos'. (Photograph courtesy of the American School of Classical Studies at Athens: Agora Excavations)

The hillock at Thermopylai where the Spartans and Thespiaians made their last stand: view north over what would mostly have been sea in 480 BC to the Othrys range. (Author's photograph)

North end of Sphakteria from Koryphasion (Pylos), with the modern town of Pylos beyond. The Spartans made their last stand on the high ground at this end of the island, and Komon and his Messenians presumably climbed the cliffs to the left. Note also the scrub which still covers much of the island. (Author's photograph)

View south from the isolated hill just north of Mantineia (Gourtsouli), with Mt. Alesion to the left and the Mytikas spur further away to the right – the battle took place somewhere in the flat ground between the two. (Author's photograph)

The acropolis of ancient Koroneia from the west. (Author's photograph)

View north from ancient Corinth over the Gulf of Corinth to the peninsula of Perachora: the fight with the *mora* would have taken place just off the picture to the left. (Author's photograph)

The remains of the monument at Leuktra, before restoration – note the typical hoplite shields. (Author's photograph, taken in 1961)

to do so. Indeed, it is worth emphasizing that far from later Spartan soldiers' finding anything incongruous or absurd in Tyrtaios' poetry, his poems were sung in the *syssitia* and on the march (Philochoros ap. Athenaios 14.630f, Lycurgus *in Leocratem*, 107).[47]

Even if we have to make some allowance for the epic colouring of Tyrtaios' language, then, we have in the surviving fragments of his poetry a precious glimpse of the Spartan army as it was at the time of the second Messenian War – an army of hoplites, except for the few and unimportant *gymnetes*, and of *homoioi*, amongst whom only the brave are to be distinguished: even the *Hippeis* are not singled out for mention, though judging from their name, they are likely to have been a very ancient institution. Unfortunately, Tyrtaios tells us nothing of the army's organization, except in the one fragment which seems to refer to the *Pamphyloi, Hylleis* and *Dymanes* fighting in separate divisions (frag. 19 West, line 8). But although the tense of the verb is uncertain, the natural assumption is that the reference is contemporary, and this presents no difficulty if the arguments advanced above are accepted, for the army of Tyrtaios' time would not have been organized in five *lochoi*, but in six *morai*, two for each of the three *phylai*. The references to 'young men' and 'older men' (frag. 10 West, lines 15 & 17; frag. 11, line 10; frag. 12, line 14), may even hint at an organization in age–classes – which is likely to be early in any case – and the passage in which the young men are exhorted not to leave the old 'to lie fallen among the front-fighters' (frag. 10 West, lines 20–2), at least suggests that it was the duty of the young men to fight in the front ranks.

The poems are slightly more informative about the equipment of Spartan soldiers at the time, though here too we must probably make some allowance for the epic language. In one passage, for example, a man's shield is said to extend from his shins to his shoulders (κνῆμαι to ὦμοι: frag. 11 West, lines 23–4), and one is reminded of Hektor's shield in the *Iliad* (6.117), which banged against his neck and his ankles (σφυρά), though if one is to be pedantic, Hektor's shield would have been slightly larger, and it is possible that early hoplite shields were larger than the later standard size.[48] Size apart, the shields are 'hollow' (frag. 19 West, line 7), i.e. convex, and round (frag. 19 West, line 15), and the term used for them is *aspides*, the normal term for the hoplite shield (cf. frag. 11 West, lines 24, 31 & 35; frag. 12, line 25; frag. 19, lines 7 & 15) – the Homeric word '*sakos*' does not occur. A possible archaizing feature is the shield-boss implied in one passage (frag. 12 West, line 25), for hoplite shields did not have bosses, whereas this was apparently a feature of many a Homeric shield. Other protective equipment included crested helm (frag. 11 West, lines 26 & 32), and corslet (frag. 12 West, line 26 – cf. frag. 19, line 17), but there does not appear to be any reference to greaves. The main offensive weapon was, clearly, the spear, and there can hardly be any doubt that this was the thrusting-spear of the hoplite: this appears from the exhortations to 'get in close' (cf. frag. 11 West, lines 12 & 29, and frag. 12, line 12), and from the lines in which a warrior is bidden 'fight a man, planting foot to foot, pressing shield to shield, crest on crest, helmet on helmet, and bringing breast to breast' (frag. 11 West, lines 31–3), if, as seems likely, the injunction is to close with the enemy, not just close up with fellow-soldiers. The sword was also used, as we have seen (frag. 11 West, lines 30 & 34), and, among the *gymnetes*, stones and javelins (frag. 11 West, lines 36–7). It is, however, very unlikely that we can trust any of the later traditions of the second Messenian War, as embodied in Pausanias, for example, except, possibly, the tradition of a battle at a 'great trench' (Pausanias 4.17.2 & 7), for Tyrtaios appears to have referred to a battle at a trench, in a lost poem (Aristotle, *Nicomachean Ethics* 3.1116b and schol. ad loc.).

As we have seen (above, p. 96), the Messenians may have occupied the Spartans right down to the end of the seventh century, but early in the following century, judging by the kings then said to be on the throne (Leon and Agesikles: Herodotos 1.65.1), we find the Spartans renewing their attacks on Arcadia, perhaps broken off after a defeat at the time of Charillos,[49] and if there is any truth in the story of the fetters they carried in the hope of taking prisoners, and in which they found themselves enchained after their defeat (Herodotos 1.66), it looks as though they hoped to turn the Tegeates into helots, like the Messenians. But unfortunately Herodotos tells us nothing about the Spartan army which suffered this, its last serious defeat for some two centuries. It is possible that they were more successful in other wars at the time, as Herodotos says (1.65.1), and one of these may have been one fought in alliance with Elis, for Strabo (8.3.30) says the Spartans co-operated with the people of Elis after their last defeat of the Messenians, and this may have been in the wars Elis fought with the sons of Pantaleon, tyrant of Pisa, the second of which ended in the total defeat of Pisa and the establishment of the people of Elis as controllers of the Olympic Games: Pausanias dates the first of these wars to 588 (6.22.3–4).

Later in the century, in the reigns of Anaxandridas and Ariston, the Spartans were finally able to defeat the Tegeates, who now became their allies

– perhaps the first members of what modern scholars call the Peloponnesian League – and although Herodotos again gives no details, at least in his story of the 'Bones of Orestes' we meet the *Hippeis* for the first time (1.67.5). Perhaps at about the same time, and possibly in 556, when the great Chilon was ephor, Spartan troops under the command of King Anaxandridas may have been instrumental in overthrowing Aischines, tyrant of Sikyon (cf. Rylands Papyrus 18), and within possibly a decade the verdict of Hysiai was finally reversed in the 'Battle of the Champions' (Herodotos 1.82), where, if the three hundred Spartan champions were really found by choosing one *enomotia* of twenty-five men from each of twelve *lochoi* (see above, p. 70), we are clearly at last dealing with an army very like the one known to Thucydides and Xenophon. It was to commemorate this battle, according to Herodotos (1.82.7–8) that the Spartans started to wear their hair long, though it is possible that in this, as in so many other things, they were just conservative, for the Achaeans in Homer already wore their hair long (cf. *Iliad* 3.43, etc.), and the story may simply have arisen because the Argives cut their hair short in sign of mourning (see plate 6). But Herodotos' story of the battle and its aftermath indicates that military fanaticism was already prevalent at Sparta, if it is true that the sole survivor of the three hundred Spartan champions, Othryades, killed himself rather than go home (Herodotos 1.82.8), despite his claim to have won the battle for Sparta in virtue of being the last man on the battlefield – the two surviving Argives had gone home, assuming that they had won. Possibly Othryades felt that the relationship between the members of his *enomotia* made it impossible for him to survive the others.

Later still in the sixth century (c.525) came the Spartan expedition to Samos, which failed to oust the tyrant Polykrates,[50] and the story of which Herodotos heard from Archias of Pitana, whose grandfather of the same name had played a heroic part in the assault (3.54–5). This story again tells us something about the fanatical courage of at least some Spartans, but unfortunately nothing about the composition or equipment of the Spartan force. The failure against Polykrates may possibly have been compensated for by success against Lygdamis, tyrant of Naxos (cf. Plutarch *Moralia* 859d). Finally, towards the end of the century, came the four Spartan interventions in Attica (Herodotos 5.63–5, 70–5), discussed at the end of the last chapter.

Even if the detailed hypotheses put forward in this chapter are not accepted, it is at least arguable that nothing precludes the possibility that the Spartan army Thucydides and Xenophon knew began to take shape in the seventh or even the eighth century, and that thereafter it remained much the same in basic organization and even in numbers. Nor should it occasion too much surprise if the army of so essentially conservative a people remained basically the same for some three centuries: after all, the Coldstream Guards were created by Cromwell in 1650, and still survive in the British Army.[51] On the contrary, it would be more surprising if the organization of the Spartan army were to be constantly changing, as some modern scholars appear to think. Of course there were changes: the primitive army, perhaps based on kinship-groups and locality, developed into one in which the various units apparently contained a cross-section of those eligible for military service, hoplite equipment and tactics were adopted, the numbers were swelled as a result of the seventh century revolution, and then, as the number of Spartiates began to decline, *hypomeiones* were accepted in increasing numbers. But Tyrtaios would in all essentials have been just as at home in the army of Xenophon's day, as its members apparently were with his songs and his ideals.

Part II

Battle

Chapter 4

Thermopylai

Thermopylai is probably the most famous fight in which the Spartan army ever took part, and it is also the earliest we can re-construct in any detail. As such, it must be included in any account of the Spartan army's achievements. But it is also a battle that passed so rapidly into the realm of legend that it is easy to forget how little we know about it – we do not know, for example, how many men Leonidas had, what his intentions were, or what led to the final catastrophe.[1] The outcome is particularly liable to distort our view of the role played by the Spartans: admiration for their courage may lead us to forget that they formed only a small part of the total number of Greeks engaged, though their king held the supreme command of the Greek army, and that even at the end they were probably outnumbered by the men of Thespiai and of Thebes. Their deaths, moreover, created a myth – the myth of the doomed army that prefers death to surrender. In reality, there is no reason to believe that Leonidas and his men thought that they were doomed, except perhaps on the morning of the final day, and even then they may have thought more of the military reasons for holding on as long as possible than of heroic gestures. It is true that Greeks of a later generation believed that the notion of 'death before dishonour' was part of the Spartan military code (cf. Thucydides 4.40.1), but this was a belief very largely created by Thermopylai itself: the fact of the matter is that since the Spartans very rarely lost battles, and even more rarely were not in a position where retreat was feasible, the question of surrender seldom arose – prisoners were allegedly taken at the 'Battle of the Fetters' early in the sixth century (Herodotos 1.66.4), on Sphakteria in 425 (Thucydides 4.38), and again at Kromnos in 365 (XH 7.4.27), so in this respect Thermopylai was the exception rather than the rule.

The battle was probably fought towards the end of August 480, and formed part of the first real clash between the invading Persian forces, led by

King Xerxes, and the Greeks who had decided to resist. The invasion was
the culmination of some twenty years of intermittent warfare, beginning
with the Athenian and Eretrian involvement in the rebellion of the Greek
states of western Asia Minor against Persian rule, early in the fifth century,
and including the Persian punitive expedition against Athens and Eretria,
which came to grief at Marathon in 490. Sparta had hitherto not actually
taken part in any of the fighting, having rejected the appeal of the Asiatic
Greeks. But when, probably in 491, King Darius had sent envoys to Greece
to demand 'earth and water' from the states of the Aegean and mainland
Greece, in token of submission, the Spartans are alleged (Herodotos 7.133.1)
to have flung his envoys down a well, telling them to get their earth and
water for the king from there. And in the following year, although their
troops had arrived too late to take part in the battle of Marathon, there is no
reason to doubt that they had genuinely wanted to do so (cf., above, p. 73).
Since Marathon, Persian retaliation had been delayed by problems
connected with the succession to Darius, and by a rebellion in Egypt, but
now, judging by the size of their forces – however much Herodotos may have
exaggerated them (cf. 7.61ff., 184–7) – and by the fact that they were led by
their king, the Persians had evidently decided to solve the Greek problem
once and for all.

The Greeks had first thought to hold the pass of Tempe, between Mt
Olympos and Mt Ossa, and had assembled there an army of 10,000 hoplites,
under the command of the Spartan polemarch, Euainetos, probably in the
late spring. However, they had abandoned the position before Xerxes even
crossed the Hellespont, on the advice of Alexander, King of Macedonia, who
warned them of the immense size of Xerxes' forces, and also because they
learned that the pass could easily be turned (Herodotos 7.172–3). Returning
to the Isthmus of Corinth, they had debated where next to try to make a
stand, and had decided to guard the pass at Thermopylai because, says
Herodotos (7.175.1), it was narrower than Tempe, was the only pass and was
nearer their own territory. Herodotos adds (7.175.2) that they knew nothing
of the track by which the position was eventually turned until they learned
of it from the people of Trachis on the spot, and this should be a reminder
that we are not dealing with people equipped with good maps, trained staff
and intelligence services, but with people who had never faced war on this
kind of scale before or fought at such a distance from their homes.
Nevertheless, it is worth stressing, in view of some modern theories that
Thermopylai was never intended to be an 'all-out effort',[2] that both here and
elsewhere (7.175.2, cf. 176.5, 177; 8.15.2) Herodotos clearly implies that the

Greek objective was to prevent Xerxes from penetrating further into Greece, and for this purpose, then as in more recent times, Thermopylai was really the only place that offered a reasonable chance between Tempe and the Isthmus of Corinth. The position actually occupied by Leonidas and his army was the so-called 'Middle Gate', where the modern monument now stands on the left of the National Highway for motorists driving south. Across the highway, the hillock where the Spartans and their Thespiaian comrades probably made their last stand is marked by a slab of pink marble bearing the famous two-line epitaph quoted by Herodotos (7.228.2).[3]

One of the reasons Thermopylai has sometimes been regarded as something less than an all-out effort is the small size of Leonidas' army. According to Herodotos it consisted of only 5,200 hoplites, *plus* the full force of the Opountian Lokrians, and even if we add 900 more Peloponnesians to bring his total of 3,100 from the Peloponnese into line with the epitaph he quotes (7.228.1), and which claimed that 4,000 men from the Peloponnese took part,[4] this is only a small proportion of the forces available, judging by the number of hoplites at Plataea in the following year. Some allowance must be made, it is true, for the number of marines serving with the fleet at the time of Thermopylai. Assuming for the sake of argument that there were at least as many on the Greek ships as there were on the Persian, the 180 Athenian triremes would have required at least 5,400 hoplites (cf. Herodotos 7.184.2), and perhaps as many as 7,200 or more.[5] But Sparta, for example, with only ten triremes at Artemision (Herodotos 8.1.2), could clearly have sent more than 300 hoplites to Thermopylai, however many marines one supposes each of her ships carried, and it is not unreasonable to suppose that the Peloponnese as a whole could have sent up to five or six times as many men as even the epitaph claimed for it.

The explanation for the small number of Spartan troops given by Herodotos (7.206.1) is that the *Karneia* prevented more from being sent at the time, but that they intended to come in full force once the festival was over – Sparta's allies are alleged to have put forward the Olympic festival as their reason for not sending more men. Herodotos sums up his view by saying that 'they sent the fore-runners (τοὺς προδρόμους) not thinking that the war at Thermopylai would be decided so quickly', (7.206.2) just as earlier (7.203.1) he says that Leonidas and those with him persuaded the Opountian Lokrians and Phokians to join them by giving out that they were the 'fore-runners' of a larger army 'expected any day'. Although this explanation should not be dismissed out of hand as a mere pretext,[6] it is not entirely satisfactory even within its own terms, for if the *Karneia* really prevented the Spartans from taking the field, why were any there? At the time of Marathon, when similar religious scruples are said to have prevented the Spartans from acceding to the request brought by Philippides (Herodotos 6.106.3), no troops were sent until the religious objection had been removed (cf. Herodotos 6.120). A possible explanation, suggested above (pp. 70–1) is that Leonidas and the 300 were somehow exempted from the taboo, Leonidas, perhaps, because he was past military age, and his men because they were chosen by lot, and hence, in a sense, with the gods' approval.[7] If this is right we may suppose that the Spartans, realizing that unless they sent *some* troops to Thermopylai, other states were unlikely to be any more forthcoming, decided to bend their religious rules a little on this occasion, whereas at the time of Marathon they could assume that the Athenians would fight in any case.

Another possibility is that the Spartans and their Peloponnesian allies, who were bound to form the hard core of any resistance to the Persians on land, were virtually incapable of really envisaging what this meant, and genuinely thought that the three or four thousand hoplites they mustered would be sufficient, assuming that they were joined by at least as many from north of the Isthmus. If we can believe the figure of 10,000 hoplites given by Herodotos (7.173.2) for the Tempe expedition – which he implies is a round number (κατὰ μυρίους ὁκίιτας) – this indicates the kind of scale the Peloponnesians had in mind, and they perhaps did not fully realize that the demands of their fleet would prevent the Athenians, who were probably present at Tempe in some force, seeing that Themistokles was their commander (Herodotos 7.173.2), from contributing any men at all. But the Boeotians were probably the crucial factor in their miscalculation, and here our judgement of the situation is bound to be blurred by hindsight. We know that the Boeotians, with the exception of the Thespiaians and the Plataeans, eventually 'medized', but was there any reason to believe that this would be the case at the time it was decided to send an army to Thermopylai? Unfortunately, Herodotos does not specify the Greek states that sent delegates to the various conferences of those determined to resist, nor does he say which states contributed contingents to the Tempe expedition, apart from Athens and Sparta herself, but Plutarch, in his essay on the *Malice of Herodotos* (31, *Moralia* 864e), claims that Thebes contributed 500 hoplites under Mnamias and if this is true, it suggests that at the time the Spartans had no reason to doubt that the Boeotians would support them in further resistance. Herodotos does say (7.205.3) that Leonidas was particularly anxious to pick up the contingent from Thebes he took with him to Thermopylai, because of serious accusations of 'medism' against the Thebans, but there is evidently a strong element of bias in Herodotos' remarks about the Thebans both here and in his account of the end of the fight at Thermopylai (7.222 & 233) – bias probably derived from an Athenian or Plataean source, as is suggested by the statement that it was the Theban commander's son who was responsible for the attack on Plataea in March 431, at the outbreak of the Peloponnesian War (Herodotos 7.233.2,cf. Thucydides 2.1.3). In reality it is possible that the Spartans were still confident that the Thebans would support them, though they presumably hoped for more than the 400 hoplites they got: their commander, Leontiades, was probably the hereditary Spartan *proxenos* at Thebes,[8] and it may have been his promises that led to the Spartan miscalculation – indeed, the presence of 700 Thespiaian hoplites in Leonidas' army may have contributed towards Leontiades' failure to deliver, for there was never any love lost between Thebes and Thespiai. If then the Spartans had originally hoped for some hoplites from Athens and, perhaps, Megara, and that the Boeotians would also contribute several thousand, they may have calculated that – with the likely response from Lokris they could at least match the 10,000 men they had had at Tempe, and although they had allegedly been warned by Alexander of Macedonia about the size of Xerxes' forces, they had never actually seen them – hence perhaps their consternation when they actually met them for the first time at Thermopylai (cf. Herodotos 7.207). Nevertheless, a suspicion must remain that the real reason for the small number of Peloponnesian troops at Thermopylai was the reluctance of Sparta and her allies to commit their forces so far to the north, and that the claims made that Leonidas and his men were only 'fore runners', and that the fall of Thermopylai was unexpectedly swift, are essentially false. One cannot help but feel that if the Spartans were prepared to send 300 men, they should have been prepared to send more, though it is arguable that there would have been an even greater disaster if they had, since there is no guarantee that the Anopaia path would have been held, even if there had been more troops there (see below, p. 112).

Whatever the true explanation of the size of Leonidas' army, we may presumably accept that he arrived at the pass with at least 4,200 hoplites (3,100 Peloponnesians and 1,100 Boeotians) – more if there were in fact 4,000 Peloponnesians – and was joined there by 1,000 Phokians and the full force of the Opountian Lokrians (Herodotos 7.202–203.1), estimated by

Diodoros (11.4.7) at 1,000 men, which seems reasonable, but by Pausanias (10.20.2) at not more than 6,000; Diodoros also adds 1,000 Malians, but it seems most unlikely that any organized body of Malian troops can have been with the Greek army once Xerxes had overrun their territory.[9] It was presumably soon after their arrival that the Greeks learned of the track by which the pass could be turned (Herodotos 7.175.2), and sent the 1,000 Phokian hoplites, who volunteered for the task, to guard it (Herodotos 7.212.2, 217.2). Apart from this Herodotos implies that the Greeks simply camped in their chosen position to wait for Xerxes' arrival. Some scholars have accepted Polyainos' story of a raid into the surrounding countryside to clear the area of provisions, but it is not even certain that the story refers to this occasion, and if it does, it is very unlikely to be true: the apparently circumstantial details do not really make sense, the story is not in Herodotos, and it is improbable in itself, for Leonidas is not likely to have dreamt of risking his men in such a raid, at night, in country entirely unknown to most of them – neither the Spartans nor the other Greek hoplites were commandos.[10]

According to Herodotos (7.207), when the Persian host drew near the pass, the Greeks, in a panic, considered withdrawing, but Leonidas, at the urging of the Phokians and Lokrians, voted to stay where they were and to send messengers 'to the cities' bidding them send to their aid, 'since they were too few to resist the army of the Medes'. This story has been doubted, because, it is argued, it is not easy to see what were 'the cities' to which Leonidas is supposed to have directed his appeal – if Peloponnesian they were too far away to be of any use, and if Boeotian Leonidas must have been aware that no more help was likely to be forthcoming. But although all such stories are suspicious, since they look like part of the legend of the overwhelming size of the Persian forces, there is nothing intrinsically improbable about this one: the Greeks may well have been filled with alarm when at last they came face to face with the Persian army and realized that they faced an array the like of which they had never seen, even if it did not run to the millions of men of Herodotos' account, and Leonidas may well have sent off an urgent appeal for more men, without really thinking of the difficulties; it is also likely enough that the Phokians and Lokrians would have been particularly insistent that the pass be held, since they would be the first to suffer if it were to be abandoned.

Xerxes' first move, according to Herodotos (7.208.1), was to send a scout to reconnoitre the Greek position: he returned having merely seen the

Spartans exercising and combing their hair in front of the ancient wall that the Greeks had repaired to use as a means of defence (Herodotos 7.176.5), and on enquiry the Persian king was told by the exiled Spartan king, Demaratos, that this meant the Spartans intended to fight to the death (7.209). Diodoros (11.5.4–5) says that Xerxes sent envoys to order the Greeks to surrender their arms and depart to their own territories, promising to grant them more and better lands if they did so. This is not, in itself, too improbable, since such diplomatic methods were part of the stock-in-trade of the Persian art of war (cf. Herodotos 6.13, 8.136ff., etc.), but in Diodoros' account Xerxes' message elicits an elaborately antithetical and most un-Laconic reply from the Spartan king – far better is Plutarch's version of the reply – though he spoils his story by implying that it was given in a letter: 'come and get them' (μόλων λάβε: *Moralia* 225d), words that are now carved on the plinth supporting the great bronze statue that forms the centre-piece of the modern monument.

The arrival of the Persian army before Thermopylai was followed by a delay of three or four days – Herodotos says (7.210.1) that Xerxes 'let four days go by', but that might include the day of his arrival. His explanation is that the Great King was waiting for the Greeks to run away, which is not as absurd as some modern commentators claim,[12] although it does seem more likely that the delay was due rather either to a desire to avoid a head-on assault while alternatives were explored, or to the difficulties the Persian fleet was experiencing, for some part of Xerxes' four-day wait before Thermopylai must surely coincide with the three-day storm, which is said to have pinned his fleet to the coast of Magnesia (Herodotos 7.191.2).[13] In the end, however, an assault was ordered, perhaps after news had at last come that the fleet had safely weathered Cape Sepias, and the Median and Kissian contingents moved forward to carry out their king's orders (Herodotos 7.210.1).

Herodotos is disappointingly vague about the epic fight that ensued, but he does make the obvious point that the Persians could not make full use of their numerical superiority because of the confined terrain, and also remarks that their spears were shorter than those of the Greeks (7.211.2). The latter fought in relays, contingent by contingent (Herodotos 7.212.2), and the Spartans at least adopted tactics that involved a series of feigned retreats followed by a swift about-turn when the enemy broke ranks to pursue (Herodotos 7.211.3). These were probably designed to nullify the effects of Persian archery by denying them a static target and by keeping the fighting fluid and at close-quarters.[14] It goes without saying that such tactics could only have been carried out by highly trained and disciplined troops, trained to move as one as the Spartans were, and one doubts whether the other Greeks were capable of them, though they may have been able to imitate them after a fashion when they saw how effective they were.

The second day's fighting was much like the first (Herodotos 7.212), but during the course of it the traitor Ephialtes came to Xerxes with the vital information about the Anopaia path probably, as has been pointed out,[15] the Persians had been aware of its existence but needed to find someone to guide them for, as anyone who has ever done any walking in Greece will confirm, it is very easy to take a wrong fork and go hopelessly astray, particularly at night.[16] The exact route of the path, particularly in its early course, has long been disputed, but most modern commentators are agreed that it descends by way of the modern village of Dhrakospilia to the vicinity of the so-called 'East Gate' at Thermopylai, and that the position occupied by the Phokians was somewhere in the vicinity of Old Dhrakospilia (Palaiodhrakospilia).[17] The mere fact of the continuing dispute about the actual route of the path shows that there are a number of possibilities, and how easy it would have been for the Persians to go astray. It is not certain how many there were with Hydarnes: Herodotos implies (7.215) that he took all 10,000 of his Immortals, and although this seems too many, some commentators may have gone too far in the other direction.[18]

The Phokians are alleged only to have become aware of the approach of the enemy because of the rustling sound their feet made tramping through the oak leaves fallen along the track (Herodotos 7.218.1), and this, if true, only goes to show how unprofessional the average Greek soldiers were, since it presumably means that the Phokians had not posted any pickets. Now, however, they hastily donned their arms, and the Persians, we are told, were hardly less alarmed at finding armed men barring their way. But, on being reassured by Ephialtes that they were not Spartans – a telling point, but one wonders how he could tell (did Spartan shields already bear the *lambda?*) – Hydarnes, too, deployed for battle (Herodotos 7.218.2). If the Phokians had stayed where they were Hydarnes might yet have found it difficult to break through, but after a volley or two his opponents retired to a nearby ridge, assuming that the Persians would follow them and determined to sell their lives dearly; the Persians, however, simply ignored them and continued on their way (Herodotos 7.218.3). Modern commentators have criticized Leonidas for not stiffening the Phokians with more experienced troops or at least putting them under a Spartan officer.[19] But this is, again, to misunderstand the nature of the Greek army: Leonidas could not just whistle up a battalion of *Chasseurs Alpins* when he learned of the Anopaia path, and the Phokians were probably as experienced in mountain warfare as any Greek troops would have been – Spartan officers would hardly have known more about it, and there is no telling whether the Phokians would have obeyed them. On this occasion the Persians displayed their 'professionalism', the Greeks their essentially 'amateur' approach to warfare.

Herodotos says (7.219.1) that the first intimation of disaster for the Greeks at Thermopylai was given by the seer, Megistias, who 'looking into the sacrificial animals declared that the death to come would be with them at dawn', and deserters, too, brought news of the turning-movement, while it was still night. Diodoros (11.8.5) names one deserter as Tyrrhastiadas of Kyme, and since he here, presumably, as elsewhere, drew upon Ephoros, who also came from Kyme, it is tempting to think that he may preserve a fragment of local knowledge; however, the tale is just as likely to be an invention of local patriotism.[20] In any case, it is quite impossible to accept Diodoros' story (11.9.4ff.) of the night-raid by Leonidas and his men on Xerxes' camp, despite its adoption by the makers of the film *The Three Hundred Spartans*, and despite some modern commentators toying with the notion that there might be some truth in it – it is typical of their curious picture of ancient Greek warfare that the famous raid carried out by the Long Range Desert Group on Rommel's headquarters should have been cited as a parallel, for this is precisely the point: the Long Range Desert Group was trained for this kind of thing, the Spartans were not.[21] Herodotos, too, clearly knew nothing of the story

Even if we dismiss Diodoros' story, it is still difficult enough to be certain what exactly happened when Leonidas finally learned definitely of the approach of Hydarnes' troops from the 'day-watchers' who came running down from the hills as day was breaking (Herodotos 7.219.1). Herodotos first says (7.219.2) that the Greeks took council and that opinions were divided, some arguing that they could not leave their position, others the opposite: in the end, he implies, some just withdrew and went off home, while others prepared to stay with Leonidas. He then goes on to say (7.220.1) that 'it is said' that Leonidas himself sent away those who went because he was anxious that they should not be destroyed, but considered that there was no possible fitting way for himself and the Spartiates who were with him to leave the post they had originally been assigned to guard.

Herodotos apparently tries to reconcile these two traditions by declaring that he himself was rather inclined to the view that Leonidas sent his allies away when he saw that they were not eager to see the danger through with him, but that it was not right for him to withdraw, and that as a result 'great glory was left to him and the well-being of Sparta was not wiped out' (7.220.2) – he explains this last statement by reference to the oracle that had foretold that either Sparta would be destroyed by the barbarians, or Lakedaimon would mourn the death of a king of the race of Herakles (7.220.4). Finally, he repeats his view that Leonidas sent the allies away rather than that they went off 'in so ill-disciplined a manner', as a result of disagreement (7.220.4), citing as evidence the fact that when Leonidas tried to send the seer, Megistias, away, he chose to stay, and sent his son instead – presumably the son was at least indirectly the source of this story (7.221).

It is clear, then, that what happened on that final morning was already the subject of controversy in Herodotos' day, and we can thus never hope to know for certain. There are, basically, two problems – one concerning those who went away, the other those who stayed – and in the case of those who went away, Herodotos presents us with simple alternatives: either they just de-camped, or they were sent away. There is no warrant in Herodotos' narrative for the modern theory that they were really sent to hold off Hydarnes and the Immortals, and the theory is improbable in itself:[22] if they were sent away, it is much more likely that Herodotos is right that Leonidas was simply concerned to save their lives, and on the whole it seems probable that they were sent, possibly after Leonidas had called for volunteers to stay and had seen how unwilling most of them were, for evidently no stigma was subsequently attached to their departure.[23]

The second problem is, if anything, even more intractable: why did Leonidas remain with the Spartans, Thespiaians and Thebans? We may, presumably, dismiss the notion, hinted at by Herodotos' mention of the oracle, that he deliberately sacrificed himself and his men as an act of *devotio,* so that Sparta herself might be saved – rather, the oracle must surely be seen as a *post eventum* attempt to boost morale after the death of the Spartan king.[24] Nor should we accept Herodotos' repeated hints that it was a matter of honour that Spartans did not retreat (7.220.1–2) – there is really no reason to doubt that Leonidas would have retreated if he could have done. If this is accepted, we must look to the military situation for an explanation, but we must not look too far: it is unlikely, for example, that the Spartan king decided to fight on as long as possible in order to give the fleet a chance either to win a decisive victory or to get through the dangerous narrows of the Euripos before the Persians blocked them, for the first presupposes the surely erroneous view that the Greeks were really seeking a decision at sea, and that it was Leonidas' role that was subordinate, and the second assumes that there really was a danger of the Persians blocking the Euripos too quickly for the Greek fleet to get through in safety.[25]

By far the most plausible explanation of what happened is that when Leonidas received the report of the day-watchers, he realized that the pass was untenable and decided to save as many of his troops as possible. We may suppose he reasoned, however, that if he and his whole army tried to retreat, the Persians, with their strength in cavalry and light troops, equipped with bows and arrows, might well catch them on the march and annihilate them. Hence a rear-guard would be necessary, in which case this would have to include himself and his Spartans at least, since he could hardly hope to be obeyed if he ordered others to stay, while he and the Spartans withdrew.[26] It has been objected that he would not have known, on receipt of the day-watchers' report, that the Phokians had failed to hold the upper path, since the day-watchers reported 'as day was breaking' (ἤδη διαφαινούσης ἡμέρης: Herodotos 7.219.1), and the Phokians were only attacked 'as dawn was breaking' (cf. ἠώς τε δὴ διέφαινε: 7.217.1). But this is mere pedantry: dawn does not 'break' instantaneously, and if the day-watchers set off immediately it became apparent that the Phokians had failed to hold the path, they could surely have run the 5 or 6 miles to Leonidas' headquarters in less than an hour, and could still have been described as 'running down from the hills as day was breaking'. Indeed, it is possibly significant that Herodotos uses the word 'dawn' (ἠώς) of the time at which the Phokians were attacked, but 'day' (ἡμέρη) of the time when the day-watchers reported. In any case, the precise timing is really irrelevant: it can hardly be doubted that sooner or later Leonidas received news that a Persian force was about to descend in his rear, and the mere fact that a large part of his army managed to withdraw is sufficient proof that he did have time to discuss what was to be done.[27]

The next problem concerns the choice of contingents to form a rear-guard. The inclusion of the Spartans was inevitable, as was argued above, but why the Thespiaians and Thebans? The choice of the 700 hoplites of Thespiai has even been used[28] as an objection to the whole idea of a rear-guard, because, it is argued, Leonidas would hardly have asked the whole hoplite army of a single state to face death with him and his Spartans. But even if it is true that Leonidas realized that the rear-guard was almost bound to be destroyed (see below), is it so inconceivable that the men of Thespiai volunteered to stay, as Herodotos says they did (7.222)? Indeed, the idea that Leonidas had a choice in the matter may be quite wrong, since even the Peloponnesian contingents might not have obeyed him.[29] if the Thespiaians really volunteered to stay, it might have been because their homeland was bound to be overrun, once Thermopylai fell, and this might also be the real reason for the Thebans staying – in their case, too, they might have feared the vengeance of their fellow-citizens, if the majority of the Boeotians were in fact inclined to medize.[30] In any case, the tradition that the Thebans were retained as hostages (Herodotos 7.222) is probably just the product of Athenian bias against the family of their commander (see above, pp. 108–109) – as Plutarch long ago pointed out (*On the Malice of Herodotos*, 31 – *Moralia* 865d), if Leonidas had really wanted to keep them as hostages, he would have been better advised to send them off under guard to the Isthmus.

The final question to be asked is whether Leonidas assumed that he and those who were staying with him, for whatever reason, were going to their deaths, or whether he thought they might still get away by holding their position only as long as their line of retreat was still open behind them. One argument that has been used in favour of the latter is that the Athenian Abronichos, who had been attached to the army to convey news of it to the fleet, is implied not to have left until all was over (Herodotos 8.21), whereas he might have been expected to have been sent off before the final battle if Leonidas assumed that he and the rear-guard had no chance.[31] But Herodotos' report of Abronichos' message is in fact extremely vague – 'he reported,' he says, 'what had happened to Leonidas and his army' – and in any case, even if Herodotos meant by this the disaster that had befallen the rear-guard, it is possible that Abronichos' message in reality was, simply, that Leonidas was about to beat a fighting retreat, for it was vital to warn the fleet that the Persians might soon be in a position to block the Euripos. Thus, whether or not he thought he had a chance, Leonidas is likely to have sent Abronichos to Eurybiades as soon as he decided his position was untenable.

Whatever the truth about the dispositions Leonidas made in the light of the information he had received from Megistias, the deserters and the day-watchers, there is no reason to doubt that in the end he was left with those who survived from his original 300 Spartiates, presumably with their attendant helots, possibly with a contingent of *perioikoi*, though Herodotos' omission of all reference to them really precludes this, and with the remnants of the 700 Thespiaians and 400 Thebans. This, at all events, is the version of Herodotos (7.222), but it is just possible that he has forgotten the smallest of all the contingents that fought at Thermopylai, the eighty gallant hoplites of Mycenae, for Pausanias (10.20.2) claims that they stayed to fight to the end with the Spartans and the men of Thespiai, and not only is this so odd a claim that it may well be true, but we may also suppose the Mycenaeans feared the vengeance of the Argives if the Persians triumphed.[32]

According to Herodotos (7.223.1), when the sun rose, Xerxes poured libations and then launched his attack, 'waiting for the time when the market-place is just about full' (i.e. about nine or ten o'clock in the morning). Herodotos claims that the king had been bidden to do this by Ephialtes (7.223.1), and implies by his remark that the descent of the Anopaia path was quicker than the ascent and march round, that Xerxes' attack was supposed to coincide with Hydarnes moving into position to block the Greeks' retreat. As it turned out, however, Xerxes' attack came well before Hydarnes' arrival. The explanation may be, simply, that it was too difficult to synchronize the attacks and that Hydarnes' march took longer than expected.[33] Alternatively, it is possible that Xerxes deliberately attacked early in order to pin the Greeks down until Hydarnes could spring the trap. The Greek response was to advance further out from their position by the Phokian wall than they had done on the previous two days, and to deploy in the wider part of the pass, and although Herodotos says (7.223.2 & 4) that this was because they knew they were going to their deaths, this is not necessarily the case: a bold front now might disconcert Xerxes' forces and deter them from pressing the pursuit too closely when the time came to retreat.[34]

Herodotos claims (7.223.3) that the losses among the Persians were even heavier than in the earlier fighting, many of the enemy being forced into the sea or trampled underfoot as their officers literally whipped them forward into the fight, and even allowing for an element of exaggeration, he may well be right: once again the Greeks were denying the Persian archers a static target at which to shoot by advancing to close quarters, and if they were deployed on a broader front – if they were formed up eight deep, for example, their line might have been about 125 shields long – the losses they would have inflicted would have been all the greater: Herodotos' account of Plataea shows just how formidable Greek hoplites were when pitted against more lightly-armed Persian infantry in a mêlée (cf. 9.62.2–3, 63.2). It is indeed possible that the Greeks were carried away, and that this was the reason for the reckless abandon with which they fought, if we are to believe Herodotos (cf. παραχρεώμενοί τε καὶ ἀτέοντες: 7.223.4), rather than their realization that death was upon them. Even now it might have been too late to retreat, but then Leonidas himself fell, and not only would this have left the Greeks momentarily leaderless, but the Spartans would never have been prepared to leave the king's body where it lay – one thinks of what apparently happened at Leuktra (cf. XH 6.4.13, and see below, p. 186). Thus, far from the Greeks' retreating, an even more ferocious struggle developed over the king's body, the Greeks eventually recovering it after four times flinging the enemy back (Herodotos 7.224–225.1) with what Herodotos describes as 'much shoving' (ὠθισμὸς ... πολλός).

At last, however, the Greeks learned of Hydarnes' approach, and withdrew back into the narrow part of the pass, crossing the Phokian wall, and taking up a position on the hillock, where, Herodotos says (7.225.2), 'the stone lion now stands as a monument to Leonidas.' Alas! the lion has long since gone, but the hillock has been securely identified[35] and is now marked again by a slab of pink marble, set on a circle of stones, and bearing the epitaph on the Spartiates quoted by Herodotos (7.228.2). Here the remnants of the Greek army took their stand, except for the Thebans who, according to Herodotos (7.225.2), broke away from the rest and ran towards the enemy, holding out their hands in token of surrender and shouting that they had only fought under compulsion: Herodotos adds the surely authentic detail that some were killed, before, on Xerxes' orders, the rest were taken prisoner and branded with the royal mark. There is not much reason to doubt that some at least of the Thebans surrendered and survived, but how much of the rest of the story is due to the bias of Herodotos' informants it is difficult to tell.[36]

The final act in the drama was probably soon over: Herodotos implies that none of the Greeks had spears left and were fighting now with swords, if they still had them, and even with hands and teeth. But the Persians in front pushed down the Phokian wall and poured through the breach, and Hydarnes and his men arrived at last to take them in the rear. Significantly, Herodotos says that 'the barbarians overwhelmed them with missiles' (κατέχωσαν οἱ βάρβαροι βάλλοντες: 7.225.3), which suggests that even now, in the end, the Persians feared to close, and having at last found a static target, preferred to shoot their way to final victory.[37] But one cannot press his account too closely since one is bound to ask how he learned the details, if all the Greeks were killed, though it is possible that some of the Thebans who survived were still near enough to see what happened, and that their story somehow found its way to Herodotos, one of whose informants, we know (cf. 9.16.1), was the Boeotian, Thersander of Orchomenos.

It is Thermopylai which, for the ancient Greeks and for later generations, exemplifies the ultimate devotion to duty of the Spartan soldier. The destruction of Leonidas and his men represented a victory for the Persians, and the publication of the oracle foretelling the death of a king of Sparta if Sparta were to be preserved (Herodotos 7.220.4), may well indicate the consternation with which the news of Thermopylai was initially received. But the epitaphs set up on the spot (Herodotos 7.228.1–3) and the way in which Herodotos writes about the episode, shows that at least when all was over the Greeks looked back on Thermopylai with pride, and it is possible that the heroic resistance there, coupled with the limited successes attained by the fleet off Artemision, was a boost to Greek morale in the fighting to come – Dunkirk is a vivid reminder of how even a defeat can restore a nation's pride and stiffen its will to resist. The receding of the sea and the building of the National Highway through Thermopylai has all but ruined the spot, but to sit on the hillock where the last stand was made and watch the sun come up over Euboea is an unforgettable experience, and however morally barren or reprehensible we may find the Spartan ideal, in the ultimate resort they and the gallant Thespiaians who died with them did die for something worthwhile. The Spartan epitaph is perhaps the most famous of all such inscriptions (Herodotos 7.228.2): 'Stranger, go tell the Lakedaimonians that here we lie, obedient to their words.'

Chapter 5

Plataea

Following the forcing of the Thermopylai pass, and the withdrawal of the Greek fleet from Artemision, all central Greece lay open to the invading Persians. The Greek fleet put in at Salamis, at the urgent request of the Athenians and now, if not before, the population of Attica was evacuated. The Persian forces poured southwards, overrunning Attica and capturing the city of Athens, empty of all save a few fanatical or dedicated defenders of the Acropolis. But three weeks or so later, towards the end of September, the Persian fleet was heavily defeated in the straits between Salamis and the mainland and Xerxes himself returned to Asia, though he left an army behind him under his brother-in-law, Mardonios. Mardonios wintered in Thessaly and after failing to win over the Athenians through the agency of Alexander, King of Macedonia, marched south again in the summer of 479, to re-occupy a once more deserted Athens. After considerable Athenian pressure (cf. Herodotos 8. 144.4–5, 9.6–7), the Spartans at last mobilized – it is somehow typical of them that they should have marched in the end without telling the Athenians, so that when Athenian envoys arrived to issue a final ultimatum, threatening to go over to the Persians, they were blandly informed that the Spartan army had already reached Orestheion on its march against 'the strangers' (Herodotos 9.11.2).

The campaign that followed, culminating in the battle of Plataea, is perhaps the most interesting of the Persian Wars since it allows us to see for the first time how easily the Persians might have won. The Greek army was again commanded by a Spartan – the regent Pausanias – and although the Spartan contingent formed less than a seventh of the whole Greek force, if Herodotos' figures are correct it was the Spartans, *perioikoi* and Tegeates who played the principal part in the victory. The 5,000 Spartans who took part, moreover, possibly formed the largest body of Spartan regular soldiers ever to take part in a single battle, and if they all really were Spartiates, as

Herodotos describes them, this was almost certainly the largest number of Spartiates ever to fight together.[1]

Plataea is a curiously neglected battle in some respects: in recent years, for example, two popular books have appeared with the titles *The Year of Salamis* and *The Year of Thermopylae*, but we have yet to see a *Year of Plataea*.[2] However, whatever some scholars seem to think, in the end Plataea was at least as 'decisive' as Salamis, since even the Peloponnese could not have been conquered by sea-power alone, and however true it may be that the Isthmus of Corinth could not have been held if the Greek fleet had been defeated, it is equally true that without Plataea all Greece north of the Isthmus might well have remained in Persian hands, with incalculable results for the future attitude of the Athenians and hence of the better part of the Greek fleet. In the end nearly all wars, except those involving islands or other states dependent on sea-power, are won and lost by the clash of armies.

Now Mardonios, having been warned by the Argives that the Spartans were at last on the move, began to withdraw from Attica to Boeotia. He turned back once on hearing that a detachment of the Spartan army had reached Megara, and his cavalry overran the Megarid – the farthest west the Persians ever came, as Herodotos says (9.14) – but when he learned that in fact the whole Greek army was assembling at the Isthmus, he promptly withdrew via Dekeleia and Tanagra to the territory of Thebes, taking up a position along the river Asopos, stretching from Erythrai, past Hysiai, to the territory of Plataea (Herodotos 9.15.3). The natural interpretation of this is that the Persians lay south of the Asopos, where Erythrai and Plataea were certainly situated, but later in the campaign they were north of the Asopos (cf. Herodotos 9.36 & 59.1), and it must be presumed that the stockade they constructed when they first arrived (Herodotos 9.15.2) also lay north of the Asopos. It seems probable, then, that Herodotos mentions Erythrai, Hysiai and Plataea in his description of the position merely to express how far it stretched, since there were no such localities on the north bank of the river to which he could allude.[3]

Herodotos says nothing of the route followed by the Greek army from Eleusis to Boeotia, except that the Greeks first learned of the Persian position along the Asopos when they reached Erythrai in Boeotia (9.19.3), and unfortunately this place has still not yet been securely located, despite the confident renaming of the modern village that used to be called Kriekouki.[4] Ancient Erythrai may have lain on the ridge now occupied by the

Pantanassa chapel, about 2 kilometres east of Kriekouki, or even further to the east, but in either event it seems more likely that the Greek army came over by the so-called Gyphtokastro pass than by one further east, and then deployed eastwards along the foothills of Kithairon. At all events, the first position of the Greek army, which was along the foothills of Kithairon (Herodotos 9.19.3), probably lay east of Kriekouki and it was here that the first fighting took place, when Mardonios launched his cavalry against the Greek position.

Some elaborate theories have been advanced to explain why Mardonios attacked with his cavalry in this way – for example that the attack was launched as the Greeks began to debouch from the hills, in accordance with the best modern principles of warfare.[5] However, Mardonios is most unlikely to have known anything about such principles and Herodotos clearly implies that he only ordered the attack when the Greeks would not come down into the plain (9.20). Nor does it make much sense to suggest that he wanted to test out his cavalry against hoplites under such conditions[6] – one would not have thought that an experienced Persian general, as Mardonios was, would have needed to experiment in this kind of way after a generation of fighting Greeks. A more Machiavellian idea is that Mardonios knew that his cavalry would fail and hoped thereby to lure the Greeks into descending into flatter country,[7] but it seems very improbable that a Persian general would have been willing to risk the possibility that some of his crack units might suffer heavy losses, with a consequent serious loss of morale, in order to lure the enemy down into just the kind of country where his cavalry would be needed.

Such notions ultimately depend upon the assumption that Mardonios wanted a battle, but it is not at all certain that this was the case. It is true that Herodotos says that the Persian general was eager for battle (cf. 9.37.1, 41.4), but it is difficult to see how he could have known this, and Mardonios' withdrawal from Attica hardly suggests that he was eager to confront the Greek army. Herodotos argues (9.13.3), and modern commentators have repeated, that Attica was not good cavalry country and that the exits from it were dangerously narrow, but the plain of Eleusis or the main plain around Athens itself are surely just as suitable for cavalry as Boeotia, as Anchimolios and the Spartans had found to their cost in the late sixth century (Herodotos 5.63.3–4), and the exits from the Theban plain were not all that good in the fifth century when the Kopais basin was still under water. Later, too, after the defeat of his cavalry and when the Greeks had moved down to the

Asopos, Mardonios made no attempt to move back from the Asopos, and although the river is not much of a barrier, if he really did want to lure the Greeks into good cavalry country, blocking their path at the Asopos was hardly the way to do it.

When a general attacks he usually wants either to destroy the enemy or to drive him back, and the natural explanation for Masistios' cavalry attack on the first Greek position is that Mardonios thereby hoped, if not to destroy the Greeks – he was probably too experienced to imagine he could achieve that in the circumstances – at least to inflict such losses upon them, and to give them such a taste of what his cavalry could do that they would withdraw. It would have been a severe psychological set-back for the Greeks, if, having once gathered the greatest army any of them had ever seen, other than the Persian, they found it could accomplish nothing, and the probability is that their army would have broken up in despair, leaving it once more open to Mardonios to continue the diplomatic warfare upon which he set considerable store, judging from his attempts to wheedle the Athenians away from their compatriots (cf. Herodotos 8.140aff., 9.4.1ff.).

Herodotos, who may have got the details from the family of the Athenian officer Olympiodoros, who played a significant part in the engagement,[9] describes how the Persian cavalry attacked by squadrons,[10] the brunt of the assault falling upon the Megarians who happened to be stationed in the most vulnerable part of the line – Diodoros, inevitably, has the attack take place at night (11.30.2). Hard-pressed, the Megarians appealed for help and Pausanias allegedly called for volunteers, whereupon the Athenians alone responded by sending a picked force of 300 men under Olympiodoros, son of Lampon, with an additional force of archers (Herodotos 9.21.3–22.1). One is bound to be suspicious of the story that only the Athenians were willing to undertake the task, but the suggestion that they did so merely because they were next in line to the Megarians[11] will not do: the only evidence that they were is Herodotos' account of the disposition of the Greek forces in the next stage of the campaign (9.28.6), and even there the Plataeans are said to have come between the Megarians and the Athenians. More likely is the explanation that the Athenians alone had archers, as Herodotos hints (9.22.1, 60.3).[12] Nor should too much emphasis be laid on Herodotos' statement that Olympiodoros' men were 'picked' (λονάδες):[13] this is much more likely to reflect the way in which Herodotos heard the story, or a compliment on his part to his informant, than to be accurate – there is no reason to believe that any such force existed in the Athenian army in the fifth century and it is difficult to see why it should.[14] In any case, it was one of the archers with Olympiodoros' force who eventually brought the fight to a successful conclusion when he hit the Persian commander's horse in the flank with an arrow (Herodotos 9.22.1). The horse reared and threw its rider, the Athenians immediately surged forward and, after striking repeatedly in vain at the Persian's corslet, at last killed him with a thrust in the eye (Herodotos 9.22.2) – Plutarch (*Aristcides* 14.5) says with the spiked butt of a javelin, which suggests that he was not killed by a hoplite, if it is true. The Persian cavalry, missing their leader's commands as they wheeled for another attack some distance away, charged *en masse* to recover the body but were eventually driven off when the rest of the Greek army came up to help the Athenians (Herodotos 9.22.3).

Whether it had been Mardonios' intention or not, the Greek success against the Persian cavalry certainly did encourage them to move to another position where, in particular, they could find better water-supplies (Herodotos 9.25.2).[15] Herodotos implies that the new position involved moving *down* from the old (cf. ἐπικαταβῆναι: loc.cit.), and says that it lay in Plataean territory. More particularly he describes it as 'near the Gargaphia spring and the *temenos* of the hero Androkrates, along hills of no great height and flat ground' (9.25.3). Unfortunately neither the spring nor the *temenos* can be securely located. The spring is usually identified either with the one now called Alepotrypi, some 500 metres south-west of the chapel of Ayios Ioannis, or the one called Rhetsi, about a kilometre south-east of the chapel. Either of these identifications would locate the Greek right wing (cf. Herodotos 9.28.2 & 49.3) more than 2 kilometres from the river Asopos, near which the Greek position is repeatedly implied to have been (cf. Herodotos 9.31.1, 36, 40 and, especially, 49.3), but the fact that the Persians were later able to spoil the spring, apparently with little or no opposition (Herodotos 9.49.2), suggests that it was actually some distance from the Spartan position, which was probably on the higher ground where the chapel of Ayios Ioannis is situated, now often called the Asopos ridge. The shrine of Androkrates, similarly, may have been some distance behind the Greek front line for Thucydides (3.24.1–2) mentions the shrine and appears to locate it on the right of the road from Plataea to Thebes, on any natural interpretation of his words, and not more than seven stades, i.e. c.1,300 metres, from the former. In both cases, however, there may have been no other landmarks nearer the river that Herodotos could have used to locate the Greek position, and we should also remember that nearly 40,000 hoplites, to say nothing of about the same number of soldier-servants, would have occupied a fairly large area when encamped. The Athenians, who were on the left of the line (Herodotos 9.28.6), were also apparently positioned on comparatively high ground, since they are said to have turned 'down into the plain' (κάτω ... ἐς τὸ πεδίον: Herodotos 9.56.2), when they set out to join the Spartans on the final morning, and it is probable that their front-line was on what is now called Pyrgos hill, to the left of the direct route from Plataea to Thebes and about 4 kilometres slightly north-west of the chapel of Ayios Ioannis. The Greek position, then, would have extended from Pyrgos hill on the left to the Asopos ridge on the right, with the centre in the relatively low ground astride the Plataea Thebes road, the whole position perhaps extending back to the shrine of Androkrates and the Gargaphia spring. This position could loosely be described as 'on the Asopos' (ἐπὶ τῷ᾽ Ασωπῷ: Herodotos 9. 31.1).[16]

Having brought the Greeks to their new position, Herodotos introduces a number of digressions – the dispute between the Tegeates and the Athenians as to which were to have the left wing (9.26–28.1), the contingents and numbers of the Greek forces (28.2–30), the corresponding totals for the Persian army (31–32), and the stories of the two seers, Teisamenos and Hegesistratos (33–38.1). Of these the two passages detailing the rival armies are the most important for our purposes. The figures for the Greek army have been doubted,[17] but there is no good reason to do so and, certainly, if one does one might as well give up any hope of estimating the size of Pausanias' army. If there really were 38,700 hoplites on the field, this was the largest hoplite army ever assembled, and this should constantly be borne in mind in attempting to determine what happened. Herodotos also reckoned that the Greeks had no fewer than 69,500 light troops, allowing seven helots to each Spartan and one batman to each of the other hoplites (9.29).[18] But it is very unlikely that there were really 35,000 helots at Plataea, despite what Herodotos says – apart from anything else, there hardly seems room for them on the battlefield or in the complicated manoeuvres that took place, and at most we should probably assume one batman to each hoplite. Their military value was probably not very high: modern scholars have suggested that they were mostly left to guard Kithairon, but this is pure supposition based on their apparent absence from the fighting in the plain and the apparent inability of the Persians to extend their raiding into the hills.[19] However, the one is better accounted for precisely by the unimportance of the soldier-servants and the second by the difficulties the Persian cavalry would soon have encountered had they ventured into the hills – they are not good cavalry country. In any case, how would the average hoplite have reacted to being deprived of his soldier-servant? Herodotos, finally, rounds off his total of hoplites and light troops (38,700 + 69,500) to 110,000, by the addition of 1,800 Thespiaians, who, he says (9.30), were present but had no arms, i.e. were not hoplites. This is curtly dismissed by some commentators[20] but it is not impossible that all the hoplites this tiny town could field had been killed at Thermopylai, and yet that other able-bodied men from the town were present in the army – its population had presumably taken refuge with the Athenians before or after Thermopylai.

It is much more difficult to arrive at a convincing total for the Persian army. Herodotos (9.32.2) says that the Persians and their Asiatic allies numbered 300,000 foot, and guesses that their Greek allies numbered 50,000 foot – he gives no figures for the cavalry in either case. These totals are obviously too high, but attempts to arrive at more realistic ones are bound up with the whole problem of the size of Xerxes' forces and are mostly pure guesswork. In the case of Plataea, the size of the stockade constructed by Mardonios, if each of its sides was really ten stades (i.e. c. 1,850m) long, as Herodotos says (9.15.3), and if it was only intended to hold the Asiatic troops, suggests a total of c. 100,000 for these latter, at most, and one very much doubts whether the medizing Greeks brought the total to more than 120,000 men.[21]

Mardonios had moved westwards up the left bank of the Asopos to cover the new Greek position (Herodotos 9.31.1), but there then followed a period of inaction lasting for eight days, according to Herodotos (9.39.11). This fits in well with the view of Mardonios' intentions suggested above (pp. 122–3), but it is, perhaps, less easy to see why Pausanias waited, since his advance to the new position suggests that he was intending to fight, as must surely have been the case. The answer is, possibly, that he was waiting for more troops to arrive, as they were all the time according to Herodotos (9.38.2, 11.1) – the contingents from Mantineia and Elis, for example, arrived after the battle (Herodotos 9.77). But delay is normal when two armies come face to face like this and Pausanias may well have preferred to wait for the Persians to attack him rather than venture to cross the Asopos.[22]

After eight days had passed, according to Herodotos, Timagenidas of Thebes advised Mardonios to 'guard the exits from Kithairon' (9.38.2), in the hope of cutting off some of the Greek reinforcements. Following this advice Mardonios sent his cavalry to the exit from the so-called 'Three

Heads' or 'Oak Heads' pass,[23] where it caught a pack-train of 500 beasts of burden bringing food from the Peloponnese to the Greek army, and annihilated it, sparing neither beast nor man (Herodotos 9.39). We can probably discount the notion that Mardonios needed such advice from a Theban, but if it is true that he waited more than a week before employing his cavalry in this way, one wonders why, since the move seems so obvious. Perhaps his cavalry needed some reorganization and time to restore its morale following the death of its commander, Masistios, or possibly the Persian general was simply hoping that the Greeks would go away.

This once again raises the question of Mardonios' intentions: it is often said that his objective was to bring the Greeks to battle in country suitable for his army, particularly his cavalry,[24] and this was the view of Herodotos (cf. 9.13.3, 41.4). But his actions, as opposed to his intentions as recorded by Herodotos, are susceptible to the interpretation that he wished to avoid battle, if possible, and only finally fought when he thought he had an opportunity too good to be missed. Thus, although the cavalry attack on the Greek supply-lines could have been intended to provoke the Greeks to battle, it is more likely to have been intended to drive them back to Kithairon in order to protect their supplies: it was followed by two more days of comparative inactivity, if we are to believe Herodotos (9.40), although the Persian cavalry continued to harass the Greeks along the Asopos. Similarly, although Herodotos says that on the eleventh day after discussing the matter with his subordinates and allies Mardonios decided to bring about a pitched battle, rejecting in particular the advice of Artabazos to withdraw to Thebes where there was an abundance of supplies for man and beast (9.41–3), the next day merely saw a continuation of the harassing tactics of the Persian cavalry (Herodotos 9.49).

One is bound to ask how Herodotos learned of discussions between high-ranking Persian generals and one suspects that this is part and parcel of his story that during the night that followed the conference Alexander, King of Macedonia, rode over to the Greek lines and told the Athenian commanders of Mardonios' intentions, advising them to hang on if the attack did not materialize because the Persians only had a few days supply of food left (9.44–5) – clearly the source of this episode, as of so many others, was Athenian, and it was designed to exonerate the King of Macedonia from the charge of medism.[25] If there was such a discussion in the Persian high-command it is more likely that Mardonios rejected the idea of withdrawing, not in favour of attacking but simply in favour of staying where he was and continuing with his attempts to persuade the Greeks to withdraw. As was argued above (p. 123), if he could have achieved this he would have won a considerable psychological victory, and it is very doubtful if the Greeks would have been able to gather another such army once the present one had dispersed, as it is likely to have done if it had withdrawn from Boeotia with nothing accomplished.[26]

Apart from personal motives and the general contempt for the Greeks as soldiers the Persians seem to have held (cf. Herodotos 7.9), there would seem to be only two reasons why Mardonios should have wished to fight a battle – one that his army really was short of supplies, the other that the situation in western Asia Minor made it necessary to finish the Greek campaign as soon as possible.[27] But neither of these motives was probably really as compelling as some think. It is probably an erroneous assumption that the Persian army was originally, to a large extent, to be supplied by sea, for although co-operation between the army and the navy was clearly a cardinal feature of the original strategy, there were periods when they were out of contact with each other for a considerable time, even in 480, and in any case the Persian navy would itself probably have needed every ounce of supplies it could carry or convoy. It should not be forgotten that the Persian fleet, even if it was only half as strong as Herodotos says, would have contained well over 100,000 men and that the fighting ships, the triremes, were not built to carry supplies for any length of time – the 'food-carrying vessels' (σιτανωνοὶ ὁλκάδες: Herodotos 7.191.1), which had accompanied the fleet, would have been there to supply the fleet itself not the army. Hence there is no reason to believe that Mardonios' army in 479 was any worse off in the matter of supplies than the full army had been during the previous year: it must always have been planned that the army should mainly live off the land and although there would certainly have been problems in feeding perhaps 100,000 extra mouths in Boeotia during the several weeks of the Plataea campaign, the Greeks would have experienced the same problems, possibly worse since they did not have a comparatively large city like Thebes at their immediate backs.

The second alleged motive for Mardonios' wishing to fight a battle as soon as possible – that the situation in Asia Minor was becoming increasingly dangerous – depends upon the assumption that Mardonios was aware of the situation there and that he would have felt under compulsion to fight because of it, but there is no real reason to believe that either was true. Herodotos has been criticized for writing about the events of 479 as though the campaigns that culminated at Plataea and Mykale were 'happening not in different continents but in different worlds.'[28] But is not this, to a large extent, a true reflection of the situation? With the Greek fleet now commanding the central Aegean, Sardes lay more than 1,000 kilometres by land from Boeotia, and it is hard to believe that Mardonios was in regular contact with Ionia. He may have felt, moreover, that his task was to hold on to those parts of Greece already conquered and to bring about the collapse of resistance elsewhere, and the avoidance of battle might have seemed desirable for both these reasons – better by far to rely upon the well-known divisiveness of the Greeks, perhaps helped on by the bribery Artabazos allegedly advised (cf. Herodotos 9.41.3).

According to Herodotos, the information brought to the Athenian commanders by Alexander of Macedonia was relayed by them to Pausanias, and he, 'in fear of the Persians' (9.46.1), proposed that – to meet the expected attack at dawn – the Athenian and Spartan contingents should exchange places. Here, although it is not impossible that Pausanias was afraid of the Persians, it is more likely that the allegation is due to the bias of Herodotos' sources. Less easy to assess are Pausanias'[1] reported public reasons for wanting the exchange – that the Athenians had had some experience of fighting the Persians whereas the Spartans had not (Herodotos 9.46.2). At least this has the merit of being true since there must have been Athenian hoplites at Plataea who had fought at Marathon only eleven years before and Aristeides himself, the Athenian commander, had been one of the ten *strategoi* at Marathon, if we are to believe Plutarch (*Aristeides* 5.1–2). But when Herodotos goes on to say that Pausanias maintained that the Spartans did have experience of fighting Boeotians and Thessalians, one begins to wonder since, as far as we know, Spartans had never fought Boeotians – unless Kleomenes' army had done some fighting in Boeotia in the late sixth century (cf. Herodotos 6.108.2) – and the only Thessalians they had ever fought had been Hippias' Thessalian allies some years later (Herodotos 5.63.2ff.) with disastrous results. Since, further, in the end, the Spartan and Athenian contingents are alleged to have reverted to their original places in the line, it is tempting to dismiss the whole episode as fiction. But one has a sneaking suspicion that something must have happened to give rise to the story and if there is any truth in it, either Pausanias genuinely felt that the Athenians, who alone had archers as we have seen, would handle the Persians better, or his purpose may have been offensive rather than defensive: it was normal for hoplites to think of winning battles on their right – to capitalize on their tendency to edge to the right because this was their unshielded side (cf. Thucydides 5.71.1) – and it is just possible that Pausanias anticipated Epameinondas in having the idea that if he could win on the left he could prevent the stalemate in which each side outflanked the other on the right and roll Mardonios' line up from his right.

In some ways more puzzling than this episode, and more important for our understanding of the campaign as a whole, is why Mardonios, having allegedly decided the previous day to fight a pitched battle, now merely sent his cavalry again to continue with its harrying of the Greek lines (Herodotos 9.49). Perhaps Herodotos meant us to understand that the marching and counter-marching involved in the exchange of positions on both sides had taken up the better part of the day and that Mardonios was thus forced to abandon his plans for an all-out attack and continue with his harassing-tactics for a further day. But it is more likely that Mardonios had in fact decided not to fight and that the whole episode of the discussion with Artabazos and the mission of Alexander is fiction. The harassing, then, continued, and was presumably intended to have the effect it did have – to force the Greeks to retreat. The alternative is that Mardonios hoped to provoke the Greeks into crossing the Asopos and fighting him on ground of his own choosing, but this is less likely: to demonstrate just how effective the cavalry could be was hardly likely to provoke the Greeks into venturing onto ground even more suitable for cavalry operations.

At all events the attacks of the cavalry were apparently even more serious on this day and, in particular, the Gargaphia spring, from which the whole Greek army now drew its water since it had been prevented from getting water from the Asopos, was temporarily put out of use; possibly the Persian cavalry succeeded in riding round the right flank of the Spartans and so reaching the spring in their rear (Herodotos 9.49.2–3). The result was that the other Greek commanders went to Pausanias to complain about this and about the lack of food, now that the supplies from the Peloponnese were no longer getting through, since those in charge of them were unable to venture down from Kithairon for fear of the Persian cavalry (Herodotos 9.50). After deliberation the decision was if the Persians continued to put off making an all-out attack, to withdraw to a place Herodotos says was called 'the island', about 10 stades (about 2 kilometres) away, in front of the city of Plataea and formed by two tributaries of the Oeroe running down from Kithairon (9.51.1–2):[29] the move was to be made during the second watch of the night to avoid the notice of the enemy, and once the island was reached, half of the army was to be sent up to rescue the supplies from Kithairon (Herodotos 9.51.3–4).

When night fell, however, according to Herodotos (9.52), and the time came for the retreat to begin, the contingents of the Greek centre, instead of making for the island made for Plataea and piled arms at the temple of Hera which stood outside it, about 20 stades (nearly 4 kilometres) from the Gargaphia spring. This inevitably raises the question whether Herodotos has correctly reported the original intention, and it is possible that Herodotos' informants once again misled him because of later bitterness against some of the Peloponnesian states, particularly Megara and Corinth:[30] it is thus possible that the centre had been intended to do precisely what it did do. On the other hand, it would not be at all surprising if part-time soldiers told to retreat at night over ground unknown to most of them did go astray: if the Greek centre had really been stationed between Pyrgos hill and the Asopos ridge, it would have been natural for it to withdraw down the main road from Thebes to Plataea.

Even more puzzling is what is alleged to have happened to the rest of the Greek army. Herodotos says (9.53.1ff.) that when Pausanias ordered the Spartans to follow those who had already retreated, Amompharetos, commander of the *lochos* of Pitana, refused to obey and that the whole Spartan army, as a result, together with the *perioikoi* and the Tegeates, stayed where it was while Pausanias and his lieutenant Euryanax[31] tried to persuade Amompharetos to move. Meanwhile, the Athenians too had stood fast and sent a mounted courier to see whether the Spartans really would move or not, and to ask Pausanias what they should do. This man was witness to the climax of a bitter argument between the Spartan commanders and was sent back to the Athenians with the request that they march towards the Spartans and conform to their movements (Herodotos 9.55.2). Dawn thus found both the Spartans and the Athenians in the same positions they had occupied the previous day.

This is the most extraordinary episode of the whole campaign and since it led directly to the battle it is important to try to determine what really happened. Perhaps the simplest solution is that Herodotos was mistaken in saying that the Greeks decided to withdraw and that what really happened was simply that the centre of the Greek army de-camped during the night, leaving the two wings in the original position: it is quite likely that if the Spartans were on the Asopos ridge and the Athenians on Pyrgos hill, the centre had suffered most severely from the harassing of the Persian cavalry during the last few days and, after all, even Herodotos believed that the centre did not adhere to the plan of retreat but 'was glad to flee from the cavalry to the city of Plataea' (9.52). But if this was the truth, it is difficult to see why Herodotos did not know it, or forbore to tell it, for he clearly took a poor view of the performance of the Greek centre and had had no hesitation in reporting a tradition that part of the Greek army at Thermopylai had simply de-camped. We must, then, accept that at least the centre of the Greek army had been supposed to retreat, even if in the event it retreated to the wrong place.

Was the original intention, however, that just the centre should withdraw, leaving the Spartans and Athenians where they were? Modern scholars have concocted a number of notional schemes designed to tempt Mardonios into attacking an apparently isolated Spartan contingent, leaving the rest of the Greek army to fall on his flank when he was fully committed to the struggle with the Spartans.[32] With respect, however, it is absurd to imagine even a Spartan general of the early fifth century dreaming up such a plan. No Greek had ever commanded an army as large as the one Pausanias commanded at Plataea or one drawn from so many different states, and even if Spartan princes were given some training in command – which is unlikely – it would have been on an altogether smaller and simpler scale. As far as we know, Pausanias himself had never before commanded an army in war. Modern scholars have cited the feigned retreats allegedly practised by the Spartans at Thermopylai as a parallel, but this is precisely the point. There Leonidas was handling a tiny force and he and his Spartans were doing something they probably had practised many times. But one wonders how many times even 5,000 Spartiates assembled to practise manoeuvres, and one suspects that their tactical training was largely at the level of the *enomotiai* and hardly ever even involved a whole *mora* at any one time. In any case, here we are mostly dealing not with trained Spartiates but with ordinary Greek hoplites whose tactical training was probably rudimentary, if they had any at all.

Herodotos' picture of chaos and confusion following the decision to retreat is thus much more likely to be close to the truth than the elaborate schemes of his modern critics. But we still have to account for the fact that whereas the centre contingents of the Greek army withdrew to Plataea, the Spartan and Athenian contingents apparently stayed where they were. Here Herodotos' explanation is usually dismissed on the grounds that no Spartan officer would have behaved in so insubordinate a way as Amompharetos is said to have done.[33] However, we know of at least one other occasion when

Spartan officers refused to obey orders – the polemarchs Aristokles and Hipponoïdas at Mantineia (Thucydides 5.71.3f.) – and it is just possible that an altercation such as Herodotos describes did take place. But the parallel is not a close one since at Mantineia the Spartan army was actually advancing into battle and there was really nothing King Agis could do to ensure that his orders were obeyed, whereas at Plataea one assumes Pausanias could simply have relieved Amompharetos of his command, though there might have been a problem if polemarchs were elected and if Amompharetos was really a polemarch (see above, pp. 31 & 67).

One radical solution to the problem is that it was not the Spartans who caused the delay but the Athenians, and that it was the Spartans who stayed where they were because the Athenians had not moved.[34] But although it would then be very easy to explain how Herodotos got it wrong, since he was fairly clearly using an Athenian source here as elsewhere, as is suggested by his cutting remark (9.54.1) that the Athenians 'understood Spartan ways of thinking – how they thought one thing and said another', this is surely too drastic an inversion of his account to be accepted. Nevertheless, it is possible that the truth is simply that the chaotic withdrawal of the centre first disrupted the Athenian retreat, and then that Pausanias was persuaded that it was, after all, a mistake to attempt to withdraw at night over unfamiliar terrain with so large a force, for if the plan had been for the Athenians to withdraw to the island it is probable that the centre, in retreating to Plataea, blundered right across their rear.

If then Herodotos is right that the Greeks decided to retreat and that the centre went astray, it is simplest to suppose that the Spartans and Athenians remained where they were because their planned withdrawal had gone wrong, and it is possible that when dawn found him still in the same place and now dangerously isolated from the rest of the Greek army, Pausanias called for volunteers to act as a rear-guard now that he was going to have to retreat in daylight, and that this is how the Amompharetos story originated.[35] It is true that the detail that Amompharetos took a rock in both hands and laid it at Pausanias' feet, declaring that 'with this pebble' (ψῆφος) he voted against running away from the 'strangers' (Herodotos 9.55.2), does not ring quite true since the Spartans did not vote with pebbles, but the other detail – that Amompharetos used the word 'strangers' (ξείνοι) for the Persians does. It is not completely impossible that the whole little scene was played out precisely for the Athenian courier who, Herodotos says, was present, and whom Pausanias now ordered to report the circumstances to the Athenians requesting them to march towards him and conform to his movements.

Whatever the true explanation for what happened, there is no reason to doubt that dawn found the Spartans still on the Asopos ridge, the Athenians still on Pyrgos hill and the contingents of the Greek centre now at the temple of Hera just outside the town of Plataea. Pausanias then gave orders to move off, keeping to the high ground with his Spartans (apart from Amompharetos' command), the *perioikoi* and the Tegeates, while the Athenians too moved down from Pyrgos hill and began to march across the flat ground towards him (Herodotos 9.56). Hitherto, everything had gone wrong for the Greek army since the defeat of Masistios' cavalry attack and one has the impression that Pausanias had been out of his depth, which is really not surprising. But now, if one can trust Herodotos' narrative, things began to change: Pausanias and his men moved off without any apparent trouble and withdrew some 10 stades (nearly 2 kilometres)[36] before halting to wait for Amompharetos and his men – there is no suggestion of panic or alarm at the situation in which they now found themselves. Amompharetos, although Herodotos believed he was still acting in as insubordinate a manner as he dared or, in fact, if he was acting as a rear-guard, handled his task with admirable precision, withdrawing at a slow pace (βάδην: Herodotos 9.57.1), and re-joining the main body at the very moment that the Persian cavalry appeared (Herodotos 9.57.3). Nor is it necessary to seek far for an explanation of the transformation in the way this part of the Greek army was now behaving. Pausanias was still, probably, handling more men than he had ever commanded in his life before, but at least operations were now on something like the normal Greek scale and above all, nearly half his army were Spartiates and the rest *perioikoi* and good, tough Tegeates – the kind of men the Spartans were used to having alongside them. Pausanias, in short, at last knew what he was doing.

His 10-stade retreat, according to Herodotos (9.57.2), brought him to 'the vicinity of the river Moloeis and the so-called Argiopian land, where also a temple of Eleusinian Demeter is situated', but none of these can any longer be securely located, which is a pity since the battle itself is said to have taken place 'right alongside the shrine of Demeter' (παρ' αὐτὸ τὸ Δημήτριον: Herodotos 9.62.2, cf. 65.2). Two inscriptions relating to a temple of Eleusinian Demeter (*IC* vii 1670 & 1671) have in fact been found in the neighbourhood of the ridge on which the chapel of the Pantanassa now stands, but this is much further than 10 stades from the likely Spartan position near the Asopos, and although Herodotos' statements of distance should not be assumed to be too precise, he is hardly likely to have said 10 stades if he meant something more like 30. In any case, the Pantanassa ridge is almost certainly the site of either Erythrai or Hysiai (see above, p. 121-2), and if Pausanias had retreated to the vicinity of either of these places, one would have expected Herodotos to say so. However, there is no necessity to believe that the shrine stood where the inscriptions were found, for such things have a notorious habit of wandering and they may have come from a location much nearer the so-called Asopos ridge where the Spartans had previously been stationed. All one can say is that the most probable site for the battle is about 2 kilometres to the north of the modern Erythrai (Kriekouki) and perhaps about a kilometre south-west of the chapel of Ayios Demetrios.[37] Somewhere here, then, Pausanias halted to wait for Amompharetos, and hardly had the latter joined him before the Persian cavalry was upon them (Herodotos 9.57.3).

According to Herodotos (9.57.3), the Persian cavalry had started out with the intention of continuing their harassing of the Greek lines – another indication, if it is true, that Mardonios still had no intention of committing his whole army to a full-scale battle. However, when they found the Greek positions along the Asopos deserted, the cavalry had ridden forward until they caught up with the Spartans. It was, then, presumably from the first cavalry patrols that Mardonios learnt that the Greeks had made off during the night, though he could now see for himself that their position was deserted (Herodotos 9.58.1). After allegedly addressing a series of gibes at the Spartans' expense to some of the Thessalians serving with him, he proceeded to lead the Persians across the Asopos at the double, following the tracks of the Greeks, and the rest of his army followed suit. However, Herodotos emphasizes (9.59.1), it was the Lakedaimonians and Tegeates alone who were the immediate object of pursuit, since Mardonios could not see the rest of the Greek army: the Athenians had 'turned into the plain' (τραπομένους ἐς τὸ πεδίον – cf. κάτω τραφθέντες ἐς τὸ πεδίον: 9.56.1), and were hidden from him by the hills – i.e. presumably, the Asopos ridge – along which the Spartans had marched (cf. Herodotos loc.cit.), while the remainder of the Greek army was now at Plataea, several kilometres away. Thus, even now Mardonios did not think he was committing his forces to full-scale battle against the entire Greek army. He thought that he was dealing solely with an isolated contingent containing less than a third of the Greek forces and that this was a golden opportunity to win a limited victory, with overwhelming force, against the best troops Greece had.

Pausanias, for his part, finding himself under attack from the cavalry immediately sent a horseman to ask the Athenians to march to his aid, or at least to send him their archers, but no sooner had they started towards him than they too found themselves under attack from the Greeks serving with the Persian army (Herodotos 9.60–61.1). This story also bears the hall mark of an Athenian source but there is no particular reason to doubt that it is true, and if it is it hardly suggests that things were going as Pausanias expected – there is no hint here that he thought he had got the Persians where he wanted them and was just summoning the Athenians to close the trap in accordance with some pre-arranged plan.

In any case if there had been a plan it had now gone wrong, and for one reason or another the Spartans, *perioikoi* and Tegeates found themselves facing the Persian army alone, in all some 11,500 hoplites and, probably, about the same number of soldier-servants armed as skirmishers with missile weapons and including helots, some of whom Herodotos believed were killed in the battle that followed (cf. 9.85.2).[38] Pausanias, in fact, had been thoroughly outmanoeuvred by his opponent. He had clearly known of no way to secure his communications and supply-route over Kithairon or to prevent the Persians harrying his army unmercifully along the Asopos, and now he had contrived to get himself isolated with less than a third of his army under command. But alarmed as he no doubt was he may well have preferred it to be this way in some respects. He probably thought he knew how to handle the now limited forces at his disposal – forces upon which he knew he could rely – and it is difficult to find fault with his handling of the final confrontation, though as usual we lack the detailed information that would enable us to pass a proper verdict on his generalship.

Herodotos is disappointingly vague about the details of the fight, but at least he lets us see how it was won. At first he declares (9.61.2) the omens were unfavourable for the Greeks to join battle and the Persians, making a hedge of their wicker shields, shot their arrows mercilessly into the Greek ranks killing many and wounding many more. It was here that the Spartan Kallikrates, the handsomest man in the Greek army, was shot in the side and died complaining that he had not struck a blow or done a deed to match his eagerness, and the detail that he was 'sitting in his rank' at the time (Herodotos 9.72.1) suggests that the Spartans sat on the ground to avoid the arrow-storm, presumably crouching under their shields. Modern commentators have cynically, but perhaps rightly, seen in the delay a deliberate manipulation of superstition to give the enemy time to mass in such numbers that they could not get away when the hoplites finally advanced.[39] But we have Xenophon's word for it that the Spartans paid such attention to their rites even in battle that at the Nemea they even found time to sacrifice a she-goat to Artemis Agrotera when the armies were less than 200 metres apart (XH 4.2.20, cf. *Anabasis* 3.2.12 and *LP* 13.8).

Another possibility is suggested by Herodotos' statement (9.62.3f.) that Pausanias was looking towards the temple of Hera at Plataea and calling upon that goddess for help when the Tegeates first leapt to their feet and advanced, and then immediately the omens came right for the Spartans. Why, one may ask, pray to Hera when you are right beside a temple of Eleusinian Demeter? Perhaps the answer is that Pausanias was looking for help from the contingents of the centre who were at the temple of Hera or, more generally, looking constantly to his left flank from where any help must come, even from the Athenians, for he probably did not know that the other Greeks were at the temple of Hera.[40] But this may again be too cynical a view. How do we know, for example, that Pausanias did not have some personal regard for Hera, or that he may not have considered the whole area as peculiarly under her protection because of her temple at Plataea?

Whatever the truth about the delay it is a telling detail, if true, that it was the Tegeates who took the initiative into their own hands (Herodotos 9.62.1), and presumably Pausanias now in any case had little option but to order a general advance. However, whether intended or not, the Persians apparently could not just melt away any longer before the advancing hoplites and continue with their missile attack from a safe distance as they would have had to do if they were to win. Instead, they found themselves involved in a stand-up fight. Even then, if Herodotos is to be believed (9.62.2ff.), a hard struggle ensued, first at the shield-hedge and then alongside the shrine of Demeter, for the Persians, casting aside their bows, grabbed at the longer spears of the Greeks and strove to break them. Eventually the sheer weight of the hoplite phalanx began to tell – as Herodotos says, the fight was a tough one 'until they reached the shoving' (ἐς ὅ ἀπίκοντο ἐς ὠθισμόν: 9.62.2). He emphasizes that although the Persians were not inferior in spirit or strength, they were 'lacking in armour' (ἄνοπλοι), and 'lacking in experience' (ἀνεπιστήμονες) – they were 'not the equals of their opponents in skill' (οὐκ ὅμοιοι τοῖσι ἐναντίοισι σοφίην: 9.62.3) – and he explains this by saying that they kept 'rushing out singly or in groups of ten, more or less' (προεξαΐσσοντες κατ' ἕνα καὶ δέκα καὶ πλεῦνές τε καὶ ἐλάσσονες συστρεφόμενοι) and that thus 'they fell upon the Spartiates and were destroyed' (ἐσέπιπτον ἐς τοὺς Σπαρτιήτας καὶ διεφθείροντο). This implies that the Greeks, by contrast, and the Spartans in particular, maintained their unbroken ranks and it is clear that this is what gave the Greeks their victory. The phalanx was irresistible against comparatively light troops who attempted to stand up to it instead of keeping their distance as, for example, Demosthenes' troops did on Sphakteria or Iphikrates' peltasts at Lechaion (Thucydides 4.33–4; XH 4.5.13ff.). At last, when Mardonios fell, and the picked troops around him were annihilated, the Persians broke – and again Herodotos emphasizes that it was their lack of protective armour that proved their undoing, 'for they were unarmoured troops trying to make a fight of it against hoplites' (πρὸς νάρ ὁπλίτας ἐόντες νυμνῆτες ἀνῶνα ἐποιεῦντο: 9.63.2).

Meanwhile, the Athenians had routed the Boeotians in a separate engagement (Herodotos 9.67), and both the latter and the Persians fled back across the Asopos, covered by their cavalry (9.68). This is the first mention of the cavalry in Herodotos' narrative since their initial pursuit of the retreating Greeks (9.57.3), and this has prompted speculation as to why it played no part in the crucial encounter, but the answer is simple: cavalry could not charge an unbroken phalanx of hoplites, and Persian cavalry-tactics – riding to within range to discharge missiles and then wheeling away, as demonstrated by Masistios' cavalry attack (cf. Herodotos 9.20ff., and note 22.3), and by the harassing along the Asopos (cf. Herodotos 9.40, and, especially, 9.49.2) – required a static target, and even then, in the end, they would probably have had to leave the job of actually routing the enemy to the infantry, whereupon they could again come into their own in the pursuit. But neither at Marathon nor at Plataea had the Greeks presented a static target: at Marathon the Athenians had charged at the double (cf. Herodotos 6.112), and here too, at Plataea, the Spartans had advanced (9.62.1) to close quarters.[41]

The Persian and Boeotian cavalry, though the latter even managed to bring off a minor victory in routing a force of Megarians and Phleiasians coming across the plain to support the Athenians (Herodotos 9.69.2), could not long delay the advance of the victorious hoplites. The final act of the drama was the storming of the Persian stockade across the Asopos where, Herodotos claims (9.70.2), the Athenian skill at siege-warfare came into its own. However, it was in fact the Tegeates who first broke in (9.70.3), and it is difficult to see how the Athenians can have been specially skilled in siege-warfare since they had never, as far as we know, taken a walled town, and certainly not in their recent history. It is more likely that since the Spartans had borne the brunt of the fighting so far, they preferred to leave it to others to finish the job.[42] Only Artabazos' division escaped the massacre, if we are to believe Herodotos (9.66). He had perhaps commanded the centre of the Persian army and seeing that all was lost, prudently made off straight for Phokis.[43]

This, then, was the battle of Plataea, which finally rid mainland Greece of the Persian menace and confirmed the verdict of Marathon as to the superiority of hoplites in a set-piece battle. With the benefit of hindsight it is easy to see that Mardonios should never have allowed himself to be drawn into such a battle, particularly after he had got the Greeks on the run. But without speculating on the possible pressures that may have made him think he had to bring about a decisive battle (see above, p. 128), it is surely easy to understand why the sight of the Spartiates, *perioikoi* and Tegeates apparently isolated from the rest of the Greek army, might have tempted him into trying to eliminate the most formidable contingents in the Greek army. Nor can he really be blamed for not realizing just how formidable 11,500 tough hoplites, nearly half of them probably among the finest infantry in the world at that time, would prove to be, for neither Marathon nor Thermopylai had really prepared the Persians for a full-scale, head-on collision with the Spartan war-machine. Indeed this was possibly the only time in history that anyone ever had to fight 5,000 of Sparta's 'peers'.

Chapter 6

Sphakteria

At Thermopylai and Plataea the Spartan army had demonstrated its discipline, cohesion and formidable fighting qualities in encounters with a more lightly-armed but more numerous and mobile enemy, equipped with long-range missile weapons. The fight on the island of Sphakteria during the summer of 425[1] was to show how it could be beaten by just such an enemy but there was, perhaps, one crucial difference. The Athenian force the Spartans had to fight on this occasion included a force of hoplites, and one nearly twice as numerous as the Spartans themselves, as well as very large numbers of light troops. Yet even then it is clear from what Thucydides says (cf. 4.34.1) that the Athenians were not at all happy at the prospect of fighting a mere 420 Spartans, though they outnumbered them by more than twenty-five to one.[2] In the long term the Spartan defeat meant little and if Sparta learnt little from it so too did her opponents, for it was still to be many years before the Spartan army was defeated in a full-scale battle, and then it was to be by hoplites not light troops.

The campaign that culminated at Sphakteria formed part of the Peloponnesian War. After the defeat of the Persian invasion in 479, the Greek states had gradually split into two rival groups, the one dominated by Athens – now the greatest sea-power in the Greek world – and comprising most of the islands in the Aegean and the states on its northern and eastern coasts, the other dominated by Sparta and including most of the Peloponnese, except Argos, with the powerful addition of Boeotia in central Greece. These two power-blocs had already clashed between 460 and 446, but had patched up relations in the Thirty Years Peace. Then, in 431, war had broken out again.

At first the war had been dominated by the strategy of the Athenian statesman Perikles, who had persuaded his fellow-countrymen to look upon the city of Athens itself, with its port the Peiraeus now linked to it by the 'long walls' as an island and not to try to defend Attica. At the same time the fleet was to be used to maintain the empire and for raids on the Peloponnese. The strategy was, one feels, a recipe for avoiding defeat rather than for securing victory, but in any case Perikles had died in 429 and within a year or two some or the new leaders of Athens appear to have taken up the idea of using the fleet to establish permanent bases, on the coast of the Peloponnese – an idea at which Perikles had hinted, if Thucydides is believed (1.142.2ff.), but only as a retaliation if the Spartans attempted to establish a base in Attica. The earliest of these bases unless one counts the island of Minoa opposite the sea-port of Megara and occupied by the Athenians in 427 (Thucydides 3.51), was the headland of Pylos, called Koryphasion by the Spartans (Thucydides 4.3.2). It lies on the west coast of Messenia at the north-west corner of the Bay of Navarino. South of the headland, and closing the bay off from the sea, lies the long, narrow island of Sphakteria.

Thucydides' account of the campaign is one of the most famous episodes in his history of the Peloponnesian War and has been the subject of much scholarly debate, but fortunately for our purposes most of the controversies do not concern the actual fight on the island.[3] The background to it is fairly straightforward. In the spring of 425 an Athenian fleet of forty ships on its way to Corfu and, ultimately, to Sicily, was driven by bad weather to shelter in the Bay of Navarino and here the ex-general Demosthenes, who had accompanied the fleet with ill defined instructions to make use of it 'around the Peloponnese', if he wished (Thucydides 4.2.4), suggested to the fleet's commanders that they fortify the headland of Pylos – Koryphasion. At first Demosthenes' suggestion was rejected, but then the ordinary rank-and-file proceeded to implement his plan during the period of enforced idleness, and when the fleet eventually went on its way Demosthenes was left behind with five triremes to guard the new fort (Thucydides 4.5.2).

The news of the Athenian landing brought the Spartan army hurrying back from its annual invasion of Attica and, Thucydides says (4.8.1), 'the Spartiates themselves and the nearest of the *perioikoi*[4] immediately marched to Pylos, although the rest of the *perioikoi* were slower to arrive since they had but lately returned from the other campaign. If Thucydides is to be believed, then, presumably something like the full levy of the regular Spartan army took part in the campaign, and that this was so is borne out by his later statement (4.8.9) that the hoplites sent over to Sphakteria were chosen by lot 'from all the *lochoi*'. If it is right to suppose that at this date the

Spartan army already consisted of *morai* and *lochoi* (see above, p. 57), the implication that 'all the *lochoi*' were present on the scene would mean that all six *morai* were also present, and since there is some reason to believe that the age-classes 'up to those thirty-five years from manhood' had been called up on this occasion (see below), the Spartan forces present would have had at least a paper-strength of 6,720 men (6 × 32 × 35).[5] We have no means of assessing the numbers of the *perioikoi* who eventually arrived, but with these and the forces of the other Peloponnesian allies it is not inconceivable that Diodoros' total of 12,000 (12.61.2) is just about right.

The Spartan plan, according to Thucydides (4.8.4ff.) was to assault the Athenian fort by land and sea, and in case the Athenian fleet returned before they had captured the fort, to block the entrances into Navarino Bay in order to deny its use to Athenian ships. In furtherance of the plan the Spartans ferried hoplites across to Sphakteria and stationed others along the coast of the mainland (4.8.7), and since there were 420 hoplites in the force that was eventually trapped on the island, and since they had been chosen by lot from all the *lochoi* (4.8.9), it has plausibly been suggested that the force was made up of twelve *enomotiai* of 35 men each, rather than that lots were literally drawn among the individual hoplites making up the whole army.[6] This hypothesis is partly supported by Thucydides' statement that the men at the first guard-post, overwhelmed right at the beginning of the Athenian assault on the island, numbered 'about thirty hoplites' (4.31.2), for it would have made sense to station a single, complete *enomotia* here, rather than 'about thirty' separate hoplites.

According to Thucydides, the Spartans intended to block up the entrances to Navarino Bay and, by stationing troops where they did, to deny the use of both the island and the mainland to the Athenians either as a base or to provide landing-places from which they could help the defenders of the fort,[7] and it is here that the principal problems in his account lie. The difficulty is that although the northern entrance to the bay is, as Thucydides says, only wide enough to allow the passage of two triremes, presumably sailing side-by-side (4.7.6),[8] and could easily have been blocked by mooring triremes close together with their rams pointing out to sea,[9] the southern entrance is far wider than he says. It would in fact have allowed something like ten times the eight or nine triremes he says to sail in side-by-side – and it could not possibly have been blocked even by mooring the entire Peloponnesian navy side-by-side in it.

There are no satisfactory solutions to these problems. Perhaps the simplest way out of the difficulty is to suppose that Thucydides or his informants just made a mistake about the width of the southern entrance - from certain angles on shore it can in fact look much narrower than it is – and that the Spartans either never intended to block the entrances or, if they did, were unable to do so in the case of the southern entrance precisely because it was far too wide – they may have failed to block the northern entrance for other reasons (see below). An ingenious solution that has recently been suggested is that the Spartan intention was to block the northern entrance and the entrance to Voïdhokilia Bay, north-east of Koryphasion, and that somehow Thucvdides confused this plan with a plan to block the entrances to Navarino Bay.[10] In any case the intention of placing hoplites on Sphakteria was clearly to deny the use of the island to the Athenians.

Meanwhile, Demosthenes, realising that he was about to be attacked in force, sent off two of his triremes to request the rest of the Athenian fleet to return, and dragged the remaining three ashore, probably at the south-east foot of his fort. He protected the ships with a palisade and armed their crews with shields mostly made of wicker, which he had got from a Messenian 30-oared privateer and light galley that had arrived on the scene.[11] There were also forty hoplites on board the Messenian vessels, so Demosthenes now had at least ninety hoplites – assuming that he had retained those from the two triremes he had sent after the rest of the fleet – some twenty archers, about 1,000 Athenian sailors and presumably some from the two smaller Messenian ships. Most of these men he stationed on the eastern side of his fortifications, facing the mainland, but sixty hoplites and a few archers he took down to the south-west corner of the promontory where a landing was most feasible (Thucydides 4.9.2).[12]

The Spartans duly made their assault by both land and sea, but it is clear that the seaward assault was the most serious, probably because it was difficult to get at the Athenian position from the landward side. Despite what has sometimes been said, the Osmanaga lagoon was almost certainly in existence in 425, and this would have restricted access to the promontory to the sand dunes skirting Voïdhokilia Bay and to the sand-bar that divides the lagoon from Navarino Bay – on a hot summer's day it is still very tiring to walk to the promontory, and the climb to the top is steep and would be difficult, if not impossible, in the face of determined opposition except in the southern corner.[13] The attack from the sea was pressed home with great gallantry where Demosthenes had expected, at the south-west corner of the promontory, and it was here that Brasidas, who was commanding a trireme, was wounded and lost his shield (Thucydides 4.11.2ff.): Thucydides says that this shield was used as part of the trophy set up on Koryphasion itself (4.12.1), but one of the other shields captured by the Athenians in this campaign can now be seen in the Agora Museum in Athens.[14] The attacks were kept up for a whole day and part of a second, but in the end all failed and the Spartans had to send off to Asine for timber to construct siege-engines (Thucydides 4.13.1).[15]

Before the Spartans could renew their assault, however, the main Athenian fleet returned, and although when they saw that the mainland and island were full of hoplites, the Athenians were forced to retire temporarily to the island of Prote, north of Pylos. When they returned next day they were able to sweep into the Bay of Navarino through both entrances and fall upon the Peloponnesian fleet. If the Spartans had really ever intended to block the channel south of Sphakteria, they had presumably abandoned the plan because it was impossible, and they had also failed to block the northern channel perhaps because it was useful to have it open while they were attacking Pylos from the sea, from its south-west corner, and the Athenian fleet arrived too soon after the failure of their attack for them to block it.[16] The Spartans seem also to have failed to post watchers along the coast to warn of the approach of the Athenian fleet and the result was that in the ensuing fight in the comparatively open waters of the bay the Athenians captured five ships and damaged others by ramming as they fled to shore or while they were being manned near the shore. But the Spartans at least managed to prevent some of the ships near the shore from being captured by rushing into the sea, even though fully armed (Thucydides 4.14.1–4).

The Athenian victory at sea, however, effectively trapped the Spartan hoplites then on Sphakteria and, after a personal visit to the scene of operations, the Spartan authorities concluded a truce with the Athenian commanders on the spot, by which they agreed to surrender all their available ships both at Pylos and in Lakonia, and not to attack the Athenian fort, provided that their men on the island were supplied with specified rations under Athenian supervision and the Athenians undertook not to attack them. In the meantime the Athenians were also to convey Spartan envoys to Athens to try to arrange a permanent peace (Thucydides 4.16).

The rations specified (Thucydides 4.16.1) were to be two Attic *choinikes* (i.e. nearly 2 kilograms) of ready-kneaded barley-meal – this would be moistened and then eaten without baking – two *kotylai* of wine (i.e. just over half a litre), which would be mixed with two or three parts water, and some meat for each hoplite, and half that for each helot, presumably each day, and it looks as though this was considered a normal daily ration by the Spartans, for Herodotos says (6.57.3) that if the kings of Sparta dined at home, they were sent two *choinikes* of barley-meal though, curiously, only one *kotyle* of wine – perhaps the wine-ration was deliberately doubled on campaign, as the Spartan equivalent of the Royal Navy's tot of rum. These rations would appear to have been on the generous side for it later transpired that the Spartan commanders on the island, as good officers should, had carefully husbanded the rations so that some of them were found by the Athenians after they had captured the island (Thucydides 4.39.2). However, after the negotiations had broken down the provisions smuggled into the island included wheat-flour, if Thucydides' language is to be pressed (4.26.5),[17] cheese, wine and 'other food', and swimmers brought skins containing poppy-seed mixed with honey and pounded linseed (Thucydides 4.26.8), so, if anything, the Spartans seem to have fared rather better after the truce than during it.[18]

When the negotiations in Athens broke down the Athenians refused to hand back the Peloponnesian ships, alleging violations of the truce, and attempted to make the blockade of the island more complete. But the rewards offered by the Spartans to helots and others to induce them to convey food to the men on the island appear to have resulted in a good supply being maintained and, meanwhile, the Athenians on their rocky, exposed and almost waterless promontory experienced hardships almost as great. In the end the stalemate was only broken, if Thucydides is to be believed, by what must surely have been one of the most extraordinary meetings of the Athenian *ekklesia* ever held, which ended in Kleon's being invested with the command (Thucydides 4.27.1ff.). However, despite his bravado, Kleon was evidently sensible enough to take the right kind of troops with him – Lemnians, Imbrians, peltasts from Ainos and elsewhere, and 400 archers (Thucydides 4.28.5) – and to associate Demosthenes with him in the command (Thucydides 4.29.1), having heard that he was already thinking of a landing on the island. Demosthenes had become increasingly worried at the sufferings of his own men and his belief in the possibility of attacking the island had been considerably strengthened by an accidental fire started by one of a party of Athenians who had landed to cook a meal – the fire had burnt off much of the scrub and brushwood that had covered the island, concealing the number and movements of the Spartans, and making movement, except by the few paths, very difficult (Thucydides 4.29.2ff.).

On Kleon's arrival the Athenians sent a herald to the Spartans on the island inviting them to surrender, but when this ultimatum was rejected, waited a day and then launched their attack (Thucydides 4.30.4ff.). The first landing was made a little before dawn on both sides of the island by about 800 hoplites, the first objective being the advanced Spartan post of about thirty hoplites (one *enomotia?*), which was probably stationed on or near the highest point of the southern third of the island (Thucydides 4.31.1). The main body of Spartans, presumably about ten *enomotiai* or 350 men strong, was in 'the middle, lowest part of the island, around the water' (Thucydides 1.31.2) – probably this means near the well of brackish water, christened 'Grundy's Well' by British scholars[19] – and another small force (one *enomotia?*) guarded the higher, northern end of the island, now inevitably called Mt Elias, where there was an old fortification. We do not know how many helots there were in addition, though there were definitely some (cf. Thucydides 4.8.9 & 16.1), nor where they were stationed, but probably each Spartan hoplite was accompanied by his own batman – it is clear from Thucydides' account of the fighting that their military value was negligible.

The Spartans evidently had no intention of attempting to contest a landing as Demosthenes had done on Koryphasion, and the probable reason is that there were too many places where an enemy could scramble ashore.[20] The posting of the pickets at the northern and southern ends of the island, on the high points, was obviously intended to provide an early warning of any landing, and the Spartans presumably hoped to be able to move their main body from its position in the lower, central part of the island to any point where a landing was attempted in time to defeat the enemy before he could properly deploy. In the event, however, the advanced guard-post at the southern end was rushed by the Athenians while the men were still in their beds or arming. This may seem surprising but events in the Falklands have shown how difficult it is to keep troops in a state of readiness for a coming attack at all times and how easy it is for a determined enemy to take defending troops by surprise at night. Thus the main body of Spartans was not able to prevent either the landing of the 800 Athenian hoplites or the landing of the rest of their forces at dawn, consisting in all, probably, of more than 10,000 men made up of 800 archers and of various other light troops including sailors from seventy ships, Messenians and the men Kleon had brought from Athens. Demosthenes had divided this heterogeneous collection into task-forces of 200 men, presumably with some archers and slingers in each group, and they proceeded to seize the high ground so as to come at the Spartans from every direction.

The main body of the Spartans, when they saw that their first guard-post had been overwhelmed and that a force was advancing upon them, formed up and advanced towards the Athenian hoplites, 'wishing to come to grips with them,' as Thucydides significantly remarks (βουλόμενοι ἐς χεῖρας ἐλθεῖν: 4.33.1): they no doubt assumed that – as in most battles – the light troops were insignificant and that they had mainly to do with the enemy hoplites, and one notes the supreme confidence with which they advanced against a force now presumably more than twice as numerous as themselves. However, the Athenian hoplites, instead of advancing in their turn stayed where they were, probably on the north-facing slopes of the hill at the southern end of the island near where the Spartan guard-post had been stationed, and meanwhile their light troops began to fire into the Spartans from flanks and rear, checking their advance and preventing them from being able to use their expertise in close combat (4.33.2). The Spartans could easily chase off any light troops they charged, but each time they did so the enemy easily escaped because they were more lightly equipped and because of the difficult terrain, which hampered the Spartans 'with their armour' (ὅπλα ἔχοντες): once out of reach the Athenian skirmishers re-formed to re-commence their attacks. The situation was very similar to that faced by the *mora* near Lechaion thirty-five years later (XH 4.5.13ff), for there too the Spartans were faced with a combination of hoplites and skirmishers, and we may guess that on Sphakteria the Spartans resorted to ordering 'those ten, or fifteen years from manhood' to charge the enemy. One may wonder what the helots were doing, in the meantime, but the only hint that they did anything is Thucydides' use of a word meaning literally 'they fought with missiles at a distance' (ἠκροβολίσαντο: 4.34.1) to describe this phase of the fighting, and although this should logically mean that the Spartan side did too, he probably meant no more than that 'they skirmished' and was not consciously thinking of any action by the helots. The probability is that the helots, who were outnumbered by more than twenty to one by the enemy skirmishers, could make no adequate reply and the Spartans may indeed have not been too happy about using them in such a situation when faced by renegade Messenians, among others.

This first phase of the fighting lasted for 'some little time', Thucydides says (4.34.1), but in the end the Spartans began to tire and found themselves unable to charge out upon their foes so swiftly, while their opponents began to gain in confidence. As Thucydides says (4.34.1), 'now that they had become accustomed to them, their enemies appeared much less terrible, since they had not suffered nearly as much as they had expected to do when they first landed, their spirits crushed by the idea that they had to face Spartans' (τῇ γνώμῃ δεδουλωμένοι ὡς ἐπὶ Λακεδαιμονίους)', – a striking tribute to the fear Spartan hoplites inspired. But the fact of the matter was that the Spartans were not used to this kind of battle and were bewildered by the clouds of dust from the recently-burned thickets, the showers of arrows and stones and the shouting of the enemy, which made their own commands inaudible. Thucydides also adds (4.34.3) that their felt caps (πῖλοι) did not protect them from the arrows and that javelins broke off in their bodies when they were hit.[21] In the end, after many of them had been wounded, they closed ranks and made for the fort at the north end of the island (Thucydides 4.35.1).

If one compares Thucydides' detailed account of this fight with Herodotos' accounts of Thermopylai and Plataea, it is possible, perhaps, to see why the Persians, though basically the same kind of troops as Demosthenes' and far stronger in archers, were apparently unable to deal with Spartan hoplites, whereas Demosthenes' men appear to have had little difficulty. It should be noted firstly that Demosthenes did have a relatively large body of hoplites, unlike the Persians, and although they evidently did not play much of a part in the actual fighting, they were always there focusing the attention of the Spartans and, presumably in a position to deliver a crushing blow if, for example, the Spartans had attempted to break up into smaller parties to deal with the skirmishers. At Thermopylai too, of course, the Persians had only been able initially to attack the Spartans head-on on a very constricted front and had apparently not been able to get away fast enough when the Spartans advanced, particularly when they adopted their feigned-retreat tactics. Thus the Persians had been constrained to fight hand-to-hand where they were at a disadvantage – it was only when the Spartans and their remaining allies made their final stand on the hillock that the Persians were at last presented with a static target for their missile-weapons. At Plataea, although we may presume the Persians had space to deploy in looser formation,[22] they still gave the Spartans and their allies the chance to come to grips with them, even planting their wicker shields in the ground instead of running away when the Greeks advanced, as Demosthenes' troops did on Sphakteria. On the other hand it seems clear from what Thucydides says that in his opinion, if the Spartans *had* been able to come to grips with the Athenian hoplites, they might well have won, even though so heavily outnumbered.

Once they reached their new position on the high point at the north end of the island the Spartans found it easier to hold out since they were no longer being attacked in flank and rear (Thucydides 4.35.3), but, in the end, the commander of the Messenians – Pausanias (4.26.2) says he was called Komon – managed to lead a detachment of archers and other light troops up behind the Spartan position and began to fire down on it from the rear. Rather than see the Spartans annihilated, Kleon and Demosthenes ordered their men to cease fire and sent a herald forward to suggest terms. Most of the Spartan survivors then lowered their shields and waved their arms in token that they agreed to talk, and after a parley between the Athenian commanders and the ranking Spartan, Styphon – their commander, Epitadas, had been killed and his second-in-command, Hippagretas, badly wounded – and after communication with the Spartans on the mainland had elicited the typical response that 'the Lakedaimonians order you yourselves to consider your own situation, provided that you do nothing dishonourable' (Thucydides 4.38.3), Styphon and his men surrendered. They had lost 128 men killed from among the hoplites – no figures are given for the helots – and 292 of them were left alive, of whom about 120 were Spartiates (Thucydides 4.38.5).

Sphakteria is usually marked down as a Spartan defeat, as of course it was, but it is arguable that in the annals of almost any other army it would have been reckoned a glorious stand against hopeless odds, even though Thucydides' account suggests that the Spartans were baffled by their opponents' tactics, and did not manage to inflict many casualties upon them. Thucydides says (4.40.1) that the fact that the Spartans handed over their weapons rather than die fighting with them in their hands was the most surprising thing that happened in the entire war, and this indicates how strong the myth about the Spartan attitude to war had grown. However, the surrender possibly suggests that even among the Spartans, a more civilized approach to warfare was beginning to appear, for it seems that those who surrendered on Sphakteria were not punished or cold-shouldered when they eventually returned to Sparta after the peace of Nikias: Thucydides says (5.34.2) that later that same year some of them actually held office, and although they were then deprived of their citizen-rights for a time, they soon recovered them. Clearly gone were the days when even the heroic survivor of the 300 champions had felt compelled to commit suicide (Herodotos

1.82.8), or when one of the two survivors of Thermopylai, Aristodemos, had been so shunned that he went berserk at Plataea (Herodotos 7.229–31, 9.31) and the other, Pantites, similarly dishonoured and, in his case, for no reason at all, had hanged himself (Herodotos 7.232). The explanation may be that there had been such a decline in the number of Spartiates that the old rules could no longer be too rigidly applied, but this is surely not the whole answer.[23]

Certainly the unfortunate Spartan prisoners did not lose their sense of humour, judging by the anecdote told by Thucydides (4.40.2). When the age-old gibe thrown at survivors was flung at them – 'I suppose it was the "best and bravest" (καλοὶ κἀναθοί) who fell' – one of them replied, 'the "spindle" (ἄτρακτος, i.e. arrow) that could pick out the brave men (τοὺς ἀναθούς) would be worth a good deal.'

Chapter 7

Mantineia

Four years after Sphakteria, the Athenians and Spartans made peace. The Athenians were worried by the threat to their empire in the northern Aegean posed by the Spartan forces now in that area, even though their brilliant commander Brasidas had been killed outside Amphipolis in 422. The Spartans, for their part, had become increasingly anxious at the growing number of bases established on the coast of the Peloponnese since 425 and by the resulting disaffection among the helots. But many of Sparta's allies, some of whom had suffered severely in the war and none of whom gained anything by the peace save peace itself, were reluctant to accept it, and in the new and fluid situation that resulted Athens, perhaps mainly due to the influence of Alkibiades, was able to at last build up a coalition of Peloponnesian states. This gave her some chance of defeating Sparta on land, the only way in which she could ever have secured real victory – as Alkibiades was later to declare, according to Thucydides (6.16.6), he had 'brought it about that the Spartans had staked their all on one day at Mantineia.'

The battle Alkibiades had in mind, fought in the summer of 418, was the classic hoplite battle and we are fortunate in having Thucydides' account of it, for although this is not without its problems most of those concern his description of the Spartan army, and we have already examined that in connection with the organization of the army in the fifth century. Here we are principally concerned with the battle itself and the conclusions previously reached about the numbers and composition of the Spartan army will be largely accepted without further argument.

The battle was brought about by Spartan fears for her principal remaining ally in Arcadia, Tegea. The forces of the coalition opposed to Sparta – Athens, Argos, Mantineia and Elis – had taken Orchomenos in Arcadia and had then begun to make preparations at Mantineia for an attack on Tegea, though Elis had withdrawn her forces since she wanted the coalition to attack Lepreon, a Spartan fortress on her own borders. Spartan sympathizers in Tegea warned the Spartans that their city was in danger of going over to the coalition, and this brought the Spartans out in full force. Thucydides describes their forces as initially consisting of 'the Lakedaimonians themselves and of the helots in full force' (τῶν Λακεδαιμονίων ... αὐτῶν τε καὶ τῶν Εἱλώτων πανδημεί: 5.64.2), and one might have assumed that this included *perioikoi*. However, there is no mention of *perioikoi* in the later detailed account of the Spartan forces at the battle (5.67.1ff.), and it is possible that Thucydides used the phrase here, and a similar one of the forces that invaded the Argolid earlier in the summer (αὐτοὶ καὶ οἱ Εἱλῶτες πανδημεί: 5.57.1), precisely to exclude the *perioikoi*. On both occasions he emphasizes the swiftness of the mobilization and it is possible that the Spartans simply did not wait for the *perioikoi* – the Pylos campaign showed that the *perioikoi* could be slower than the Spartans (cf. Thucydides 4.8.1) – or, possibly, as was argued above (p. 20–21), the *perioikoi* were not used against Peloponnesian enemies at this time: the specific references to the helots on both occasions may be intended to emphasize that no *perioikoi* were present – the forces consisted exclusively of Spartans and helots.[1] The remark that they were in 'full force' (πανδημεί) is absolutely justified if all forty age-classes were originally present, and the two age-classes just below military age.

The whole army advanced as far as Orestheion on the border with Arcadia[2] and from there a sixth part, consisting of the older and younger men, was sent back to guard the homeland while the rest proceeded to Tegea to *rendez vous* with their Arcadian allies. Possibly, as was suggested above (p. 55), the sixth part consisted of eighteen-and nineteen-year-olds and the last five age-classes, leaving 'those up to thirty-five years from manhood' (i.e. the age-classes from twenty to fifty-four inclusive), as in the Leuktra campaign (cf. XH 6.4.17). From Tegea the Spartans and their allies marched northwards into the territory of Mantineia and began to ravage the land from a base near a shrine of Herakles (Thucydides 5.64.5). This has not been securely located but was probably south of Mantineia and just north of the mountain spur now called Mytikas. The enemy responded by deploying 'in a strong position, which was difficult to approach' (Thucydides 5.65.1), and which was probably on the lower slopes of the hill now called Alesion – Thucydides subsequently (5.65.4 & 6) refers to the position as on a hill (λόφος).[3] The Spartans immediately advanced to the attack and had got within missile-range when one of the older men[4] shouted to King Agis that he appeared to 'have it in mind to cure wrong with wrong' (Thucydides 5.65.2), alluding to the king's alleged failure earlier that summer to crush the Argive army, for which he had been heavily censured (cf. Thucydides 5.60.2ff.).

Agis then withdrew to Tegeate territory and began to divert the water of a stream into Mantineian territory in the hope of forcing the enemy to come down into the plain to stop it being flooded (Thucydides 5.65.4). It was possibly the stream now called Sarandopotamos, which flows eastwards from north of Tegea and Agis may have tried to divert it into the Zanovistas, which flows northwards into Mantineian territory to disappear into the swallow-holes known locally as 'katavothres'.[5] The coalition forces were, however, astonished at the sudden withdrawal of the Spartan army and the Argives in particular began to blame their generals for again letting the enemy escape, as they were thought to have done earlier that summer, in the Argive plain (Thucydides 5.60.5–6). As a result, the generals, in some confusion, led the army down off the hill into the plain, where they camped, intending to follow the enemy next day (Thucydides 5.65.5–6).

Next day, accordingly, the Argives and their allies deployed for battle, since they meant to fight if they contacted the enemy, and the Spartans, returning from their diversion-operations towards their old camp at the Herakleion, saw their opponents 'a little distance away and all already in line-of-battle'. Thucydides claims (5.66.2) that the Spartans were more startled at this moment than they could ever remember, and this remark has caused considerable controversy since they ought to have seen the enemy army long before Thucydides implies that they did and indeed ought to have left scouts on the hills when they retired precisely to observe the enemy's movements.[6] One solution is that the Spartans could not see the enemy army because of the Pelagos wood, which Pausanias (8.11.1) says lay across the road from Mantineia to Tegea, beyond the temple of Poseidon Hippios, which in turn lay not more than 7 stades (c. 1,300m) from Mantineia (cf. Polybius 9.8.11). The wood also reached the other road south from Mantineia – to Pallantion – about 30 stades (c. 5.5km) from Mantineia and so, presumably, just north of the Mytikas spur. However, it is very difficult to believe that if there was a wood there in 418, and if it was for this reason that the Spartans were surprised by their sudden sight of the enemy, Thucydides would not have known this. Alternative explanations are that the allied army moved at night or that some ridge or spur jutting into the plain obscured the view of the advancing Spartans. But even if the enemy had moved at night the Spartans should still have been able to see them for a considerable distance as they advanced now that it was daylight, and there really is no spur to obstruct the view of anyone moving up the Tegea–Mantineia road.

Possibly too much has been made of the passage. Part of the doubts about it stem from the constant modern belief that Greek armies in general, and the Spartan army in particular, must have behaved as modern armies are supposed to do and would therefore have left scouts on the hills to observe enemy movements and would have screened its advance with patrols. But for every example of scouts or patrols that can be quoted one can cite examples of even the Spartans being taken by surprise, and if Agis here had failed to take the necessary precautions it would only have been in keeping with the level of competence he displayed in the battle itself.[7] Another possibility is that Thucydides was misled by his informants. They may, for example, have exaggerated the unexpectedness of the appearance of the enemy – the fact of the matter is that the Spartans were able to deploy for battle and even to encourage each other with their war-songs and reminders of their prowess, while the enemy generals harangued their men (Thucydides 5.69). Alternatively, Thucydides may have misunderstood his informants: the Spartans may not have been so much surprised at coming so unexpectedly on the enemy as at the enemy's having come down off the hill so soon, for they would not have expected the diversion of the water as yet to have had any appreciable effect. In other words, the Spartans may have realized that the enemy was there quite early in their approach, but have been surprised at this development, their surprise increasing still further when they got near enough to see that the enemy was in battle array.

At all events, once it was realized that the enemy had descended into the plain and was deployed for battle, the well-drilled Spartan war-machine slipped smoothly into gear, the king's orders being rapidly passed down the chain of command from polemarchs to enomotarchs (Thucydides 5.66.2). Thucydides says that the *Skiritai*, 600 in number (5.67.1 & 68.3), were stationed on the left wing (5.66.2), and this suggests that they had been leading the column of march, as they are said to have done in the fourth century (*LP* 13.6), and that the column deployed into line to the left, as again was fourth century practice (*LP* 11.8). Next to the *Skiritai* were placed Brasidas' old soldiers (the '*Brasideioi*') and the *neodamodeis*, together numbering 512 men according to Thucydides (cf. 5.68.3), but in reality perhaps double that number (above. pp. 53–54). After them, Thucydides says (5.67.1), 'the Lakedaimonians themselves ranged their *lochoi* in line', and since he says later (5.68.3) that there were seven *lochoi* in all, apart from the *Skiritai*, he almost certainly means that the *Brasideioi* and *neodamodeis* formed one, 'the Lakedaimonians themselves' the other six.[8] We have, however, seen reason to believe that Thucydides confused *morai* and *lochoi* here, and that what he should have said was that after the *Brasideioi* and *neodamodeis* – perhaps forming what was called a *lochos* – 'the Lakedaimonians themselves ranged their *morai* in line'. If this is right, there were not just six *lochoi* of Spartans at Mantineia but twelve, numbering 6,144 men, and probably the 300 *Hippeis* who surrounded the king somewhere in the middle of the line (Thucydides 5.72.4), should be added to that number, rather than thought of as belonging to one of the six *morai* (see p. 180 n.7).

After the 'Lakedaimonians themselves' came hoplites from Heraia, Mainalia and Tegea, for whom Thucydides gives no numbers. We would hardly expect more than a few hundred from the two former places at most, but Tegea should have been able to muster two or three thousand for a battle fought so close to home – she had sent 1,500 hoplites to Plataea in 479 (Herodotos 9.28.3) and was to send perhaps as many as 2,400 to the Nemea in 394 (cf. XH 4.2.19). Finally, beyond the Tegeates on the extreme right of the hoplite phalanx were what Thucydides calls (5.67.1) 'a few Lakedaimonians'. Thus, with the *Skiritai*, *Brasideioi* and *neodamodeis*, and Spartans coming to something over 8,000 men (600 + 1,024? + 6,444? + a few), the whole Spartan phalanx including the allies would have come to between ten and eleven thousand hoplites. The Spartans themselves were ranged at an average depth of eight, according to Thucydides (5.68.3), as were the *Brasideioi* and *neodamodeis*, if they are to be included in his seven '*lochoi*', so assuming the same depth for the *Skiritai*, the Spartan part of the phalanx would have had a front of just over 1,000 shields, the allies of perhaps 375. In addition there was a small force of cavalry on each flank, numbers and composition unknown (Thucydides 5.67.1).[9]

There is one final puzzle about these dispositions – the number, nature and purpose of the few Lakedaimonians on the extreme right of the hoplite phalanx. As to their number there is a slight implication in what Thucydides says that they were at least fewer than the *Skiritai*, but beyond this we have no means of telling how numerous they were. If thirty-five age-classes had remained after the departure of the 'older and younger' at Orestheion, as suggested above, and yet each *enomotia* in the *lochoi* of Spartans only contained an average of thirty-two men (Thucydides 5.68.3), this leaves some 576 men spare ($12 \times 16 \times 35 = 6,720 - 12 \times 16 \times 32 = 6,144$): some of these were probably the 'older' men set to guard the baggage-train (Thucydides 5.72.3), but the others may well be the few Lakedaimonians placed on the extreme right. This was not only the post of honour but was also tactically important. Presumably the Spartans anticipated that their right would outflank the enemy on their left, and although this would probably not mean hard fighting it was important that there should be reliable and steady men there to exploit any advantage.

The allies for their part ranged their forces with the Mantineians, in whose territory the battle was to be fought, on the right then their Arcadian allies, then the thousand picked Argives followed by the rest of the Argives, next the troops from Kleonai and Orneai and finally the Athenians, there were also some Athenian cavalry on the left but apparently none on the right. Apart from the number for the picked Argives, Thucydides gives no figures for the allied side, though we can probably infer from, an earlier reference to 1,000 Athenian hoplites and 300 cavalry (5.61.1) that their numbers were about the same at Mantineia. For the numbers of the other contingents we can only guess. The Mantineians may have numbered about 3,000 (cf. Diodoros 12.78.4 and Lysias 34.7), the main body of Argives three or four thousand, and the Arcadians and the men of Kleonai and Orneai perhaps 1,000 in all.

When the lines had been ranged to the generals' satisfaction and they had delivered their customary exhortations, the advance began the Argives and their allies moving forward energetically and with passion, the Spartans slowly and to the sound of their pipers so as to march 'evenly' (ὁμαλῶς) to the rhythm and not break ranks (Thucydides 5.70). It was at this point that Agis tried to bring about the most extraordinary manoeuvre of the whole battle. All hoplite armies, we are assured by Thucydides (5.71.1), tended to edge to the right because the men on the extreme right were anxious to avoid giving the enemy a chance to outflank them on their shield-less side, and their neighbours wanted to keep close-up to them. Now Agis, worried that the Mantineians appeared to be outflanking the *Skiritai* on his left, ordered them and the *Brasideioi* and *neodamodeis* next to them to shift to the left in order to cover the Mantineians, and the polemarchs, Hipponoïdas and Aristokles, to take what Thucydides calls two *lochoi* from the right and plug the gap opening between the *Brasideioi* and *neodamodeis* and those next in line to them (Thucydides 5.71.2–3).

Presumably, as we have seen, Thucydides meant that Hipponoïdas and Aristokles were to take the two *lochoi* from the right of the main body of Spartan troops not from the few Lakedaimonians on the extreme right,[10] and presumably he also meant that they were to take two of the six *lochoi* that he implies formed this main body. But if in fact the main body consisted of six *morai*, the question arises whether Agis intended to transfer two of these from right to left or whether in this part of his narrative Thucydides is correctly using the term *lochos* to mean half a *mora*. Unfortunately it is not possible to say how large a gap Agis thought he had to fill, though it may be possible to arrive at a very rough estimate of the size of the gap as it eventually became. Two of Thucydides' *lochoi*, each with their sixteen *enomotiai* ranged in four files, would have had a front of 128 shields; two *morai*, each containing two such *lochoi*, would, of course, have had double that frontage. However, as was argued above (see p.54), it is hardly likely that Agis seriously considered transferring one third of his Spartan troops from right to left as they were advancing upon the enemy, so it is possible that only two *lochoi* were involved, and not necessarily *lochoi* that were contiguous. In any case, as it turned out Hipponoïdas and Aristokles refused to obey the king's order and one must presume that for a time the gap continued to widen before the king ordered the *Skiritai*, *Brasideioi* and *neodamodeis* to close-up to their right again, and the battle began before they were able to do it (Thucydides 5.72.1).

The result was that the right wing of the Mantineians routed the *Skiritai* and the *Brasideioi* and *neodamodeis*, presumably taking them in both flanks and, more seriously, the Mantineians and their Arcadian allies and the 1,000 picked Argives charged into the gap in the Spartan line (Thucydides 5.72.3). This information enables us to make a rough estimate of the size of the gap as it then was for, assuming that the Spartans' opponents were drawn up eight deep as the Spartans themselves were, the 1,000 picked Argives would have had a front of 125 shields, the Arcadian allies of the Mantineians perhaps sixty to seventy, and the Mantineians themselves, assuming that they were about 3,000 in number, 375. However, of the Mantineians, rather more than half would have been opposite the *Skiritai*, *Brasideioi* and *neodamodeis*, assuming that there were 1,024 of the latter, and some at least of the remainder presumably stretched beyond the left flank of the *Skiritai*. If we assume that about three-quarters of the Mantineians were thus engaged with the *Skiritai* and their comrades, or stretched beyond them on their left, their front opposite the gap would have been composed of about another ninety to 100 shields. In short, the gap would have been approximately equal to a front of 285 shields.[11]

On the left then the Spartans were defeated. The right wing of the Mantineians curled round the left of the *Skiritai* while on their right the *Brasideioi* and *neodamodeis* were similarly taken in flank by the left wing of the Mantineians, their Arcadian allies and the 1,000 picked Argives as they charged into the gap in the Spartan line – the Spartans were driven back upon their wagon-train where some of the 'older men' set to guard it were slain – these may have been men in their fifty-third to fifty-fifth years, as suggested above (p. 55).[12] As Thucydides says (5.72.4), 'in this part of the field the Lakedaimonians were defeated', but it is noticeable that instead of exploiting their advantage by wheeling to catch the victorious Spartans on their shieldless side as they came back across the field – which is what the Spartan right was to do to them – even the 1,000 picked Argives hared off in pursuit as far as the wagons. The allied right thus made little or nothing of its victory, unlike the Spartan right, and instead laid itself open to counter-attack. The Spartans were clearly much more firmly under control than their opponents.

Elsewhere too it was a very different story. The rest of the Argives, the Kleonaians, the Orneatai and the Athenians ranged opposite the Spartans themselves, hardly waited to come to grips, if we are to believe Thucydides (5.72.4), but immediately gave way, some even being trampled underfoot in their anxiety to escape the enemy's clutches – the rout was particularly marked in the centre where King Agis himself was, and 'around him the 300 so-called *Hippeis*'. It is clear from this that any damage the reputation of the Spartans may have suffered by the surrender on Sphakteria was more than outweighed by the reality of having to face them in battle and that the *Hippeis* were not just young dandies picked for their family connections.

The Athenians on the allied left in particular faced disaster on both flanks – on the left where the Tegeates, the other Arcadian allies of the Spartans and the Spartans themselves who protruded beyond them, were sweeping round to take them in flank, and on the right where they had shared in the rout of the main body of the Argives and their allies. In Thucydides' opinion (5.73.1) they would have suffered more than any other contingent in the allied army but for the presence of their cavalry. However, they were also saved by Agis's anxiety about his own left and his order to his whole army to go to its aid. What happened is not exactly clear. Thucydides says (5.73.3) that the Athenians and the Argives with them escaped in safety, 'as the [Spartan] army went past and wheeled away from them' (ὡς παρῆλθε καὶ ἐξέκλινεν ἀπὸ σφῶν τὸ στράτευμα), and this suggests that the Athenians and Argives made good their escape before the Spartans were in a position to take them in flank, and so were beyond reach when the Spartan line pivoted to its left.

The victorious Mantineians and their comrades, however, seeing the whole Spartan army now bearing down upon them, also turned to fly, the Mantineians losing heavily, the picked Argives coming off comparatively unscathed, presumably not so much because they were the better soldiers as because they too mostly got away before the Spartans completed their wheel, whereas the Mantineians were attacked on their shieldless side as they tried to run past (cf. XH 4.2.21–2). The losses on the allied side were 700 of the Argives, Orneatai and Kleonaians, 200 Mantineians and 200 Athenians and Aiginetans, including both Athenian generals, and might have been worse, Thucydides implies (5.73.4), but for the Spartan habit of not pursuing a beaten enemy too far. Diodoros (12.79.6) has an odd story that Agis was ordered to allow the 1,000 picked Argives to escape by one of the 'advisers' attached to his staff, named Pharax, but although Pharax may have been real enough – this was the name of the father of the ranking Spartan officer at the end of the fight on Sphakteria (Thucydides 4.38.1) – and although advisers had been attached to Agis after his much-criticized campaign against Argos earlier in the year (Thucydides 5.63.4), Diodoros' story seems unlikely to be true. In fact, too much should not be made of this alleged Spartan unwillingness to pursue a beaten army, despite what Plutarch says in his life of Lykourgos (22.9–10): such a pursuit could not be carried out by hoplites without serious risk of their breaking ranks and so exposing themselves to sudden counter-attacks, and the Spartans were probably very well aware of this.[13] On the Spartan side the losses among their allies were said to be hardly worth mentioning and their own were said to be about 300, though Thucydides records that it was hard to learn the truth (5.74.3). As we have seen (above, p. 20) one monument of the battle survives in the form of an inscription recording the death 'in war at Mantineia' of one Eualkes, perhaps a *perioikos* from Geronthrai serving as a volunteer with the king's staff (*IG* V i 1124).

This then was the battle of Mantineia – a battle the Spartans might so easily have lost if their opponents had been able to exploit their break-through in the left centre of the Spartan line. Thucydides indeed remarks

(5.72.2) that the Spartans had the worst of it in every respect as far as 'skill' (ἐμπειρία) was concerned, but that they showed that they were no less superior in 'manhood' (ἀνδρεία), whereas at Sphakteria, for example, it had been precisely their 'ἐμπειρία' that the Spartans are said to have been unable to exploit because they could not get to grips with their elusive opponents (Thucydides 4.33.2). But although Thucydides uses the same word in both cases, he clearly means something different in each. On Sphakteria it was the skill of Spartan hoplites in a stand-up fight that was in question including, presumably, both tactical skill and skill with their weapons, but there was clearly nothing wrong with their skill in this sense at Mantineia – there it was the skill of their king that had let them down, or that of the polemarchs who had refused to obey his orders. Skill in the former sense was something that the Spartans could and did learn from their youth, but in the latter sense it was something probably no ancient general learned except by experience – there were no Staff Colleges even in Sparta, and even Spartan armies were commanded by men who reached that position for reasons other than professional expertise.

Nevertheless, it is possible that the success of Agis's wheeling-manoeuvre was noted and that the Spartans later deliberately set out to exploit the advantage to be gained from the tendency, noted by Thucydides (5.71.1), of hoplite armies to edge to the right. The danger was that since each army would tend to get outflanked on its left, the result would virtually be stalemate, but Mantineia had shown that if one could check one's pursuit of the beaten enemy left, and wheel to the left, one could ignore defeat on one's own left and catch the victorious enemy right on its shieldless side as it returned from the pursuit. At all events the new tactics were brilliantly exploited at the Nemea in 394 and it is possible that Kleombrotos was in the act of trying the same kind of manoeuvre at Leuktra when Epameinondas' massed attack hit his line (see pp. 184).

As for Mantineia, it effectively meant the end of the growing opposition to Spartan within the Peloponnese and is arguable that it thus put paid to any chance of Athens winning the Peloponnesian War, since Athens could only have defeated Sparta in the end by defeating her on land. The immediate effects of the battle are best summed up by Thucydides who says that: 'by this one action, the Spartans removed the reproaches cast at them for cowardice due to the disaster on the island and for their other folly and slowness. Humbled they might seem by Fortune but in spirit they were still the same' (5.75.3).

Chapter 8

The Nemea, Koroneia & Lechaion

The battle usually known as the battle of the Nemea river (see below), fought in 394, was the last clear-cut victory won by the Spartan army and is one of the most interesting of all hoplite fights. The Spartans, having alienated in one way or another most of the allies who had helped them to defeat the Athenians in the Peloponnesian War, now found themselves facing a coalition of Boeotians, Euboeans, Athenians, Corinthians and Argives, together with some of the smaller states of central Greece. In 395, at the beginning of what came to be known as the Corinthian War, they had despatched forces into Boeotia, but in a skirmish outside the walls of Haliartos Lysander, hero of the final victory over Athens, had been killed and shortly afterwards King Pausanias, who was thought to have failed properly to support Lysander, had been exiled. The Spartans had then sent for the other king, Agesilaos, at that time campaigning in Asia Minor, but in the meantime, in the spring of 394, mobilized an army under Aristodemos, a member of the same royal house as Pausanias (the Agiadai), and guardian of his young son Agesipolis (XH 4.2.9). They were probably anxious to redress the harm done by the débâcle in Boeotia as soon as possible and were therefore not prepared to wait for Agesilaos' return. They may also have learned that their enemies, perhaps encouraged by the apparent failure of the Spartan army in Boeotia, were airily discussing ways and means of defeating the Spartans before they could gather their allies. Thus Timolaos of Corinth is said by Xenophon (XH 4.2.11–12) to have likened the Spartans to a river, smaller at source, or to wasps, easier to destroy in their nest. But although the strategy advocated by Timolaos anticipated that of Epameinondas twenty-four years later, this time the Spartans were too quick for it.

The opposing armies approached each other along the south shore of the Gulf of Corinth,[1] the Spartans coming from the west, their opponents from the east. There is some controversy about the exact location of the battlefield,[2] but Xenophon's account of the preliminaries to the battle and its aftermath leaves little doubt that it was fought between the river now again called the Nemea (formerly Koutsomadiotikos) and the Rachiani or Longopotamos. Both Strabo (8.6.25) and Livy (33.15.1) give the Nemea river as the boundary between the territory of Sikyon and that of Corinth, so when Xenophon says (XH 4.2.14) the Spartans invaded by way of Epieikeia (ἐμβαλόντων δὲ αὐτῶν κατὰ τὴν Ἐπιείκειαν – i.e. invaded Corinthian territory), although the whereabouts of Epieikeia is unknown they must be presumed to have crossed the river Nemea and this is borne out by the fact that they came under fire from enemy light troops on the hills to their right, and having marched down nearer the sea, began to ravage and burn (XH 4.2.14–5). Hence, when the enemy withdrew and encamped, 'placing the stream-bed in their front' (ἔμπροσθεω ποιησάμενοι τὴν χαράδραν: XH 4.2.15), this stream-bed cannot be that of the Nemea, but must be one further to the east, probably that of the Rachiani (Longopotamos), which is in any case more of an obstacle.[3] That the enemy camp was beside a stream-bed nearer Corinth than the Nemea is confirmed by Xenophon's statement (XH 4.2.23) that after the battle the defeated troops fled first to Corinth and then returned 'to their old camp', because the gates of Corinth were closed against them, for it is only about 6 kilometres from ancient Corinth to the lower course of the Rachiani but 13 or 14 to the Nemea – too great a distance for the defeated army to march over twice after the battle. The enemy camp then was almost certainly on the right bank of the Rachiani and the battle probably took place between it and the Nemea, for although Xenophon does not specifically say that the allies re-crossed the stream-bed that lay in front of their camp before the battle, he does make it clear that they took the initiative and advanced, led by the Boeotians (XH 4.2.18). The Spartans, for their part, were encamped at a distance of 10-stades (about 1,850 metres: XH 4.2.15), and since at first they were unaware that the enemy were advancing, presumably the latter had advanced rather more than halfway between the two camps when battle was finally joined. In short the battle probably took place something like a kilometre west of the Rachiani in the neighbourhood of the modern village of Assos. However, it is usually known as the battle of the Nemea (river) and it would be silly to try to re-name it the battle of the Rachiani or Longopotamos, or something of that sort.

The Spartan army, according to Xenophon (XH 4.2.16), consisted of up to 6,000 Lakedaimonian hoplites, 3,000 from Elis and her neighbours, 1,500 from Sikyon and 3,000 from Epidauros, Trozen, Hermione and Halieis. In addition there were some 600 Lakedaimonian cavalry,[4] 300 Cretan bowmen and not less than 400 slingers from the borders of Elis, whose communities had gone over to Sparta some five years before (cf. XH 3.2.25 & 30). Xenophon has, however, clearly omitted the contingent from Tegea, which he mentions in his account of the battle (XH 4.2.19), possibly a contingent from Mantineia, from where he says the Spartans picked up troops on their march to the Corinthian Gulf along with Tegeates (XH 4.2.13), and possibly a further contingent from Achaea, for he mentions Achaeans in a later passage (XH 4.2.18), and although this may refer primarily to the 1,500 Sikyonians, he also mentions men from Pellene in yet another passage (4.2.20). However, it seems unlikely that contingents from Tegea, Mantineia and Achaea can have amounted to as many as 9,500 men, as has been claimed,[5] thus enabling Xenophon's total for the hoplites on the Spartan side (13,500) to be reconciled with Diodoros' 23,000 (14.83.1). It is true that the Tegeates eventually faced four Athenian regiments totalling 2,400 men, and might thus have had about the same number, and it is equally true that Mantineia could probably have provided as many or more, but it is unlikely that something like 3,000 hoplites or more could have been received from Achaea, excluding Sikyon. More tempting is the suggestion[6] that Diodoros has got his totals for the two armies the wrong way round and should have said that there were 15,000 hoplites on the Spartan side, 23,000 on the other, for Xenophon's total for the allied hoplites in fact comes to 24,000 and he was obviously in some doubt whether there really were as many as 7,000 Argives (XH 4.2.17). However, to allow a mere 1,500 hoplites to the missing contingents from Tegea, Mantineia and – at least – Pellene in Achaea, seems too little. It seems more likely that we should add about 5,000 to Xenophon's totals for the hoplites on the Spartan side, bringing them to between 18,000 and 19,000 men.

Unfortunately too Xenophon does not specify how many of his 6,000 Lakedaimonians were regular Spartan soldiers, nor how many *morai* were present. However, one *mora* was almost certainly stationed at Orchomenos in Boeotia at the time (cf. XH 4.3.15) and it is possible that the *mora*, which is said to have crossed over 'from Corinth' in time to join Agesilaos at Koroneia (Xenophon loc.cit.), was also absent from the Nemea, though it is much more likely that it was present and was sent to join Agesilaos after the victory.

In this case, there would probably have been five *morai* at the Nemea and assuming that thirty-five age-classes were called up for the campaign, as they were for Leuktra (cf. XH 6.4.17), and that – as was argued in the first chapter – there were thirty-two *enomotiai* in each *mora*, five *morai* would have contained 5,600 hoplites: this is near enough to 6,000 to suggest that all Xenophon's 'hoplites of the Lakedaimonians' were regular Spartan soldiers, and if the 300 *Hippeis* were also present the totals become even closer. There is thus no need to postulate that there were large numbers of *perioikoi* or *neodamodeis* present on the field.[7] We have already seen reason to believe that the Spartans would not use *perioikoi* against Peloponnesian enemies at this time (see above. pp. 20–21), and there were already many *neodamodeis* serving in Asia Minor in any case (cf. XH 3.1.4 & 4.2).

For the enemy Xenophon gives 6,000 Athenian hoplites, about 7,000 Argives, 5,000 Boeotians, 3,000 Corinthians and 3,000 Euboeans, making a total of 24,000 hoplites; in addition, he says there were 1,550 cavalry and a considerable number of light troops (XH 4.2.17). As was said above, Diodoros makes the total 15,000 hoplites for the allies, but although Xenophon obviously had some doubt about the Argive total (cf. Ἀρνείων δ 'ἐλένοντο περὶ ἐπτακισχιλίους: 4.2.17), it is impossible to reconcile his total with Diodoros' and it is obvious that Xenophon's is to be preferred. Thus, even if the Spartans had some 5,000 more hoplites on their side than Xenophon says, they were still considerably outnumbered and this makes their victory all the more remarkable.

The dispositions of the two sides had an important bearing on the outcome and we can reconstruct them in some detail from Xenophon's narrative. The Spartans themselves occupied the right of their army (XH 4.2.18), with the Tegeates next to them (cf. 4.2.19), and immediately one notices the difference from Mantineia. There the Spartan right had consisted of the Tegeates and a few Lakedaimonians (Thucydides 5.67.1), suggesting that this flank was then considered of less importance. On the Spartan left were the 'Achaeans' opposite the Boeotians (XH 4.2.18), probably mostly Sikyonians, but with some troops at least from Pellene – they are later found opposite those from Thespiai (XH 4.2.20) – and possibly from other small towns in Achaea. This would leave the 3,000 from Elis and its neighbourhood, the 3,000 from Epidauros and other towns in the Argolid, and possibly 2–3,000 Mantineians, to occupy the rest of the Spartan line.

On the allied side we know that the Athenians occupied the left (XH 4.2.19) and the Boeotians the right (XH 4.2.18), that the Corinthians were next to the Boeotians, and the Argives next to them (cf. XH 4.2.22). But it is not certain where the Euboeans were. Since they are not mentioned in the account of the rout it is likely that they were next to the Athenians and so escaped with them (cf. XH 4.2.21). In the case of the allies too we can say how long a front each contingent occupied, except for the Boeotians, for we know how deep they were drawn up. Xenophon says (XH 4.2.13) that there had been some discussion among the allies as to how deep they should form their phalanx, and when he says that the Boeotians disregarded 'the depth of sixteen' (τοῦ εἰς ἐκκαίδεκα: 4.2.18), he implies that this was the depth agreed upon and adopted by the rest. If this is right the Athenians would have presented a front of 375 shields, the Euboeans one of 187 or 188, the Argives one of about 437 and the Corinthians again one of 187 or 188. Thus the allies, apart from the Boeotians, would have had a front of 1,188 men. Unfortunately Xenophon does not say how deep the Boeotians eventually decided to make their line but it must clearly have been deeper than sixteen shields. If they made it twenty-five shields deep, as the Thebans had done at Delion in 424 (Thucydides 4.93.4), their front would have been of 200 shields giving the whole allied army a front of about 1,388 shields.

Xenophon does not say how deep the Spartans made their line, but since their enemies are said to have agreed on a depth of sixteen to prevent their being outflanked (XH 4.2.13), they presumably thought that the Spartans were unlikely to draw up only eight deep as they had done at Mantineia (Thucydides 5.68.3), since this would have given them a longer front, even if they were only 13,500 strong. Before the Boeotians broke the agreement the allies would have assumed that they would have a front of 1,500 shields. It is true that the Spartans did succeed in outflanking them, but this seems to have been largely due to the way both armies 'led to the right' when they advanced (XH 4.2.18–19). It is not even certain that all the contingents on the Spartan side would have been drawn up in the same depth: the Spartans, for example, may have been drawn up with a depth of twelve shields, as at Leuktra (cf. XH 6.4.12), giving them a front of just under 500 shields if there really were 5,900 of them' but, on the other hand, if we are to interpret strictly Xenophon's statement that the 'Achaeans' were opposite the Boeotians, and if by the 'Achaeans' he meant just the 1,500 Sikyonis together with a few hoplites from Pellene, then the 'Achaeans' cannot have been drawn up twelve deep: if they were eight deep they would have presented a front just about as long as the 5,000 Boeotians assuming the latter were twenty-five deep. However, there are too many variables here: there may have been more than 1,500+ 'Achaeans', for example, and the Boeotians may have overlapped them considerably on their left.

According to Xenophon (XH 4.2.18), it was the Boeotians who took the initiative in bringing about the battle. While they were on the left of the allied line, opposite the Lakedaimonians, they were not at all anxious to fight – an indication, if it is true (Xenophon did not like Boeotians), of the reputation enjoyed by the Spartans at this time – but when they found themselves on the right, opposite the Achaeans, they immediately gave the word to make ready – this suggests that some agreement had also been reached that the various national contingents should take the right and the command in rotation. The Boeotians, however, disregarded the agreement to form up sixteen deep and instead, in Xenophon's words (loc.cit.), 'made their phalanx really deep' (βαθεῖαν παντελῶς ἐποιήσαντο τὴν φάλαννα) – perhaps twenty-five deep, as suggested above. When they moved off, furthermore, 'they led to the right in order that they might extend beyond the enemy with their wing' (ἦγον ἐπὶ τα δεξιά, ὅπως ὑπερέχοιεν τῷ κέρατι τῶν πολεμίων: Xenophon loc.cit.), and in this they were followed by the Athenians in order to avoid becoming separated and, obviously, though Xenophon does not say so, by the other contingents between the Boeotians and Athenians.

We cannot be sure exactly how the Boeotians and their allies carried out this manoeuvre but we should at least suppose that they did the same thing as the Spartans, for Xenophon uses exactly the same phrase of them (ἦγον δὲ καὶ οἱ Λακεδαιμόνιοι ἐπὶ τὰ δεξιά: 4.2.19). Xenophon's language suggests that we are not dealing with a simple matter of both armies edging to the right in the manner described by Thucydides in his account of Mantineia (5.71.1), but with something more deliberate and this is borne out for the Spartans by Xenophon's remark that the word was passed along to follow the leading unit (παρεννύησαν μὲν ἀκολουθεῖν τῷ ἡγουμένῳ). But the desired result could still have been achieved either by marching forward at an angle to the right of the direct line of approach or by the two phalanxes turning to the right and marching off in column for some distance before turning left again into line-of-battle. Xenophon's remark about passing the word to 'follow-the leading unit' has been held to indicate the latter, but certainty is not possible.[8]

The result of this sideways movement, however achieved, was that the Spartans extended their right wing so far beyond the enemy left that only six of the Athenian tribal regiments were eventually opposite them, the other four being opposite the Tegeates (XH 4.2.19). Since there were 6,000 Athenians on the field (XH 4.2.17), the six regiments opposite the Spartans would have contained some 3,600 men who would have had a front of 225 men, if they were formed sixteen deep – the other four regiments would have contained 2,400 men with a front of 150. Thus, if the Spartans were ranged twelve deep, as suggested above, with a front of 500 men, we can calculate that about 275 of their files were beyond the left of the Athenian line.

The two armies closed until they were less than a stade (less than 200 metres) apart, then the Spartans sacrificed a goat to Artemis the Huntress and continued the advance, 'wheeling round their overlapping wing to encircle the enemy' (or 'in a circle': τὸ ὑπερέχον ἐπικάμψαντες εἰς κύκλωσιν: XH 4.2.20). Here the phrase Xenophon uses is one he also uses in the *Anabasis* (1.8.23) to describe a manoeuvre at Kounaxa and in his fictional account of the upbringing of Cyrus (*Cyropaedia* 7.1.5), where he makes use of the Greek letter *gamma* (Γ) as a simile for the end-product of the manoeuvre. What seems to be meant is that the overlapping part of the phalanx – at the Nemea the Spartan right – pivoted at a point opposite the end of the enemy phalanx (here their left), and wheeled to form a new front at right angles to the remainder of the army.[9] The result of this at the Nemea was that the six Athenian regiments that faced the Spartans broke before their attack losing particularly heavily on their left to the flank attack, and that the Spartans then began to sweep across the field from their right to left, with their remaining units presumably now also wheeling to the left one by one, as the Athenians gave way before them.

Meanwhile, however, to the left of the Spartans their allies had in turn all given way, except, intriguingly, the men from Pellene, who are said to have fought it out with the soldiers of Thespiai where they stood (XH 4.2.20). Thus, as the Spartans began their new advance most of their opponents, apart from the six Athenian regiments they themselves had routed, had gone off in pursuit of the fleeing left wing of the Spartan army. The remaining four Athenian regiments, which had defeated the Tegeates, managed to escape the onslaught without losing any more men than they had lost at the hands of the Tegeates because the Spartans had passed across their rear before they began to return from the pursuit (XH 4.2.21), and the same may be true of the Euboeans, who are not mentioned in Xenophon's account after their listing as part of the allied army. But the other allied contingents were caught by the Spartans as they now tried to retreat back across the field. The first to suffer were the Argives. Xenophon says (XH 4.2.22) that 'as the first polemarch was about to engage them head-on, someone is said to have shouted to let the front ranks go by', and this suggests that the 'first polemarch', who was probably the commander of the 'first' *mora*, on the extreme right of the Spartan line, was about to continue his wheel so that his men would have been facing back the way they had come and would thus have met the Argives head-on, and that the man who shouted advocated an attack on the right flank of the enemy – their shieldless side – as they ran by.[10] At all events this is what happened: the Spartans struck the shieldless side of the fleeing Argives and caused many casualties, and the same thing happened to the Corinthians and Thebans as the relentless Spartan advance continued. According to Xenophon (XH 4.3.1) the Spartans later claimed that only eight of their own men were killed as against 'very many' (παμπληθεῖς) of the enemy, though they admitted that 'not a few' (οὐκ ὀλίγοι) of their allies had fallen – Diodoros (14.83.2) says that 'of the Lakedaimonians and their allies' 1,100 men fell, for 2,800 of the Boeotians and their allies.

The Nemea has been regarded as an old-fashioned battle,[11] but it seems clear that the rolling-up of the enemy line was deliberate in comparison with what happened at Mantineia, as was the shift to the right which brought it about. The Spartans were now apparently prepared to accept defeat on their own left wing – in this case perhaps all the more willingly since it only involved allied troops – relying on the assumption that the enemy would only exploit their own success in outflanking the left of the Spartan line to the extent of defeating the troops opposite them. Even if one finds the sacrificing of allied troops distasteful, from the purely military point of view there is nothing crude about the Spartan tactics and one cannot help but be impressed by their discipline. It is clear that at every moment of the battle their officers had them completely in hand and could manoeuvre them about the battlefield in unbroken formation (cf. συντεταγμένοι ἐπορεύοντο: XH 4.2.21). It was this machine-like precision that made the Spartans so formidable in a set-piece engagement and when, as here, it was allied to good tactics, the result was devastating. If anyone appears old-fashioned in this battle it is the enemy not the Spartans.

While the battle near the Nemea was being fought and won the Spartan king Agesilaos was marching home from Asia Minor. He was at Amphipolis when word was brought to him of the victory, but this apparently made no difference to his plans. He had to fight his way through Thessaly, winning a victory near Mt Narthakion, south-west of Pharsalos (XH 4.3.3ff.), which indicates that he followed the route from Pharsalos to Lamia through the

Fourka pass, but thereafter he apparently encountered no opposition until he reached Boeotia, at the time of the eclipse of the sun on 14 August, 394 (XH 4.3.10). Diodoros records the capture of Herakleia by the Boeotians and Argives under the year 395/4 (14.82.6–7), but unless we are to assume that the garrison was not strong enough to prevent the Spartans using Thermopylai, he must have misplaced the incident[12] for there can hardly be any doubt that Agesilaos used the pass, though thereafter he may have taken the quickest feasible route into Phokis – for example through the Klisoura pass from Molos to Dhrimaia via Mendhenitsa – for the Opountian Lokrians were hostile (cf. XH 4.3.15). In Phokis he would have been joined by the contingent of Phokian hoplites that fought with him at Koroneia (XH loc.cit.) and possibly by the *mora*, which had been sent to join him probably after the battle near the Nemea – the safest and easiest route for this force would have been across the Gulf of Corinth to Itea and thence by way of Amphissa into Phokis over the Amvlema pass. Finally, on entering Boeotia, he would have been joined by a contingent from Orchomenos and by half the *mora*, which had been stationed there since the previous year (cf. XH 4.3.15).

Unfortunately no ancient source gives a total for either army in the clash that followed and we are reduced to guesswork. Agesilaos had with him a *mora* and a half of Spartans and, assuming that these were at full campaign strength, this would give him about 1,680 Spartan troops. In addition he had the *neodamodeis* he had commanded in Asia, originally 2,000 in number (XH 3.4.2), those that remained of the 10,000 mercenaries, including Xenophon himself who had marched with Cyrus to Kounaxa and who were now commanded by the Spartiate, Herippidas (cf. XH 3.4.20), men from some of the Greek cities in Asia Minor and of those in Europe he had won over as he marched home, and contingents from Phokis and Orchomenos. In all he may have had something like 15,000 hoplites, probably less, and in addition, Xenophon says (XH 4.3.15), he had many more peltasts than his opponents but about the same number of cavalry, though he irritatingly gives no figures.

Xenophon lists the opposing forces as consisting of Boeotians, Athenians, Argives, Corinthians, Ainianians, Euboeans and both Opountian and Ozolian Lokrians, but again without giving any numbers. We can, however, probably assume that the Boeotians were in greater strength than at the Nemea, since the battle was fought in their territory – perhaps then 6,000 rather than 5,000 – and that the Athenians and Euboeans, who lived nearby and had escaped relatively unscathed from the Nemea, fielded about the same number (6,000 and 3,000, respectively), though the Athenians may have been fewer in view of their evident alarm for the safety of Athens at about this time.[13] But it seems unlikely that the Argives and Corinthians had sent as many as 10,000 men between them (7,000 + 3,000), in view of their losses at the Nemea and the danger to their own territories from the victorious Spartan army, and although the presence of contingents from both Lokrian peoples might have compensated to some extent, they were probably not very numerous – the contingent of Ainianians presumably consisted of light troops. All in all then the allies probably had something like 20,000 hoplites.[14]

Xenophon also says little about the dispositions on either side. Agesilaos himself commanded the Spartan right (XH 4.3.16) and presumably had the Spartan regulars under his direct command while the contingent from Orchomenos was on the left of his line. On the allied side the Thebans were on the right, facing the Orchomenians, while the Argives had the unenviable task of facing the Spartans. The encounter took place, according to Xenophon (loc.cit.), in the plain of Koroneia, with Agesilaos and his army coming from the Kephisos and his opponents from Helikon, and this has been interpreted to mean that the lines faced respectively south and north, with the Theban wing perhaps resting approximately on the site of the modern village of Mamoura.[15]

Both in his life of Agesilaos (2.10) and in the *Hellenika* (4.3.17), Xenophon, who was an eyewitness, mentions the deep silence in which the two sides approached each other, but when they were about a stade apart the Thebans broke into a double, shouting their war-cry, and when the lines had closed to within three *plethra* of each other (half a stade, or about 90 metres), Herippidas' mercenaries, followed by the Ionians, Aeolians and Hellespontines from the centre of Agesilaos' line, ran forward in turn (XH 4.3.17), and soon the two armies had closed to spear-thrust. On the Spartan right the Argives are said not even to have waited to receive the attack but to have fled to the slopes of Helikon, while those next to them in the allied line were rapidly overcome by Agesilaos' centre. But as some of the mercenaries were already garlanding the king, someone brought the news that the Thebans had cut their way through the Orchomenians and were among the baggage-train (XH 4.3.18).

Immediately Agesilaos, in Xenophon's words (loc.cit.), 'counter marched his phalanx and led it against them', presumably using the Lakonian form of counter march (see above, p. 35), whereby each man in the file about-turned, and while the original rear-man (now in front) stood fast, the original file-leader (now at the rear) led his men to take up their places again, in their original order, in front of the rear-man, thus giving the impression of advancing. The Theban contingent was now separated from the rest of their allies by the whole of Agesilaos' army, but apparently did not hesitate, 'wishing to break through to their own men,' says Xenophon (loc.cit.), 'they closed up and stoutly advanced'. Presumably this means that they either massed in deeper formation or, perhaps more probably, simply closed-up – the later tactical writer, Asklepiodotos, says that the closest order was when men locked shields and stood only one cubit apart (*Taktika* 4.1), or in other words the distance from one man's left shoulder to the next man's left shoulder was approximately 18 inches or about 46 centimetres.

Xenophon says (XH 4.3.19) that Agesilaos could at this point have let the Thebans go by and then fallen on their rear but chose instead to meet them head on. It is possible that Xenophon is here being defensive about his hero and modern scholars have suggested that Agesilaos was motivated by personal hatred of the Thebans.[16] But either a flank attack, as at the Nemea, or a rear attack, as Xenophon suggests, though less risky, did not give the Spartans the chance of annihilating victory, and it is arguable that Agesilaos was correct in choosing the course he did. He must have outnumbered the Thebans – presumably Xenophon means the whole Boeotian contingent – by more than two to one and he must have thought that he had a splendid opportunity of knocking out Sparta's most dangerous foe in one decisive engagement.

It was probably mainly the fact that in the ensuing clash the two sides were facing in the opposite direction to the way they had faced at the beginning of the battle, which led Xenophon to describe it as 'like no other of those in our time' (XH 4.3.16, *Agesilaos* 2.9), although the tone of his description suggests that the final clash also left an impression of unusual ferocity upon him: '(the king) crashed against the Thebans face to face,' he says (XH 4.3.19), 'and smashing their shields together, they shoved, fought, slew and died' – in the *Agesilaos* (2.12) he adds that 'there was no shouting, nor yet silence, but the kind of noise that anger and battle would produce'.[17] In the end, according to Xenophon, some of the Thebans broke through to the slopes of Helikon but many were killed as they made off, while Agesilaos himself was wounded.

Plutarch (*Agesilaos* 18.3–4), alleging that the fiercest fighting involved what he calls the fifty 'volunteers' who acted as the king's bodyguard, claims that in the end the Spartans were compelled to open their phalanx and let the Thebans through and that they then followed up to take the Thebans in flank as they loosened their order after their apparent break through. Frontinus (*Strategemata* 2.6.6) and Polyainos (2.1.19) also both say that the Spartans deliberately opened ranks to let the Thebans through, though they then say the Spartans attacked them from the rear, which is precisely what Xenophon says Agesilaos had originally decided not to do (XH 4.3.19). Xenophon was an eyewitness of the battle and his version should be preferred. By claiming that his hero tried to prevent the Thebans' escape and failed, he does nothing to enhance his reputation – rather the reverse – and in any case, to part ranks in the heat of battle to let several thousand men go through would probably have been beyond even the Spartans.[18] Eighty Thebans who had apparently got left behind took refuge in the temple of Itonian Athena (XH 4.3.20, cf. Plutarch *Agesilaos* 19.1–2), which has been plausibly located at the site of the present-day chapel of the Metamorphosis, about a kilometre east-north-east of the village of Mamoura,[19] but Agesilaos ordered his men to let them go.

According to Diodoros (14.84.2), more than 600 of the Boeotians and their allies fell for only 350 on the Spartan side, but although Agesilaos claimed the victory, ordering a trophy erected next day and a parade of his troops garlanded with pipers sounding, and although the Thebans conceded defeat by sending heralds to ask that they might bury their dead under truce (XH 4.3.21), Plutarch may well be right – though he was a Boeotian – that the Thebans were elated at the outcome of the battle since their own contingent, they claimed, had been undefeated and had twice broken through those opposed to them (*Agesilaos* 18.4). Certainly Agesilaos made no attempt to follow up his victory. He himself returned home by way of Delphi without venturing further into Boeotia, and although an army was left behind under the polemarch Gylis, it too withdrew to Phokis and contented itself with invading Lokris, where Gylis was killed. In the long term the Spartans should have taken more note, one feels, of the effect of a charge of close-packed Theban hoplites in depth.

After Koroneia, there were no more set-piece battles in the Corinthian War but four years later occurred the famous fight on the road from Sikyon to Lechaion, in which a *mora* of the Spartan army lost almost half its number at the hands of Iphikrates' peltasts. In the meantime the war in mainland

Greece had increasingly centred round Corinth – hence its name. Thus, in 392, the polemarch Praxitas, with two *morai* under command, and aided by treachery, had penetrated the 'long walls' linking Corinth to its sea-port on the Gulf of Corinth, Lechaion, and had gone on to capture Lechaion itself and two small forts in the direction of Megara (XH 4.4.7ff.), though by the end of the year the section of the walls demolished by Praxitas had been re-built by Athenian troops and Lechaion itself re-captured. It was now that Iphikrates and his mercenaries became prominent, though at first they were wary of clashing with Spartan troops after some of them had been caught and killed by young Spartan hoplites on one of their raids into Arcadia (XH 4.4.16). In 391 Agesilaos, in co-operation with his brother Teleutias commanding at sea, re-captured the long walls and retook Lechaion (XH 4.4.19), and next year he was back to raid the Perachora peninsula where the Corinthians were reported to be keeping most of their livestock. It was while he was there that the Spartan king learned of the disaster that had befallen the *mora* on the Lechaion road (XH 4.5.7).

What had happened (XH 4.5.11ff.) was that all the Amyklaians in the Spartan army had been given furlough to go home and celebrate the festival of the Hyakinthia, and the polemarch in command of the *mora* at Lechaion had decided to escort them past Corinth and part of the way to Sikyon. When about 20 or 30 stades (3.7–5.5km.) from Sikyon, the polemarch turned back with his infantry, ordering the cavalry *mora* attached to his command to continue to escort the Amyklaians as far as they wanted. Xenophon emphasises (4.5.12) that the Spartans were aware of the presence of numerous hoplites and peltasts in Corinth, but because of their previous successes contemptuously assumed that no-one would attack them. However, when Iphikrates and the Athenian hoplite commander Kallias saw the *mora* approaching and realised how few the Spartans were and that they were not accompanied by either peltasts or cavalry, they decided to attack. They calculated that they would be able to aim javelins at the Spartans' unshielded side if they proceeded along the road, and if they attempted to pursue, the peltasts would easily be able to escape them (XH 4.5.13).

The fight that followed was very similar to the one on Sphakteria, thirty–five years before, save that this time the Spartan hoplites at least had somewhere to go. Kallias drew up his hoplites not far from the city walls of Corinth, thus presumably inhibiting the Spartans from pursuing the peltasts too far since, once they broke ranks in pursuit, there would always be a danger that they might be attacked by the Athenian hoplites before they could re-form. In the same way Demosthenes on Sphakteria had deployed his 800 hoplites to support his light troops (cf. Thucydides 4.33.1–2). Meanwhile, Iphikrates led his peltasts into the attack, perhaps at first not pressing too closely for the Spartans were apparently able to get the first of their wounded carried away safely to Lechaion (XH 4.5.15). This may even have made the polemarch over-confident, for if the *hypaspistai* could get away, supporting the wounded, one would have thought that the whole *mora* could equally well have escaped by marching resolutely for Lechaion. Instead the polemarch reverted to the well-tried technique of ordering those 'ten years from manhood' (i.e., perhaps, his front two ranks) to charge and drive the peltasts away.

The inevitable happened. The peltasts, skilfully handled on this occasion, simply ran away and when the Spartan hoplites began to retire – presumably before they came too close to Kallias' hoplites – the peltasts came at them again now that they were scattered, killing nine or ten immediately with their javelins. The polemarch then ordered those 'fifteen years from manhood' to charge, but their losses were even heavier. At this point the Spartan cavalry arrived on the scene, but although the polemarch ordered another charge by his hoplites, in co-operation with the cavalry, the latter, according to Xenophon (4.5.16), mis-managed the attack. Instead of pursuing the peltasts at full gallop the Spartan troopers merely kept pace with their hoplites, presumably for fear of becoming isolated, and so failed to catch the fleeing enemy.

One must assume that all this time the Spartans had been gradually edging towards Lechaion, and eventually they reached a hillock about 370 metres from the sea and about 3 kilometres from Lechaion. Their friends there had by now realized their plight and put out in small boats along the coast, but instead of marching in an orderly way down to the sea, the remnants of the *mora* now apparently broke, seeing even the Athenian hoplites at last advancing upon them. Some managed to run down to the sea and were presumably picked up by the boats, others managed to escape to Lechaion with the cavalry, but, all told, they lost 250 killed out of the c.600 hoplites with which they had started (XH 4.5.17), though it is interesting that Xenophon says nothing of any prisoners.

There is no doubt that the defeat of the *mora* was a serious blow to Sparta in the short term, as is shown by Agesilaos' endeavours to minimize its effects on his return-march to Sparta by entering ostensibly friendly cities as late as possible and leaving as early as possible in the morning, and by marching past Mantineia in particular while it was dark – he was worried especially about the possible effects on his own men if they saw the delight of the Mantineians at their misfortune (XH 4.5.18). But although Iphikrates followed up his success by re-capturing three of the Spartan-held fortresses in the Corinthia, and the Spartans seem to have avoided operations in the Corinthia for the duration of the war, they held on to Lechaion and were not deterred from successful operations elsewhere, in Akarnania and the Argolid. In the long term the defeat was not decisive since the war was to be decided by the intervention of the king of Persia and operations at sea, and the defeat of the *mora* certainly did not encourage Sparta's enemies to try conclusions again with her army.

Chapter 9

Leuktra

After the fight on the Lechaion road, the focus of the Corinthian War increasingly shifted to Asia Minor and after Persia had intervened on Sparta's behalf, it was finally brought to an end by the so-called King's Peace, or Peace of Antalkidas, in 386.[1] Four years later a Spartan force under Phoibidas, ostensibly on its way to Chalkidike, seized the Kadmeia, the acropolis of Thebes itself, at the instigation of a pro-Spartan faction led by Leontiades and when in 379 King Agesilaos finally brought Sparta's erstwhile ally Phleious to heel, and in Chalkidike, Olynthos came to terms, Sparta reached the zenith of her power in mainland Greece (cf. XH 5.3.27). But her empire soon crumbled. The same year saw Thebes freed by patriotic exiles and Sparta rapidly found herself faced by another coalition based on a renewed Athenian confederacy after Athens had been deeply offended by an ill-conceived raid on Attica by the Spartan general Sphodrias. The desultory warfare that followed was interrupted by an abortive peace in 375, during which the Thebans, increasingly at odds with Athens and her allies, re-established the Boeotian confederacy. But by 371 the principal belligerents all had their problems and were willing to discuss a new peace, particularly since the Spartans had again secured Persian backing as they had done in 387/6.

Initially all went well and peace was concluded at a conference held at Sparta. But the Thebans were apprehensive about the status of the Boeotian League, which could be held to infringe the provision in the peace-treaty that all Greek states were to be autonomous, and although they had sworn to the peace as Thebans, they requested that the treaty be altered to show that it was the Boeotians and not just the Thebans who had sworn to it. Agesilaos, however, refused to allow this and when the Thebans, led by Epameinondas, continued to insist, the king erased their name from the list of signatories, thus effectively isolating them from the rest of Greece.[2]

Since 375 the Spartans had maintained a considerable military presence in Phokis and northern Boeotia, where Orchomenos had remained hostile to Thebes. Originally the Spartan forces had consisted of four *morai*, together with allied contingents, under Agesilaos' colleague Kieombrotos (cf. XH 6.1.1), but although Xenophon implies that they had been there ever since, it seems very unlikely that so large a part of the Spartan army can have been so far from home for five years and it is possible that only two *morai* were retained in the area in rotation (cf. Plutarch *Pelopidas* 16.1–2). It was this force that Plutarch says (op.cit., 16–7) was routed by the Theban general Pelopidas, in command of a body of cavalry and the hoplites of the crack unit of the Theban army, the so-called 'Sacred Band' (ἱερὸς λόχος), in a skirmish at Tegyra, possibly in 375 (cf. Diodoros 15.81.2, and, for the date, 15.37.1–2): Pelopidas' victory was no doubt exaggerated by Theban tradition and it is clear that the Spartan force was not destroyed. Now in 371, if not before, it was brought back up to a strength of four *morai*, with King Kieombrotos again in command and, following the fracas at the peace-conference, the Spartans ordered him to invade Boeotia unless the Thebans duly acquiesced in the dissolution of the Boeotian Confederacy. This the Thebans naturally refused to do and so Kieombrotos prepared to invade Boeotia from the north down the Kephisos valley.

Faced with this threat the Boeotians mustered their federal army and with 6,000 hoplites took up a strong position between Koroneia and Lake Kopais (Diodoros 15.52.27; Pausanias 9.13.3), much as they had done when faced with Agesilaos' invasion in 394. They probably also sent another force, perhaps 1,000 hoplites strong, under the Boeotarch, Bakchylidas, to guard the passes over Kithairon and a smaller force, under Chaireas, to guard a route through the mountains south of Helikon (cf. Pausanias 9.13.3 & 13.1). Unlike Agesilaos, however, Kleombrotos was evidently unwilling to try to force a passage through at Koroneia and instead turned back on his tracks and made his way through the mountains to Thisbe, thus turning the Koroneia position (XH 6.1.3). There is some doubt about his exact route but Pausanias (9.13.3) says he went by way of Ambrossos, which lay near the modern village of Distomon, so he probably followed the route from Lebadeia to Delphi until he turned off for Ambrossos. From there he may have followed the relatively easy route to Stiris, and thence made his way via the sites of the modern villages of Kyriaki and Koukoura to Thisbe. It was perhaps somewhere between Kyriaki and Koukoura that there took place the skirmish with the Boeotian detachment under Chaireas, recorded by Pausanias (9.13.1).[3]

From Thisbe Kleombrotos could have marched straight to the plain of Thebes via Thespiai, but instead he made his way to Kreusis (Livadhostro) on the Gulf of Corinth, where he captured twelve Theban triremes (XH 6.4.3 – ten according to Diodoros 15.53.1). This diversion is probably to be explained by the Spartan king's desire to re-establish communications with the Peloponnese with a view either to the possibility of receiving reinforcements or to securing his line of retreat, should it prove necessary.[4] The diversion undoubtedly gave the Boeotians more time to react to the Spartan move but Kleombrotos can hardly have hoped to surprise the enemy by entering the Theban plain from a different direction, since ultimately his march could hardly be concealed – in the event his brush with Chaireas must have given the game away, if it had not been given away before – and the Boeotians could easily march to bar his path. Presumably then the flank-march itself had been partly, if not primarily, designed to re-establish communications with the Peloponnese, if also to give Kleombrotos at least the freedom of manoeuvre, which the terrain near Koroneia would have denied him. At all events from Kreusis he turned north, possibly up the ancient road running over the eastern shoulder of Mt Korombili, past the site of the chapel of Ayios Mamas, to descend into the valley of the upper Asopos, whence another easy route leads to Thebes. Here the Spartan army camped in a position overlooking the plain of Leuktra, probably just south of the flat ground between the fork in the Kreusis-Thespiai road and the now restored monument.[5] The Boeotians, meanwhile, had probably learned of the Spartan flank-march from Chaireas, if not before, and marched from Koroneia to bar entry to the Theban plain, probably ordering the Boeotarch, Bakchylidas guarding Kithairon to join the main body as soon as possible. The main army presumably took the route past Thespiai to Leuktra, where they finally came in sight of the Spartan army and camped opposite it.

Unfortunately, we do not know how many men there were on either side at this crucial battle, though the secondary sources are agreed that the Boeotians were outnumbered. Xenophon says nothing except that there were four Spartan *morai* (XH 6.4.17), and that the *enomotiai* were formed up in three files of not more than twelve men each (6.4.12) – in fact, since thirty-five of the forty age-classes had been called up (XH 6.4.17), the paper-strength of each *enomotia* should have been thirty-five. Assuming then that there were thirty-two *enomotiai* in each *mora*, the main body of Spartan troops would have had a paper-strength of 4,480 hoplites, to whom we should probably add 300 *Hippeis* (cf. XH 6.4.14, and see above, p. 14), and perhaps four to five hundred cavalry.[6] This agrees well enough with the most reasonable total for Kleombrotos' army given by the secondary sources – Plutarch's 10,000 hoplites and 1,000 cavalry (*Pelopidas* 20.1), for the Spartans certainly had some other troops with them. Xenophon himself mentions mercenaries, Phokian peltasts and cavalry from Herakleia and Phleious (XH 6.4.9), Pausanias (8.6.2) says Arcadians fought at the battle, and there were probably hoplites from Phleious and Herakleia at least, as well as their cavalry. Indeed it is possible that Kleombrotos' army in 371 contained 'the proportionate levy of the allies', as it had done in 375 (cf. XH 6.1.1: 'τῶν συμμάχων τὸ μέρος', i.e. two-thirds, the corresponding proportion to four *morai* of Spartan troops), in which case there could easily have been over 5,000 allied hoplites present.[7] But in any case Plutarch's figures are far more realistic than Frontinus's 24,000 infantry and 1,600 cavalry (*Strategemata* 4.2.6), or Polyainos' overall total of 40,000 men, for the Spartan side (2.3.8 & 12).

As for the Boeotians, Diodoros gives them 6,000 hoplites commanded by six Boeotarchs at Koroneia (15.53.2), and if we can trust his and Pausanias' story of the disagreement between the six Boeotarchs before the seventh, Bakchylidas, joined them (Diodoros 15.53.3; Pausanias 9.13.3), it is plausible to suggest that Bakchylidas' detachment brought the number up to 7,000. Of these 4,000 were probably Thebans, the rest from the other three federal units of the Boeotian League,[8] and this may be where Frontinus gets his figure of 4,000 for the Boeotian infantry and cavalry combined, of which 400 were cavalry – the latter figure too may really reflect the Theban contribution to the cavalry, in which case the true total for the whole of the Boeotian cavalry will have been 700. But the Boeotians were almost certainly without allies (cf. XH 6.4.4), and Diodoros' statement that they were joined by Jason of Pherai before the battle must be rejected in the light of Xenophon's evidence (XH 6.4.20ff.), as must his even more absurd story that Kleombrotos first retreated from Leuktra but returned to fight the battle when joined by reinforcements under Agesilaos' son Archidamos (15.54.2–7). Xenophon says that the Spartans retreating from the defeat met Archidamos at Aigosthena (XH 6.4.26).

It would seem that neither side was particularly eager for battle. According to Xenophon (XH 6.4.4–6), Kleombrotos' 'friends' urged him not to compound his earlier failures against the Boeotians by allowing them to escape now and that it was this that spurred him to fight. The Boeotians, on the other hand, may well have been dismayed at the prospect of fighting the

Spartans with the odds against them, even if they outnumbered the Spartans themselves, and Diodoros and Pausanias both tell a circumstantial story of disagreement among the Boeotarchs, which was only resolved when Bakchylidas joined the other six and gave his vote for fighting (Diodoros 15.53.3; Pausanias 9.13.3). All the sources also make much of the various omens of victory or disaster that were manifested to either side, some suggesting that some or all were deliberately manufactured by Epameinondas and his friend Pelopidas (cf. Diodoros 15.53.4ff.; Plutarch *Pelopidas* 20.3–4; Frontinus *Strategemata* 1.11.16; Polyainos 2.3.8). The most amusing – and perhaps the most likely to be authentic because the most unusual – is the story told by Frontinus (op.cit. 1.2.7) that Epameinondas' chair collapsed under him and when his men were dismayed at the omen he declared, 'No! We are just being forbidden to sit!'

We have three accounts of the battle itself – by Xenophon, Diodoros and Plutarch – and too much has perhaps been made of the discrepancies between them, particularly if one bears in mind that Xenophon writes exclusively from the Spartan point of view. He does not even mention Epameinondas, for example, and says nothing about tactics on either side. And Plutarch is naturally to a certain extent concerned in his life of Pelopidas with the doings of his hero, who commanded the Theban Sacred Band. His life of Epameinondas, unfortunately, has not survived. In particular, although it is arguable that we should not accept anything from the secondary sources that conflicts with what Xenophon, our primary source, actually says, it is surely dangerous to argue from his silence that any given additional piece of information from a secondary source must be wrong. In fact, the only serious discrepancy between the three accounts is that Diodoros has the Spartan phalanx attack on both wings in crescent formation (15.53.3), and this is almost certainly untrue. It is either due to his mistaken belief – or, of course, that of his source – that both Kleombrotos and Agesilaos' son Archidamos were present at the battle,[9] or may be a muddled reflection of Xenophon's statement (XH 6.4.9) that the battle opened with an attack by some of Sparta's mercenaries and allies who may be presumed to have been on their left (see below) on the Boeotian camp-followers and others reluctant to fight as they tried to leave the field.

The dispositions of the two sides are reasonably clear in general. Xenophon implies that Kleombrotos and the *Hippeis* were on the Spartan right (XH 6.4.14), and presumably almost the whole right half of the Spartan army was composed of the four *morai*, with the king and the *Hippeis* perhaps between the first and second *morai* counting from the right.[10] The left would then have been composed of the mercenaries and allied troops. Xenophon also says (XH 6.4.12) that the Spartan *enomotiai* were drawn up 'not more than twelve deep', which would mean a front of about 400 shields for the Spartan half of the army, assuming that it contained 4,780 hoplites.

On the other side it is clear that the Thebans were on the left and the rest of the Boeotians on the right (cf. XH 6.4.13), and if we are to accept Xenophon's account at its face value, the Thebans were massed 'not less than' fifty shields deep (XH 6.4.12). Four thousand Theban hoplites massed fifty deep would only have had a front of eighty shields, which may seem somewhat improbable in itself and it has been argued that it is difficult to account for the Spartan losses if the Theban front was so short.' But it may not merely be a coincidence that the Spartans directly opposed to the Thebans would originally, at least, have numbered 960 men, if the Thebans had a front of eighty shields (80 x 12), and that the Theban blow apparently fell where the king and the *Hippeis* had taken their stand. It is by no means inconceivable that the *Hippeis* and the files that stood to either side of them were virtually annihilated, and this would account for almost all the losses amongst both the Spartiates and the 'Lakedaimonians as a whole' (see below). The massed Theban formation was the culmination of a development that can be traced back at least as far as Delion in 424, when the Thebans on the Boeotian right had been massed twenty-five deep (Thucydides 4.93.4). Thus, at the Nemea, the Boeotians had made their phalanx 'really deep' (βαθεῖαν παντελῶς: XH 4.2.18), and certainly deeper than sixteen, and this deep formation may explain how the Thebans at Koroneia and the Sacred Band at Tegyra had been able to smash through the Spartan forces opposed to them, though the sources only mention their close order (cf. XH 4.3.18, Plutarch *Pelopidas* 17.2). It has been suggested[12] that these deep formations enabled the men in the rear ranks to act as a reserve to be employed in a secondary role once the enemy had been pinned by the front ranks but if so, there is no evidence that this redeployment was ever carried out and it is more likely that it was just the extra weight that seemed tactically desirable. Indeed, one has a sneaking suspicion that the deeper formation may originally have been adopted because of the inferiority of Boeotian hoplites, just as the attack in column was thought suitable for the raw levies of revolutionary France.

One uncertainty about the Theban dispositions at Leuktra concerns the position occupied by the Sacred Band. One theory is that it was originally stationed behind the Theban phalanx and that it then took the Spartan right wing in flank when the latter was about to attack the left flank of the Theban phalanx.[13] But this goes far beyond any of the evidence and it seems very unlikely that Epameinondas would have stationed his finest troops behind his phalanx on the off-chance that they might be able to catch the Spartans in flank, and Plutarch does, after all, say that Pelopidas managed to catch the Spartans before Kleombrotos 'stretched out' his wing (πρὶν ἀνατεῖναι τὸν Κλεόμβροτον τὸ κέρας: *Pelopidas* 23.2 – see below). It makes much more sense of what Plutarch says about Pelopidas and his command if the Sacred Band was stationed somewhere in the front of the Theban phalanx, and perhaps it made up the front three or four ranks of the whole phalanx, forming in a very real sense its 'cutting edge'.

There is considerable uncertainty about the tactics of the two sides, especially the Spartans. Xenophon says little or nothing but at least he makes it clear that the Theban attack fell on the Spartan right (XH 6.4.14), and in this Diodoros and Plutarch do not disagree. These later authors clearly drew on the same basic tradition about the Boeotian tactics, though Diodoros' version is partly contaminated by his erroneous view that the Spartans advanced in crescent formation, with both wings advanced. He says (15.55.2) that Epameinondas picked the best men from his whole army and placed them on one wing, intending to settle the issue there, whereas the other wing was ordered to avoid battle and gradually withdraw before the enemy's advance – the result was that he made his phalanx 'slanting' (λοξήν). Despite the doubts of some scholars,[14] this is perfectly acceptable provided that we interpret the reference to the 'picked men' (ἐπίλεκτοι) on Epameinondas' left as referring either to the positioning of the Theban contingent as a whole or to that of the Sacred Band, and take the role assigned to the right to be just to hang back when the left advanced, rather than literally withdraw when it came into contact with the enemy – the latter is due to the mistaken notion that it would have had to contend with an advancing Spartan left wing.

Plutarch's version, perhaps derived from Kallisthenes,[15] clearly follows basically the same tradition, even to the extent of using the same word slanting to describe the Boeotian phalanx, but seems to suggest that this oblique approach was not merely designed to defeat the Spartan right without the left's being able to interfere, but actually to draw the Spartan right away from the left (cf. *Pelopidas* 23.1: 'ὅπως τῶν ἄλλων Ἑλλήνων ἀπωτάτω γένηται τὸ δεξιὸν τῶν Σπαρτιατῶν'), and perhaps ultimately take it in flank (cf. ibid.: '… καί τὸν Κλεόμβροτον ἐξώση προσπεσὼν ἀθρόως κατὰ κέρας').[16] But in general it is clear that the great innovation in Epameinondas' tactics was that they were designed to defeat the Spartans themselves on their right, where hitherto they had been accustomed to winning their battles, as at Mantineia and the Nemea, and by 'refusing' the left to deny the enemy any chance of retrieving the situation there, though there was in any case little chance of that happening since the Spartan left was occupied by their allies. The most vivid illustration of the tactics is the story Polyainos tells (2.3.15) of how Epameinondas caught a snake and by crushing its head showed his men how useless the rest of it was, and even Xenophon hints at these tactics when he says (XH 6.4.12) that the Thebans calculated that if they could defeat the part of the Spartan army around the king, all the rest of it would be easy to overcome.

It is very much more difficult to see what the Spartan tactics were and it is possible that Xenophon's silence on the subject is to be explained by their absence.[17] However, although Diodoros' talk of a Spartan advance in crescent formation is almost certainly nonsense, Plutarch's version of the Spartan tactics is circumstantial and, although difficult to interpret, seems to make some sense. It may go back to a good source and there is no real reason to reject it just because of Xenophon's silence. According to Plutarch, when the Spartans realized what the Thebans were doing, 'they began to make changes in their own formation' (μετακινεῖν τῇ τάξει σφᾶς αὐτούς) – specifically, 'they started to fold back (or "unroll") their right and lead it round so as to wheel (or "encircle") and envelop Epameinondas in strength' (τὸ δεξιὸν ἀνέπτυσσον καὶ περιῆνον ὡς κυκλωσόμενοι καὶ περιβαλοῦντες ὑπὸ πλήθους τὸν Ἐπαμεινώνδαν). The main uncertainty here is the meaning of 'ἀνέπτυσσον καὶ περιῆνον': the root-meaning of the verb 'ἀναπτύσσειν' is 'to fold back' – hence 'unroll' a scroll, as in Herodotos (1.125.2), or 'open' doors, as in Euripides (*Iphigeneia in Tauris* 1286). In a tactical sense Arrian uses it to mean 'extend' a phalanx by thinning its depth (*Anabasis* 3.12.2, *Tactica* 9.5), and although this could hardly be the meaning here, since the Spartans are unlikely to have thought of thinning their line still further in the face of the massed Theban attack, the notion of 'extending' the line could be correct. Thus, it has been suggested that Plutarch is simply referring to some such manoeuvre as the Spartans successfully carried out at the Nemea when they 'led to the right' and so overlapped the enemy line (cf. XH 4.2.19).[18] But to suppose that the Spartan right merely turned to the right and began to march off in column hardly conveys the notion of 'folding back', which is

present in other passages in which Plutarch uses the word 'ἀναπτύσσειν' (cf.,
e.g., *Comparison between Lykourgos and Numa* 3.7, *Moralia* 979b), or for that
matter, in the passages in which Xenophon uses it in a military context
(*Anabasis* 1.10.9, *Cyropaedia* 7.5.3).

A more plausible hypothesis perhaps is that Kleombrotos tried to do what
Agis had attempted at Mantineia, namely transfer men from the left of the
Spartan wing of his army to its right so as to outflank the Thebans,
Plutarch's 'ἀνέπτυσσον' referring to the process of withdrawing men from
the left behind the right – thus 'folding back' the right – and 'περιῆνον' to
the further process of 'leading them round' to the right of the line.[19] This has
the merit of keeping close to a likely meaning of the crucial words in
Plutarch and of having the Spartans attempt to do what they had done on
previous occasions. However, the manoeuvre envisaged would have had the
effect of partly reversing the left and right wings of the Spartan phalanx,
which is something that would probably not have been thought desirable
particularly since it would have moved the king further away from the
critical point in the battle (cf. *LP* 11.9), even though the men transferred and
those who remained in position would still have been in the same positions
relative to themselves. Moreover, this interpretation does not really explain
why Plutarch says that the Spartan intention was to envelop Epameinondas
'in strength' (ὑπὸ πλήθους: *Pelopidas* 23.2), since the depth of their line
would remain unaltered.

A possible compromise is that the Spartans tried to do two things at once
– increase the depth of their phalanx and 'lead it round' to take the
advancing Thebans in flank. They saw that the Theban phalanx was both
very deep and, as a consequence, very short and they thought they could
both deepen their own and still leave it long enough to overlap the Theban
left. Thus they 'began to fold back the right' by withdrawing files or units
(e.g. *enomotiai*) from the left of their line of four *morai* and stationing them
behind the right-hand *morai*, while possibly at the same time they 'began to
lead round' the right hand *morai*, i.e. move them to the right, preparatory to
wheeling them to envelop Epameinondas in strength, as Plutarch says.

It is clearly not possible to be quite certain what the Spartans intended, if
only because their intentions were, in the event, frustrated. The battle
opened, Xenophon implies (XH 6.4.8), about midday, after King
Kleombrotos had taken his morning meal – it was said that as a result he and
his men were a little 'high' on the wine they had drunk. Even before this,
perhaps, the first fighting had taken place when Sparta's mercenaries, under

Hieron, the Phokian peltasts and the cavalry of Herakleia and Phleious, attacked the Boeotian camp-followers and others reluctant to fight as they tried to leave (XH 6.4.9) – the latter are said to have included the contingent from Thespiai (cf. Pausanias 9.3.18; Polyainos 2.3.3).[20] Xenophon says that the result of this episode was merely to make the Boeotian army larger than it would otherwise have been, since those who had been trying to leave now re-joined the rest. Next, in Xenophon's account (XH 6.4.10), the Lakedaimonian and Theban cavalry, which had been stationed in front of their respective phalanxes, fought a brisk skirmish that ended in the rout of the Lakedaimonians (XH 6.4.13). This raises the question why cavalry had been placed in front of the infantry phalanxes instead of on the wings as was usual – the cavalry of Herakleia and Phlious was presumably on the Spartan left wing and the rest of the Boeotian cavalry on their right. The most probable explanation is that the intention was to screen the movements of the opposing phalanxes. Xenophon notes (XH 6.4.10) that the ground between the two armies was flat and Epameinondas is alleged to have used cavalry to create a dust-screen at the second battle of Mantineia in 362 (Frontinus *Strategemata* 2.2.12; Polyainos 2.3.14).[21]

Xenophon is severely critical of the Spartan cavalry at the time of Leuktra (XH 6.4.10–11), perhaps because of its poor showing at this crucial battle. It was soon trounced by the Theban cavalry and sent reeling back into its own hoplites. Some of it may have escaped through the gap on the left of the Spartan half of the phalanx, if such a gap had been opened by the attempt to extend the phalanx to the right,[22] but others fell foul of the Spartan hoplites themselves (XH 6.4.13). However, it was too late to do anything for now, as Xenophon says (ibid.), 'the Theban *lochoi* fell upon them.' According to Plutarch (*Pelopidas* 23.2), it was the action of Pelopidas and the Sacred Band that was crucial and although he may have exaggerated his hero's role, there is no real reason to doubt that Pelopidas may have seen the turmoil in the Spartan ranks and ordered his crack troops to break into a double, catching the Spartans before they could either swing their wing forwards or reverse the movement and re-form their line, as Plutarch says (ibid.).

The Theban attack thus caught the Spartans in confusion, caused partly by their own cavalry, partly by whatever manoeuvre they were attempting on the right – Xenophon even says (XH 6.4.13) that Kleombrotos had begun the advance 'at first before the army with him so much as realized that he was advancing', which, if true, shows vividly how badly the Spartans had been caught napping on this occasion. To make matters worse the enemy probably first hit the Spartan line near where the king himself stood, for Xenophon's account suggests that he was mortally wounded early in the fight. But despite their confusion and the fall of their king – the first to be killed in battle since Leonidas – it is clear that initially the Spartans held their own for, as Xenophon argues (XH 6.4.13), they were able to carry the king, still living, from the field and they could not have done this had their front not still been holding – Plutarch, in an interesting passage (*Pelopidas* 23.3), stresses that Spartan training was designed to ensure that they could fight in any order or formation. But the fall of the king and the death of many of those near him, including the polemarch Deinon (XH 6.4.14), must have added to the confusion, and no phalanx twelve deep – or even twenty-four deep, if the left had been 'folded back' behind the right – could ultimately hope to prevail against one fifty deep, unless it could curl around and take the massed formation in flank, and this the Spartans had tried but failed to do. One would like to believe that at the supreme moment Epameinondas did shout, as Polyainos says (2.3.2), 'grant me one pace forward, and we'll have victory,' but, at all events, the Spartan right at last gave way followed by the left, though Xenophon claims that even then discipline was maintained –Diodoros (15.56.2) and Plutarch (*Pelopidas* 23.4) suggest a larger element of flight.

Xenophon says (XH 6.4.15) that 'of the Lakedaimonians as a whole' (συμπάντων Λακεδαιμονίων) nearly a thousand were killed, 'and of the Spartiates themselves, there being some 700 there, about 400 were killed,' and his phraseology suggests that the 400 Spartiates should be included in the overall total. In any case the catastrophic losses among the Spartiates are probably to be explained by the virtual annihilation of the *Hippeis*, all 300 of whom must have been Spartiates, in the desperate struggle to rescue the mortally wounded king – the other 100 who fell presumably belonged to ordinary *enomotiai* to left and right of the *Hippeis*, which were also probably almost annihilated – indeed, there were probably very few casualties except where the great mass of Thebans hit the Spartan line. Diodoros (15.56.4) says that 'not less than 4,000 Lakedaimonians' fell in the battle, which can hardly be accepted in view of Xenophon's testimony unless we are to suppose that the figure includes losses amongst Sparta's allies and they seem to have played little or no part in the fighting, except in the skirmish on the left before the real battle started. But at least Diodoros' figure of 300 for the losses on the Boeotian side is more credible than Pausanias' forty-seven (9.13.12), though this was perhaps the number of men from the Sacred Band who were killed. Whatever the truth about the losses on either side the Spartans acknowledged defeat in the traditional way by asking for a truce to recover their dead (XH 6.4.15), though the Thebans forbore to attack their camp, allegedly on the advice of Jason of Pherai (XH 6.4.22ff.), who then negotiated a further truce to allow the Spartans to depart. They retreated at night via Kreusis to Aigosthena where they met Archidamos and the relief force (XH 6.4.26).

In view of the doubts about what exactly happened at Leuktra, we cannot be sure precisely why the Spartans were defeated and it is by no means certain that it was due entirely to the brilliance of Epameinondas and the old-fashioned ways of his opponents. It is true that the 'slanting phalanx', whatever precisely that means, probably nullified the Spartan superiority in numbers, but there is some suggestion in the sources that the allies of the Spartans and the Thebans, on their left and right wings respectively, were reluctant to fight in any case (cf. XH 6.4.9 & 15: *Pausanias* 9.13.8–9, 12), and if the battle was really a question of Thebans against Spartans, the two sides were more evenly matched (4,000 Thebans against 4,780 Spartans) – indeed, if there really were only sixteen *enomotiai* in each of the Spartan *morai*, as is generally believed, the Spartans were outnumbered (2,540 to 4,000). Epameinondas' oblique approach may in fact have been designed partly to detach the Spartans from their allies, as Plutarch suggests (*Pelopidas* 23.2). It is certainly true that Epameinondas' placing of his best troops on his left was a brilliant innovation and it is possible that Pelopidas' crucial charge formed part of his original plan. But he could not have foreseen that the Spartan cavalry would collide with their infantry, nor that their infantry would fall into confusion as a result of trying to change formation, and to that extent he was lucky.

Moreover, if Plutarch's account of what the Spartans were trying to do can be accepted, it is at least clear that they did not just stolidly wait while their opponent ran rings around them. Whatever precisely we make of what Plutarch says the Spartans were trying to carry out some deliberate manoeuvre, and there was still nothing amateurish about their tactical training – it surely took far less training to advance even 'obliquely' as one hoplite in a mass fifty deep[23] than to take part in manoeuvres to increase the depth of a phalanx, move it to the right and wheel it to take an enemy in flank. What stands out is not so much the old-fashioned way in which the Spartans fought as their apparent continuing assumption that it really did not matter what their opponents did and that they could move their forces about the battlefield at will, in the face of the enemy – an assumption that had so nearly proved disastrous at Mantineia. Too many victories are often bad for armies, and for far too long the Spartans had been the only 'professionals' in Greece. Now, however, they finally faced an opponent who seems to have learned from past defeats and who took the initiative himself, refusing to allow the Spartans to dictate how the battle went and allowing them no time to retrieve the situation.

But what finally stands out is the sheer fighting quality of the Spartan hoplites who, perhaps still only twelve deep and in confusion, held up an enemy force massed fifty deep for some considerable time, and the courage of those Spartiates who stood to fight it out to the death. Brutal and barren though their ideals might be, nobody in the end could say that they had forsaken them, for their losses were out of all proportion to those of the rest of the army.

In the end too Leuktra was decisive, not so much because the Spartan army had been destroyed, or even because this defeat put an end to its victories – there were Spartan victories to come – but because it put an end to the myth of Spartan invincibility. Sparta's position in Greece had long rested on what amounted to a gigantic bluff, since her man-power resources, in terms of actual citizen-soldiers, had never really been sufficient to sustain that position. But behind the bluff there had always remained in the last resort the reality of the Spartan army, which many feared to face. Leuktra showed that it could be beaten in fair fight and thus encouraged Sparta's enemies to risk action against her even if it meant fighting her army. The inevitable result was the breakaway of the Arcadians from her control, the Theban invasion of the Peloponnese and the freeing of Messenia, events that effectively put paid to Sparta's status as a great power.

Part III

Epilogue

Chapter 10

After Leuktra

Leuktra, of course, was not the end of the Spartan army. Although the surviving polemarchs had conceded defeat by asking for a truce to recover the Spartan dead, the Boeotians did not attempt to attack the Spartan camp and, after a further truce had been negotiated, the defeated *morai* slipped away with their usual quiet efficiency. At Aigosthena they were met by a relief army consisting of the remaining Spartan troops and contingents of the Peloponnesian allies and the whole force then withdrew to Corinth, whence the various contingents dispersed to their homes (XH 6.4.18, 25–6). Assuming that Xenophon's figures for the losses in the battle apply only to the four *morai* that had taken part, and the *Hippeis*, the Spartans should still have had almost 7,000 hoplites immediately available and presumably the 600 or so *hypomeiones* who had been killed could easily be replaced. It would have been more difficult to replace the 400 Spartiates, but there would have been some young Spartiates now reaching their twentieth birthdays and presumably some men, hitherto *hypomeiones*, who now became Spartiates in virtue of inheriting *klaroi* from the fallen. In the meantime too more *hypomeiones* could no doubt have been recruited. However, it appears that one concession was made to the exigencies of the situation. Those who had shown cowardice at Leuktra – the *tresantes* – were for once not visited with the full penalties that custom required, after no less a person than Agesilaos himself had advised that 'the laws must be allowed to sleep for a day' (Plutarch *Agesilaos* 30. 2–4).

Despite Xenophon's references to the 'desertion' of Lakedaimon at the end of 370 (XH 6.5.23 & 25) then, it was probably not so much the losses Sparta had sustained that affected the attitude of the Greeks to her, as the fact of her defeat in a set-piece battle. If one compares what Thucydides says (5.75.3) about the effect of the Spartan victory at Mantineia, one can imagine what the effect of her defeat at Leuktra would have been. The most serious developments were in Arcadia where Mantineia and Tegea both broke away in 370, in company with other smaller communities, to form an Arcadian League (XH 6.5.3–9). This was dangerous for Sparta not only because a united Arcadia could prove a formidable enemy in itself but because the Arcadian defection cut Sparta off from other allies – thus troops from Corinth, the Argolid and Achaea had to come to Sparta by sea via Prasiai at the end of 370 or the beginning of 369 (XH 7.2.2–3). The Spartan response was to invade Arcadia in full force under Agesilaos and it seems likely from what Xenophon says (cf. XH 6.5.16 especially) that they would have liked nothing better than another Mantineia. However, the Arcadians and their allies preferred to wait for the arrival of the promised Boeotian aid and although Agesilaos remained right into the middle of winter, he was eventually compelled to withdraw (XH 6.5.10–21). It was in the course of this campaign that he conducted his masterly retreat from an awkward situation near Mantineia by the use of the *anastrophe* (XH 6.5.18–9, see above, pp. 36–37). But the most significant thing about the campaign is that in the absence of contingents from their allies – they only had a few troops from Heraia and Lepreon (XH 6.5.11) and were later joined by some cavalry from Phleious (XH 6.5.17) – the Spartans seem to have been over-anxious for the arrival of a contingent of mercenary peltasts from Orchomenos in Arcadia (cf. XH 6.5.11ff.) and, perhaps for the first time (see above. pp. 20–21) had to use *perioikoi* against Peloponnesian enemies (cf. XH 6.5.21).

By far the most ominous result of the campaign, however, was the arrival of the Boeotian army at Mantineia shortly after Agesilaos' return home. According to Xenophon (XH 6.5.23–4), the Thebans were not at all anxious to invade Lakedaimon. They had come to help the Arcadians, the enemy was now nowhere to be seen and Lakonia was considered very difficult to attack. But their allies pointed out the number of their troops compared with the dearth of men in Lakedaimon and when emissaries arrived from Karyai and other perioecic communities, promising to join them, the Thebans, led by Epameinondas, were finally convinced. For the first time in six centuries the Spartans were faced with invasion.[1]

Unfortunately, Xenophon gives no figures for the forces of the Thebans and their allies and although Diodoros and Plutarch give figures ranging from 50,000 to 70,000 men (Diodoros 15.62.5; Plutarch *Agesilaos* 31.1, *Pelopidas* 24.2), these must be exaggerations – the true figure can hardly have been in excess of 30,000.[2] Nevertheless, the Spartans could not hope to match this kind of number in the absence of substantial help from their allies and, as we have seen, what help they obtained from this source had to come by a roundabout route and cannot have been large. We have no means of telling how large a force could be mustered from the *perioikoi*, but one doubts that it could have been much larger, if at all, than the numbers the Spartans themselves could put into the field, and although it is clear that by no means all the *perioikoi* sided with the invaders (cf. XH 6.5.32), it is equally clear that some did (loc.cit.). The Spartans were probably only too well aware of this disaffection and to muster a large force of *perioikoi* probably seemed, therefore, dangerous in the circumstances, particularly since the *perioikoi* would in any case have been worried for their own homes. Thus the Spartans had to fall back on calling for helot volunteers – and then, typically, became alarmed at the numbers that came forward (6,000 according to Xenophon: XH 6.5.29). There was, thus, never any question of attempting to face the invaders in pitched battle and after failing to hold the passes with *neodamodeis* and other irregular forces, commanded by Spartiates (XH 6.5.24, 26–7; Diodoros 15.64.2), the Spartans settled for trying to hold Sparta itself.

Xenophon has little to say about the defence, except to emphasize that Sparta still had no walls and that the Spartiates themselves were very few in number (XH 6.5.28), but it is sad to learn that the women of Sparta, for all their vaunted injunctions to their menfolk to return with their shields or on them, now found the sight of the smoke rising from burned houses and farms unbearable (loc.cit.) – much of this property, of course, was owned by them (Aristotle *Politics* 1270a23ff.). The only military detail of interest in Xenophon's account is the reference to a force of '300 of the younger hoplites' (XH 6.5.31), which might be to a new corps of *Hippeis* or, if an ambush is not considered a suitable operation for the 'Guards', possibly we may discern here yet another of the forces of 300 that occur so frequently in Spartan military history and which may have been constituted by taking one *enomotia* of twenty-five men from each of the twelve *lochoi* (see above, pp. 70–71). Diodoros' account of the invasion of Lakedaimon is virtually worthless (15.65), but Plutarch provides some more details, though not about the Spartan army itself – particularly interesting is his report of a conspiracy of 200 of 'those in Lakedaimon who had long been disaffected and criminal' – probably to be identified as *hypomeiones* (*Agesilaos* 32.3)[3] – and the tradition that there was an even wider conspiracy of Spartiates (op.cit. 32.6), though it can hardly be true that more than 200 Spartiates were quietly done away with without due process of law – after Leuktra there can hardly have been as many as a thousand left. Plutarch also reports (op.cit. 32.7) that some of the helots and *perioikoi* recruited into the army deserted during the attack on Sparta, which, if true, shows that at least some of the latter were there. But by far the most serious consequence of the inability of the Spartans to meet the invaders in the field was the loss of Messenia, which Xenophon notoriously does not mention (cf. Diodoros 15.66; Plutarch *Agesilaos* 34.1, *Pelopidas* 24.5; Pausanias 4.26. 3–27. 9).[4]

Later in 369 Spartan troops took part in the defence of the Corinthia against the second Boeotian invasion of the Peloponnese[5] but failed to prevent Epameinondas' breaking through in a surprise dawn attack (XH 7.1.15–17).[6] Since the Spartan force was commanded by a polemarch (XH 7.1.17), it may have consisted of a *mora* of regular troops and the same may have been true of the garrison of Messenian Asine, defeated by Lykomedes and the Arcadians earlier in the year, for its commander too is implied to have been a polemarch (XH 7.1.25).[7] Although, as was pointed out in the first chapter, *morai* are not mentioned by Xenophon after the Leuktra campaign, these references to polemarchs are some indication that the Spartan army was still organized in the old way.

By the summer of 368 too the Spartans had recovered sufficient of their confidence to stage something of a counter-attack against the Arcadians. Archidamos, Agesilaos' son, first stormed Karyai, which lay near the modern village of Arachova on the northern frontier of Lakonia[8] and then invaded Parrhasia. Here, just north of the future site of Megalopolis, Archidamos turned at bay to face an army of Arcadians and Argives and won what became known as the 'Tearless Battle' since, according to tradition, not a single Spartan (Spartiate?) was killed (cf. XH 7.1.28–32; Plutarch *Agesilaos* 32.3; etc.). It is in his account of the preliminaries to this battle that Xenophon mentions *lochoi* in the Spartan army for the first time but, as was argued in the first chapter, this is probably just a coincidence, and there is no real reason to believe that the Spartan army had been re-organized before this campaign. Nor had the attitude to it of other Greek soldiers changed appreciably since Leuktra, if it is true, as Xenophon alleges (XH 7.1.31), that only a few of the enemy even waited for the Spartans to come within spear-thrust, whereas the Spartan officers are alleged to have had difficulty in restraining their men from 'pushing to the front'. It was after this Spartan victory that the Arcadians founded Megalopolis to guard this part of Arcadia against just such attacks (Diodoros 15.72.4; Pausanias 8.27.3ff.).

For the next few years we know of no military operations in which the Spartans were involved, but in 365 they recaptured Sellasia, lost in the invasion of 370/69 (XH 7.4.12), and later in the same year they captured Kromnos in Arcadia and garrisoned it with 'three of the twelve *lochoi*' (XH 7.4.20).[9] This threat to their communications with Messenia, however, brought a swift response from the Arcadians and their allies and the Spartan force in Kromnos soon found itself under siege. The Spartans tried to draw the Arcadians off by ravaging the Skiritis and adjacent parts of Arcadia – an indication that the Skiritis had now passed out of Spartan control – but the Arcadians refused to be drawn and the Spartans then had to try to raise the siege by direct action. Archidamos, who was again in command, tried to capture a hill which commanded part of the Arcadian siege-works but was defeated and himself wounded in the skirmishing that followed and forced to withdraw (XH 7.4.20–5). Subsequently the Spartans did manage to capture a part of the siege-works in a night attack and extricate most of the garrison of Kromnos, but over a hundred prisoners were taken, including both Spartiates and *perioikoi* (XH 7.4.27).

Three years later the changing situation in the Peloponnese led to a final full-scale Boeotian intervention, culminating in the second battle of Mantineia. Before the battle Epameinondas, then encamped at Tegea, received intelligence that Agesilaos had left Sparta with the Spartan army to join his allies at Mantineia and thought he saw a chance to surprise Sparta itself in the absence of any defenders. Agesilaos, however, learned in time of the Boeotian intentions and managed to get back to Sparta with three-quarters of the army, though he sent 'three of the twelve *lochoi*' on to the rendezvous at Mantineia (XH 7.5.7–10). Once again Xenophon emphasizes the fewness of the Spartiates but their desperate and spirited defence proved enough to deter the Boeotians and Epameinondas withdrew after penetrating into the outskirts of Sparta (XH 7.5.11–14). According to Plutarch (*Agesilaos* 34.6–8), it was for his part in this defence that Isidas, son of Phoibidas, was garlanded by the ephors and then fined 1,000 *drachmai* for daring to risk his life 'without armour'.

Unfortunately Xenophon never even mentions the Spartans in his account of the battle of Mantineia, which took place after Epameinondas had abandoned his attack on Sparta (XH 7.5.18–27), but although it has been claimed that the whole Spartan army under Agesilaos' command took part,[10] there is no ancient evidence for this and the implication of Xenophon's narrative is rather that only the three *lochoi* absent from the defence of

Sparta, took part in the subsequent battle (cf. XH 7.5.10). Later sources say that the Spartans were stationed on the right wing alongside the Mantineians and their Arcadian allies (cf. Diodoros 15.85.2), and they seem to have borne the brunt of the massed Theban attack (Diodoros 15.86. 2ff.). The Thebans appear to have broken through (cf. Diodoros 15.87.1–2; Plutarch *Agesilaos* 35.1), but in the moment of victory Epameinondas fell, mortally wounded, and his men abandoned the pursuit. Plutarch (loc.cit.) quoted the fourth century author Dioskorides to the effect that the Theban general was killed by a Spartan called Antikrates, but there was evidently some doubt about this.[11]

The Spartans have often been criticized for not adhering to the 'common peace' concluded by many of the Greek states after Mantineia, but since acceptance of the peace involved acceptance of the independence of Messenia (cf. Polybios 4.33.8–9; Diodoros 15.89.1–2; Plutarch *Agesilaos* 35), such criticism is hardly justified. It would surely be asking too much of any nation to acquiesce in the loss of territory it had ruled for more than two centuries, if not three, a scant seven years after the original loss and the situation in the Peloponnese had, if anything, recently changed in Sparta's favour.

Xenophon ends his history of Greece with his account of the battle of Mantineia and thereafter almost nothing is known about Sparta for a century or more, let alone about the Spartan army – it is typical of Spartan 'history' at this time that not a single action is recorded of Kleomenes II, son of Kleombrotos, who succeeded his elder brother Agesipolis II in 370, though he is alleged to have reigned for over sixty years (cf. Diodoros 20.29.1). Diodoros (16.39.1–7) records a series of engagements in Arcadia under the year 352/1, during the reign of Agesilaos' son Archidamos III which formed part of the so-called Sacred War, but no details emerge of the Spartan forces involved and Diodoros merely describes troops sent earlier to aid the Phokians as 'soldiers' (στρατιῶται: 16.37.3), and a later force as 'hoplites' (16.59.1).

As the ally of the Phokians in the Sacred War, Sparta was technically the enemy of Philip II of Macedonia, but she took no part in the resistance to Philip's aggression, which culminated at the battle of Chaironeia in 338. However, after his victory Philip entered the Peloponnese at the invitation of Sparta's enemies and through the League of Corinth, which Sparta, alone of all the Greek states, refused to join (Justin 9.5.3, cf. Arrian 1.16.7), granted disputed territories on Sparta's borders to her enemies. But although he invaded Lakonia, even Philip forbore to attack Sparta. Five years later in 333 we hear of Spartan co-operation with Persia at the time of Issus, but the only recorded Spartan operations were in Crete (Arrian *Anabasis* 2.13.5–6; Diodoros 17.48.1; Curtius 4.1.38ff.). Then, when Alexander embarked on the conquest of the further parts of the Persian Empire in 331, Agesilaos' grandson Agis III raised the standard of revolt against the Macedonians and was killed in battle near Megalopolis by Alexander's viceroy Antipater (Diodoros 17.62–3; Pausanias 3.10.5; Curtius 6.1.21). We know nothing of Agis' army but it is clear that some Spartan attitudes were still the same as they had been earlier, for it emerges from a later passage in Diodoros (19.70.5) that there was a question whether those who had survived the battle should suffer loss of their rights as citizens, and the prince Akrotatos incurred great hostility for opposing the proposal that they should not.

An interesting development in these years is the employment of Spartan kings and princes by other states as *condottieri*. This suggests firstly that the reputation of Spartan soldiers still stood high but secondly that Sparta herself increasingly came to need mercenaries and hence the money to pay for them. The first royal Spartan to act in this capacity was no less a person than King Agesilaos himself who, now in his eighties first served the rebel Persian satrap Ariobarzanes (Xenophon *Agesilaos* 2.26–7), and then, after Mantineia, went out to Egypt to command mercenaries for the nationalist leader Tachos (Diodoros 15.92.2ff.; Xenophon *Agesilaos* 2.28ff.; Plutarch *Agesilaos* 36ff.), amassing no less a sum than 230 talents – he died on his way home to Sparta (361/0). It may seem surprising that a king of Sparta should play such a role and Plutarch clearly regarded it as a disgrace (cf. *Agesilaos* 36.1), but there seems no doubt that he had the official sanction of the state and that his mission was regarded as the sending of help to an ally (cf. Diodoros 15.92.2) – he was, for example, accompanied by thirty Spartiate advisers just as he had been on his mission to Asia Minor over thirty years before (Plutarch *Agesilaos* 36.3). The 1,000 hoplites who accompanied him, however (Diodoros 15.92.2), were presumably not regular Spartan soldiers. They were probably not just mercenaries – Diodoros distinguishes them from the mercenaries placed under Agesilaos' command by Tachos (loc.cit.) – and may have been *neodamodeis*.

Agesilaos' example was followed by his son Archidamos who fought in Crete on behalf of Lyktos (Diodoros 16.62.4), and then went on to Italy to fight for Sparta's old colony Taras against the Lucanians. He was allegedly killed in battle on the same day that Chaironeia was fought in Greece

(Diodoros 16.63.1, 88.3), and one cannot help but feel that he ought to have been there. Some years later Akrotatos, the elder son of Kleomenes II, who had offended many younger Spartans by insisting that those who had survived the defeat at Antipater's hands should suffer the full penalties described by custom (Diodoros 19.70.5), went to help Akragas against Agathokles, allegedly without the ephors' consent (Diodoros 19.70.6), but his boorish and brutal behaviour antagonized the Sicilians and he had to return to Sparta under a cloud (Diodoros 19.71.1–5). His younger brother Kleonymos too piqued at being passed over for the crown in favour of his elder brother's son Areus fought for Taras as a mercenary and began to carve out a little kingdom for himself in southern Italy and across the Adriatic in Corfu (Diodoros 20.104–5), before securing the help of the greatest of the *condottieri*, Pyrrhus of Epirus, in an attempt to wrest the crown of Sparta from his nephew (see below). He also has the distinction of being the first Spartan to have dealings with Rome, or at least the first to secure a mention in Livy. After being defeated in battle near Thurii by the consul M. Aemilius Paullus, according to one of Livy's sources, or having withdrawn at the advance of the dictator C. Iunius Bubulcus Brutus, according to others (Livy 10.2.1–3), he had the temerity to attack Livy's birthplace Patavium (Padua) – Livy says that there were many Patavians alive in his day who had seen the spoils taken from Kleonymos' army hanging in the ancient temple of Juno and that the naval fight was annually commemorated by a mock ship-battle on the river that flowed through the city (10.2.4ff.). Kleonymos' son Leonidas finally saw service with Seleukos II of Syria before becoming king of Sparta in 259 (Plutarch *Agis* 3.6).

But perhaps the most famous of these Spartan mercenary captains, though apparently not a member of either of the royal families, was Xanthippos, who in 255 helped the Carthaginians to defeat Regulus during the course of the First Punic War (Polybios 1.32.1ff.). Diodoros (23.14.1) says he was a Spartiate and this is confirmed by Polybios' remark (1.32.1) that he had 'shared the Lakonian *agoge*', though the latter might mean that he was a *mothax*. He is said by Polybios (1.36.2 4) to have returned to Sparta after Regulus' defeat, but Diodoros (23.16) evidently knew of a tradition that he was treacherously murdered by the Carthaginians while serving in Sicily. In any case he presumably knew Hannibal's father Hamilcar Barca and Sosylos, the Spartan historian who taught Hannibal Greek (Cornelius Nepos *Hannibal* 13.3), may have been one of his men. It is interesting to reflect that some of Sparta's military lore may thus have passed to perhaps the greatest general of antiquity (cf. Vegetius, *Prologue to Book 3*).

Side-by-side with the phenomenon of the Spartan *condottiere* goes the development of Tainaron as a great centre for the hiring of mercenaries, presumably with the approval of Sparta, which both needed mercenaries itself and was probably a fruitful source of supply. Perhaps the first hint that Tainaron had taken on this role is Arrian's statement (*Anabasis* 2.13.6) that when – at the time of the battle of Issus in October 333 – King Agis III of Sparta received thirty talents and ten triremes from the Persians, he sent them to his brother Agesilaos at Tainaron with orders to pay his crews and proceed to Crete. Diodoros says (17.48.1) that Agis later engaged the mercenaries who escaped from Issus, though his figure of 8,000 is almost certainly exaggerated. By the time of Alexander's death in 323, Tainaron had clearly become known as the best market for mercenaries in the Greek world, for those discharged by Alexander's satraps, at his orders, flocked there to find employment (Diodoros 17.111.1) – 8,000 were later hired by the Athenians for the Lamian War (Diodoros 18.9.1–3), and a further 2,500 were available for service in Cyrenaica (Diodoros 18.21.1–2). In 315 Antigonos Monophthalmos' general Aristodemos was able to hire as many as 8,000 mercenaries from the Peloponnese in Lakonia, presumably at Tainaron, and in this case Diodoros says specifically that he received the permission of the Spartans (19.60.1). Twelve years later the Spartan prince Kleonymos hired 5,000 mercenaries at Tainaron for his Italian venture (Diodoros 20.104.1–2).[12]

Sparta played little part in the wars of the *Diadochoi* but it was then that the Spartans at last surrounded their ancient settlements with some kind of continuous fortifications. Justin (14.5.6) says it was when Kassander was threatening Greece in 318 but Pausanias (1.13.5) suggests that it was in the war with Demetrios Poliorketes in 294 – even then it would seem that the fortifications in question consisted of ditches and stockades rather than walls, which were not in fact completed until over a century later. Demetrios' attack on Sparta followed his defeat of the Spartan army under Archidamos IV near Mantineia and a second victory outside Sparta itself. It seemed that nothing could save Sparta this time but at the last moment Demetrios was diverted by attacks upon his territories in Asia Minor and Cyprus by Lysimachos and Ptolemy I Soter (Plutarch *Demetrios* 35), and once again the town of Sparta remained inviolate.

Twenty years later Pyrrhos of Epiros took up the cause of Kleonymos, younger son of Kleomenes II, who had been passed over for the crown in favour of his elder brother's son Areus. Pyrrhos' army included the first elephants the Spartans had ever had to face, though no doubt some of them had come across the beasts while on mercenary service. Plutarch has a spirited account of the hasty defences they constructed and of the heroic fight that followed, led by the crown prince Akrotatos. Eventually Pyrrhos too abandoned his attempt when the Spartans were reinforced, first by a force of Antigonos Conatas' mercenaries sent from Corinth and then by Kleonymos' rival, King Areus himself returning providentially from Crete – it was soon after his attack on Sparta that the great Epirote general lost his life in Argos (Plutarch *Pyrrhos* 26ff.).

Areus was perhaps the last king of Sparta with pretensions to interfere outside the confines of the Peloponnese. He first built up an alliance of Peloponnesian states, including Elis, Achaea and some of Sparta's old Arcadian allies, and then in 266 joined Athens and Ptolemy II of Egypt in their struggle against Antigonos Conatas known as the Chremonidean War. Areus marched to Athens' aid when Antigonos laid siege to the city (Pausanias 3.6.4), but was forced to retreat for lack of supplies, and was killed in battle near Corinth (Pausanias 3.6.4–6; Justin 26.2.1; Plutarch *Agis* 3.4). Thereafter, as far as we know, no Spartan army ever again operated outside the Peloponnese and succeeding generations of Spartans were evidently hard put to make headway against even single states within the Peloponnese. Five years after his father's death, for example, Areus's son Akrotatos was himself killed in battle against Megalopolis (Pausanias 8.27.11).[13]

It was probably mainly in an attempt to counteract this growing weakness that King Agis IV of the Eurypontidai and King Kleomenes III of the Agiadai attempted a wholesale economic and social revolution. Plutarch would have us believe (cf., e.g., *Agis* 3.1, 4–5) that when Agis came to the throne about 244 the Spartans had sadly fallen away from their old ideals, and some modern scholars believe that the old system had almost completely broken down.[14] It is, indeed, possible that as the Spartans became increasingly aware of their impotence in the new world of 'super-powers' like Macedonia, they began to see less and less point in adhering to old practices that seemed to have lost their usefulness and perhaps too the economic and social trends already visible in the fifth century had so widened the gap between rich and poor and so reduced the numbers of those who could afford the old life that it had virtually withered away. However, some at least of what Plutarch has to say looks like conventional moralizing, probably derived from Phylarchos, and one wonders whether Phylarchos had done much more than refurbish some of the criticisms of Sparta already advanced by Aristotle.[15]

Agis IV in any case was done to death before he could fully implement his designs though, if we are to believe Plutarch (*Agis* 14), even what he did accomplish had so profound an effect on the discipline and spirit of the Spartan army that it astonished the contingents of other states when Agis led it to the aid of the Achaean defence of the Isthmus against the Aetolians in the autumn of 243.[16] Whether or not it had been revived by Agis, the reign of Kleomenes III (235–22) certainly saw a final flowering of the old Spartan martial prowess (cf. Polybios 2.51.; Plutarch *Kleomenes* 4ff., *Aratos* 36ff.), with great victories over the Achaeans at Mt Lykaion, at Leuktra near Megalopolis and, later, near Dyme, and although hardly any details of the Spartan forces involved are given in the sources, in one passage of Plutarch's life of Kleomenes there is a tantalizing reference to a force of 'a few horsemen and 300 foot' (4.3). Is this, one wonders, a last glimpse of the *Hippeis* or, possibly, one of those task-forces made up of twelve *enomotiai* chosen from 'all the *lochoi*'?

It was after his early successes, probably in the autumn of 227, that Kleomenes finally carried out his revolution in Sparta, and if Plutarch is to be trusted (*Kleomenes* 11.2), this included a change in the equipment of the Spartan army. Kleomenes taught his men, he says, 'to use the *sarisa*[17] with both hands instead of the spear and to carry the shield with a strap (δἴόχάνης) instead of an armband (μὴ διὰ πόρπακος)'. Thus the Spartans finally ceased to be hoplites, in the strict sense, and it is possible that Kleomenes also reorganized the army at the same time for Plutarch in his account of one of the king's later campaigns refers to two '*tagmata*' of Lakedaimonians (*Kleomenes* 23.4). However, Plutarch's language here can obviously not be pressed – one would have to be certain that his source was reliable on technical military terms and Polybios' alleged reference to a *mora* of 900 men (ap. Plutarch *Pelopidas* 17.2) may have referred to a period after Kleomenes' army-reforms.[18]

At all events the 'New Model' Spartan army continued to enjoy success for a number of years: probably in 226 it routed the Achaeans again near Dyme (Polybios 2.51.; Plutarch *Kleomenes* 14; Pausanias 7.7.3), and after an abortive attempt to patch up a peace Kleomenes proceeded to win over, by force or persuasion, city after city in the northern Peloponnese including Argos, Phleious and even Corinth. However, in the end the very extent of his success was perhaps Kleomenes' undoing, for the Achaeans appealed to Antigonos Doson, King of Macedonia, and the appeal was accepted, possibly because Antigonos was suspicious of Kleomenes' relations with Ptolemy Euergetes of Egypt (cf. Polybios 2.51). Even then Kleomenes' attempt to hold the Isthmus might have been successful (cf. Polybios 2.54.), but the defection of Argos threatened his rear and he withdrew to Sparta. The final confrontation came at Sellasia, probably in 222,[19] where Kleomenes' army was overwhelmed. The sources, unfortunately, give no details of the Spartan army at this crucial battle, though Plutarch again tantalizingly suggests a measure of continuity with the old Sparta where he mentions the *krypteia* (*Kleomenes* 28.3), and the 6,000 'Lakedaimonians' who allegedly took part (Plutarch *Kleomenes* 28.5), whatever their composition, certainly seem to have fought with all the old fanatical courage. At one point, Plutarch says (*Kleomenes* 28.4), the impetus of the charge 'of those Spartiates about the king' drove the Macedonian phalanx, 10,000 strong, back nearly a kilometre, though this must be an exaggeration and even Polybios, who had no use for Kleomenes or the Spartans of his time, refers to their 'spirit' (εὐψυχία: 2.70.) in this hopeless fight against odds, from which only 200 of the 6,000 survived, according to Plutarch.

After Sellasia, for the first time in seven centuries Sparta was actually occupied by an enemy, but in a few days news of an attack on their own country sent the Macedonians scurrying home. Sparta was left under the control of one Brachylles, a Boeotian, as governor (cf. Polybios 20.5.12), but with what Polybios is pleased to term its 'ancestral constitution' restored (2.70.1) – in practice this meant the abolition of the monarchy in favour of rule by ephors and *Gerousia*. Within two years, however, the pro-Macedonian ephors and their supporters in the *Gerousia* were murdered, and the monarchy revived. Kleomenes had been killed in exile in Alexandria, but there was no difficulty in finding an Agiad heir – he was called Agesipolis – and although Polybios sneeringly says (4.35.14) that the Eurypontid choice – Lykourgos – gave each of the ephors a talent to become a descendant of Herakles and king of Sparta, this is probably no more than the product of hostile propaganda. Lykourgos was certainly the 'strong man' of the new regime: he eventually expelled his colleague and ruled alone (cf. Livy 34.26.14), and under him the Spartans fought Argos and the Achaean League (Polybios 4.36), and later Messene and Tegea (Polybios 5.17), eventually provoking Philip V of Macedonia to invade Lakonia in 218. Lykourgos fought quite a skilful rear-guard action against overwhelming odds, but was unable to prevent the Macedonians' ravaging most of his country (Polybios 5.18–24), though Philip made no attempt on Sparta itself.

Lykourgos died some time before the winter of 211/10 and was succeeded by his infant son Pelops (cf. Livy 34.32.1–2), but real power lay in the hands of the so-called 'tyrant' Machanidas, who was probably, in fact, regent for Pelops. Machanidas was killed in 207 at yet another battle of Mantineia, which is the subject of one of Polybios' best battle-narratives (11.11–18). But the Spartans of an earlier day would have been hard put to recognize Machanidas' army with its siege-engines and catapults (Polybios 11.11.3), and its phalangites armed with the *sarisa* (Polybios 11.15.6), and they would have thoroughly disapproved of 'Lakedaimonians' who advanced to the attack without orders (loc.cit.).

Machanidas was succeeded as regent by Nabis, who finally got rid of Pelops, according to Diodoros (27.1). Although habitually called 'tyrant' by Livy, presumably following Polybios, Nabis styled himself 'king' as we know from inscriptions on bricks and elsewhere (*IG* V i 885; *Sylloge* 3.584), and from coins, and he evidently claimed descent from the exiled king Demaratos, who accompanied Xerxes to Greece and warned him about the 8,000 Spartans like the ones he had just faced at Thermopylai (Herodotos 7.234.2): Nabis' father was also called Demaratos (*Sylloge* loc.cit.). Under him there was a last dying flicker of the old Spartan spirit. As an enemy of the Macedonians and of the Achaean League he was an ally of the Romans in their first war against Philip V – the so-called First Macedonian War – but in the second, principally no doubt because by then the Achaeans had changed sides, he supported Philip, and after the latter's defeat and the proclamation of the 'freedom of the Greeks' in 196, Flamininus himself led a Roman army into Lakonia. According to Livy (34.37. 1ff.), the Spartan assembly almost unanimously rejected the terms offered by the Romans, after they had overrun Lakonia and moved on Sparta, and it was only after five days of skirmishing and three of siege, in which the Spartans faced 50,000 men, that they eventually capitulated.

Three years later when Greece was again in turmoil and Antiochus of Syria was expected to come to the aid of the Aetolian League against Rome, the Aetolians encouraged Nabis to try to recover some of the coastal towns of which Sparta had been deprived in 195. He stormed Gytheion and fought a successful engagement at sea against a squadron of Achaean ships (Livy 35.25.2–36), but while Gytheion was still under siege Philopoimen mustered the Achaean army and invaded Lakonia from the north by way of Karyai

(Livy 35.27.11ff.). After some bitter fighting, in which Livy alleges he lost three-quarters of his men (35.30.11), Nabis took refuge in Sparta and could do nothing but look on while his country was systematically ravaged for a month, before Philopoimen led his army home (Livy 35.30.12). This can be regarded as the last fight of the Spartan army[20] for, some months later, Nabis was treacherously murdered by Aetolian soldiers ostensibly sent to his aid. The enraged Spartans turned on the Aetolians and massacred them and even made a show of restoring the old monarchy in the person of a boy called Lakonikos, whom Livy describes as a member of the royal line (35.36.7–8) – which, he does not say – but Philopoimen seized the opportunity created by the confusion caused by Nabis' death and the arrival of a Roman fleet off Gytheion to browbeat the Spartans into joining the Achaean League.

Of Lakonikos, last king of Sparta, nothing more is heard.

Notes

Chapter 1

1. Plutarch's estimate was presumably based on a genealogical calculation – perhaps eighteen generations back from Agesilaos to the twin sons of Aristodemos, from whom the two Spartan royal houses were supposed to have been descended, giving 600 years at three generations to the century. But, the archaeological evidence, such as it is, does suggest that historical Sparta was founded about the middle of the tenth century: cf. Cartledge, 81–92. Note that all dates in this book are BC, unless otherwise stated.
2. See above. pp. 74–5.
3. Cf., e.g., the Athenians on Sphakteria (Thucydides 4.34.1), the Argives and their allies at Mantineia (Thucydides 5.72.4), the Boeotians at the Nemea (XH 4.2.18), the Arcadians at the 'Tearless Battle' (XH 7.1.31). In one of Lysias' speeches (16.17) the Athenian Mantitheus openly admits that he is not the kind of man who 'does not consider it a terrible thing to fight the Lakedaimonians.'
4. Cf. Eupolis fr.359 (Kock) ap. Eustathius on *Iliad* 1.293, referring to Kleon's fear of the *lambdas*, and see L. Lacroix, *Études d'archéologie classique*, 1 (1955–6), 89–115.
5. Presumably the story cannot be strictly true, since most, if not all, the allied hoplites would have been comparatively well off, and very few would have literally practised a trade – if they were anything, they would have been farmers (cf. Adcock, 5). On the other hand, none of them would have practised for war most of their lives as the Spartans did, and a passage in Xenophon (XH 7.4.34) is evidence that not all hoplites could afford to serve without pay.
6. Adcock. 10.
7. For the purpose of this book it does not matter whether or not the treatise on the *Constitution of the Lakedaimonians*, attributed to Xenophon, is by him or not, since it is presumably roughly contemporary. I am inclined to think that it is not by Xenophon: see K.M.T. Chrimes, *The Respublica Lacedaimoniorum Ascribed to Xenophon* (Manchester, 1948), and Appendix VII of her book *Ancient Sparta* (Manchester, 1949).
8. This disposes of the view of Beloch and Toynbee – cf. Toynbee 375 and n.8 – that Xenophon refers to three *lochoi* in XH 7.4.20 and 5.10 because it was less cumbersome than to refer to a *mora* and a half; nor is Toynbee's argument that Archidamos is said to walk along 'in front of the *lochoi*' when addressing his men, because there were too many men in a *mora* to hear him all at once, any more convincing.
9. Ct., e.g., Michell, 246.
10. *HCT* iv 216.
11. Kromayer, *Klio* 3 (1903), 187; Busolt, *Hermes* 40 (1905), 426.

12. Cf. G.T. Griffith & N.G. L. Hammond, *A History of Macedonia* II (Oxford, 1979), 529ff.

13. Cf. H.T. Wade-Gery, *Essays in Greek History* (Oxford, 1958), 82.

14. Cf. Toynbee, 378–9.

15. Cf. Toynbee, 396, though I think his explanation of how the author of the *Constitution* may have come to make his mistake, is over-elaborate.

16. Despite Chrimes, 378ff., I see no reason to doubt that the *Skiritai* were called after the district – cf. *HCT* iv, 103–4, where it is also suggested that Diodoros may have confused the *Skiritai* with the *Hippeis*. E.L. Wheeler, *Chiron* 13 (1983), 7, assumes that the *Skiritai* were cavalry, but Thucydides 5.67.1, where they are listed separately from the cavalry on either flank at Mantineia, shows that at least in 418, they counted as infantry.

17. Cf. Anderson, 245–9. On the *Hippeis* see H. Jeanmaire, *Couroi et Courètes* (Lille, 1939), 541ff., and M. Detienne, *La Phalange: Problèmes et Controverses*, in *Problèmes de la Guerre en Grèce Ancienne* (ed. J.P. Vernant, Paris 1968), 135ff., though I would not accept Detienne's identification of the *Hippeis* with the 300 Champions in 546 or with the 300 at Thermopylai. Jeanmaire identifies the *Hippeis* with the *krypteia* (op.cit., 550ff.), but although this is plausible in view of the rôle of the *hippagretai* in the arrest of Kinadon, I find his identification of the *Hippeis* with the 'little assembly' of XH 3.3.8 less convincing: the context suggests the 'little assembly' is the *Gerousia*.

18. When the Spartans raised a force of cavalry in 424, Thucydides regarded it as unprecedented (cf. 4.55.2), and there is no mention of cavalry in Tyrtaios: see P.A.L. Creenhalgh, *Early Greek Warfare* (Cambridge, 1973), 97ff., 147; Snodgrass, 85; Cartledge, *JHS* 97 (1977), 18–19 n. 60.

19. Cartledge, 313–4, but I think he makes too much of the passage – in particular, is there any reason to believe that these troopers had been 'enrolled specially' for this occasion? It is, however, interesting that Kinadon – who I would argue is an example of an 'inferior' who served as a hoplite – is implied by Xenophon (XH 3.3.5) to have been of robust physique.

20. Toynbee, 369–71.

21. Cf. Toynbee, 369, and refs. in n.5. He suggests that each of his 'homoian' *enomotiai* consisted of a pair of *syssitia*, but even if all the members of a fifteen-strong *syssition* were of military age, two would still only have made three-quarters of an *enomotia*, and Toynbee has to introduce the further complication that even a 'homoian' *enomotia* did not consist entirely of *homoioi*.

22. It may be relevant that there normally appear to have been eleven couches in standard sanctuary dining-rooms (R.A. Tomlinson, *Greek Sanctuaries* (London, 1976), 42–4.

23. Oliva, 166–70.

24. Cf., e.g., Michell, 238ff.; Andrewes, *HCT* iv 74; Jones, 61; Hooker, 130; Cartledge, 254ff. Toynbee, 38Iff., presents the most elaborate hypothesis. Recently Cawkwell (*CQ* 33, 1983, 385ff.) has even suggested that Spartiates and *perioikoi* were brigaded together at Plataea, with the latter in the rear ranks, but this is to make too much of Herodotos' failure to mention a grave for the *perioikoi*.

25. Cf. L.H. Jeffery, *The Local Scripts of Archaic Greece* (Oxford, 1961), No. 60.

26. Cartledge, 257.

27. This is the reading of the MSS and of Harpokration, s.v. μόραι, but Stobaeus read 'τῶν ὁπλιτικῶν μορῶν' (i.e. the hoplite *morai*) and this is accepted, e.g., by Marchant in the Oxford Text.

28. A possible exception is Thucydides 5.54.1 where he says of the army which accompanied King Agis in his abortive campaign of 419 that 'no one knew whither they were

marching, not even the cities from which they had been sent' (οὐδὲ αἱ πόλεις ἐξ ὧν ἐπέμφθησαν). But although Ste. Croix argues (345–6) that by 'αἱ πόλεις' Thucydides must mean the perioecic cities, it is possible that he means the cities of the allies, as Gomme and Andrewes take it (*HCT* iv 73–4), and one does wonder whether it would have been an occasion for remark if perioecic contingents had not known where they were going.

29. Toynbee tries to get round this by suggesting that some *perioikoi* served in Spartan *enomotiai* – he suggests that there were eight in each – and some in separate contingents. But this is over-complicated and still does not meet the objection that *perioikoi* would probably not have been full-time soldiers in the way that Spartiates were, as he seems uncomfortably aware (384–5). Cartledge, too, seems to realize that there is a problem here (cf. *JHS* 97, 1977, 17 n.52), and also notes the difficulty created by Xenophon's statement that 'gentlemen-volunteers' of the *perioikoi* served in the Olynthos campaign, when no regular Spartan units were present (289) – Cawkwell (*CQ* 33, 1983, 398) misinterprets this passage. At least some of the evidence that Toynbee cites to show that *perioikoi* served in the *morai*, shows no such thing: the *perioikoi* mentioned in XH 6.5.21, e.g., are not said to have served in the *morai*, and the non-Spartiate 'Lakedaimonians' who fought at Leuktra (XH 6.4.16), are not said to have been *perioikoi*.

Similarly, when Xenophon says in the *Symposium* (8.35) that young Spartans were ashamed to desert their comrades even when they were stationed alongside 'strangers' (ξένοι) and not with their lovers, there is nothing to suggest that he meant *perioikoi* by strangers, and the context – pace S. Hodkinson, *Chiron* 13 (1983), 256 n.36 – rather suggests that he meant, simply, men they did not know.

30. Cf. Cartledge, 315–7, and refs, there; Ste Croix, 331–2.
31. Since there were 700 Spartiates in the army at Leuktra (XH 6.4.15), of whom 300 were probably *Hippeis*, each of the four *morai* there probably contained about 100 Spartiates, but since only thirty five of the forty age-classes had been called up (XH 6.4.17), each *mora* at full strength would have contained c.114, giving c.684 in all six *morai*, c.984 in the whole army, including the *Hippeis*, to whom should be added those 'in office' at the time (cf. XH 6.4.17). Thus, in all, there would probably have been about 1,000 Spartiates of military age.
32. Cf. Cartledge, 314. Cartledge himself argues that Kinadon and the other 'enlisted men' must have been few, because he said 'the masses' would get their weapons from the iron store. But by 'the masses' Kinadon could have meant primarily the helots, possibly even *perioikoi* and *neodamodeis* who were not in service at the time – one is even tempted to see in his use of the expression, the contempt felt by even an 'inferior' Spartan for those who were not Spartans, though the expression is, presumably, Xenophon's own. I agree with Cartledge, 313, that Kinadon's remark that he wished to 'less than no one in Lakedaimon' indicates that he was an 'inferior' – cf. also the word 'ἐλασσωθήσεσθαι' ('lessened') in Thucydides 5.34.2, where he is talking about the fears of those who had surrendered on Sphakteria. Recently Cawkwell (*CQ* 33–NS–1983, 392–3) has rightly stressed the complexities of Spartan society – cf. Athenaios 6.271e–f.
33. Cf. Michell, 47 & 89; Toynbee, 324, 345 & nn., 350 n.3. For the contrary view see Chrimes, 221ff.; Oliva, 174ff.; Jones, 37–8; Cartledge, 314–5; and see also D. Lotze, *Historia* 11 (1962), 427–35.
34. On the navarchy see B.R. Sealey, *Klio* 58 (1976), 335–58.
35. I owe this splendid translation to Cartledge, 268. For the suggestion that the helot-harmosts were *mothakes* see K.W. Welwei, *Unfreie in antiken Kriegsdienst* I (Wiesbaden,

1974), 132. On Spartan prosopography see P. Poralla, *Prosopographie der Lakedaimonier bis auf die Zeit Alexanders des Grossen* (Breslau, 1913). On the value of family distinction in determining a Spartan's career see S. Hodkinson, *Chiron* 13 (1983), 260ff.

36. Cf. Toynbee, 339–40.

37. The MSS have '... τε καὶ ὁμοίως σφίσι ξυγγενεῖς': emendations are 'ὁμοίοις' (Bekker) and 'ὁμοῖοι' (Rauchenstein).

38. Cf., e.g., John Keegan, *The Face of Battle* (London, 1976), 186–92. Where officers stood is uncertain: they must surely have stood in the phalanx and not in front of it, and passages in *LP* 11.9 suggest that they normally took station on the right of the units they commanded. Hodkinson, op.cit., 265ff., suggests that the pressures to which Spartans were subjected had a stultifying effect upon them when it came to exercising independent command, but they do not seem to have been worse than other Greeks, and they were much in demand.

39. Cf. Keegan, op.cit., 113–4.

40. On the *agoge* see Chrimes, 118ff.; Michell, 165ff.; Toynbee, 317ff.; Jones, 34ff.; Hooker, 137ff.; and Cartledge, *JHS* 97 (1977), 16 & nn.44–7, and *PCPhS* (NS) 27 (1981), 17–36; Hodkinson, op.cit., 239ff.

41. The only evidence seems to be Plutarch's report of disaffection among 'those in Lakedaimon who had long been disaffected and criminal' – possibly to be identified as *hypomeiones* – during Epameinondas' first invasion (*Agesilaos* 32.3), but one can hardly believe that there was an even more widespread conspiracy among the Spartiates themselves, at the time, as he later claims (op.cit., 32.6).

42. But cf. what Keegan says, op.cit., 192.

43. On arms-drill see Anderson, 84–93. On drill-masters see E.L. Wheeler, *Chiron* 13(1983), 1–20.

44. Anderson, 144–6, takes it in the former way, but the Loeb translation, e.g., has 'veered to the right'.

45. Liddell & Scott, s.v. ἐξελίσσω IIa, cite this passage as an example of the meaning 'deploy' and the Loeb translation has 'wheeled', but the meaning is, clearly, 'countermarched' as in the later tactical writers (cf., e.g., Asklepiodotos 10.13).

46. Anderson, 107.

47. See Anderson, 105ff.

48. Cf. Anderson, 104, and 291 n.41.

49. This is how Anderson (107–9) interprets *LP* 11.10, but it is odd that the author should suddenly switch from talking about meeting a threat from a phalanx in front to meeting one from light troops on the right, without warning. As it stands, the passage dealing with the threat from the left means, 'if the enemy approach from the left, neither do they allow this, but push them back – (or, in one MS, 'run forward') – or wheel the *lochoi* to face the enemy,' but both readings seem very weak.

50. Cf. Anderson, 248.

51. Cf. John Buckler, *The Theban Hegemony 371–362 BC* (Cambridge, Mass., and London, 1980), 63 and 290 n.26. Thucydides describes the king's position at Mantineia as 'in the middle' (τῳ μέσῳ: 5.72.4).

52. On the shield see Anderson, 14–20; Snodgrass, 53–5; Cartledge, *JHS* 97 (1977), 12–3; Peter Connolly, *Greece and Rome at War* (London, 1981), 51–4. When not in use shields were covered – Anderson loc.cit.

53. Chrimes, 362ff.; Anderson, 20–8.

54. Anderson, 26, also cites *Anabasis* 1.2.15–6 as evidence that hoplites did not wear body-armour in the late fifth century, but there, of course, the hoplites in question are not

Spartans. *Anabasis* 4.1.8 mentions a 'Lakonian' who was shot through his '*spolas*', which was a kind of linen or leather jerkin. For the Spartan military cloak see Cartledge, *JHS* 97 (1977), 15 & n.38.

55. See Snodgrass 90–1; Connolly op.cit., 54–9.
56. Anderson, 27–9; Cartledge, *JHS* 97 (1977), 14 & n.27.
57. But cf. Keegan, op.cit., 114.
58. Would that Keegan had extended his book back in time to include a hoplite battle, but I take comfort from the fact that he, like myself, has never been in a battle. Perhaps the chapters in Rider Haggard's *King Solomon's Mines* which describe the great battle between the rival forces of Ignosi and Twala (Chapters 13 & 14) best convey what a hoplite battle might have been like – indeed, Rider Haggard surely had Thermopylai in mind when he wrote Chapter 14 – 'The Last Stand of the Greys'.
59. C.L. Cawkwell, *Philip II of Macedon* (London, 1976), 150–3. For a good summary of the usually accepted view of hoplite fighting see Adcock, 3–5, and for an able defence of this view see A.J. Holladay, *JHS* 102 (1982), 94–7. Cawkwell claims (op.cit., 152) that at Delion the *othismos* only came when the Thebans on the right began to win (Thucydides 4.96.4), but he appears to have overlooked Thucydides 4.96.2. On the alleged secondary role of the rear ranks in deep phalanxes see pp. 180–1.

Chapter 2

1. Cartledge, 256, argues for a *terminus ante queen* of 425, following Toynbee (373f., 376f., 382f., and 391), who links his alleged army-reform to the earthquake of c.465, though Cartledge (ibid. & 221–2) rightly points out that the earthquake's effects can be greatly exaggerated.
2. Michell, 244.
3. Cf. *HCT* iv 110ff.; Toynbee, 396ff.; Cartledge, 254–5; Ste. Croix, 331–2. Kagan, *The Peace of Nicias and the Sicilian Expedition* (Ithaca and London, 1981), 123–5, seems as confused about *morai* and *lochoi* as Thucydides perhaps was. Cawkwell, *CQ* (NS) 33 (1983), 385ff., defends Thucydides' numbers, arguing that the Spartan army 'appeared greater' because its front was longer, and that the seven lochoi did not include the *Brasideioi* and *neodamodeis*. But that Thucydides was not just thinking of a longer front is shown by his calculation of numbers, and to introduce a seven-*lochoi* army is to further complicate the issue. The polemarchs may have been staff-officers attached to the king, but their place in the command-structure suggests that they commanded specific units.
4. This is Forrest's solution – cf. 134.
5. When writing about numbers, and especially in connection with the Spartan army, it is all too easy to get confused, as I am only too well aware – I would hesitate to claim that all the calculations in this book are correct! Thus, Michell, 240, calculates that eight ranks of 448 men 'makes 3,840' when in fact it only makes 3,584, and then tries to account for an extra 266 men, when he should be only accounting for 256!
6. Cf. *HCT* iv 119–20. Michell, 242, is inclined to think that these two *lochoi* were the 'few Lakedaimonians' on the extreme right, but a third, or even a sixth, of the Spartan troops, is hardly a 'few', and the implication is that they were fewer than the 600 Skiritai, in which case two *lochoi* of even 512 men could not have come from them.
7. It could be argued that since Thucydides omits the *Hippeis* from his calculation of the number of Spartan troops present, whereas he mentions the 600 Skiritai, the *Hippeis* must have formed part of one of his seven *lochoi*. But, as was argued above (p. 15), it is difficult to see how the *Hippeis* can have formed part of one of the ordinary units, and it is more likely that Thucydides simply forgot them in his calculations.

8. Michell, 234–7, is an extreme example of this tendency. I do not find the argument that 'in warfare the Spartans were τεχνῖται (LP 13.5) and should move with the times' (*HCT* iv 114), convincing: moving with the times did not require constant reorganizing of the army (see above, pp. 7–8, 48, 101–102).

9. *HCT* iv 114; Cartledge, 256.

10. Toynbee, 376–7; Cartledge. 256.

11. Cf. note 24 on p. 206. Even the usually careful Cartledge says (256), '(Thucydides) tells us that of the 292 survivors from the 420 about 120 were Spartiates, the rest *Perioikoi* (4.38.),' although Thucydides does not specifically mention *perioikoi* anywhere in 4.38.5.

12. This is indicated by the well-known story told by Thucydides in 4.40.2 – see above, p. 150: the point of the story is that the enemy arrows had not picked out the καλοὶ κἀναθοί, and there is thus no reason to believe that proportionately more Spartiates than non-Spartiates had been killed.

13. Cf. Cartledge, 227, though I do not understand how he *knows* that by 'ἑαυτῶν' here, and by 'αὐτοί' and 'αὐτῶν' at 5.57.1 & 64.2, Thucydides 'is describing a mixed force of Spartiate and Perioikic hoplites.'

14. See above, p. 19 & p. 206 n.23.

15. Cf. Chrimes, 86ff; CM. Tazelaar, *Mnemosyne* 20(1967), 127ff. *Contra*: Michell, 171ff.; Toynbee, 161–2.

16. Hooker, 172, suggests that the words in Herodotos' text may conceal some obscure Spartan term; Toynbee, 319 n.4, guessed that what Herodotos wrote was 'ἥρωες/ἥρωας': I wonder whether it might have been 'ἵππεες/ἵππεας'. Cawkwell's solution to the problem of why there was no grave for the *perioikoi* is that they served in the rear ranks of the Spartan phalanx, and thus none of them were killed (op.cit., 387), but this is far-fetched.

17. Chrimes, 318.

18. Wade-Gery, *CAH* iii, 560, cf. *CQ* 38 (1944), 119ff, and *Essays in Greek History*, 37–85; Michell, 235ff.; Jones, 31–2; Toynbee, 371–2; Cartledge, 207, 256. Forrest, 42ff., is rightly sceptical. For my view cf. Chrimes, 314–5.

19. Cf. *Photios*, ed. S.A. Naber (Amsterdam, 1965), 395 n.7.

20. Chrimes, 163ff. A *phyle* of *Mesoatai* is mentioned in an unpublished inscription of Antonine date in the Sparta Museum: I owe this reference to Dr. A.J.S. Spawforth.

21. For Pitana cf. Herodotos 3.55.2; for Mesoa and Limnai Strabo 8.5.3; for all four Pausanias 3.16.9. Pausanias has the form 'Kynosoureis' for the ethnic, but inscriptions preserve the name 'Konooureis' (cf. *IG* V i 480 & 566 – the reading is restored in 681 & 684), and the obe was probably called 'Konooura', though for an epigraphic use of 'Kynosoura' see *BCH* Suppl. 1, 238. The words 'ὠβα Λιμναέων' occur on IG V i 688.

22. Chrimes, 165–6.

23. Huxley, 48–9, suggests that there were nine *obai* after the reform embodied in the *rhetra*, on the basis of the well-known fragment of Demetrios of Skepsis (ap. Athenaios 4.141e–f) describing the arrangements for the Karneia. Demetrios, however, clearly did not mention *obai*, and the arrangements he describes do not necessarily presuppose that there were nine such units. In any case, the arrangements at the Karneia may only have reflected the way the boys were organized for the *agoge* (see below, p. 214 n.30), and Demetrios was writing some 500 years after the probable date of the *rhetra*. The mysterious *oba* of 'Arkaloi' apparently mentioned in a now lost inscription (*IG* V i 722: cf. A.J. Beattie, *CQ – NS – 1*, 1945, 46ff.), seems to me too problematical to be brought into the discussion.

24. There are also the five *agathoergoi* of Herodotos 1.67.5, and the five arbitrators who allegedly awarded the island of Salamis to Athens – one of whom, to make coincidence complete, is also said to have been called Amompharetos (Plutarch *Solon* 10.4).

25. Chrimes 392 and n.3.

26. For these names see Chrimes, 86ff., and n.4 on 86.

27. In Chapter 3 (above, p. 89) I suggest that there may originally have been three *lochoi* of Pitana.

28. If only five men left the corps each year, this suggests that five men entered it each year from the youngest age-class, but even if all forty age-classes were thus represented in the corps – which seems unlikely in view of the evidence that it was a body of young men – the total number would still only have been 200. Perhaps Herodotos misunderstood something that he was told e.g. that *each* of the three *Hippagretai* chose five men from the youngest age class each year to replace the five oldest men in each group of 100 (cf. *LP* 4.3 and Herodotos 6.56). This would mean that each of the age-classes represented in the corps, would have been represented by fifteen men, and thus that only the first twenty age-classes would have had to be represented to make up the total of 300. However, one doubts that even men in the age-classes 30–39 still served in the *Hippeis*, and there is the further complication – for what it is worth – that one of the ancient commentators on Aristophanes *Lysistrata* 453 possibly implies that there were four *lochoi* in the *Hippeis*.

29. For other suggestions as to what the *triakades* may have been see How & Wells i 88 on Herodotos 1.65.5; Huxley, 124 n.316; Chrimes, 393; Michell, 236.

30. See above, p. 17, and cf. Forrest, 45–6. King Agis was only legislating for 4,500 Spartiates, whom he proposed, according to Plutarch, to divide into fifteen *syssitia* 'by two hundreds and four hundreds' (κατὰ διηκοσίους καὶ τετρακοσίους). This suggests that there may originally have been thirty *syssitia*, and it is just possible that Plutarch's statement that Agis' fifteen were to consist of 200 and 400 members – which is mathematically impossible – reflects an earlier system in which there had been fifteen *syssitia* of 200 members and fifteen of 400, which would have produced a total of 9000 Spartiates. The larger *syssitia* could then have been the earlier, the smaller those formed after Polydoros had added 3,000 new *klaroi* (cf. Plutarch *Lykourgos* 8.3). But it is much more likely that the archaic and classical *syssitia* were much smaller – see above, p. 17. Perhaps Plutarch should have written 'εἰς τριακόσια νενέσθαι φιδίτια κατὰ πεντεκαίδεκα' (… to form 300 *phiditia* by fifteens), when talking of Agis IV's reform.

31. Cf., e.g.. Hooker, 164; M. Detienne, *La Phalange: Problèmes et Controverses* (ap. J.P. Vernant, *Problèmes de la Guerre en Grèce Ancienne*, Paris 1968), 134.

32. It is sometimes said that Spartiates were not eligible to attend the assembly until they were thirty – e.g. Forrest, 52 – but the only evidence seems to be Plutarch *Lykourgos* 25.1, and as Ste. Croix has pointed out (347), the passage refers only to those under thirty being debarred from the *agora* in the sense of market-place. There was a similar prohibition against early marriage among the Zulus – cf. Donald R.Morris, *The Washing of the Spears* (London 1965), 51. For a comparison of the Spartan and Zulu military systems see W.S. Ferguson, *Havard African Studies* 2 (1918), 197–234.

33. His half-brother, Kleomenes, was evidently reigning, with full powers, by c.519 at latest (cf. Herodotos 6.108 and Thucydides 3.68.5), possibly by c.525 (cf. Plutarch *Moralia* 223d), which suggests that he was born not later than c.550, possibly c.555, and Leonidas was evidently born soon afterwards (cf. Herodotos 5.41).

34. Sealey, *Klio* 58 (1976), 339, suggests Anchimolios may have been the first *navarch*.

35. Cf. D. Daube, *The Duty of Procreation* (Edinburgh, 1977), 11, and Cartledge, 309–11.

36. Cf. Cartledge, 169–70.
37. Cf. Forrest, 137; Cartledge, 167–8, 316.
38. Cartledge, 317–8.
39. Cartledge, 168, suggests that this is where the 'ancient portion' (ἀρχαῖα μοῖρα) of Aristotle fr.611.12 Rose and Plutarch *Moralia* 238e, was located.
40. Unless some of the disaffected elements who plotted against the state in 370/69, according to Plutarch (*Agesilaos* 32.3), were *hypomeiones* see above, pp. 193–4 and p. 208 n. 41.

Chapter 3

1. Cf., e.g., C.G. Starr, *Historia* 14 (1965), 257–72; M.I. Finley, *Sparta*, ap. J.P. Vernant, *Problèmes de la Guerre en Grèce Ancienne* (Paris, 1968), 143.
2. On the Dorians see, e.g., V. R.d'A. Desborough, *The Last Mycenaeans and their Successors* (Oxford, 1964), 251–2; A.Snodgrass, *The Dark Age of Greece* (Edinburgh, 1971), 8–10, 177–9, 300–4, 311–12; Cartledge, 73ff.; and for an eccentric view J. Chadwick, *La Parola del Passato* 31 (1976), 103–17, accepted by, e.g.. Hooker, 41–6.
3. Cf. V.R.d'A.Desborough, *Protogeometric Pottery* (Oxford, 1952), 283–90, and *The Greek Dark Ages* (London, 1972), 240–3; J.N. Coldstream, *Greek Geometric Pottery* (London, 1968), 212–4, and *Geometric Greece* (London, 1977), 157–9; Cartledge, 75ff.
4. Cf., e.g., Thucydides 5.112.2 and 1.12.3, and cf. Herodotos 2.145.4.
5. Of course, if the genealogy of the Eurypontidai has been fabricated in its early stages, as suggested above, we are dependent on that of the Agiadai, and it is questionable whether even this is accurate for the earliest period. However, assuming it to be roughly right, it could give a reasonably accurate date for the beginnings of historical Sparta: if, for example, we knew no more of the date of William the Conqueror than that he reigned twenty-eight generations before the present queen, a calculation based on allowing three generations to the century would lead us to believe that he reigned about the middle of the eleventh century AD, which would not be far out.
6. Cf. Chrimes, 205ff.; Toynbee, 329ff.; R.F. Willetts, *Ancient Grete: A Social History* (London, 1965), 58ff., 95ff., 110ff.
7. Cf. Cartledge, 103. Huxley, 22, suggests that it was now that the Skiritis also became subject to Sparta, and that further expansion in this direction may have been halted by a defeat at the hands of Tegea in the reign of Charillos, which later became confused with the defeat early in the sixth century (Pausanias 3.7.3) – Charillos was even alleged to have been taken prisoner (Pausanias 8.5.9, cf. 48.4).
8. Cf. J.N. Coldstream, *Geometric Greece* (London, 1977), 157–60; Cartledge, 109ff.; Hooker, 47ff. Cartledge (97, 106–7) is sceptical about the 'tradition' embodied in Pausanias, but I do not find his arguments cogent, and his picture of Spartan influence extending as far as Helos before the eighth century, seems to me less plausible than Pausanias'.
9. Cf. C.A. Roebuck, *A History of Messenia from 369 to 146 BC* (Chicago, 1941), 122ff; *BSA* 61 (1966), 115–6.
10. Alkamenes' son, Polydoros, is associated with Theopompos in Pausanias' account of the First Messenian War (4.7.7–8, 8.10), but one suspects that he did not really come to the throne until after the war, and was only associated with Theopompos in the reforms that led to the *rhetra* (cf. Plutarch *Lykourgos* 6.4, and above p. 91ff). Elsewhere (*Moralia* 739f), Plutarch associates Theopompos with Alkamenes, and there was evidently a tradition that the former lived to an immense age, being succeeded by his grandson or

even great-grandson (Pausanias 3.7.5), though Herodotos thought his son, Anaxandridas, reigned as king (8.131.2–3).

11. Cf. L.H.Jeffery, *Archaic Greece* (London, 1976), 114; Cartledge 103ff. If Charillos was held to have usurped power in some sense, this might explain Aristotle's curious classification of him as a 'tyrant' whose tyranny changed into 'aristocracy' (*Politics* 1316a33–4).

12. Cf. Cartledge, 106.

13. On the rites of Artemis Orthia see Chrimes, 118ff., 248ff.; Hooker, 52ff.; Michell, 175–7.

14. For the view that Lykourgos was originally a god see E. Meyer, *Forschungen zur alten Geschichte* I (Halle, 1892), 211–86; Toynbee, 274ff.; Oliva, 63ff.

15. Cf. V. Ehrenberg, *Neugründer des Staates* (Munich, 1925), 13, 30, 49.

16. Cf. Pindar *Isthmian* 6(7) 18ff., and schol. ad loc. = Aristotle frag. 532 Rose. On the Aigeïdai see Huxley, 22–4 & 49; Toynbee, 175–7 & 214–20.

17. *Pace* M. Detienne, *La Phalange: Problèmes et Controverses* (ap. *Problèmes de la guerre en Grèce ancienne*, ed. J.P. Vernant, Paris 1968), 139. For the date of the First Messenian War see J. Kroymann, *Sparta und Messenien* (Berlin, 1937), 13–7, and H.T. Wade-Gery, *The Rhianos Hypothesis* (ap. *Ancient Society and Institutions*, Oxford 1966), 296, and for the date of the beginning of hoplite warfare J. Salmon, *JHS* 97 (1977), 85–92. A possible relic of the war is the skeleton of a warrior buried in a pithos at Nichoria in Messenia, which I saw unearthed while taking part in the excavations there in 1969: cf. J.N. Coldstream, *Geometric Greece* (London, 1977), 163–4.

18. Cf. K.J. Neumann, *Historische Zeitschrift* 96 (1906), 25ff.

19. Cf. Chrimes, 392ff.; Forrest, 29ff., 44ff.; and see Demetrios of Skepsis ap. Athenaios 4.141e–f.

20. See B.C. Dietrich, *Kadmos* 14 (1975), 133–42, for the argument that the Hyakinthia were a Dorian cult.

21. Though Amyklaians were clearly 'Spartans' in some sense, they seem to have retained a separate identity: they were apparently not admitted to the cult of Artemis Orthia, whereas they were admitted to that of Athena Poliachos (Cartledge, 106), and they retained their own special festival of the Hyakinthia (cf. XH 5.4.10, etc., and see also n.31 below).

22. On the possibility that the Aigeïdai were involved in the plot that led to the foundation of Taras see Toynbee, 215ff.; for the cult of Hyakinthos at Taras see Polybios 8.30.1.

23. For Timomachos' corslet see the references in n.16 above, and for the equipment of the primitive Spartan army Cartledge, *JHS* 97 (1977), 18–9, and notes thereto, though I am not convinced, as he apparently is (n.61), that the 'Dipylon' shield was not 'a figment of the artistic imagination' – cf. P.A.L. Greenhalgh, *Early Greek Warfare* (Cambridge, 1973), 63–70.

24. Here I am broadly in agreement with Cartledge, *JHS* 97 (1977), 18–24, and John Salmon, op.cit., 85–92, as against, particularly, Snodgrass, *JHS* 85 (1965), 110–22. I am not sure, however, that hoplite equipment was devised for phalanx fighting, and not the other way round: is it not possible that the hoplite-shield, in particular, with its characteristic double-grip, was devised because it was less tiring to carry a shield with its weight falling, essentially, on the shoulder rather than the wrist, as was the case with the central hand-grip shield, even with the additional support of a shoulder-strap? If so, the phalanx may have emerged after the adoption of the equipment, though the latter was probably not the only reason for the adoption of phalanx tactics.

25. Salmon, op.cit., 90.

26. Cf. *Palatine Anthology* 14.73, Aristotle *Politics* 1310b16–28; A. Andrewes, *Classical Quarterly* 43 (1949), 74–7, *The Greek Tyrants* (London, 1956), 39–40; Salmon, op.cit., 92–3.

27. Cf. Wade-Gery, *Classical Quarterly* 43 (1949), 79–81; Cartledge, *JHS* 97 (1977), 75 n.1. T. Kelly, *American Journal of Philology* 91 (1970), 31–42, and *A History of Argos* (Minneapolis, 1976), 86–8, argues that the battle is not historical, but a new fragment of Tyrtaios (*Pap.Ox.* 3316) apparently confirms that the Spartans were involved with the Argives at the time – see Cartledge, 126. For the location of the battlefield see now W.K. Pritchett, *Studies in Ancient Greek Topography. 3. (Roads)*, Berkeley & Los Angeles, 1980.

28. See the articles by Cartledge and Salmon cited in n.24 above. Even though the connection between Orthagoras and the army at Sikyon, and that of Kypselos with the Corinthian army, is tenuous (cf. Jacoby FGH 105F2 and Nikolaos of Damascus, *FGH* 90F57–8, Aristotle *Politics* 1305a7ff. and 1315b27–8), it is suggestive.

29. Cf. Aristotle *Politics* 1306b27ff. and 1313a26ff.; Antiochos of Syracuse and Ephoros ap. Strabo 6.3.2–3; Pausanias 3.3.2–3; Plutarch *Lykourgos* 5–6, and esp. 6.4–5. Thucydides' date for the beginning of *eunomia* at Sparta – 'about four hundred years to the end of this war' (i.e. the Peloponnesian War) – might be based on a calculation of ten generations of forty years from King Pausanias back to Polydoros, or twelve generations from Agis II to Charillos.

30. Cf. Huxley, 43ff., and in general for my view of the date of the *rhetra* W.G. Forrest, *Phoenix* 17 (1963), 157–79, and *History of Sparta*, 58. I do not think that the arrangements for the Karneia described by Demetrios of Skepsis (ap. Athenaios 4.141e–f) can be used to reconstruct the archaic Spartan army, for although Demetrios describes the arrangements as a 'μίμημα τῆς στρατιωτικῆςἀγωγῆς'. this does not mean that they reflected the army's *organization*, but, if anything, 'the military training-system'. The probability, in fact, is that Demetrios meant that the arrangements were 'a symbol of the *agoge*', in which case they presumably reflected the way the *boys* were organized. But, in any case, Demetrios was writing in the 2nd century, and who knows how much the arrangements at the Karneia may have changed by then?

31. Cf. Wade Gery, *Essays in Greek History* (Oxford, 1958), 37–85. The Amyklaians present a problem on my interpretation, of course, since even if they belonged to the three *phylai*, they presumably did not belong to any of the four *obai*. However, all we really know about the status of the Amyklaians is that by the fourth century they were to be found serving in the *morai*: we do not know their exact status at the time of the *rhetra*, and they might originally have had one analagous to that of Roman *cives sine suffragio*, for example, and hence not have been catered for in the *rhetra*'s arrangements for the Spartan assembly.

32. Cf. the 'ἀρχαῖα μοῖρα' of Aristotle frag.611.12 Rose ap. Herakleides Lembos 2.7, and Plutarch *Moralia* 238e, and see Cartledge, 165ff.

33. Cartledge, 127 & 134, seems inclined to think that Tyrtaios was referring to contemporary demands for land-distribution, but if the poem on *Eunomia* cited by Aristotle was the one in which the poet paraphrased the *rhetra*, he certainly harked back to the past in it – perhaps, indeed, his argument was that his contemporaries should look to the past for a solution to their problems.

34. Even if it is true that the Spartan state later issued equipment to its hoplites – see W.K. Pritchett, *The Greek State at War I* (California, 1971), 4 n.3; M.I. Finley, *The Use and Abuse of History* (London, 1975), 166ff; Cartledge, 185 & 314 – I cannot believe that this was true of pre-*rhetra* Sparta.

35. Cf. A.J. Holladay, *JHS* 102 (1982), 99.

36. Cf. the story in Aristotle *Politics* 1313a25ff., and compare the role of Hindenburg in the establishment of the German republic in 1918 – see John Terraine, *To Win a War* (London, 1978), 245–54.

37. For the view that only certain Spartans were eligible for the *gerousia* and for its power, see Aristotle *Politics* 1265b35ff., 1270b24–5, 1270b36ff., 1294b29 31, 1306a18–9. If one takes the view, as I do, that Tyrtaios frag.4 West paraphrases both the *rhetra* and the amendment allegedly made by Theopompos and Polydoros, it is hardly possible to deny that they are both part of the original *rhetra*, and I am not convinced that the amendment in fact gives the *gerousia* and kings an effective veto – it depends on the meanings of 'ἀφίστασθαι' and 'ἀποστατῆρας', and we really do not know what these words mean. I think they might mean 'divide' and 'dividers', i.e. refer to arrangements for *voting* (cf. Thucydides 1.87.1–3).

38. Cf. Cartledge, *JHS* 97 (1977), 27.

39. Cf. Cartledge, 169–70. I agree with Cartledge that we must assume that the *klaroi* were distributed on each occasion once and for all, and that Plutarch was wrong to say (*Lykourgos* 16.1) that a new-born male Spartiate, once accepted by the elders of his *phyle*, was assigned one of the *klaroi*. In fact, the *klaroi* must have passed from father to son, as Plutarch himself implies elsewhere (*Agis* 5.2).

40. Assuming that the *klaroi* were to be hereditary – see n.39 above – it would surely have been realized that some would inevitably be inherited by boys too young for immediate military service.

41. Cartledge, 126, distinguishes the two, but Theopompos could, surely, still have been alive in 669, and Pausanias does say (3.7.5) that he was too old to take part in the war over Thyreatis in his time. Dare one suggest that the curious story of the murder of Polydoros by 'Polemarchos' (Pausanias 3.3.3) may have arisen because Polydoros was done away with by the polemarchs after Hysiai?

42. Cf., e.g., Huxley, 53; Forrest, 67; Cartledge, 126–7.

43. Cartledge, *JHS* 97 (1977), 26 n.167, quotes with approval Lloyd-Jones' remark (*The Justice of Zeus*, 45) that 'when Jaeger claims that Tyrtaios was trying to substitute a city-state morality for an aristocratic morality in Sparta, he has failed to notice that in Sparta the two kinds of morality were not distinct.' But even though all Spartiates were, in a sense, 'aristocrats', and this would have become more and more true as their numbers declined, there always seems to have been an aristocracy within the Spartiate body, as Cartledge himself is, of course, aware (cf., e.g., 343), and as the evidence about the *gerousia* cited in n.37 above, shows. See also L.F. Fitzhardinge, *The Spartans* (London, 1980), 157ff.

44. Cf. A. Snodgrass, *JHS* 85 (1965), 116; M.I. Finley, *The Use and Abuse of History* (London, 1975), 161; Toynbee, 256ff.; Fitzhardinge, op.cit., 127. I agree with Cartledge, *JHS* 97 (1977), 26, that 'the supposed ambiguities and contradictions in Tyrtaios melt away ... when it is perceived that they arise from his attempt to pour new spiritual wine into old linguistic bottles.'

45. There is apparently a reference to '*gymnomachoi*' in the new papyrus fragment of Tyrtaios (*Pap. Ox.* 3316).

46. Cf. the slaves allegedly killed at Marathon (Pausanias 1.32.3), and the helots killed at Plataea (Herodotos 9.85.2). I am not at all sure that Toynbee was right (256 n.17) to accept Kiechle's view (*Lakonien und Sparta*, 192–3) that the *gymnetes* were Spartiates – surely they were 'inferiors' at least?

47. Cf. Cartledge, *JHS* 97 (1977), 26.

48. Those on the Protocorinthian aryballos from Rhodes now in Berlin (Salmon, *JHS* 97, 1977, 86 fig.1), and on the Chigi vase (op.cit., fig. 2) certainly appear to reach from the shoulders to the knees at least: see Pl. 5.
49. Huxley, 22 – cf. n.7 above. It is possible that the defeat of Sparta near Orchomenos, referred to in Theopompos *FGH* 115F69, belongs to the early 6th century. On the history of these years see D.M. Leahy, *Phoenix* 12 (1958), 141ff.
50. Cf., now, Cartledge, *Classical Quarterly* 32 (1982), 243ff.
51. Cf. Antonia Fraser, *Cromwell Our Chief of Men* (London, 1963), 363.

Chapter 4
1. On the difficulties of reconstructing ancient battles see N. Whatley, *JHS* 84 (1964), 119–39. I agree with almost everything Whatley says, though I believe that he is, perhaps, slightly too sceptical, and even he does not think the attempt should not be made (cf. 119). On the date of Thermopylai see Burn, 403–5, and Hignett, 448–52, who effectively demolish the view of Labarbe (*BCH* 78, 1954, 1–21), accepted by Pritchett (*AJA* 62, 1958, 203).
2. Cf., e.g., M.H. Jameson, *Hesperia* 29 (1960), 205. Another view – cf., e.g., Adcock, 41 – is that Thermopylai was to be held in order to give the Greek fleet a chance to win a decisive victory: this, too, I find too sophisticated a strategy for the Greeks of 480.
3. Cf. S.Marinatos, *Thermopylae* (Athens, 1951); *JHS* 59 (1939), 199f.; *AJA* 43 (1939), 699–700. For the Anopaia path see W.K. Pritchett, *AJA* 62 (1958), 203–13, and *Studies in Ancient Greek Topography I* (California, 1965), 71–9; Burn, 407–11; Hignett, 361–70; Green, 114–7.
4. One suggestion – e.g. Green, 111 & 140 – is that the missing 900 were helots, but Herodotos implies that there was only one helot in attendance on each Spartan at Thermopylai (7.229.1), and it is extremely unlikely that the epitaph would have referred to helots. Another possibility is that Herodotos omitted a contingent from Elis (cf. Hignett, 116), but the people of Elis would, above all, surely have been debarred from fighting during the Olympic festival. Diodoros (11.4.5, cf. Ktesias 25) adds 1,000 'Lakedaimonians' by which he presumably means *perioikoi*, but although one might have expected a contingent of *perioikoi*, it would, perhaps, have been odd if they had fielded three times as many troops as the Spartans themselves, and there really is no place for them in the story of the final day.
5. I agree with Burn, 367–8, and Hignett, 466–7, as against J.S. Morrison & R.T. Williams, *Greek Oared Ships 900–322 BC* (Cambridge, 1968), 131 – accepted by, e.g.. Green, 109, and Peter Connolly, *Greece and Rome at War* (London, 1981), 13 & 265 – that Greek triremes of 480 had at least as many marines as the Persian triremes are alleged to have had – the Chiot warships at Lade c.496 each had 40 marines on board (Herodotos 6.15.1).
6. Cf. Marathon (Herodotos 6.106), and see Thucydides 5.54 for a series of incidents which show how seriously the Dorians of the Peloponnese still took the Karneian month as late as 419.
7. There is also the question how Eurybiades and those who served with him on the Spartan ships at Artemision, came to be exempted from the taboo. But perhaps the majority of the marines were *perioikoi*, and the crews helots, or the taboo may not have been held to apply to service at sea, which was presumably not envisaged when the taboo originated. For a perioecic naval commander cf. Thucydides 8.22.1 and for helot sailors XH 7.1.13.

8. The Leontiades who admitted Phoibidas to the Kadmeia in 382 (XH 5.2.25ff.), was presumably a member of the same family (cf. John Buckler, *The Theban Hegemony*, Cambridge, Mass., 1980, 42).

9. G. Busolt, *Criechische Ceschichte*,² ii (Gotha, 1895), 675 n.2.

10. Cf. Polyainos 1.32.3. Burn, 381, and Green, 114, are among those inclined to accept the story, but, for example, who are 'those in the city' (οἱ κατὰ τὴν πόλιν) who are said to have been deterred from coming out? Burn suggests the inhabitants of Lamia, Labarbe (*BCH* 78, 1954, 4–6) those of Trachis, but Leonidas would hardly have been worried about these utterly minor towns.

11. E.g. Hignett, 119.

12. E.g. Hignett, 143.

13. The precise chronology of the Thermopylai-Artemision campaign is the subject of controversy – see, e.g., Hignett, 379–85. I used to believe (cf. *Hermes* 92, 1964, 278 nn. 1 & 4) that the first sea-fight took place on the day the Persian fleet reached Aphetai, in which case the last three days of Xerxes' wait before Thermopylai would have exactly coincided with the storm. Now I am reluctantly coming round to the conclusion that a day or days intervened between the arrival of the Persian fleet at Aphetai and the first battle, partly because of Herodotos 7.196, partly because of the difficulty in believing that the 200 Persian ships detached to round Euboea could have reached the likely location of the Hollows before dawn on the day of the second sea-fight, if they had not left Aphetai before the afternoon of the day before – for the location of the Hollows see H.J. Mason & M.B. Wallace, *Hesperia* 41 (1972), 128–140.

14. It is instructive to compare Thucydides' account of the fight on Sphakteria: there the Spartans were prevented from coming to close quarters – see 4.33 and above. pp. 119–20.

15. See, e.g.. Burn, 413.

16. I once walked from Olymbos to Spoa on the island of Karpathos, with Dick Hope Simpson, under instructions, simply, to keep to the central spine of the island, and ended up, at night, on the wrong side of the ridge.

17. For the Anopaia path see the references in n.3 above.

18. Hignett, 363, e.g., suggests 2,000. Diodoros (11.8.5) says 20,000!

19. Cf., e.g., Burn, 418; Hignett, 141; Green, 116; but see R. Hope Simpson, *Phoenix* 26 (1972), 4 n.23.

20. Green, n. on 139, is inclined to accept the story of Tyrrhastiadas -Hignett, 377, is sceptical.

21. It is, inevitably. Green who cites the Long Range Desert Group's exploit as a parallel (139) – for the exploit see Desmond Young, *Rommel* (London, 1950), 111–2, and David Irving, *The Trail of the Fox* (London, 1977), 107–8. The incident took place in November, 1941, not in 1942, as Green states.

22. For the theory see J.B. Bury, *BSA* 2 (1895/6), 98ff. *Contra*: Pritchett, *AJA* 62 (1958), 211 n.8; Burn, 417 n.23; Hignett, 374–6; J.A.S. Evans, *GRBS* 5 (1964), 233.

23. Green, 140, suggests that Leonidas called for volunteers, and Herodotos 7.220.2 hints that this may be true; Hope Simpson, op.cit., 5, points out that no official blame or stigma appears to have attached to the Peloponnesians.

24. Cf. J.A.R. Munro, *JHS* 22 (1902), 316; Green, 67–8, is inclined to accept the oracle as genuine.

25. For criticisms of these views of Munro (*JHS* 22, 1902, 318) and Miltner (*Klio* 28, 1935, 228ff.) see Hignett, 377–8.

26. Cf. A.W. Gomme, *JHS* 53 (1933), 21 n.19; Burn, 417–8.

27. Beloch (Griechischc Geschichte² ii.2.91–105 – accepted by Hignett, 373–4) argued on the basis of the timing implied by Herodotos that Leonidas only learned of the success of the turning-movement too late for an orderly retreat, and that he and those with him were caught before they could escape, whereas the rest had fled at the first hint of danGer. But this is belied by Herodotus' narrative, and the last fighting would surely have taken place east of the Middle Gate if Leonidas and his men had been caught escaping. A pupil of mine, a serving officer in the Cheshire Regiment, told me that the British Army still orders a 'stand to' at 'first-light', when in the field, and that this can last for anything up to an hour.

28. Cf. Hignett, 376. Delbrück, typically, asserted that the Thespiaians were in fact caught retreating (*History of the Art of War*, tr. Walter J. Renfroe, Jr., Westport, Connecticut, 1975, I, 97 n.3).

29. Thus the Corinthians refused to obey Kleomenes c.505 (Herodotos 5.75.1), and the other Peloponnesian contingents, apart from the Tegeates, apparently disobeyed Pausanias at Plataea (Herodotos 9.52).

30. Cf. Diodoros 11.4.7; Burn, 417; Green, 140. The difficulty about supposing that the choice of the Thespiaians and Thebans was solely conditioned by the thought that their homes were bound to be overrun, is that one would have thought this consideration would have applied even more strongly to the Lokrians.

31. Cf. J.R. Grant, *Phoenix* 15 (1961), 26; Hope Simpson, op.cit., 9.

32. Hignett, 146 n.5, argues that the reference to the contingent from Mycenae in Pausanias 2.16.5 does not mean that it, too, stayed with Leonidas, which is true, but he seems to have overlooked Pausanias 10.20.2 where this is explicitly stated. Diodoros (11.9.2) says that Leonidas only had 500 men left, including the Thespiaians, after the departure of the allies, but this seems too few, and Diodoros, in any case, appears to have forgotten the Thebans.

33. Cf. Hope Simpson, op.cit., 10.

34. Hope Simpson, loc.cit.

35. By S. Marinatos' excavation in 1939 – see n.3 above.

36. For the branding of prisoners – which was also a Greek habit – see the note on this passage in How & Wells, ii, 232.

37. Green, 142.

Chapter 5

1. If I am right – see above, p. 52 – there were at least 6,144 Spartan soldiers at Mantineia, and it is possible that the 6000 'Lakedaimonians' at the Nemea in 394, were also all Spartans (see above, pP. 10–11); even Agesilaos' army in Boeotia in 377, if it really did contain five morai, probably had more than 5,000 Spartans. If, of course, Herodotos' use of the term '*Spartiatai*' for the 5,000 at Plataea is to be pressed, this is the largest body of Spartiates ever mentioned – but see above, pp. 24 & 59.

2. I hesitate to mention Ernie Bradford's '*The Year of Thermopylae*' (London, 1980) with Peter Green's '*The Year of Salamis*', since despite my doubts about many of the latter's views, it is, basically, a scholarly work in its use of evidence and argument, apart from being splendidly written.

3. Cf. George Grote, *A History of Greece* (London, 1862), vol. iii, 496; How & Wells, ii, 292f.; etc. Hignett, 296, prefers the idea that the Persians were first south of the Asopos and then withdrew north of it, but if Mardonios had in fact spent a night at Tanagra, as Herodotos says he did (9.15.1), he had already crossed the Asopos.

4. For the location of Erythrai see Hignett, 425–6. I am inclined to locate it on the Pantanassa ridge – see Hope Simpson & Lazenby, *The Catalogue of the Ships in Homer's Iliad* (Oxford, 1970), 24 – for Skolos see 21.

5. For the principle cf. Delbrück, *History of the Art of War* (trans. Renfroe, Westport, Connecticut, 1975), 93.

6. Even Hignett toys with this notion – see 299. Green, 245, contradicts himself within ten lines: he says, first, that Mardonios 'wanted to see how his cavalry would shape up, over rough ground, against a disciplined line of Greek spearmen,' and then adds, surely rightly this time, that 'he knew perfectly well that the chances of a cavalry charge succeeding under such conditions were minimal.'

7. This is Green's second suggestion (loc.cit.).

8. Cf. G. Busolt, *Griechische Geschichte*[2] (Gotha, 1895), ii 724 n.3; A. Hauvette, *Hérodote, historien des guerres médiques* (Paris, 1894), 453; H.B. Wright, *The Campaign of Plataea* (New Haven, 1904), 51; Burn, 509–10; Green, 233.

9. Cf. Busolt, op.cit., 727 n.2.

10. Cf. 'προσέβαλλον κατά τέλεα': Herodotos 9.20. Burn, 516, translates 'discharging their missiles by squadrons,' but although the root meaning of 'βάλλειν' is, of course, 'to throw', 'προσβάλλειν' usually means, simply, 'to attack'. It is illuminating to read Green's account of this episode (245–71) alongside that of Herodotos.

11. R. Macan, *Herodotos. The Seventh, Eighth & Ninth Books* (London, 1908), 631B; How & Wells, ii, 294; Burn, 516.

12. Cf. Herodotos 9.29.2, where he calculates the number of the Greek light troops as 69,500, whereas at 7 helots to each Spartiate, and one soldier-servant to each of the other hoplites, the figure should be 68,700. This has suggested that the Athenian archers numbered 800; cf. E. Meyer, *Geschichte des Altertums*[,] (Stuttgart, 1901), iii, 360 and n., 408 and n.

13. Burn, e.g., says (517), 'it looks like a task-force specially adapted for advanced-guard action,' and, worse still, Green (246) describes it as 'a special Athenian commando force of three hundred light infantry and archers, which had been posted well ahead of the main line, perhaps as shock troops.' This is not only pure fantasy, but nonsense at that – 'light infantry' would hardly be 'shock troops'!

14. If all ten Athenian *phylai* were represented at Plataea, each *taxis* would have contained about 800 men, since there were 8,000 Athenians in all (Herodotos 9.28.6), and Olympiodoros' force may really have been half a *taxis*, perhaps called a *lochos* – Herodotos (9.21.3) uses the word 'ἐλοχήγεε' of him, and Plutarch (Aristeides 14.3) describes him as the 'keenest of the *lochagoi*'. Diodoros (11.30.4) says his men constituted Aristeides' bodyguard, but this looks like confusion with the 300 Spartan *Hippeis*.

15. Having spent some time looking for Mycenaean sherds along the foothills of Kithairon, east of Kriekouki, I can confirm how dry this area is.

16. For the topography of the second Greek position see Burn, 519–22, and Hignett, 301–11. Grundy's solution to the problems (*The Great Persian War and its Preliminaries*, London 1901, 466ff. and 473f.), is unnecessarily elaborate. Ufer in *Antike Schlachtfelder* (ed. J. Kromayer), vol. iv (Berlin, 1924–31), 127ff., suggested that the Gargaphia spring should be located on the north slope of the Asopos ridge, referring to one of the two springs described by Grundy, *The Topography of the Battle of Plataea* (London, 1894), 17. Burn, 522 n.26, points out that the name 'Apotripi' used by some modern scholars (e.g. Hignett, 302, 304 & 428, and map p. 290), is almost certainly a corruption of 'Alepotrypi'. For the Pyrgos hill position see J.A.R. Munro, *JHS* 24 (1904), 159ff.,

Green, 248, but to calculate that this must have been where the Greek left wing was stationed on the basis of the number of hoplites they had, allowing a depth of eight shields, is going too far, since, apart from anything else, it is unlikely that the whole Greek army was ever drawn up in phalanx formation in this position – see N. Whatley, *JHS* 84 (1964), 124, for the difficulties in being too precise about such positions. Hignett, 418–21 (cf. 430–1), is rightly sceptical about the value of any topographical information in Plutarch's life of Aristeides, for the Plataea campaign.

17. Cf. Hignett, Appendix XII, 435–8.
18. Herodotos miscalculates here – cf.n.12 above.
19. Cf., e.g.. Burn, 521, and Green, 244.
20. E.g. Hignett, 435.
21. On the basis of the size of the stockade, Burn, 511, suggests 60–70,000 men for the Asiatic troops, inclusive of cavalry; on the same basis, Peter Connolly, *Greece and Rome at War* (London, 1981), 29, suggests a total of 120,000, apparently for the whole army, including cavalry.
22. On the usual delay before battle see Whatley, op.cit., 137.
23. On the passes see Hignett, 422–4, and references there.
24. Cf., e.g., Hignett, 292, 296, 298, 301; Green, 243, 245, 255.
25. Cf. Hignett, 316.
26. One is tempted to bring in here, as evidence for dissensions amongst the Greeks at this time, Plutarch's story of the right-wing plot in the Athenian camp (*Aristeides* 13), but the story is probably an invention – see Hauvette, op.cit., 148 & 465, and How & Wells, ii 306.
27. Cf. Hignett, 318ff., and refs. there; Green, 255ff.
28. The words are Hignett's, 318.
29. On the location of 'the island' see especially G.B. Grundy, *The Great Persian War and its Preliminaries* (London, 1901), 481ff.
30. Cf. Burn, 531, but see Hignett, 327–8.
31. The existence of Euryanax, and Herodotos' description of him as 'the son of Dorieus, a man of the same house (as Pausanias)' (9.10.3), has created problems, for if Euryanax was really the son of the Dorieus who was Leonidas' elder brother, then one would have thought that he and not Leonidas would have become king of Sparta. It has been suggested (How & Wells, ii, 290) that Dorieus, by going abroad, had forfeited his right to the throne or renounced it, or that Euryanax' father was a different Dorieus (Hignett, 286–7). It is more likely, however, that it is the same Dorieus but that he was considered illegitimate – there were clearly doubts about his birth (cf. Herodotos 5.41) – or that Euryanax himself was illegitimate (cf. M.E. White, *JHS* 84, 1964, 150(e).
32. Cf. Burn, 530–4; Green, 262–5.
33. Cf., e.g.. How & Wells, ii 311; Green, 263. Hignett, 329, who cites the parallel from Thucydides, cautions against dismissing Herodotos' story out of hand.
34. This is the suggestion of Munro, *JHS* 24 (1904), 164, cf. *CAH* iv, 335.
35. Cf. W.J. Woodhouse, *JHS* 18 (1898), 52ff.
36. This is the reading of Herodotos' MSS – cf. Burn, 532 n.56. The distance is the same as that to the 'island' (9.51.1), but the Spartans were now presumably retreating in a different direction, since it was daylight, keeping as far as possible to comparatively high ground 'for fear of the cavalry,' as Herodotos says (9.56.1–2): Pausanias clearly did not reach the 'island' or Herodotos would have said so.
37. For the location of the temple of Eleusinian Demeter see Hignett, 431–4.

38. Herodotos, of course, believed that Pausanias had some 41,500 light troops, including 35,000 helots, but there can surely be no question of this huge number of men taking part in the battle.
39. Grundy, op.cit., 502; Burn, 535; Hignett, 336; Green, 266.
40. Cf. Hignett, 338.
41. Cf. Hignett's admirable discussion, 335–6. Green (297 n.14, cf. 262) accepts as an 'undoubtedly correct crumb of information' Diodoros' assertion (11.31.5–6) that the battle was fought in a limited space, but Diodorus' account of the campaign is hopelessly confused: he telescopes the second and third position of the Greeks, or rather omits the second altogether.
42. Herodotos' claim here is reminiscent of the reason Thucydides' gives for the Spartan appeal to Athens for help against the helots on Mt Ithome in the 460's (1.102.2), and one wonders whether Herodotos has not transferred back to the time of Plataea a reputation for skill in siege-warfare which the Athenians only acquired later through the sieges of places like Sestos, Eion, Byzantion, Naxos and Thasos.
43. On Artabazos see Burn, 536–7, 539–40, though he perhaps goes too far beyond the evidence.

Chapter 6
1. For the time see Comme, *HCT* iii, 478.
2. The Spartan hoplites numbered 420 (Thucydides 4.8.9), the Athenian 800 (Thucydides 4.32.1); for a breakdown of the whole Athenian force see J.B. Wilson, *Pylos 425 BC* (Warminster, 1979), 104–5 – he concludes that 'we cannot put the Athenian numbers much lower than 11,000.'
3. For the topography of Pylos see R.M. Burrows, *JHS* 16 (1896), 55ff., *JHS* 18 (1898), 147ff.; G.B. Grundy, *JHS* 16 (1896), 1ff., *JHS* 18 (1898), 232ff. and *Thucydides and the History of His Age* (Oxford, 1948), ii 122–33; Gomme, *HCT* iii, 482–6, and nn. ad locc; W.K. Pritchett, *Studies in Ancient Greek Topography I* (Berkeley, 1965), 6–29; Wilson, op.cit., 47ff. *passim*.
4. Presumably 'οἱ ἐγγύτατα τῶν περιόικων' means 'the nearest of the *perioikoi*' to Pylos, e.g. from places like Methone, Asine and Aulon: these may well normally have been exempted from serving with Spartan forces because of the necessity for keeping an eye on the Messenian helots, and hence were not among those Lakedaimonians who had 'lately returned from another campaign'.
5. I find Wilson's note here (op.cit. 85–6) somewhat muddled: he seems to miss the clue provided by the reference to 'all the *lochoi*', and tries to estimate the numbers needed for the various requirements the Spartans had. I would argue that Thucydides' use of the word 'Σπαρτιᾶται' in 4.8.1 is another example of the meaning 'Spartans' as opposed to *perioikoi*, not 'Spartiates' in the strict sense see above, pp. 24 & 57.
6. Cf. Toynbee, 376–7.
7. This is Wilson's interpretation of the relevant passage in Thucydides 4.8.8 – op.cit. 78–80.
8. See now Wilson, op.cit., 76–8.
9. Wilson is, surely, right (op.cit., 73–4), as against Gomme, *HCT* iii, 443–4, that Thucydides did not mean that the intention was to *sink* triremes broadside on to the open sea, but he misses the use of 'βύζην' by Appian (*Punika* 123), where it must mean something like 'packed close together.' Wilson is also right to stress that Thucydides does not say the entrances could be *blocked* by two triremes and by eight or nine, respectively: in fact they would have needed more to block them than could have sailed

through under oar – even the northern entrance would have required five or six (Wilson, op.cit., 74 n.5 & 77).

10. See Wilson, op.cit., 73ff.

11. Wilson, op.cit., 50, seems to think that these Messenians were 'semi-free' Messenians from western Messenia itself, but is it not more likely that they were from Naupaktos? (see Gomme, *HCT* iii, 445).

12. Wilson argues (op.cit., 65–6; cf. Gomme, loc.cit.) that when Thucydides says Demosthenes stationed facing the mainland 'τοὺς μὲν οὖν πόλλους τῶν ἀόπλων καί ὡπλισμένων', he implies that the Athenian commander had more than 120 hoplites at least, at his disposal, since he took 60 down to the southwest shore with him. Logically this may be so, but the contrast between the thousand men Demosthenes placed facing the mainland, and the sixty+ he took with him, is so great that I am not sure we should press logic here too far: even if Demosthenes in fact took the majority of the hoplites with him, he left far more men altogether, up on the hill.

13. Wilson, op.cit. 136, says that the 'Osmyn Aga lagoon' was dry land in 425, but see *The Minnesota Messenia Expedition* (Minnespolis, 1972), 44–6. In general, Wilson's account of the topography of Koryphasion is first class (see, esp., 54–61 & 136–7).

14. See T.L. Shear, *Hesperia* 6 (1937), 346–8.

15. I.e., presumably, towers, or something more substantial than just ladders – see Wilson, op.cit., 51.

16. Cf. Wilson, op.cit., 83.

17. Cf. Comme ad loc.

18. Alkman, fr.55D is evidence for the use of poppy and flax-seed as food by the Spartans. Poppy-seeds, in particular, contain a considerable quantity of oil, without any narcotic properties, sometimes used for adulterating olive-oil. Gomme (*HCT* iii, 467), referring to Theophrastos, *History of Plants* 9.12.3–4, says that poppy-seeds would not be a useful food, since they were chiefly used as a purge, but one suspects the Spartans might have needed that too!

19. Cf. G.B. Grundy, *Thucydides and the History of His Age* (Oxford, 1948), ii 130, and for further useful information about other possible sources of water on the island see Gomme, *HCT* iii 730–1, and Pritchett, *Studies in Ancient Greek Topography I* (Berkeley & Los Angeles, 1965), 25–7.

20. See Wilson, op.cit. 106 ff., where the author's personal knowledge of the terrain is put to excellent use.

21. This is Wilson's interpretation of the phrase 'δοράτιά τε ἐναπεκέκλαστο βαλλομένων' in 4.34.3; Gomme, ad loc, seems to accept that the javelins broke off in the cuirasses of the Spartans. I do not know where Gomme gets the notion that the *pilos* was a *steel* cap: surely even if it was not made of felt as the term itself implies, it would have been made of bronze, and in that case I am not so sure that it would have kept out an arrow – see Wilson, op.cit., 114–5.

22. See above, p. 221 n.41.

23. Cf. Cartledge, 311.

Chapter 7

1. Gomme (*HCT* iv 79) thought that the reference to helots in Thucydides 5.57.1 and 5.64.2 must be to 'a larger and, perhaps, a special force,' and not merely to the usual servants of the hoplites; Andrewes, in his additional note (loc.cit.), argues that the Spartan order-of-battle says nothing of any force of helot origin except the *Brasideioi* and *neodamodeis*, and wonders whether Thucydides refers to these, but the difficulty with

this is that they are not referred to in the account of the earlier campaign. K.W. Welwei (*Unfreie in antiken Kriegsdienst*, vol. i, Wiesbaden 1974, 127) suggests that there was a specially large force of helots in charge of the baggage-train. However, Thucydides was, surely, emphasizing the size of the Spartan forces, not that of the body of helots.

2. For the topography see W. Loring, *JHS* 15 (1895), 47ff., and E. Meyer, *RE* 18, 1014–6. Meyer is probably right that Orestheion lay near the site of the future Megalopolis, and that it was the same place as Pausanias' Oresthasion/Oresteion (8.3.1–2).

3. Cf. J. Kromayer, *Antike Schlachtfelder* (Berlin 1903–31), iv 208.

4. Gomme (*HCT* iv 93) suggests that this 'older man' (τῶν πρεσβυτέρων τις) may have been one of the ten Spartiate 'advisers' (ξύμβουλοι) sent to accompany Agis after the Argos debacle (cf. Thucydides 5.63.4), or a senior officer, presumably because Thucydides says 'the older men' in general had been sent home from Orestheion. But it is not necessary to assume that he uses the word 'older' in exactly the same sense in both passages. This man could, surely, have been a member of one of the age-classes 50–54. W.J. Woodhouse, *King Agis of Sparta* (Oxford, 1933), 111–3, thinks that this uphill attack of Agis was a feint.

5. See G. Fougères, *Mantinée et l'Arcadie Orientale* (Paris, 1898), chapter ii, and Gomme's note ad loc. (*HCT* iv 97–8); but cf. also W. K. Pritchett, *Studies in Ancient Greek Topography I* (Berkeley & Los Angeles, 1965), 122–34, and *II* (1969), 42.

6. See W.J. Woodhouse, *BSA* 22 (1916–8), 51–84, and *King Agis of Sparta*, 42–56; Kromayer, op.cit., iv 212–3; A.W. Gomme, *Essays in Greek History* (Oxford, 1937), 140–1, and *HCT* iv 100; Andrewes, *HCT* iv 100–2; D. Kagan, *The Peace of Nicias and the Sicilian Expedition* (Ithaca & London, 1981), 119ff.

7. *Pace* Woodhouse, *King Agis of Sparta*, 80–2. Andrewes (*HCT* iv 100–1) argues that 'Agis could not have failed to keep a watch on his enemies' movements' and that 'Greek military history is full of scouts,' but the Pylos campaign provides two examples of the Spartans' failing in this respect – when the Athenian fleet returned and when the Athenian hoplites surprised the first Spartan guard post on Sphakteria (see Thucydides 4.14.1 & 32.1), and for other examples of Spartan forces' being surprised in various circumstances see XH 6.5.17 and 7.1.16. For some apposite comments on the failure of ancient armies to scout properly see W.K. Pritchett, *Studies in ancient Greek Topography 3* (Berkeley & Los Angeles, 1980), 365ff.

8. See J. Beloch, *Die Bevölkerung der griechisch-römischen Welt* (Leipzig, 1886), 140; Gomme, *HCT* iv 112. Cawkwell (*CQ* – NS – 33, 1983, 386) argues that this view is 'ill-grounded', but it makes more sense than to introduce a seven-*lochoi* Spartan army for the first and only time.

9. Thucydides does not say where these cavalry forces were from: Sparta herself had raised a force of cavalry in 424 (Thucydides 4.55.2).

10. Cf. above, p. 209 n.6.

11. It must be emphasized that this gap is not necessarily what King Agis thought he had to fill, and therefore should not be used to calculate the size of the force he tried to send to plug it, for his left may have shifted further to his left than he had anticipated. Woodhouse, op.cit., 80–2, would have it that Agis deliberately left a gap in his line to entice the enemy to charge into it. For an even more eccentric view see D. Gillis, *Rendiconti dell' Instituto Lombardo, Classe di Lettere, Scienze morali e storiche*, 97 (1963), 199–226.

12. This is better than Gomme's explanation (*HCT* iv 93) that they were 'older men (perhaps *perioikoi* and helots only) already detailed, from the beginning when the march out of Sparta began, to look after the 'train'.'

13. Cf. Gomme, *HCT* iv 125, and for examples of victorious troops being caught when they pursued too far see, e.g., XH 2.4.31–3, 5.3.3–6, 5.4.41–6. Kagan (op.cit., 129–30) accepts Diodoros' story of the intervention of Pharax.
14. Cf. Anderson, 141–2.

Chapter 8

1. The Loeb translator has a note (Xenophon Hellenika I–IV, bottom 286) that when Xenophon says (XH 4.2.13) the Lakedaimonians, having picked up the Tegeates and Mantineians, 'ἐξῆσαν τὴν ἀμφίαλον', he means the shore of the 'Argolic Gulf', but surely the Corinthian Gulf is meant.
2. See W.K. Pritchett, *Studies in Ancient Greek Topography II* (Berkeley and Los Angeles, 1969), 77–83. Anderson, 143, puts the battle in the wrong place.
3. Pritchett, op.cit., 78.
4. The Loeb edition of the *Hellenika* has 'περὶ ἑξακοσίους' for the number of Lakedaimonian cavalry in the text, but translates 'about 700'; Anderson, 143, has '600', Charles D. Hamilton, *Sparta's Bitter Victories* (Ithaca & London, 1979), 221, has '700 horsemen'. The correct reading is 'περὶ ἑξακοσίους' and this means 'about 600'.
5. Cf. Kromayer, *Antike Schlachtfelder* (Berlin, 1931), iv 595–6; Anderson, 143; Pritchett, op.cit., 74; Hamilton, op.cit., 221.
6. Cf. *Revue des études anciennes* 27 (1925), 273–8.
7. As Anderson, e.g., does (143 & 240): Anderson, of course, believes that a *mora* was only c.600 strong.
8. Anderson, 145, argues, possibly correctly, that the orders given on the Spartan side to 'follow the leader' suggest a move to the right in column, but on the previous page says of the Boeotians that they merely 'advanced obliquely to the right'. I think Xenophon's use of the same phrase to describe both manoeuvres, even though he says nothing about 'following the leader' in the case of the Boeotians, must mean that they were thought to have done the same thing.
9. Cf. Anderson, 145–6 and n.9 on 309, which refers to *Cyropaedia* 7.1.5 and 181–4 in his own text.
10. Anderson, 146–7, cites Thucydides 5.65.2 as a parallel and suggests that the man who shouted out at the Nemea wanted to avoid a head-on encounter. This is true, up to a point, but the cases are essentially different: in the Thucydides episode Agis was about to lead his men *uphill* against the enemy, and the man who shouted at him wanted to avoid an encounter altogether in those conditions – at the Nemea the man who shouted did not want to avoid a fight, he simply wanted to take the enemy in flank rather than head-on.
11. E.g. by M. Cary, *Cambridge Ancient History* V (Cambridge, 1927), 47, and by W. Kaupert in Kromayer *Schlachtenatlas zür antiken Kriegesgeschichte* (Leipzig, 1922–9), iv, text to Blatt v, col. 29: cf. Anderson, 141, and n.2 on 308–9; Adcock, 88.
12. Cf. E. Harrison, *CQ* 7 (1913), 132.
13. Cf. the decree for the refortification of the city and the Peiraeus, dating from the last month of the archonship of 395/4, and therefore probably shortly after the Nemea battle (Tod *GHI* ii 107).
14. Cf. W.Kaupert, op.cit., iv col.32.
15. Cf. Pritchett, op.cit., 93–4.
16. See Pritchett, op.cit., 94, and cf. Plutarch *Agesilaos* 18.2.
17. Compare Appian's description of the encounter between two veteran legions in the civil war of H3 (*Civil Wars* 3.68).

18. Anderson, 153, notes the difficulty, but claims that Agesilaos' men did succeed in 'opening their ranks to let the Thebans go by.'
19. Pritchett, op.cit., 85–9.

Chapter 9
1. On this period see now Charles D. Hamilton, *Sparta's Bitter Victories* (Ithaca & London, 1979), though his attempts to discern factions behind every twist and turn of the tangled history of these years perhaps goes too far.
2. On the peace conference see John Buckler, *The Theban Hegemony 371–362 BC* (Cambridge, Mass., & London, 1980), 48–54.
3. On the route followed by Kleombrotos from Ambrossos to Thisbe see Buckler, op.cit., 57–9, and refs, there.
4. Cf. Buckler, op.cit., 59.
5. See especially W.K. Pritchett, *Studies in Ancient Greek Topography I* (Berkeley & Los Angeles, 1965), 56–7, and Buckler, op.cit., 59.
6. Since there were probably five *morai* at the Nemea, and they were accompanied by 600 'Lakedaimonian' cavalry (XH 4.2.16), it is tempting to suggest that the four at Leuktra were accompanied by c.480.
7. Cf. C.L. Cawkwell, *CQ* (NS) 22 (1972), 257 n.5. Cawkwell, of course, in my view, halves the number of troops in the four *morai*.
8. On the army of the renewed Boeotian League see Buckler, op.cit., 23–4. Anderson's discussion of the size of the Boeotian army, among others, is vitiated by his failure to realize that the new League only had seven federal districts, not eleven (197–8).
9. See J. Wolter in *Antike Schlachtfelder in Griechenland*, ed. J. Kromayer & G. Veith (Berlin, 1903–31), iv 309. The suggestion that the Spartan line became crescent-shaped when the Theban attack fell on the centre (W. Judeich, *Rheinisches Museum für Philologie* 76, 1927, 196) is unacceptable because the Theban attack fell not on the Spartan centre, but on their right (cf. XH 6.4.14). Cawkwell's suggestion, op.cit., 262, that 'the Peloponnesian line bent moon-shaped round their struggling cavalry,' seems little better.
10. This is Buckler's suggestion – op.cit., 63-based on LP 13.6 (op.cit., 290 n.26), but it should be noted that that passage appears to refer to the king's position *on the march* – see pp. 38–40. For the emendation 'ἱππεῖς' for 'ἵπποι' in XH 6.4.14 see above, p. 14.
11. Cf. Anderson, 203 & 215. A.M. Devine, *Phoenix* 37 (1983), 201ff., suggests that the 50–deep formation consisted of only a wedge of 1,376 Thebans, with the Sacred Band at its apex, but this is to place too much reliance on the late evidence of Arrian (*Tactica* 11.2) and Aelian (*Taktike Theoria* 47.4).
12. Cf. Cawkwell, op.cit., 261, and *Philip of Macedon* (London, 1978), 154–5.
13. This was suggested by H.A.T. Köchly & W. Rüstow, *Geschichte des griechischen Kriegwesens* (Aarau, 1852), 171ff., and followed by Anderson, 213–6, but see J. Buckler, *Symbolae Osloenses* 55 (1980), 76–9.
14. Cf., e.g., Anderson, 207–9.
15. Cf. Buckler, op.cit., 75–6.
16. The whole passage means: 'In the battle, while Epameinondas was drawing his phalanx aslant to the left, in order that the right of the Spartiates might be as far as possible from the other Greeks, and that he might push Kleombrotos back by falling in close order on his flank …' (the Loeb translation has 'in column' for 'κατὰ ικέραϲι' here, but it surely means 'on the flank').
17. This seems to be the point of Cawkwell's remarks in *CQ* (NS) 22 (1972), 262 and n.3.
18. Cf. Anderson, 211–12.

19. Cf. Buckler, *Symbolae Osloenses* 55 (1980), 79–86.
20. On the Thespiaians at Leuktra see Buckler, *Wiener Studien* 90 (1977), 76–9.
21. Cf. Köchly & Rüstow, op.cit., 171ff.; Judeich, op.cit., 194–5; followed by Anderson, 213–6, etc. Delbrück (*History of the Art of War*, trans. Renfroe, Westport, Connecticut, 1975, 168–9) managed to manufacture out of Xenophon's statement that the ground between the two armies was flat, a natural obstacle on the Theban left and Spartan right, to explain the position of their cavalry.
22. Buckler, *Symbolae Osloenses*, loc.cit., 89, and *Theban Hegemony* 64 and 291 n.29, makes much of this gap, but it was clearly of little significance in the event: the important thing was the collision of the Spartan cavalry with their own hoplites. *Pace* Cawkwell, *CQ* (NS) 22 (1972), 262, and Buckler, *Symbolae Osloenses*, loc.cit., 89, I cannot see how we can be certain that this was the result of deliberate planning by Epameinondas.
23. Cawkwell, op.cit., 262 and n.4, emphasises the high state of training in the Theban army, but the evidence he cites from the *Hellenika* (6.5.23 & 7.5.19) refers to a time *after* Leuktra. Cawkwell also – 265 – criticizes what he calls 'conventional, conservative Spartan warfare.'

Chapter 10

1. See now John Buckler, *The Theban Hegemony 371–362 BC* (Cambridge, Mass., & London, 1980), 74ff.
2. Reasonable totals might be c.6,000 Boeotians, 5,000 Arcadians, 5,000 Argives, 3,000 Eleians, 3,000 Euboeans, 1,000 Phokians, 2,000 Lokrians, 1,000 Acarnanians, 1,000 Herakleians and Malians, and 1,000 Thessalians (cf. XH 6.5.23).
3. Cf. Cartledge, 298.
4. It is usually thought that the loss of Messenia was a crippling blow to Sparta – cf., e.g., Ste. Croix, 93 and n.11; Cartledge, 299 – but Jones, 134 & 137, takes a different view, and if when Aristotle says (*Politics* 1270a30–1) that there were 'not even 1000' Spartans (i.e. Spartiates), he was speaking of his own time, as, e.g., Ste.Croix thinks (332), there had not been much of a decline in numbers since Leuktra, and it is possible that by 369 there were not many Spartiates left who depended solely upon *klaroi* in Messenia. Cartledge, however, thinks that Aristotle's figure was simply based on what Xenophon says about the number of Spartiates at Leuktra (308). By c.244, Plutarch says (*Agis* 5.4), there were not more than 700 Spartiates left, of whom perhaps 100 possessed 'land and *kleros*', where he perhaps meant 'land *in addition to* kleros'.
5. For the date see Buckler, op.cit., 233–42.
6. Op.cit., 90ff.
7. Cartledge, 300, evidently accepts the MSS reading 'πολέμαρχον Σπαρτιάτην γεγενημένον' here, which means '... the polemarch who had become a Spartiate,' and suggests that the man in question, Geranor, may originally have been a '*nothos*' or '*trophimos*'. However Dindorf's emendation 'Σπαρτιάτην πολέμαρχον' is often accepted, which means that Geranor was a Spartiate, and had *become* polemarch, perhaps suggesting that there was something unusual about his appointment, or, simply, that he had recently been chosen for the office, perhaps, e.g., to replace Deinon, the polemarch killed at Leuktra (XH 6.4.14).
8. Cf. W. Loring, *JHS* 15 (1895), 54–8.
9. The exact location of Kromnos is uncertain: see M. Jost, *Revue des Études Anciennes* 75 (1973), 252.
10. E.g. by Buckler, op.cit., 213–6; *contra*: Anderson, 222. For the whole campaign see Buckler, op.cit., 208–19.

11. Plutarch (*Agesilaos* 35.1) argues that Antikrates must have used a sword because the Spartans called his descendants 'Machairiones' (i.e. 'Swordsmen'); Diodoros, oddly enough, does say that most of the spears were broken at the first onset between Spartans and Thebans, and that they then used swords (15.86.2), but says clearly that Epameinondas was wounded by a spear (15.87.1). Pausanias (8.11.5) says that the Mantineians claimed that Epameinondas was killed by one of them, called Machairion (Swordsman), whereas the Spartans said he was a Spartan. However, he goes on to state (8.11.6) that the Athenians claimed, and the Thebans confirmed, that it was the Athenian, Grylos, Xenophon's son, who killed the Theban general, and cites as his evidence the 'painting of the battle' at Mantineia, and the fact that the Mantineians honoured Grylos with a public funeral and a monument on the spot, whereas, despite the talk about Mac hairion, they showed no such honour to a man of that name.
12. On all this see M. Launey, *Recherches sur les armées hellènistiques* (Paris, 1949–50), i 113ff.
13. Pausanias confuses this Akrotatos with his grandfather of the same name, the elder son of Kleomenes II: it was the latter who never inherited the crown – the grandson succeeded Areus after his death in 264.
14. Cf., e.g., Cartledge, 319–20.
15. Cf. Chrimes, 5ff.
16. Pausanias (8.10.5–8) tells a circumstantial story of the defeat and death of Agis IV in battle near Mantineia, against the combined armies of Mantineia, Megalopolis and Sikyon, in which Aratos and the Achaeans deliberately fell back in the centre, and when the Spartans followed, they were taken in flank and rear by Aratos' allies. This battle is not mentioned in any other source, and can hardly stand against Plutarch's account of Agis' death at Sparta, but it is just possible that there was such a battle before Agis' death.
17. This word is usually spelt 'sarissa' with a double 's', but 'sarisa' with a single 's' seems to be the correct form – see Liddell Scott s.v.
18. Busolt, *Hermes 40* (1905), 420, suggested the reference was to the army of Kleomenes III; another possibility is Nabis' army.
19. For the date of Sellasia see Walbank, *A Historical Commentary on Polybius I* (Oxford, 1957), 272. For a different view of the chronology see Chrimes, Appendix II, 431–4.
20. Nevertheless, as late as the third century AD, we hear of Spartan troops in Caracalla's army (cf. Herodian 4.8.2–3 & 9.4), and it is possible that the Romans deliberately refurbished the legend of Spartan military prowess in order to rally the Greeks, as Dr. A.J.S. Spawforth suggests in his doctoral thesis. *Studies in the History of Roman Sparta* (Birmingham, 1982). One of the units in Caracalla's army was even called the 'Pitanate lochos' (Herodian 4.8.3)!

Glossary of Greek Terms

agoge – 'training system', particularly the system to which the youth of Sparta was subjected – though the first extant use of the word as applied to Sparta seems to be Polybios 1.32.1

agora – market-place or civic centre of a Greek community.

choinix – a measure, especially of corn (= c. 2 pints).

damos – Doric dialect form of *demos* = 'people').

deme(s) – the 'villages' or 'parishes' into which some Greek states were divided, especially Attica.

drachme (-ai) – a silver coin.

ekklesia – the assembly of adult male citizens at Athens, Sparta and elsewhere.

enomotarch – commander of an enomotia.

enomotia – at full strength, a unit of forty men in the Spartan army.

ephor(s) – the highest civilian officals in the Spartan state.

gerontes – 'elders', members of chief deliberative and judicial council at Sparta, the *gerousia*.

gerousia – the chief deliberative and judicial council of Sparta.

gymnetes – lightly armed skirmishers.

helot(s) – serfs who farmed the estates of Spartans.

Hippeis – 'horsemen' – a term used of aristocratic groups in various Greek states: at Sparta the Royal Guard.

homoios (-oi) – 'equals' or 'peers' – term used of full Spartan citizens.

hoplite(s) – heavy-armed infantry soldiers of the line.

hypaspistai – 'shield-bearers', probably = helot batmen in the Spartan army.

hypomeion, (-eiones) – 'inferiors', second-class Spartan citizens.

klaros (-oi) – Doric dialect form of '*kleros*' = 'land-lot' i.e. the estates assigned to Spartan citizens by the state.

kome (-ai) – 'villages', a term often applied to the constituent parts of a Greek state.

kotyle (-ai) – dry or wet measure (= c.½ pint).

lambda – the Greek letter 'L' (Λ or λ).

lochagos – commander of a lochos.

lochos (-oi) – in the Spartan army a unit of 640 men, when at full strength; also used as a unit of various sizes in other armies.

mora (-ai) – the largest units in the Spartan army, containing 1,280 men when at full strength.

mothax (-akes) – 'warriors' (?), a term used of inferior Spartans brought up with the sons of wealthier patrons.

neodamodeis – 'new citizens', helots freed for service in the army.

oba(-ai), obe(s) – the wards or villages of Sparta.

phalanx – a line of battle.

pentekonter – commander of a *pentekostys*.

pentekoster – alternative spelling of the above.

pentekostys – in the Spartan army a unit of 160 men, when at full strength.

perioikos(-oi) – 'dwellers round', members of the semi-independent communities on the fringe of Spartan territory in Lakonia and Messenia.

phyle(-ai) – a group of clans or families in many Greek states (often translated 'tribe(s)').

polemarch – 'war leader', at Sparta commander of a mora.

polis – a city or state.

rhetra – a 'saying', term used of an enactment of the Spartan ekklesia.

sigma – the Greek letter 'S' (Σ, σ or ς).

stasis – civil discord or disturbance.

strategos(-oi) – 'general(s)'.

syssition(-ia) – the military messes at Sparta.

taxis – a unit in the Athenian and other Greek armies.

taxiarchos – commander of a *taxis*.

temenos – shrine, precinct or sanctuary dedicated to a deity or hero.

tresantes – 'tremblers', term used of cowards in Sparta.

Index

Abronichos, 116

Abydos, 32

Achaea, Achaeans, 10–11, 101, 163–6, 192, 200–204

Achilles, 98

Acrocorinth, xiv

Aelian, 26

Aeolis, Aeolians, 170

Aeschylos, 68

Aetolia, Aetolians, 50, 201, 203–204

agathoergoi, 68, 211 n.24

Agathokles, 198

age-classes (at Sparta), 9–10, 12, 15–17, 18, 22, 51, 59, 68–9, 71, 73–4, 82, 99, 142, 152, 155, 164, 178

Agesikles, 85, 100

Agesilaos I, 85

Agesilaos II, 3–5, 7, 10–16, 19, 21–2, 24, 27–8, 31–4, 36–7, 41–3, 46, 48–9, 73, 78, 85, 89, 161, 163, 168–73, 176, 177, 191–7, 199

Agesilaos (grandfather of Leotychidas II), 85

Agesilaos (brother of Agis III), 199

Agesipolis I, 13, 19–21, 27, 31, 45, 161,

Agesipolis II, 85, 196

Agesipolis III, 85, 202

Agi(a)dai, genealogy of, 85; *see also* 84, 86–7, 161, 200

Agis I, 85, 93

Agis II, 5, 20, 30–4, 52, 54, 56–7, 84–5, 93, 133, 153–4, 156–60, 184, 206 n.28, 214 n.29

Agis III, 85, 197–9

Agis IV, 17, 69, 75–6, 85, 95, 200–201, 211 n.30, 227 n.16

agoge, 23, 25, 27, 34, 82, 86–7, 92, 198, 208 n.40, 214 n.30

Aidolios (lochos), 65

Ainos, 145

Aischines, 101

Akarnania (Akarnanians), 49–50, 175, 226 n.2

Akragas, 198

Akrotatos (King), 85, 198, 227 n.13

Akrotatos (Prince), 85, 197, 200, 227 n.13

Alepotrypi spring, ix, 124

Alesion, Mt, xii, 152

Alexander I (of Macedonia), 106, 109, 120, 127, 129–30

Alexander III (the Great), 197, 199

Alexandria, 202

Alkamenes (King), 83, 85

Alkamenes (Spartan officer), 29

Alkibiades, 78, 151

Alkman, 222 n.18

Alpenoi, 72

Ambrossos, xviii, 177, 225 n.3

Amompharetos (Spartan officer), 29, 31, 61–4, 67, 72, 89, 131–5

Amompharetos (arbitrator), 211 n.24

Amphipolis, 48, 151, 168

Amphissa, 169

Amvlema pass, 169

Amyklai, Amyklaians, 12, 18, 64–6, 83, 88–90, 92–3, 173

anastrophe, 36, 42, 192

Anaxander, 85

Anaxandridas (Agiad king), 74, 85, 100–101

Anaxandridas (son of Theopompos), 85, 213 n.10

Anaxibios, 31

Anaxilaos, 85
Anchimolios, 73–4, 122, 211 n.34
Androkrates, *temenos* of, ix, 124–5,
Anopaia path, 109, 112–13, 117, 216 n.3
Antalkidas, 32, 176
Antalkidas, Peace of, 48
Antigonos Doson, 202
Antigonos Gonatas, 200
Antigonos Monophthalmos, 199
Antikrates, 196, 227 n.11
Antiochos III of Syria, 90
Antipater, 197–8
Antisthenes, 4
Aphetai, 217 n.13
Aphetais street, 86
Arachova (Karyai), 194
Arakos, 27
Arcadia, Arcadians, 5, 21, 42, 48, 50, 54, 59,
    61, 86, 96, 100, 151–2, 156–8, 173, 179,
    188, 192, 194–6, 200, 205 n.3, 226 n.2
Archelaos, 83, 85–6, 93
archers, 5, 44, 72, 111, 117, 123–4, 129,
    136, 143, 145–6, 148–9, 219 n.12
Archias of Pitana, 64, 66, 101
Archidamos I, 85
Archidamos II, 85
Archidamos III, 20, 28–9, 49, 61, 85,
    179–80, 187, 194–5, 205 n.8
Archidamos IV, 85, 196–9
Archidamos V, 85
archons (Athenian), 66
Areus I, 85, 198, 200
Areus II, 85
Arginusae, 78
Argiopian land, the, 134
Argive Heraion, 73
Argos, Argives, xi, 3, 9, 21, 31, 45–6, 52, 56,
    61, 73, 80, 83, 86, 90–1, 94, 96, 101, 117,
    121, 140, 151, 153, 156–9, 161, 163–4,
    165, 167–70, 194, 200–202, 205 n.3, 226
    n.2
Arimas (lochos), 65
Arimnestos (Plataean), 63,
Arimnestos (Spartan), 62, 71
Ariobarzanes, 197
Aristeides, 129
Aristodemos (hero), 84–5, 205 n.1
Aristodemos (survivor of Thermopylai),
    72–3, 149,

Aristodemos (Regent), 27, 34, 161
Aristodemos (General of Antigonos
    Monophthalmos), 199
Aristokles, 31, 53–4, 56, 133, 156–7
Ariston, 85, 100
Aristophanes, 64–5
Aristotle, 4, 17, 22–3, 31, 65, 67, 74–6, 83,
    86–7, 90, 92–6, 100, 193, 201
Arkaloi, alleged *oba* of, 210 n.23
Arrian, 64, 183, 196–7, 199
Artabazos, 127, 129–30, 139, 221 n.43
Artemis Agrotera (the Huntress), 45, 167
Artemis Orthia, vii, 34, 66, 86–7, 213 n. 13
    & 21
Artemision, battle of, 107, 119–20, 216 n.7
Asia Minor, 6–7, 19, 27, 31, 48–9, 60, 78,
    106, 120, 128, 161, 164, 168–9, 176, 197,
    199
Asine (Messenian), 194, 221 n.4
Asklepiodotos, 36, 171
Asopos ridge, ix, 124–5, 131, 134–5
Asopos river (Boeotia), 121–4, 126–7, 130,
    134, 136, 138, 178, 218 n.3
Asopos river (nr. Thermopylai), viii
Assos, xiv, 162
Athenaios, 26, 34, 43, 45, 83, 92, 99,
Athene, 45
Athene (Itonian), 172
Athene Poliachos, vii, 86, 213 n.21
Athens, Athenians, 5–6, 28–30, 46, 48–50,
    52, 56–62, 66–7, 73, 75–80, 97, 106–109,
    116, 120–9, 131–8, 140–9, 151, 156,
    158–61, 163–7, 169–70, 173–4, 176,
    199–200, 205 n.3
Attica, 66, 73–4, 77, 101, 120–2, 141, 176
Ayios Ioannis (St John), chapel of, ix, 124–5

Bakchylidas, 177–80
blazons, 3, 40, 112, 205 n.4
Boeotia, Boeotians, 10–11, 13, 21, 41, 43–4,
    47–8, 61, 108–10, 116, 119, 121–2,
    128–9, 138, 140, 161–6, 168–9, 171–2,
    176–82, 185–6, 191–2, 194–5, 202, 205
    n.3, 226 n.2
Brachylles, 202
Brasidas, 29–30, 32, 48, 53, 58–60, 77, 143,
    151, 154
Brasideioi, 53–4, 154–8, 209 n.3, 222 n.1
Brutus, C. Iunius Bubulcus (dict. 302), 198

Caesar, 12
Carthage, Carthaginians, 198
Cassius Dio, 22
Castor, 45
cavalry (Spartan), 3, 13–16, 42, 44, 50, 60,
    73, 81, 173–4, 177, 179, 185, 187, 206
    n.16 & 18, 225 n.6, 226 n.22
Chabrias, 48
Chaireas, 177–8
Chaironeia, 196, 198
Chalkidike, 28, 30, 48, 59, 176
Champions, Battle of the, 69, 71, 80, 101,
    206 n.17
Charillos (Charilaos), 86–7, 93, 100, 212
    n.7, 213 n.11, 214 n.29
Chilon (ephor), 87, 101
Chilon (4th century), 29
Chorsiai, xviii
Chremonidean War, 200
Coldstream Guards, 102
Corfu *see* Kerkyra
Corinth, Corinthians, 42, 49, 59, 91, 94–5,
    106–107, 121, 131, 161–5, 168–70, 172–3,
    175–6, 178, 191–2, 194, 196, 200–201,
    218 n.29
Corinth, Gulf of, xiv, xviii, 161, 163, 169,
    173, 178
Corinth, league of, 196
Corinthian war, 161, 172
Cornelius Nepos, 198
corslet, 41, 90, 100, 124
Crete, Cretans, 83, 163, 197, 199–200
Cromwell, 102
Curtius, 197
Cyprus, 199
Cyrenaica, 199
Cyrus, 167, 169

Darius, 106
Deinon, 186, 226 n.7
Dekeleia, 78, 121
Delion, battle of, 47, 165, 181, 209 n.59
Delphi, 45, 172, 177
Demaratos, 4, 69, 71, 95–6, 111, 203
Demeter (Eleusinian), temple of, 134, 137,
    220 n.37
Demetrios, Ayios (St.), chapel of, 135
Demetrios of Skepsis, 83, 199, 210 n.23,
    213 n.19, 214 n.30

Demosthenes, 50, 58, 138, 141, 143, 145–6,
    148–9, 174, 222 n.12
Derkylidas, 7, 48
Dhamasta, viii
Dhrakospilia, viii, 112
Dhrimaia, 169
Dienekes, 5, 72
Diodoros, 10–13, 30, 35, 40, 50, 52, 61, 72,
    75, 110–11, 113, 123, 142, 156, 159,
    163–4, 168–9, 172, 177–80, 182–3, 186,
    192–4, 196–9, 203
Diogenes Laertius, 87
Dioskorides, 196
Dipaia, 61
Distomon, 177
Dorian invasion, 82, 212 n.2
Doris, 59
Doryssos, 85
Dryoskephalai ('Oak Heads') pass, ix, 126–7
Dunkirk, 119
Dymanes, 66, 83, 88–9, 93, 99

earthquake (at Sparta), 23, 75, 209 n.1
Echestratos, 83, 85
Edolos (lochos), 64
Egypt, 106, 197, 200, 202,
eirenes, 62–3
Eleusis, 121
Eleutherai, ix, 48
Eleven, the (at Athens), 66
Elis, Eleians, 60, 100, 126, 151–2, 163–4,
    200, 216 n.4, 226 n.2
enomotarch(s), *enomotarches (-ai),*
    enomotarchos (-oi), 6–7, 9, 11, 13, 29–30,
    33, 38, 51–2, 154
enomotia (-iai) composition of, 6–7, 9–13,
    15–18, 30, 35, 38, 51–2, 55, 57, 63,
    67–71, 89–90, 101, 132, 142, 146, 156–7,
    164, 178, 181, 184, 186–7, 193, 201, 206
    n.21, 207 n.29
Epameinondas, 3, 42, 47, 50, 96, 130,
    160–1, 176, 180, 182–7, 192, 194–6, 208
    n.41, 227 n.11
Ephialtes (of Trachis), 112, 117
ephor(s), 14, 19, 24–5, 29–32, 41, 66, 87,
    101, 195, 198, 202
Ephoros, 11, 90, 93, 113
Epidauros, 83, 163–4
Epieikeia, 12, 162

epistoleus, 27–8
Epitadas, 30, 149
Epitadeus, 30, 75
Erasinos river, 73
Eretria, Eretrians, 106
Eros, 45
Erythrai (in Boeotia), ix, 121, 135, 219 n.4
Etna, 66
Euainetos, 67, 106
Eualkes, 20, 53, 159
Euboea, Euboeans, 9, 29, 32, 60, 119, 161, 164–5, 167, 169, 226 n2
Eudamidas (Spartan general), 32
Eudamidas I, 85
Eudamidas II, 85
eunomia, 84, 92, 94, 214 n.33
Eunomos, 84–5
Eupolis, 205 n.4
Euripides, 183
Euripos, the, 115
Eurotas, vii, 3, 43, 76
Euryanax, 131, 220 n.31
Eurybiades, 116, 216 n.7
Eurykrates, 85
Eurykratides, 85
Euryleon, 88, 90
Euryphon, 84–5
Eurypontidai, genealogy of, 85
  see also, 84, 86–8, 200, 212 n.5
Eurysthenes, 84–5
Eurytos, 72
Eustathius, 205 n.4

'Fetters', battle of, 105
'first' polemarch, 33, 44, 167
Flamininus, T. Quinctius (cos. 198), 203
Fourka pass, 169
Frontinus, 10, 36, 172, 179–80, 185

Gargaphia spring, ix, 124–5, 130–1, 219 n.16
Geranor, 29, 226 n.7
Geronthrai, 20, 83, 93, 159
gerontes, 19, 95
gerousia, 202, 206 n.17, 215 nn.37 & 43, 216 n.5 & 6
Gorgopas, 24
'Grundy's Well', 146
Grylos, 227 n.11

Gylippos, 26–7
Gylis, 19, 24, 49, 172
gymnetes, 98–100, 215 n.46
Gyphtokastro pass (Dryoskephalai pass), 122
Gytheion, 78, 203–204

Hades, 72
Haliartos, xvii, xviii, 161
Halieis, 163
Hamilcar Barca, 198
Hannibal, 198
harmost(s), 28, 32, 78, 207 n.35
Harpokration, 206 n.27
Hegesistratos, 125
Hektor, 97, 99
Helikon, Mount, xviii, 170–1, 177
Hellanikos, 93
Hellespont, Hellespontines, 106, 170
Helos (Lakonian), 84, 93, 212 n.8
helots, 18, 22–6, 28, 40, 43, 53, 59–60, 62, 73, 76–8, 80, 86, 93, 100, 116, 125, 136, 145–7, 149, 151–2, 194, 215 n.46, 216 n.4 & 7, 221 n.38 & 41 & 4, 222 n.1
Hera, temple of (at Plataea), 131, 134, 137
Heraia, 52, 155, 192,
Herakleia (Trachis), 28, 169, 179, 185, 226 n.2
Herakles, xi, 88, 114, 202
Herakles, shrine of (near Mantineia), 152
Herippidas, 169–70
Hermione, 163
Herodotos *passim;* Spartan army in, 60–74
Hesychios, 26, 65–7
Hiero of Syracuse, 66
Hieron (Spartan mercenary commander), 185
hippagretai, 13–14, 70, 206 n.17, 211 n.28
Hippagretas, 30, 149
hipparmostes, 16
Hippeis (at Sparta), 9–11, 13–15, 18, 21, 30, 34, 51–4, 58, 65, 68–71, 73, 75, 83, 96, 99, 101, 155, 158, 164, 178, 180–1, 186, 191, 193, 201, 206 nn.16 & 17, 207 n.31, 209 n.7, 211 n.28
Hippias (tyrant of Athens), 74, 129
Hippokratides, 85
Hipponoïdas, 31, 53–4, 56, 133, 156–7
Hollows of Euboea, 217 n.13

Homer, 91, 97, 99–101
homoioi ('peers'), 22, 24, 29, 95–7, 99, 206 n.21
hoplites;
    battle tactics of, 45–50, 52, 55, 57–62, 72–3, 75–80, 88, 94, 97–100, 102, 106–11, 115, 117, 122, 125–6, 129, 132, 136–44, 146–9, 151, 155–6, 159–61, 163–5, 169–70, 172–4, 177–9, 181, 185, 187–8, 191, 193, 196–7, 201
    origins of, 91–3
    in Tyraios, 98–100
    and *passim* elsewhere
Hyakinthia, Hyakinthos, 12, 66, 90, 173, 213 nn.20, 21 & 22
Hydarnes, 112–14, 117–18
Hylleis, 66, 83, 88–9, 93, 99
Hyllos, 88
hypaspistai, 40, 44, 174
hypomeion (-es), 22–6, 32–5, 50, 60, 77, 79–81, 102, 191, 193, 207 n.32, 208 n.41, 212 n.40
Hysiai, battle of, 91, 96, 101, 214 n.27, 215 n.41
Hysiai (Boeotian), 121, 135

Imbros, Imbrians, 145
Immortals, the, 112, 114
Ionia, Ionians, 129
Iphikrates, 5, 11, 18, 49, 138, 172–5
Isidas, 41, 195
'Island', the, ix, 130–1, 133, 220 nn.29 & 36
Isokrates, 19, 61
Issus, battle of, 197, 199
'Isthmos' (Ithome?), 61
Isthmus (of Corinth), 77, 106–108, 116, 121, 201–202
Italy, 90, 93, 197–8
Itea, 169
Ithome, Mount, 76, 84, 221 n.42

Jason of Pherai, 179, 187
Juno, 198
Justin, 196, 199–200

Kadmeia, the, 176, 217 n.8
Kallias, 173–4
Kallikrates, 63, 136,
Kallikratidas, 26–7

Kallisthenes, 11, 182
Kapareli, xix
Karneia, the, 70, 83, 92, 107–108, 210 n.23, 214 n.30, 216 n.6
Karpathos, 217 n.16
Karyai, 192, 194, 203,
Kassander, 199
Kephisos, river, xvii, 170, 177,
Kerkyra (Corfu), 7, 141, 198
Kinadon, 13, 19, 24–6, 33, 50, 79, 206 nn.17 & 19, 207 n. 32
King's Peace, 176
Kithairon, xviii, xix, 48, 122, 125–7, 130–1, 136, 177–8, 219 n.15
klaros (-oi), 74, 76–8, 93–6, 191, 211 n.30, 215 nn.39 & 40, 226 n.4
Kleandridas, 26,
Klearchos, 28
Klearidas, 48
Kleisthenes (tyrant of Sikyon), 66
Kleombrotos (King), 28, 44, 48, 85, 160, 177–80, 182, 184–5, 196,
Kleombrotos (Prince), 85
Kleomenes I, 73–4, 85, 129, 211 n.33, 218 n.29
Kleomenes II, 85, 196, 198–9, 227 n.13
Kleomenes III, 76, 85, 200–202
Kleon, 48, 145–6, 149, 205 n.4
Kleonai, 52, 156, 158–9
Kleonymos (son of Sphodrias), 28, 34
Kleonymos (Prince), 85, 198–200
Klisoura pass, 169
Knemos, 59
Komon, 149
Konooura (obe), Konooureis, vii, 64–6, 85–6, 88–9, 92–3, 210 n.21
Kopais, Lake, xvii, xviii, 122, 177,
Korombili, Mount, xix, 178
Koroneia, battle of, 5, 27, 36–7, 41, 47–9, 163, 169–70, 172, 179, 181
Koroneia (town), xvii, xviii, 177–8
Koryphasion (Pylos), 141, 143–4, 146,
Koukoura, xviii, 177
Kounaxa, 7, 36, 167, 169
Kreusis (Livadhostro), xix, 41, 178, 187
Kriekouki, ix, 121–2, 135
Krommyon, 12
Kromnos, 19–20, 29, 49, 105, 195, 226 n.9
krypteia, the, 202, 207 n.17

Kynosoura (obe) *see* Konooura
Kynourian land, the, 80
Kypselos, 214 n.28
Kyriaki, xviii, 177
Kythera, 60, 79

Labotas (harmost), 28
Labotas (King), 83, 85, 87
Lade, battle of, 216 n.5
Lakedaimon, 3, 24
Lakedaimonians defined, 18
    elsewhere *passim*
Lakonia, Lakonians, 28, 36, 64, 76–8, 80,
    82–4, 90–1, 93, 95, 144, 170, 192, 194,
    197–9, 202–203
Lakonikos, 204
Lakrates, 34
Lamia, 168, 217 n.10
Lamian War, 199
Lampon, 123
Lebadeia, xviii, 177
Lechaion, xiv, 5–6, 9, 11–12, 27, 34, 40,
    49–50, 63, 81, 138, 147, 172–6
Leipsydrion drinking song, 97
Lemnos, Lemnians, 145
Leon, 85, 100
Leondari, 83
Leonidas I, 27, 45, 68, 70–2, 74, 85, 105,
    107–10, 112–19, 132, 186, 211 n.33
Leonidas II, 85, 198
Leontiades (5th century), 109
Leontiades (4th century), 176, 217 n.8
Leotychidas I, 85
Leotychidas II, 27, 71, 84–5
Lepreon, 53, 60, 152, 192
Leuktra (Arcadian), 201
Leuktra (Boeotian), battle of, 4, 6–12,
    14–19, 23–4, 27, 30, 33–4, 37–8, 44,
    47–8, 50, 55, 58, 75, 96, 118, 152, 160,
    164–5, 178–9, 181, 185, 187–8, 191, 194,
    201, 207 n.29 & 31
Leuktra (the place), xviii, xix, 177–8
Limnai (obe), Limnaeis, vii, 64–6, 83, 86,
    88–9, 92–3, 210 n.21
Livy, 162, 198, 202–204
lochagos (-oi), 29, 61, 64, 89
lochos (-oi);
    number of in morai, 6–8
    first mentioned in *Hellenika*, 194

in Thucydides, 51–3, 55
in Herodotos, 60–5, 91–2
alleged five-lochoi army, 61, 64–6
see also, 9, 11, 13, 20, 38, 54, 57, 67,
    69–71, 75, 89, 96, 99, 101, 131, 141–2,
    155–7, 185, 193, 195, 205 n.8. 209 n.9
Lokris, Lokrians (Opountian), 19, 24, 49,
    107, 109–10, 169–70, 172, 218 n.30, 226
    n.2
Loutraki, 43
Lucania, Lucanians, 197
Lycurgus (Athenian orator), 99
Lygdamis, 101
Lykaion, Mount, 201
Lykomedes, 194
Lykourgos (lawgiver), 14, 17, 31, 34, 38, 40,
    43, 45, 55, 62, 67, 69–70, 74–5, 84–7,
    92–5, 159, 184, 213 n.14
Lykourgos (King), 202–203
Lyktos, 197
Lynkos, 59
Lysander, 26–7, 29, 32, 60, 161
Lysimachos, 199
Lysias, 156, 205 n.3

Macedonia, Macedonians, 15, 36, 106, 109,
    120, 127, 129, 197, 200, 202–203
Macedonian War, the first, 203
Machairiones, 227 n.11
Machanidas, 85, 203
Magnesia, 111
Mainalia, 52, 155
Malea, Cape, 78
Malis, Malians, 110, 226 n.2
Malis, Gulf of, viii
Mamas, Ayios (Chapel of), xix, 178
Mamoura, xvii, 170, 172
Mantineia, Mantineians, 52, 61, 126,
    151–61, 163–5, 175, 192, 195–6
Mantineia, First battle of, 5–6, 8–10,
    13–14, 20, 27, 30–1, 33–4, 37, 45, 47,
    51–5, 57, 60, 80, 133, 151–61, 165–6,
    168, 183–4, 188, 191, 196, 205 n.3, 206
    n.16, 218 n.1
Mantineia, Second battle of, 46, 185, 195
Mantineia, Third battle of, 203
Mantitheus, 205 n.3
Marathon, battle of, 44, 47, 56, 69, 73, 106,
    108, 129, 138–9

Mardonios, 62–3, 120–4, 126–30, 132, 135, 138–9

Masistios, 123, 127, 134, 138

Megalopolis, 194, 197, 200–201, 223 n.2

Megara, Megarians, 49, 109, 121, 123, 131, 138, 141, 173

Megistias, 45, 113–14, 116

Menares, 85

Mendhenitsa, 169

Mesoa (obe), Mesoatai, vii, 64, 66, 86–9, 92–3, 210 n.20 & 21

Mesoates (lochos), 65, 87

Messenia, Messenians, 29–30, 61, 69, 71, 76–7, 83–4, 88, 90, 93–4, 95–7, 100, 141, 143, 146–7, 149, 188, 194–6, 223 n.11, 226 n.4

Messenian War, the first, 86, 88, 90, 94, 212 n.10, 213 n.17

Messenian War, the second, 96, 99–100

Messoages (lochos), 64–5, 67

Metamorphosis, chapel of the, xvii, 172

Methone (Messenian), 30, 221 n.4

Minoa, 141

Mnasippos, 7

Molobros, 30

Moleis, river, xiii

Molos, 169

Moni Panayias, viii

mora, morai;
   composition of, 6–8
   numbers in, 8–11
   origins of, 53–4
   see also, 12–16, 18–20, 25, 30, 39–40, 43–4, 49–51, 53–5, 61, 63, 67–9, 71, 73–5, 81, 83, 88–90, 96, 99, 132, 142, 147, 155, 157, 163–4, 168–9, 172–5, 177–81, 184, 187, 191, 194, 201, 205 n.8, 206 n.27, 207 n.29 & 31, 209 n.3, 218 n.1

mothax (-akes), 26–9, 34, 198, 207 n.35

Muses, the, 45

Mycenae, 90, 117, 218 n.32

Mykale, 129

Mytikas, xi, 152–3

Nabis, 85, 203–204

Narthakion, Mount, 168,

Nauplion, 73

navarch(s), 27–8, 30–2, 59, 207 n.34, 211 n.34

Navarino, bay of, x, 141–4

Naxos, 101

Nemea, battle of the, xv, xvi, 5, 10, 16, 27, 33, 35, 37, 46, 56–7, 137, 155, 160, 162–4, 167–71, 181, 183, 205 n.3, 218 n.1

Nemea river, xiv, 161–2

neodamodeis, 9, 13, 18–19, 22, 24, 29, 53–4, 60, 77–8, 154–8, 164, 169, 193, 197, 207 n.32, 209 n.3, 222 n.1

Neopolitoi (phyle), 65

Nestor, 97

Nikander, 85

Nikias, 35

Nikias, peace of, 29, 77, 149

'Oak Heads' pass *see* Dryoskephalai oba, obai, 64–6, 86–9, 92–3, 127, 210 nn. 21 & 23, 214 n.31

Oeroe, river, ix, xix, 130

Oinoe, 12

Olpai, 58–9

Olympia, 34, 45

Olympiodoros, 123–4, 129 n.14

Olympos, Mount, 106

Olynthos, 13, 19–21, 31–2, 48, 53, 176, 207 n.29

Onchestos, xvii

Oneion, Mount, 42

Orchomenos (Arcadian), 42, 48, 151, 192

Orchomenos (Boeotian), xvii, 36, 119, 163, 169–70, 177

Orestes, bones of, 101

Orestheion, 55, 120, 152, 155, 223 n.2

Orneai, 52, 156

Orthagoras, 214 n.28

Osmanaga (Osmyn Aga) lagoon, x, 143, 196 n.13

Ossa, Mount, 106

Palaiodhrakospilia, viii, 112

Pallantion, xi, 153

Pamisos, river, 84

Pamphyloi, 66, 83, 88–9, 93, 99

Pantaleon, 100

Pantites, 72, 150

Parrhasia, 77, 194

Patavium (Padua), 198
Patrokles, 80
Paullus, M. Aemilius (cos. 302), 198
Pausanias (author), 66, 83–6, 88, 90–1, 93,
  95–6, 100, 110, 117, 149, 153, 177,
  179–80, 185–7, 194, 197, 199–201
Pausanias (King), 21, 34, 85, 161, 214 n.29
Pausanias (Regent), 27, 31, 34, 44, 61–3, 72,
  85, 120, 123, 125–6, 129–37
Peiraeus, 28, 34, 140, 224 n.13
Peisander, 28
Pelagos wood, the, xi, 153
Pellene, 163–5, 167
Pelopidas, 10–11, 29, 50, 177, 179–82,
  184–7, 192, 194, 201
Peloponnese, Peloponnesians, 21, 53, 59, 61,
  83, 107–10, 116, 121, 127, 130–1, 140–2,
  144–5, 151–2, 160, 164, 178, 188, 191–2,
  194–6, 199–201, 218 n.29
Peloponnesian League, 27, 101,
Peloponnesian War, 3, 8, 10, 13, 27–8, 44,
  48, 59, 75, 77–8, 109, 140–1, 160–1,
Pelops (King), 85, 203
peltasts, 5, 11, 18, 44, 47–50, 138, 145, 169,
  172–4, 179, 185, 192
pentekonteres, 6, 51–2
pentekosteres, 6–8, 13, 30, 45,
pentekostys (-yes), 6–11, 13, 30, 51–2, 67–8,
  89–90,
Perachora, 43, 49, 173
Perikles, 4, 26, 140–1
perioikos (-oi), 13–14, 18–26, 28, 52–3,
  57–9, 61–2, 93, 116, 120, 131, 134, 136,
  139, 141–2, 152, 159, 164, 192–5, 206
  nn.24 & 28, 207 nn. 29 & 32, 210 nn.11,
  13 & 16, 216 n.7
Persia, Persians, 4–5, 48, 63, 71–2, 105–108,
  110–13, 115–31, 133–40, 148, 175–6, 197,
  199
Persian Wars, 59, 75, 81, 120
Phalaros, xvii
Pharax, 28, 30, 159
Pharis, 83, 93
Pharsalos, 168
Pheidon, 91
Phigalia, 96
Philip II of Macedonia, 196
Philip V of Macedonia, 202–203

Philochoros, 99,
Philopoimen, 203–204
Phleious, 21, 42, 176, 179, 185, 192, 201
Phoibidas, 32, 41, 48, 176, 195, 217 n.8
Phokis, Phokians, 48, 107, 109–10, 112–13,
  115, 117–18, 139, 169, 172, 177, 179, 185,
  196, 226 n.2
Photios, 11–12, 65
phratriai, 89
Phylarchos, 26–7, 34, 201
phyle (-ai), 62, 64–6, 83, 88–9, 92–3, 99,
  210 n.20, 214 n.31, 215 n.39, 219 n.14
piloi, 58
Pindar, 66
pipes, pipers, 29, 35, 45–6, 56, 156, 172
Pisa, 100
Pitana (obe), Pitanatai, 64–6, 86–9, 101, 210
  n.21
Pitanate lochos, 61, 64–7, 89, 92, 131, 211
  n.27, 227 n.20
Plataea, Plataeans, ix, 48, 56, 108–109,
  120–40,
Plataea, battle of, 4, 27, 40, 44, 61, 63–4, 69,
  71–2, 75, 77, 107, 117, 120–40, 148, 150,
  155, 206 n.24
Plato, 4, 35, 46, 71
Pleistarchos, 27, 85
Ploas (lochos), 64–5
Plutarch, 3–4, 10–11, 17, 26, 29–31, 34,
  40–1, 43, 45, 50, 61–2, 69–70, 72–5,
  84–7, 89, 92–5, 97, 101, 108, 111, 116,
  124, 129, 159, 172, 177, 179–87, 191–202
polemarch(s), 6–8, 13–14, 19, 24, 27, 29, 31,
  33, 39, 44–5, 49, 51, 53–4, 56, 67, 74,
  106, 133, 154, 156, 160, 167–8, 172–4,
  186, 191, 194, 215 n.41, 226 n.7
Pollis, 28
Pollux, 45
Polyainos, 4, 10, 17, 36, 47, 86, 110, 172,
  179–80, 183, 185–6
Polybios, 11, 75, 196, 198, 201–203
Polydektes, 85
Polydoros, 74, 85, 88, 92, 94–5, 212 n.10,
  214 n.29, 215 nn. 37 & 41
Polykrates, 101
Pontos, 43
Poseidon Hippios, temple of (near
  Mantineia), 153

Poseidonios, 72
Prasiai, 192
Praxitas, 173
Prokles, 84–5
Prote, 144
Prytanis, 84–5
Ptolemy I Soter, 199
Ptolemy II Philadelphos, 200
Ptolemy II Euergetes, 202
Punic War, the first, 198
Pylos, x, 8, 21, 43, 57–8, 60, 65, 77–8, 141, 144, 152, 223 n.7
Pyrrhos, 199–200

Rachiani (Longopotamos), xiv, 162
Ramphias, 28
rations (Spartan), 43, 144–5
Regulus, M.Atilius (cos.II 256), 198
religion, 44–5, 70–1, 108
Rhetsi springs, 124
rhetra, the, 66, 75, 87, 92–5, 97, 210 n.23, 212 n.10, 214 nn.30 & 31
Rommel, Field-Marshal, 113, 217 n. 21

'Sacred Band', 177, 180–2, 185–6, 225 n.11
Sacred War (4th century), 196
Salamis, 29, 120–1
Samos, 101
Sarandopotamos, xi, 153
Sardes, 129
Sarinas (lochos), 65
sarisa, 201, 203, 227 n.17
Seleukos II, 198
Sellasia, 195
Sellasia, battle of, 202, 227 n.19
Sepeia, battle of, 73
Sepias, Cape, 111
shield, 40
Sicily, Sicilians, 27, 59–60, 78, 141, 198
Sidous, 12
Sikia channel, x
Sikyon, Sikyonians, xiv, 3, 59, 66, 83, 91, 94–5, 101, 162–5, 172–3, 214 n.28
Simonides, 87
Sinis (lochos), 64–5
Siphai, xviii, xix
Skiritai, 9, 11, 13, 21, 39, 42, 51–4, 65, 154–8, 206 n.16, 209 nn.6 & 7

Skolos, 219 n.4
Soös, 84, 86
Sosibios, 92
Sosylos, 198
Sparta, Spartans *passim*
Spartiates, 15, 19
    definition of, 19
    see also, 15, 20, 22–7, 29–32, 34, 57–9, 61–2, 69, 71, 74–6, 78–81, 95–7, 102, 113, 116, 118, 120–1, 132, 134, 137, 139, 141, 149–50, 181, 186, 188, 191, 193, 195, 202
spear, 40
Spercheios river, viii
sphaireis, 65
Sphakteria, x, 5–6, 27–8, 30, 40, 43, 48, 50, 57, 59, 69, 75, 79–81, 105, 138, 140–51, 158–60, 173–4, 205 n.3, 217 n.14
Sphodrias, 28, 34, 176
Stenyklaros, 69, 71
Sthenelaidas, 29
Stiris, xviii, 177
Strabo, 15, 90, 93, 96, 100, 162
Styphon, 28, 30, 149
sword (Spartan), 40
Syracuse, 66
Syria, 198, 203
syssition (-ia), 17–18, 22–3, 25, 68–9, 75–6, 78, 82, 88, 95, 99, 206 n.21, 211 n.30

Tachos, 197
Tainaron, 199
Tanagra, 121, 218 n.3
Tanagra, battle of, 59–61, 77
Tantalos, 80
Taras (Tarentum, Taranto), 84, 90, 92–3, 197–8, 213 n.22
Taygetos, 83
'Tearless Battle', 5, 46, 50, 81, 194, 205 n.3
Tegea, Tegeates, xi, 4, 11, 21, 52, 72, 100, 120, 125, 131, 134–9, 151–5, 158, 163–4, 166–7, 192, 195, 202, 212 n.7, 218 n.29
Tegea, battle of, 61
Tegyra, battle of, 29, 50, 177, 181
Teisamenos, 125
Teleklos, 83, 85, 93,
Teleutias, 27, 48, 173
Tellis, 29

Tempe, 67, 106–109
'tent companions', 29, 31, 44
Thebes, Thebans, 3–4, 10, 13–15, 23, 28,
    33, 36, 47, 105, 108–109, 114–18, 121–2,
    124–8, 131, 165, 168, 170–2, 176–88, 192,
    196, 218 n.30
Themistokles, 108
Theopompos (author), 96
Theopompos (King), 84–6, 88, 92, 95, 212
    n.10, 215 nn.37 & 41
Theopompos (polemarch), 29
Thermopylai, viii, 3–5, 27, 34, 44–5, 68–72,
    79, 105–20, 126, 132, 139–40, 148–9, 169,
    203, 206 n.17
Thersander, 119
Thespiai, Thespiaians, xviii, xix, 28, 48,
    105, 107–109, 114–17, 119, 126, 164, 167,
    178, 185, 218 n.30, 226 n.20
Thessaly, Thessalians, 72, 74, 120, 129, 135,
    168, 226 n.2
Thibron, 60, 78
Thisbe, xviii, 177–8, 225 n.3
'Three Heads' pass *see* Dryoskephalai
Thucydides *passim*
Thurii, 198
Thyrea, Thyreatis, 80, 96, 215 n.41
Timagenidas, 126

Timolaos, 161
Timomachos, 90, 213 n.23
Trachis, viii, 72, 106, 217 n.10
'Trench', Great, battle of, 100
'*tresantes*', 191
triakades, 68–9, 83, 90, 211 n.29
Tripolis, xi
Trozen, 163
Tyrrhastiadas, 113, 217 n.20
Tyrtaios, 45, 66, 76, 82–4, 86–8, 91–2, 94,
    97–100, 102, 206 n.18

Vegetius, 199
Voïdhokilia bay, x, 143
Volimnos, 83

women (Spartan), 34, 64, 193

Xanthippos, 198
Xenophon *passim*
Xerxes, 4, 71, 95–6, 106–107, 109–13,
    117–18, 120, 126, 203

Zakynthos, 59
Zanovistas, xi, 153
Zeus, 45
Zeuxidamos, 85